TEACHER'S GUIDE
with TESTS & MULTILEVEL ACTIVITY CD-ROM

FOUNDATIONS

Second Edition

W9-BSY-833

Donated by
Pearson Education
Upper Saddle River, NJ

Steven J. Molinsky • Bill Bliss

PEARSON
Longman

Foundations, Teacher's Guide with Tests & Multilevel Activity CD-ROM, second edition

Copyright © 2007 by Prentice Hall Regents
Pearson Education, Inc.
All rights reserved.
No part of this publication may be reproduced, stored in a
retrieval system, or transmitted in any form or by any means,
electronic, mechanical, photocopying, recording, or otherwise,
without the prior permission of the publisher.

Pearson Education, 10 Bank Street, White Plains, NY 10606

Editorial director: Pam Fishman
Vice president, director of design and production: Rhea Banker
Director of electronic production: Aliza Greenblatt
Director of manufacturing: Patrice Fraccio
Senior manufacturing manager: Edith Pullman
Director of marketing: Oliva Fernandez
Production editor: Diane Cipollone
Text composition: TSI Graphics
Text design: TSI Graphics; Warren Fischbach; Wendy Wolf
Cover design: Wanda España, Wee Design Group;
    Warren Fischbach; Wendy Wolf

ISBN 978-0-13-227554-5; 0-13-227554-6

Longman on the Web
Longman.com offers online resources for teachers and students.
Access our Companion Websites, our online catalog, and our
local offices around the world.
Visit us at longman.com.
Printed in the United States of America
4 5 6 7 8 9 10 – VOLA – 14 13 12 11 10

Contents

To the Teacher

Foundations is an all-skills, standards-based program for beginning-literacy and low-beginning learners of English. Its simple format, easy-to-use photo dictionary lessons, and dynamic communication activities offer students a lively and motivating introduction to basic English for essential life skills. The program builds a language *foundation* to prepare students for future success at the Book 1 level of instruction. For additional vocabulary enrichment, *Foundations* correlates unit-by-unit with the *Word by Word Basic* Picture Dictionary.

The text and accompanying workbooks provide a careful research-based sequence of lessons that integrates vocabulary, life skills, and a gentle introduction to very basic grammar. Standards-based lessons are designed to help students develop key competencies included in CASAS, BEST Plus, EFF, SCANS, California Model Standards, Florida Adult ESOL Competencies, and other national, state, and local curriculum frameworks and assessment systems. A Scope & Sequence chart on the pages that follow includes a correlation to key curriculum standards and frameworks.

Program Components

- The *Foundations* Student Book offers fifteen standards-based units organized by topics and integrating all-skills language instruction with essential life skills.

- The Activity Workbook provides valuable supplemental practice with vocabulary, reading, writing, listening, numeracy, and test preparation (Audio CDs included).

- The Literacy Workbook offers fundamental practice with the alphabet, letter and number formation, and basic reading, writing, and listening skills—ideal support for literacy-level students in multi-level beginning classes (Audio CD included).

- This Teacher's Guide with Tests & Multilevel Activity CD-ROM offers step-by-step teaching strategies, multilevel expansion activities, and hundreds of reproducible CD-ROM files containing activity masters, tests, evidence-based reading instruction activities, and worksheets. (A complete description of the Teacher's Guide and CD-ROM features follows below.)

- The Audio Program for the student book includes word practice with vocabulary in the unit-opening photo dictionary lessons, speaking practice with all conversations, and recordings for all listening activities (on Audio CDs and Cassettes).

- Vocabulary Photo Cards are a motivating visual resource for vocabulary practice, pair work, group activities, and games.

- Color Transparencies of full-page illustrations in unit review lessons stimulate active full-class vocabulary practice and lively class discussions, games, and other activities.

Student Book Overview

Photo Dictionary Lessons

Each unit of *Foundations* begins with a two-page Vocabulary Preview in an easy-to-use photo dictionary format. These lessons offer students a clear visual reference and study tool for previewing and mastering more than 350 key words that occur in the units—especially helpful preparation for the beginning-literacy and low-beginning learner.

Two-Page Lesson Format

The core lessons in each unit follow a convenient two-page lesson format that is consistent and predictable and that provides sufficient practice for students to achieve the lesson objectives. This format is specifically designed to provide a successful learning experience for students with limited prior experience using a textbook.

Guided Conversations

Guided conversations are the dialogs and exercises that are the essential learning devices in *Foundations*. Model conversations depict situations in which people use the key vocabulary of each lesson. In the exercises that follow, pairs of students create their own conversations by placing new vocabulary items into the framework of the model. Highlighted words in color and "skeletal dialogs" with blanks help students focus on key vocabulary and practice new conversations.

Follow-Up Exercises and Activities

After each lesson's guided conversation practice, follow-up exercises and activities provide all-skills practice and lively learning through action.

- Language in Motion activities get students moving around the classroom as they pantomime actions, ask each other questions, gather information, and do other movement activities.

- Games motivate active learning through small-group and full-class practice designed to stimulate classroom interaction.

- Writing activities offer basic practice with authentic life-skill writing tasks.

- Listening exercises develop students' aural comprehension skills. (An audio program is available, and listening scripts are provided in the appendix.)

- **Mini grammar lessons** offer practice with key grammatical structures. (Grammar is not emphasized in *Foundations*; it is highlighted when basic structures are needed for communication practice.)

- **Community Connections** activities introduce civics topics related to community life and help students connect to community services.

- **Numbers lessons** in every unit provide a careful introduction to basic numeracy and math skills.

- **Language Experience Journal** writing activities prompt students to write basic sentences to apply each unit's vocabulary and topics to their own lives.

Unit Activities

Each unit ends with a series of activities designed to reinforce and build upon the language skills in the preceding lessons.

- **Different Cultures, Different Ways** sections provide photos from around the world to stimulate cross-cultural discussions about how people's lives are different in other countries and cultures.

- **Information Gap** activities promote teamwork as students work in pairs to complete tasks by sharing information and cooperating.

- **Vocabulary lists and Language Skill checklists** help students review words they have learned and keep track of the skills they are developing.

- **Full-page illustrations** stimulate a range of vocabulary review activities and games for individual students, pairs, small groups, and the entire class.

Suggested Teaching Strategies

We encourage you, in using *Foundations*, to develop approaches and strategies that are compatible with your own teaching style and the needs and abilities of your students. You may find it helpful to incorporate some of the following suggestions. More specific step-by-step instructions for all lessons are provided in this Teacher's Guide.

Vocabulary Preview (Photo Dictionary lessons)

1. **PREVIEW:** Activate students' prior knowledge of the vocabulary by having them look at the illustrations and identify the words they already know.

2. **PRESENT:** Point to each illustration or say its number, say the word, and have the class repeat it chorally and individually. (You can also play the word list on the Audio Program.) Check students' understanding and pronunciation of the vocabulary.

3. **PRACTICE:** Have students practice as a class, in pairs, or in small groups. Say or write a word, and have students point to the item in their books or tell the number. Or, point to an illustration in the book or give the number, and have students say the word.

(Additional activities and games customized for each Vocabulary Preview Lesson are provided in this Teacher's Guide.)

Guided Conversations

1. **SETTING THE SCENE:** Have students look at the model photograph in the book. Set the scene: Who are the people? What is the situation?

2. **LISTENING:** With books closed, have students listen to the model conversation—presented by you, by a pair of students, or on the audio program. Check students' understanding of the situation and the vocabulary.

3. **CLASS PRACTICE:** With books still closed, model each line and have the whole class practice in unison.

4. **READING:** With books open, have students follow along as two students present the model.

5. **PAIR PRACTICE:** In pairs, have students practice the model conversation.

6. **THE SKELETAL DIALOG:** Write the "skeletal dialog" on the board. Fill in the replacement from Exercise 1 to show students how the guided conversation method works. Call on a few pairs of students to practice the new Exercise 1 dialog using the skeletal framework on the board.

7. **VOCABULARY PRESENTATION:** Present the new vocabulary words in the exercises. Point to the photograph of each item, say the word, and have the class repeat it chorally and individually. Check students' understanding and pronunciation of the vocabulary. (You can also use the Vocabulary Preview lesson at the beginning of the unit if it contains these new words.)

8. **EXERCISE PRACTICE:** (optional) Have pairs of students simultaneously practice all the exercises.

9. **EXERCISE PRESENTATIONS:** Call on pairs of students to present their conversations to the class.

Community Connections

Have students do the activity individually, in pairs, or in small groups and then report back to the class.

Different Cultures, Different Ways

Have students first work in pairs or small groups, reacting to the photographs and responding to the questions. Then have students share with the class what they have talked about.

Put It Together!

In these paired information gap activities, Student A has information that Student B doesn't have, and vice versa. Students ask each other questions in order to fill in the missing information.

Language Experience Journal

Have students begin a Language Experience Journal in a composition notebook. Depending on your students' writing abilities, either have them write in their journals or dictate sentences for you to write. Then students should read what they have written to a classmate. (If time permits, you may also want to write a response in each student's journal, reacting to what the student has written.) If you are keeping portfolios of students' work, these journal entries serve as excellent examples of students' progress in learning to write in English.

Talk About It! (Full-Page Illustrations)

Use the richly-detailed illustration to review the vocabulary and conversations in the unit. (Color overhead transparencies of these illustrations are also available.) Have students first work in pairs or small groups to talk about the illustration and answer the questions posed at the bottom of the page. Then discuss as a class. Students may enjoy practicing conversations based on the characters and situations and then presenting their conversations to the class. The Teacher's Guide suggests a variety of activities and games customized for each full-page illustration lesson.

Teacher's Guide Overview

- **Step-by-step teaching instructions** for each lesson provide instructional strategies for using the text with students at a wide range of literacy and beginning levels.

- **Timing suggestions** help new and experienced teachers with lesson planning.

- **Hundreds of multilevel games and communication activities** create a lively, participatory classroom especially appropriate for low-beginners with a range of active learning styles.

- **Unit achievement tests** (provided as reproducible masters) assess learner progress and prepare students for success on standardized tests. An introduction to the test section offers suggestions

for using the tests and strategies for developing students' test-taking skills.

- **An Activity Handbook** provides a variety of games and activities for use with the *Foundations* Vocabulary Photo Cards.

Multilevel Activity CD-ROM Overview

The CD-ROM included with this Teacher's Guide provides a wealth of downloadable, printable instructional resources for use with the *Foundations* program, including activity masters, tests, and an Activity Bank with hundreds of supplemental worksheets offering practice in preliteracy, literacy, evidence-based reading instruction, handwriting, vocabulary, and numeracy. These resources are organized in a set of convenient folders designed for easy access and flexible use. They may be reproduced for classroom use only in conjunction with the *Foundations* instructional program.

Assessment Folder

- A **Needs Assessment** questionnaire in an easy pictorial format enables students to indicate their needs and interests to guide the teacher's lesson planning.

- A **Performance-Based Lesson Assessment** form is a tool for evaluating and documenting student participation and performance with a simple scoring rubric. The form contains text fields that enable instructors to enter up to 23 student names prior to printing the form. (The full version of Adobe Acrobat is required in order to retain the names entered in form fields by saving the file. Saving forms without the full version of Adobe Acrobat will NOT retain the data within the form fields.)

- A **Learner Progress Chart** enables students to record their test scores and chart their progress.

Tests Folder

- **Unit Achievement Tests** assess student progress and prepare students for standardized tests. Reproducible resources include a two-page test for each unit, listening scripts, an answer sheet, and an answer key. (For convenience, these tests also appear as reproducible masters in the Teacher's Guide.)

- **Teacher Notes about Testing** offer suggestions for using the tests and strategies for developing students' test-taking skills.

Activity Masters
- **Activity Masters** include ready-to-use word cards and activity sheets for the multilevel activities and games suggested throughout this Teacher's Guide.

Flash Cards and Labels
- **Flash Cards** on reproducible masters provide an economical vocabulary study tool for students.
- **Classroom Labels** with large print can be posted next to key classroom objects and furnishings.

Worksheets Activity Bank
- **Phonemic Awareness** activities offer students systematic, explicit instruction in how to detect the individual speech sounds that make up words. Activities include phoneme isolation, phoneme identification, phoneme categorization, phoneme blending, and phoneme segmentation. Since this form of systematic instruction may be unfamiliar to many teachers, the CD-ROM includes step-by-step instructions for these activities.
- **Basic Reading Practice** activities provide evidence-based reading instruction in decoding, concepts of print (letters/words/sentences), and fluency. The decoding activities are phonics-based and introduce students to fundamental concepts and skills including short and long vowels, consonant blends, consonant digraphs, vowel digraphs, vowel diphthongs, and rhyming words. Teacher instructions are provided for these activities.
- **Preliteracy Practice** worksheets are designed for students who do not have basic literacy skills in any language. The worksheets provide a careful sequence of instruction that develops basic preliteracy concepts and skills, including identification of same and different shapes, sizes, and alphabet letters. Pre-Writing worksheets offer practice with basic elements of letter formation, and Basic Writing worksheets provide tracing and copying practice with upper case letters, lower case letters, and numbers.
- **Literacy Practice** worksheets develop students' letter recognition and word recognition skills through common picture-based literacy-level test formats.
- **Vocabulary Practice** worksheets review key unit vocabulary through a variety of exercise formats including word choice, sentence completion, and cloze reading. Students also practice common abbreviations and word categorization.
- **Handwriting Practice** worksheets help learners master manuscript and cursive letter formation through tracing and copying activities.

- **Number Practice** worksheets develop students' numeracy skills and provide tracing and copying practice with numerals.

"Resources by Unit" Folder
- For convenience and ease-of-use, all resources that are organized by type in their respective folders may also be accessed by unit. Instructors can therefore find the various resources related to a specific unit in one convenient folder.

Hours of Instruction

The *Foundations* program is designed to provide 90–225+ hours of classroom instruction in low intensity programs and up to 450 hours of instruction in high intensity programs (i.e., programs offering more than 15 hours of class time per week). Programs can adapt their use of the Student Book, Activity and Literacy Workbooks, Teacher's Guide suggestions, and CD-ROM resources to meet the requirements of their program schedules as well as to meet the needs and availability of their students.

- **90–120 hours:** The Student Book serves as the main instructional resource. Teachers should use the Getting Ready activities suggested in this Teacher's Guide as needed to prepare students for the lessons. As time permits, teachers should consider using at least one Expansion Activity to reinforce or review a lesson before moving on to the next lesson in the text. The Activity and Literacy Workbooks should be used primarily outside of class. The Workbooks include Answer Keys and Audio CDs in order to serve as effective home-study materials that extend classroom learning and promote student persistence. The various worksheets provided on the Multilevel Activity CD-ROM can be used as additional take-home work. These worksheets are also ideal materials for students to use with a tutor or other helper outside of class. (Average class time per unit: 6–8 hours. Not recommended.)

- **120–165 hours:** The Student Book lessons should be introduced using the Getting Ready activities in this Teacher's Guide, and one or more Expansion Activities should be used to reinforce or review each lesson. Students will need to do most supplementary Workbook practice outside of class, but there should be some class time available to "go over the homework" together. Many teachers prefer to at least do the Workbook listening activities during class time. The worksheets on the Multilevel Activity CD-ROM can be used at home, with a tutor or helper, or during class as time and resources permit. (Average class time per unit: 8–11 hours. Recommended for low-beginning level classes. Beginning-literacy level classes would benefit from additional hours if available.)

- **165–225 hours:** This is a more appropriate range of hours of instruction for low intensity programs. The Student Book lessons should be introduced using the Getting Ready activities, at least one Expansion Activity should be used to reinforce a lesson, and another Expansion Activity should be used in a subsequent class as time permits in order to consolidate student mastery of the lesson. Some supplementary Workbook practice can occur in class, and some practice should occur at home. Some of the worksheets on the Multilevel Activity CD-ROM should be used during class time as appropriate, while other worksheets can be used as additional take-home work. (Average class time per unit: 11–15 hours. Recommended.)

- **225–450 hours:** A high intensity program providing more than 15 hours of instruction per week for a total of 225–450 hours should provide sufficient class time for comprehensive use of all components of *Foundations*. This should include many of the activities recommended in the Teacher's Guide and allow adequate class time for completion of Workbook practice and use of most worksheets on the Multilevel Activity CD-ROM, including some individualized, pair, and small-group instruction during class time. (Average class time per unit: 15–30 hours. Optimal.)

Intensity and Duration of Instruction

Beginning-literacy and low-beginning students clearly benefit from a maximum number of hours of instruction per week, but ironically, these students are often enrolled in under-resourced programs that can only provide minimal hours of classroom time. These students' life circumstances and work requirements also commonly prevent them from attending language classes as intensively and frequently as they would like. As noted in the above section, 165–225 hours of instruction is a reasonable time range to allow students in low intensity programs at this level to make progress and to be able to demonstrate learning gains through testing. Programs that are unable to offer this amount of instruction in a program term should consider spreading the Beginning Literacy or Low Beginning curriculum over two terms instead of one, thereby doubling the duration of this level of instruction to partially compensate for the lesser intensity of the instruction. If you need to advocate for this, you should consider providing your program administrator or funding agency with a complete set of the *Foundations* program components in order to demonstrate the extent of the learning challenge facing students at this level.

In conclusion, we have attempted to offer students of English at the beginning-literacy and low-beginning level a communicative, meaningful, and lively way of learning the basic vocabulary and language they need to communicate in essential life-skill situations. Through listening, speaking, reading, writing, discussion, movement, games, and other activities, our goal has been to meet the needs of students with different learning styles and particular abilities and strengths.

While conveying to you the substance of *Foundations*, we hope that we have also conveyed the spirit: that instruction in basic language, vocabulary, and life skills can be dynamic and interactive . . . responsive to our students' differing learning styles . . . relevant to our students' lives . . . and fun!

Steven J. Molinsky
Bill Bliss

Scope and Sequence

LANGUAGE SKILLS & STANDARDS-BASED OBJECTIVES

UNIT	KEY TOPICS	LISTENING & SPEAKING	READING & WRITING	NUMERACY/ MATH
1 **Personal Information & Family** *Text Page 2*	• The alphabet • Numbers 0–10 • Introduce yourself • Spell your name • Telephone numbers • Addresses • Family members	• Greeting people • Introducing yourself • Spelling name aloud • Listening to names spelled aloud & choosing correct written form • Asking & answering questions about name & spelling, address, & telephone number • Repeating information to check understanding • Listening to phone numbers & apartment numbers & choosing correct written form • Introducing family members • Talking about a family photo	• Identifying & writing alphabet letters • Reading information on a form • Filling out a form with personal information (name, address, telephone, cell phone, e-mail) • Writing telephone numbers • Identifying abbreviations for states • Interpreting a family tree diagram • Writing about family members	• Numbers 0–10 • Telephone numbers • Numbers in addresses (street numbers, apartment numbers, zip codes) • Using numbers to indicate age • Social security numbers
2 **The Classroom** *Text Page 18*	• Classroom objects • Classroom actions • Numbers 11–19	• Identifying classroom objects & locations • Locating classroom objects • Identifying classroom actions • Giving & following simple classroom commands • Listening to & identifying classroom objects & actions • Describing objects & people's actions in a classroom scene	• Making a list of objects • Reading an inventory list of objects • Writing a description of a classroom	• Numbers 11–19 • Using numbers to indicate quantity • Using numbers to take inventory
3 **Everyday Activities & Weather** *Text Page 32*	• Describe everyday activities • Numbers 20–100 • Describe weather • Interpret a weather map	• Talking about everyday activities • Inquiring by phone about a person's activities • Listening to & identifying everyday activities • Describing the weather • Listening to & identifying weather descriptions • Asking & answering personal information questions	• Arranging a list of events into chronological order • Interpreting a weather map • Reading weather information in a newspaper • Making a list of cities & weather conditions • Writing about daily activities	• Numbers 20–100 • Temperatures • Using numbers to indicate age • Using numbers to indicate address
4 **Numbers, Time, Calendar, Money** *Text Page 46*	• Cardinal numbers 1–100 • Time • Days of the week • Ordinal numbers • Months of the year • Coins & currency	• Asking & answering addition problems • Listening & identifying numbers, times • Asking & telling time • Saying days of the week & months of the year • Making an appointment over the telephone • Asking & answering about where you live • Saying a date • Asking & giving information about birthday • Listening & identifying dates • Saying names & values of coins & currency • Listening & identifying amounts of money • Asking & giving information about a transportation schedule	• Reading addition problems • Writing numbers • Reading clock times • Recognizing abbreviations of days of the week & months of the year • Writing days of the week & months of the year • Writing time information on a calendar • Writing dates of birthdays & holidays • Writing about daily schedule	• Cardinal numbers 1–100 • Ordinal numbers • Addition • Pronouncing numbers • Listening & identifying similar numbers • Saying large address numbers & room numbers • Telling time • Identifying times on schedules • Using ordinal numbers to indicate order, dates, birthdays • Coin & currency values • Adding coin & currency values

CURRICULUM STANDARDS & FRAMEWORKS

BASIC GRAMMAR*	COMMUNITY/ CIVICS & CULTURE	EFF	SCANS	CASAS	LAUSD	FLORIDA	
						FOUNDATIONS	LOW BEGINNING
• WH-Questions: *Who, What, How* • Personal pronouns: *I, you, he, she* • Possessive adjectives: *my, his, her*	• Emergency telephone numbers: Police, Ambulance, Fire, Poison control center • Greeting people in different cultures	• Interact in a way that is friendly • Identify community resources • Identify family relationships • Respect others & value diversity • Cooperate with others • Work together	• Sociability • Acquire information • Communicate information • Work with cultural diversity	0.1.2, 0.1.4, 0.2.1, 0.2.2	*Beg. Literacy:* 1, 2, 3, 4, 5 *Beg. Low:* 1, 2, 4, 6, 7, 9, 58	5.01, 5.02, 6.04, 8.01, 10.02, 12.01, 14.01, 15.02, 15.03, 15.04, 15.05, 15.06, 15.07, 16.01, 16.02, 16.04, 16.05, 16.06, 16.10, 16.11	5.01, 5.02, 6.04, 10.02, 14.01, 15.02, 15.05, 15.06, 15.07, 16.01, 16.02, 16.04, 16.05, 16.06, 16.10, 16.11
• Verb: To be • Yes/No questions • WH-Questions: *What, Where, How many* • Prepositions of location: *on, next to* • Articles: *a, an* • There is / There are • Imperatives	• Visiting a classroom in another school • Comparing classrooms in different countries	• Manage resources: Identify those resources you have; Determine where they are • Give direction • Respect others & value diversity • Cooperate with others • Work together	• Basic skills • Identify resources • Work with cultural diversity • Participate as a member of a team	0.1.2, 0.1.5	*Beg. Literacy:* 8, 9, 11 *Beg. Low:* 12, 13, 15, 16, 17, 18	5.01, 8.01, 15.03, 15.04, 15.06, 15.07, 16.02, 16.04, 16.05, 16.06, 16.08, 16.09, 16.10, 16.11	5.01, 8.01, 15.02, 15.06, 15.07, 16.02, 16.04, 16.05, 16.06, 16.08, 16.09, 16.10, 16.11
• Simple present tense • Present continuous tense • WH-Questions: *What, How old*	• Using newspaper weather maps & weather reports • How household chores are shared in different cultures	• Meet family needs & responsibilities • Organize activities • Identify family relationships • Gather information • Understand &, interpret numbers • Respect others & value diversity • Cooperate with others • Work together	• Basic skills • Identify goal-relevant activities • Work with cultural diversity • Participate as a member of a team	0.1.2, 0.1.4, 0.2.1, 0.2.4, 1.1.5, 2.1.8, 2.3.3, 7.5.5, 7.5.6, 8.2.3	*Beg. Literacy:* 5, 6 *Beg. Low:* 9, 11, 12, 13, 28, 29	5.01, 5.02, 8.01, 13.01, 14.01, 15.03, 15.04, 15.06, 15.07, 16.01, 16.02, 16.05, 16.06, 16.07, 16.09, 16.11	5.01, 5.02, 7.08, 13.01, 14.01, 15.02, 15.06, 15.07, 16.01, 16.02, 16.05, 16.06, 16.07, 16.09, 16.11
• WH-Questions: *How much, What* • Can	• Making appointments • Writing days & times of work & school schedules • Using a transportation schedule • Concepts of time & punctuality in different cultures	• Acquire information • Understand, interpret, & work with numbers • Use math to solve problems • Manage resources: Allocate time • Respect others & value diversity • Cooperate with others • Work together	• Basic skills • Acquire & communicate information • Sociability: Demonstrate friendliness • Self-management • Work with cultural diversity • Participate as a member of a team	0.1.2, 0.2.1, 1.1.6, 2.3.1, 2.3.2, 6.1.1	*Beg. Literacy:* 6, 12, 13 *Beg. Low:* 3, 4, 25, 26, 30	5.01, 5.02, 8.01, 8.02, 8.03, 8.05, 11.01, 15.03, 15.04, 15.06, 15.07, 16.01, 16.02, 16.05, 16.06, 16.08, 16.10, 16.11	5.01, 5.02, 8.01, 8.02, 8.03, 8.04, 15.02, 15.06, 15.07, 16.01, 16.02, 16.05, 16.06, 16.08, 16.10, 16.11

---

* Basic grammar structures are included in a careful progression for introductory exposure, not mastery.

EFF: Equipped for the Future (Content standards, Common activities, & Key activities for Citizen/Community Member, Worker, & Parent/Family role maps; EFF communication skills are covered in every unit)

SCANS: Secretary's Commission on Achieving Necessary Skills (U.S. Department of Labor)

CASAS: Comprehensive Adult Student Assessment System

LAUSD: Los Angeles Unified School District content standards (Beginning Literacy, Beginning Low)

FLORIDA: Adult ESOL Standardized Syllabi

(‡Florida benchmarks 17.01, 17.02, and 17.03 are covered in every unit and therefore are not included in the listings above.)

LANGUAGE SKILLS & STANDARDS-BASED OBJECTIVES

UNIT	KEY TOPICS	LISTENING & SPEAKING	READING & WRITING	NUMERACY/ MATH
5 Home *Text Page 64*	• Rooms in the home • Home appliances & features • Types of housing	• Identifying rooms in the home • Identifying home appliances & features • Asking for information about an apartment • Asking & answering questions about home activities • Identifying furniture • Asking for & giving instructions • Talking about types of housing in the community	• Understanding number information in a story • Writing a description of your home	• Cardinal & ordinal numbers review • Understanding number information in a story
6 Community *Text Page 76*	• Places in the community • Asking for & giving location	• Identifying places in the community • Asking & answering questions about destination • Listening & identifying places in the community • Asking & giving the location of places in the community • Getting someone's attention politely	• Reading & writing missing words in a cloze paragraph about people's activities • Writing missing letters in words • Reading street names • Writing addresses of community services • Writing about your neighborhood • Interpreting a simple street map	• Ordinal numbers in names of streets
7 Describing *Text Page 88*	• Describing people: Age, Height, Hair color, Eye color, Marital status • Describing feelings • Countries & languages • Titles	• Describing people by physical characteristics • Asking & answering questions about age, height, hair color, eye color, weight • Making a request at work • Asking & telling what someone looks like • Listening & identifying a person by a physical description • Asking & giving personal information: marital status, country of origin, language spoken • Inquiring about & describing feelings	• Reading & writing missing words in a cloze paragraph about family members' activities • Completing a chart about family members • Completing a chart with descriptive information about people • Making a list of students, their countries, & their languages • Filling out a personal information form • Writing about yourself	• Using numbers to indicate age, height, weight
8 Food *Text Page 102*	• Common foods • Expressing food needs • Food containers & quantities • Ordering food in a restaurant	• Identifying food items • Expressing food needs • Listening & identifying food items • Locating food items in a store • Identifying food containers & quantities • Ordering food items in a fast-food restaurant or coffee shop • Taking customers' orders at a food service counter • Identifying units of measure • Making a polite request	• Categorizing: Listing words in correct groups • Writing missing letters in words • Making a list of food stores & foods purchased there • Making a list of fast-food restaurants & foods eaten there • Interpreting abbreviations for food measurements (lb., qt., doz.) • Making a food shopping list • Writing about favorite food	• Aisle numbers in stores • Food quantities (quart, pound, half a pound, dozen, half a dozen)

BASIC GRAMMAR	COMMUNITY/ CIVICS & CULTURE	EFF	SCANS	CASAS	LAUSD	FLORIDA	
						FOUNDATIONS	LOW BEGINNING
• Has • There is / There are • WH-Questions: *How many, Where* • Imperatives	• Types of housing in a community • Comparing different kinds of homes around the world	• Give direction • Meet family needs • Identify community resources • Respect others & value diversity • Cooperate with others • Work together	• Basic skills • Acquire & communicate information • Work with cultural diversity • Participate as a member of a team	0.1.2, 0.1.4, 1.4.1	*Beg. Low:* 12, 13, 21, 38, 39	4.01, 8.01, 11.06, 15.03, 15.04, 15.06, 15.07, 16.01, 16.02, 16.04, 16.05, 16.06, 16.07, 16.08, 16.09, 16.11	4.01, 8.01, 11.06, 15.02, 15.06, 15.07, 16.01, 16.02, 16.04, 16.05, 16.06, 16.07, 16.08, 16.09, 16.11
• WH-Questions: *Where* • Present continuous tense • Verb: To be • Prepositions of location: *next to, across from, between, on* • There is	• Places & services in the community • Addresses of key community services used (bank, clinic, library, drug store, post office, supermarket) • Different kinds of places where people shop around the world • Interpreting a simple street map	• Identify community resources • Seek & receive information • Gather information • Interact in a way that is courteous • Respect others & value diversity • Cooperate with others • Work together	• Basic skills • Acquire & communicate information • Understand a social system (community) • Work with cultural diversity • See things in the mind's eye • Participate as a member of a team	0.1.2, 0.1.4	*Beg. Literacy:* 5, 11 *Beg. Low:* 22, 23, 24	5.01, 15.03, 15.04, 15.06, 15.07, 16.01, 16.02, 16.05, 16.06, 16.08, 16.09, 16.11	5.01, 15.02, 15.06, 15.07, 16.01, 16.02, 16.05, 16.06, 16.08, 16.09, 16.11
• Verb: To be • WH-Questions: *What, Where* • Subject pronouns • Adjectives	• Different ways that people in different cultures show their feelings	• Gather information • Identify family relationships • Interact in a way that is friendly • Respect others & value diversity • Cooperate with others • Work together	• Basic skills • Acquire & communicate information • Sociability • Work with cultural diversity • Participate as a member of a team	0.1.2, 0.2.1, 0.2.2, 1.1.4	*Beg. Literacy:* 7 *Beg. Low:* 6	5.02, 5.03, 14.01, 15.01, 15.02, 15.03, 15.04, 15.05, 15.06, 15.07, 16.01, 16.02, 16.05, 16.06, 16.07, 16.08, 16.10, 16.11	5.02, 5.03, 14.01, 15.01, 15.02, 15.05, 15.06, 15.07, 16.01, 16.02, 16.05, 16.06, 16.07, 16.08, 16.10, 16.11
• Singular/Plural • Articles: *A, an* • There is/There are • Verb: To be • Imperatives	• Listing food stores & restaurants used in the community & foods obtained there • Different kinds of foods people around the world eat	• Manage resources: Identify those resources you have • Meet family needs & responsibilities • Seek & receive assistance • Gather information • Identify community resources • Interact in a way that is courteous • Interact in a way that is helpful • Respect others & value diversity • Cooperate with others • Work together	• Basic skills • Identify resources • Acquire & communicate information • Serve clients/customers • Work with cultural diversity • Participate as a member of a team	0.1.2, 0.1.4, 1.1.7, 1.3.7, 1.3.8, 2.6.4, 4.8.3	*Beg. Literacy:* 5, 14 *Beg. Low:* 14, 32, 35, 37	5.01, 5.03, 7.06, 7.08, 11.02, 15.03, 15.04, 15.06, 15.07, 16.01, 16.02, 16.05, 16.06, 16.08, 16.09, 16.11	5.01, 5.03, 7.09, 7.11, 11.02, 15.02, 15.06, 15.07, 16.01, 16.02, 16.05, 16.06, 16.08, 16.09, 16.11

LANGUAGE SKILLS & STANDARDS-BASED OBJECTIVES

UNIT	KEY TOPICS	LISTENING & SPEAKING	READING & WRITING	NUMERACY/ MATH
9 Clothing, Colors, & Shopping *Text Page 118*	• Clothing items • Asking for clothing in a store • Colors • Clothing sizes • Problems with clothing • Prices	• Identifying clothing items • Locating clothing items in a store • Listening & identifying clothing items • Identifying colors • Describing what a person is wearing • Expressing clothing size needed to a store salesperson • Expressing problems with clothing • Asking the price of items in a store • Offering assistance to customers as a salesperson • Expressing needs to a salesperson in a store	• Writing plural forms of nouns • Writing missing letters in words • Writing on a chart items of clothing, stores where purchased, & their locations • Reading store display signs with prices • Writing about a favorite clothing item • Reading a clothing store directory to determine location of items	• Numbers in clothing sizes • Prices • Using ordinal numbers to indicate floor of a building
10 The Bank & the Post Office *Text Page 132*	• Bank items • Checks • Making change • Postal items • Obtaining post office services	• Identify bank items & forms • Listening & identifying bank items & forms • Identifying post office items & services • Requesting post office items & services • Paying for goods & services • Giving & receiving correct change during transactions	• Writing information on a chart about banking services used • Reading & writing bank checks • Reading signs in a post office • Identifying return address & mailing address on an envelope • Completing a chart indicating a schedule of opening & closing times • Writing about strategies for controlling expenses & saving money • Interpreting a fast-food menu	• Indicating amount of money on a check • Writing opening & closing times on a schedule • Making change • Subtraction • Identifying prices on a fast-food restaurant menu
11 Health *Text Page 144*	• Parts of the body • Ailments • Medicine • Making a doctor's appointment • Staying healthy • Dosage information on medicine labels	• Identifying parts of the body • Asking about another person's health • Describing ailments, symptoms, & injuries • Listening & identifying ailments, symptoms, & injuries • Indicating what hurts to medical personnel • Asking for & giving advice about over-the-counter medicine • Locating items in a drug store • Using the telephone to make a medical appointment • Expressing sympathy • Calling for an ambulance • Understanding a doctor's medical advice • Repeating information to check understanding • Asking & answering questions about health habits • Understanding a pharmacist's dosage instructions for prescription medicines	• Reading signs in drug store aisles to locate products • Writing information on a chart about pharmacist recommendations for common ailments & symptoms • Reading & writing missing words in a cloze paragraph about staying healthy • Writing survey information about students' health habits on a chart • Understanding dosage instructions on medicine labels • Writing about remedies used for common ailments & symptoms • Reading a drug store directory to determine location of items	• Indicating time when making an appointment • Interpreting numbers in medical advice (e.g., sleep 8 hours, eat 3 meals) • Interpreting numbers in dosage instructions for medicine • Aisle numbers in stores
12 School *Text Page 158*	• School personnel & locations • School subjects • Extracurricular activities • Class schedules	• Identifying school personnel • Identifying school locations • Identifying school subjects • Telling about favorite school subject • Identifying extracurricular activities • Listening & identifying school subjects & extracurricular activities • Describing after-school plans • Talking about a class schedule	• Writing information on a chart about students' favorite school subjects • Writing information on a chart about names of schools in the community, their locations, & their students • Interpreting a class schedule • Writing a description of places & people in your school	• Cardinal & ordinal numbers review • Interpreting numbers in a class schedule (periods, classroom numbers, class times)

CURRICULUM STANDARDS & FRAMEWORKS

BASIC GRAMMAR	COMMUNITY/ CIVICS & CULTURE	EFF	SCANS	CASAS	LAUSD	FLORIDA	
						FOUNDATIONS	LOW BEGINNING
• Singular / Plural • Adjectives • Too + adjective	• Listing clothing stores in the community, their locations, & types of clothing purchased there • Different kinds of special clothing people in different cultures wear on special days	• Seek & receive assistance • Identify problems • Identify community resources • Gather information • Understand & work with numbers • Respect others & value diversity • Cooperate with others • Work together	• Basic skills • Identify resources • Acquire & communicate information • Serve clients/customers • Work with cultural diversity • Participate as a member of a team	0.1.2, 0.1.4, 1.1.9, 1.2.1, 1.3.7, 1.3.9, 4.8.3	*Beg. Literacy:* 5, 8, 13, 14 *Beg. Low:* 14, 31, 32, 33, 34	5.01, 5.03, 8.05, 11.01, 11.03, 11.04, 15.01, 15.03, 15.04, 15.06, 15.07, 16.01, 16.02, 16.05, 16.06, 16.07, 16.08, 16.09, 16.10, 16.11	5.01, 5.03, 8.04, 11.01, 11.04, 15.01, 15.02, 15.06, 15.07, 16.01, 16.02, 16.05, 16.06, 16.07, 16.08, 16.09, 16.11
• WH-Questions: *Where, What, How much* • Want to	• Listing banks & banking services students use • Obtaining services at the post office • Interpreting a posted schedule of opening & closing times at a community location • Different kinds of coins & bills in different countries, & their values	• Meet family needs & responsibilities • Identify community resources • Gather information • Seek & receive assistance • Understand, interpret, & work with numbers • Use math to solve problems & communicate • Manage resources • Respect others & value diversity • Cooperate with others • Work together	• Basic skills • Acquire & communicate information • Allocate money • Self-management • Work with cultural diversity • Participate as a member of a team	0.1.2, 1.3.1, 1.3.3, 1.8.2, 2.4.1, 2.4.2, 2.4.4, 2.5.4, 6.1.2	*Beg. Low:* 8	5.01, 8.01, 8.05, 8.06, 8.07, 11.01, 11.05, 12.03, 15.03, 15.04, 15.06, 15.07, 16.01, 16.02, 16.05, 16.06, 16.08, 16.09, 16.10, 16.11	5.01, 8.04, 8.05, 8.06, 8.07, 12.03, 15.02, 15.06, 15.07, 16.01, 16.02, 16.05, 16.06, 16.08, 16.09, 16.11
• WH-Questions: *What, Where, How many* • Have / Has • Should • Can • Want to • Past Tense	• Locating products in a drug store • Visiting a local drug store & obtaining pharmacist recommendations for over-the-counter medicine • Calling for an ambulance • Different remedies for common medical problems in different cultures	• Seek & receive assistance • Guide & support others • Gather & use information • Interact in a way that is friendly & courteous • Give direction • Provide for family members' safety & physical needs • Understand, interpret, & work with numbers & symbolic information • Respect others & value diversity • Cooperate with others • Work together	• Basic skills • Acquire & communicate information • Identify resources • Serve clients/customers • Sociability: Demonstrate empathy • Self-management • Work with cultural diversity • Participate as a member of a team	0.1.2, 0.1.4, 1.3.7, 2.1.2, 3.1.1, 3.1.2, 3.1.3, 3.3.1, 3.3.2, 3.3.3, 3.5.9	*Beg. Literacy:* 9 *Beg. Low:* 12, 21, 32, 43, 44, 45, 46	5.01, 5.02, 5.03, 6.01, 6.04, 7.01, 7.02, 7.03, 7.04, 7.07, 15.03, 15.04, 15.06, 15.07, 16.01, 16.02, 16.05, 16.06, 16.10, 16.11	5.01, 5.02, 6.01, 6.04, 7.01, 7.02, 7.03, 7.04, 7.05, 7.06, 7.10, 10.02, 15.02, 15.06, 15.07, 16.01, 16.02, 16.05, 16.06, 16.10, 16.11
• WH-Questions: *Who, Where, What, Which* • Have	• Listing different types of schools in the community, their locations, & the students who attend • Different types of school buildings & classrooms around the world	• Gather information • Identify community resources • Manage resources: Allocate time • Respect others & value diversity • Cooperate with others • Work together	• Basic skills • Identify resources • Sociability • See things in the mind's eye (Interpret a chart) • Allocate time • Understand a social system (school) • Work with cultural diversity • Participate as a member of a team	0.1.2, 2.5.5	*Beg. Literacy:* 15 *Beg. Low:* 12, 16, 17	5.01, 5.03, 8.01, 15.03, 15.04, 15.06, 15.07, 16.01, 16.02, 16.04, 16.05, 16.06, 16.08, 16.09, 16.11	5.01, 5.03, 15.02, 15.06, 15.07, 16.02, 16.04, 16.05, 16.06, 16.08, 16.09, 16.11

Scope and Sequence

LANGUAGE SKILLS & STANDARDS-BASED OBJECTIVES

UNIT	KEY TOPICS	LISTENING & SPEAKING	READING & WRITING	NUMERACY/ MATH
13 Work *Text Page 170*	• Occupations • Job skills • Help Wanted signs & want ads • Places at work • Safety warnings & signs • Work schedules & paychecks	• Identifying occupations • Describing occupation & place of work • Expressing job goal during an interview • Listening to job goals & selecting related Help Wanted signs & want ads • Identifying job skills & work activities • Indicating job skills during an interview • Expressing self-confidence during an interview • Calling in sick • Asking the location of workplace departments & facilities • Warning a co-worker of a safety hazard • Interpreting warning & safety signs at work	• Reading Help Wanted signs • Writing missing letters in words • Reading want ads • Filling out a job application form • Writing information on a chart about students' job skills • Interpreting a workplace floor plan diagram • Reading & copying Help Wanted signs in the community • Interpreting workplace warning & safety signs • Reading a work schedule • Reading a paycheck & pay stub • Reading & writing missing numbers in a cloze paragraph • Writing a description of a workplace • Indicating job skills on a checklist	• Identifying telephone numbers in classified ads • Interpreting times in a work schedule • Interpreting numbers, dates, & dollar amounts on a paycheck & pay stub
14 Transportation *Text Page 188*	• Locating places • Asking for & giving directions • Types of public transportation • Traffic signs • Driving safety warnings	• Identifying modes of travel • Getting someone's attention politely • Asking for & giving directions to a place • Listening & identifying correct locations on a map • Asking for & giving information about local transportation & routes • Listening & identifying correct destination signs on buses & trains & correct street signs • Asking passengers on local transportation where to get off for a destination • Asking & telling about about modes of transportation used • Warning a driver about an upcoming traffic sign • Asking & telling about a bus schedule • Repeating to confirm information	• Interpreting a simple street map • Reading destination signs on buses & trains • Reading street signs & station signs to locate destination • Writing classroom survey results on a chart • Writing information on a chart about public transportation used • Interpreting traffic signs • Drawing traffic signs & writing their meanings • Interpreting a bus route schedule • Writing about how you get to places in the community	• Identifying bus numbers • Interpreting numbers on street signs & traffic signs • Counting student responses to a survey & entering the information on a chart • Interpreting times on a bus schedule
15 Recreation & Entertainment *Text Page 202*	• Recreation & entertainment activities • Expressing likes • Expressing future plans • Telling about past activities • Calendars & schedules	• Asking & telling about recreation & entertainment activities • Expressing likes • Listening & identifying recreation & entertainment activities • Asking & telling about plans to do a future activity • Asking & telling about a past activity • Listening & distinguishing present & past tense statements	• Writing missing letters in words • Writing survey information about students' free time activities on a chart • Writing information on a chart about places for recreation & entertainment • Interpreting a monthly calendar with activities listed • Reading a paragrapn with accompanying graphic • Writing about plans for next weekend • Reading personal schedule information on a daily calendar	• Counting student responses to a survey & entering information on a chart • Using a calendar • Interpreting time information on a daily calendar schedule

CURRICULUM STANDARDS & FRAMEWORKS

BASIC GRAMMAR	COMMUNITY/ CIVICS & CULTURE	EFF	SCANS	CASAS	LAUSD	FLORIDA Foundations	FLORIDA Low Beginning
• Verb: To be • Can • WH-Questions: *What, Where* • Prepositions of location: *across from, next to, between*	• Finding & interpreting Help Wanted signs in the community • Discussing different types of jobs & workplaces in the community • Men's & women's jobs in different cultures, & changes that are occurring	• Identify goals • Develop & express sense of self • Gather information • Seek & receive assistance • Give direction • Take responsibility for assuring work safety • Understand, interpret, & work with numbers • Respect others & value diversity • Cooperate with others • Work together	• Basic skills • Identify human resources (occupations, work skills) • Identify goal-relevant activities • Self-management: Assess self accurately • Self-esteem • Understand a social system (workplace) • See things in the mind's eye (Interpret a diagram; Interpret a sign with symbols; Draw a sign with symbols) • Work with cultural diversity • Participate as a member of a team	0.1.2, 4.1.2, 4.1.3, 4.1.6, 4.1.8, 4.3.1, 4.3.3	*Beg. Literacy:* 5, 10 *Beg. Low:* 11, 12, 14, 48, 49, 50, 51, 52, 53, 54, 56	1.01, 1.02, 1.03, 1.04, 1.07, 2.01, 2.02, 2.03, 2.04, 2.05, 3.03, 5.01, 5.02, 10.01, 15.03, 15.04, 15.05, 15.06, 15.07, 16.01, 16.02, 16.03, 16.05, 16.06, 16.08, 16.09, 16.11	1.01, 1.02, 1.03, 1.04, 1.07, 2.01, 2.02, 2.03, 2.04, 2.05, 3.03, 5.01, 5.02, 10.01, 15.02, 15.05, 15.06, 15.07, 16.02, 16.03, 16.05, 16.06, 16.08, 16.09, 16.11
• WH-Questions: *How, Where* • Imperatives • Prepositions of location: *across from, between, next to, on the left, on the right* • Exclamations	• Asking the location of places in the community • Interpreting a simple street map • Asking for information about public transportation routes • Listing places in the community accessed by public transportation, modes of transportation used, route numbers, & locations • Interpreting traffic signs • Interpreting a bus route schedule • Transportation in different places around the world	• Give direction • Seek & receive assistance • Interact in a way that is friendly, courteous, & helpful • Gather information • Identify community resources • Guide others • Understand, interpret, & work with numbers • Respect others & value diversity • Cooperate with others • Work together	• Basic skills • Acquire & communicate information • See things in the mind's eye (Interpret a map) • Identify resources • Sociability: Demonstrate understanding, friendliness • Work with cultural diversity • Participate as a member of a team	0.1.2, 0.1.3, 0.1.6, 1.9.1, 1.9.4, 2.2.1, 2.2.2, 2.2.3, 2.2.4, 2.5.4	*Beg. Literacy:* 5, 10 *Beg. Low:* 11, 13, 23, 24, 42, 48, 49	5.01, 9.01, 9.02, 9.03, 9.04, 15.03, 15.04, 15.06, 15.07, 16.01, 16.02, 16.05, 16.06, 16.08, 16.09	5.01, 9.02, 9.03, 9.04, 9.05, 15.02, 15.06, 15.07, 16.02, 16.05, 16.06, 16.08, 16.09
• Like to • Future: Going to • Past tense	• Listing places for recreation & entertainment in the community • Different ways people in different cultures spend their free time	• Interact in a way that is friendly • Gather information • Identify community resources • Manage resources: Allocate time • Plan: Develop an organized approach of activities & objectives • Plan: Set a goal • Respect others & value diversity • Cooperate with others • Work together	• Basic skills • Sociability: Demonstrate friendliness • Acquire & communicate information • Identify goal-relevant activities • Identify resources • Self-management • Work with cultural diversity • Participate as a member of a team	0.1.2, 0.1.4, 0.2.4, 2.6.1, 3.5.8, 3.5.9	*Beg. Low:* 12, 13, 14	3.03, 5.01, 5.03, 8.01, 14.07, 15.03, 15.04, 15.06, 15.07, 16.01, 16.02, 16.05, 16.06, 16.08, 16.09, 16.11	3.03, 5.01, 5.03, 14.07, 15.02, 15.06, 15.07, 16.01, 16.02, 16.05, 16.06, 16.08, 16.09, 16.11

UNIT 1 PERSONAL INFORMATION & FAMILY

LESSONS & UNIT ACTIVITIES	OBJECTIVES	TEXT	TEACHER'S GUIDE
Vocabulary Preview	The alphabet • Numbers 0–10 • Personal information	2–3	2–3
LESSON 1 Hello. My name is . . .	Introduce yourself	4–5	4–5
LESSON 2 How do you spell it?	The alphabet • Spell your name	6–7	6–8
LESSON 3 What's your telephone number?	Numbers 0–10 • Telephone numbers	8–9	9–11
LESSON 4 What's your address?	Addresses • Numbers 1–10	10–11	12–13
LESSON 5 This is my wife.	Family members	12–13	14–16
LESSON 6 NUMBERS: How old . . .?	Numbers 0–10	14	17–18
Language Experience Journal	Drawing a family tree • Writing a story about family	14	18
Different Cultures / Different Ways	Greeting people in different cultures	15	19
Put It Together	Information Gap / Teamwork activity	15–16	19
Vocabulary Foundations / Language Skill Foundations	Review & skills checklist	16	19–20
Talk About It!	Review, conversations, activities, & games	17	20

UNIT RESOURCES

Audio Program:
Audio CD 1: Tracks 2–20
Audio Cassette 1A

Workbooks:
Activity Workbook
Literacy Workbook

Lesson Planner CD-ROM:
Activity Masters 1–6
Activity Bank Unit 1 Worksheets

Transparency: Color Overhead for Unit 1, page 17

UNIT 1 VOCABULARY PREVIEW

THE ALPHABET (PAGE 2)

PREVIEW THE ALPHABET
5 MINUTES

Activate students' prior knowledge of the alphabet. Have students tell you letters of the alphabet in English they know. As they tell you each letter, write it on the board in capital letters. (*Note*: Write the letters in alphabetical order, leaving room for missing letters.)

PRESENT THE ALPHABET
10–15 MINUTES

1. Write the alphabet in capital letters on the board. Point to each letter and say its name or call on a student to say its name. Have the class repeat.

   Alternative: Repeat the letters students gave you during the Preview, and fill in the remaining letters so that you have the complete alphabet on the board.

2. Point to individual letters. Have the class say the letter name chorally.

3. Point to individual letters. Call on individual students to name them. Pay special attention to the names of the vowels. Make sure that students know how to name the vowels in English.

4. Repeat steps 1–3 with alphabet letters written in lower case on the board.

5. Using the alphabet on student book page 2, point to each letter, say the letter, and have the class repeat it chorally and individually. (You can also play the audio program.)

PRACTICE THE ALPHABET
5–10 MINUTES

As a class, in pairs, or in small groups, have students practice the alphabet in either or both of the following ways:

- Say or write a letter, and have students point to the letter in the student book.
- Point to a letter in the student book, and have students say its name.

NUMBERS 0–10 (PAGE 2)

PREVIEW THE NUMBERS
5 MINUTES

Activate students' prior knowledge of numbers 0–10 by doing either or both of the following:

1. Gesture counting to ten with your fingers. Have students tell you the numbers they know and write them on the board.

2. Have students look at the numbers on student book page 2 while they cover the words at the bottom of the page. Have students identify the numbers they already know.

PRESENT THE NUMBERS
10 MINUTES

Using the numbers on student book page 2, point to each number, say the word, and have the class repeat it chorally and individually. (You can also play the audio program.)

PRACTICE THE NUMBERS
10–15 MINUTES

As a class, in pairs, or in small groups, have students practice the numbers in either or both of the following ways:

- Say or write a number in words, and have students point to the number in the student book.
- Point to a number in the student book, and have students say its name.

PERSONAL INFORMATION (PAGE 3)

PREVIEW
5–10 MINUTES

1. Write two columns on the board: <u>first name</u> and <u>last name</u>. Write your first name and last name in the appropriate column.

   a. Explain that a first name is used with friends and with classmates, and that a last name is used with a title (Mr., Mrs., Ms., or Miss) in more formal situations.

   b. Have students give you their first and last names. Write them in the columns on the board. Be sure to clarify that the first name they give you is what their husband, wife, mother, or father would call them.

2. Have students look at the illustrations on student book page 3 while they cover the words at the bottom of the page. Have

students identify the words they already know and write them on the board. (Prompt students by asking what information people put on an envelope. Also, ask students if they have a telephone, a cell phone, and an identification card such as a social security card.)

PRESENT
10 MINUTES

Using the illustrations on student book page 3 or the words you had written on the board during the Preview activity, point to each item or say its number, say the word, and have the class repeat it chorally and individually. (You can also play the audio program.) Check students' understanding and pronunciation of the vocabulary.

PRACTICE
5–10 MINUTES

As a class, in pairs, or in small groups, have students practice the vocabulary in either or both of the following ways:

- Say or write a word, and have students point to the item in their books or tell the number.
- Point to an illustration in the book or give the number, and have students say the word.

SPELLING PRACTICE
5–10 MINUTES

Say a word, and have students spell it aloud or write it. You can also spell a portion of a word on the board, and have students come to the board to complete it.

EXPANSION

1. **Alphabet Match Game** ✶
   ACTIVITY MASTERS 1–4

   a. Make copies of Activity Masters 1–4 and cut them into cards. Depending upon the number of students in the class, give half the students a Capital Alphabet Letters Card and the other half a corresponding Lower Case Alphabet Letters Card.

   b. Have students look at their card and name the letter. Then have students circulate around the room, showing one another their alphabet cards until they find their match.

   c. When students have found their match, have them come show you. Then give each student another alphabet card to keep the game going. Continue until you have completed all the alphabet cards.

2. **Number Match Game** ✶✶
   ACTIVITY MASTERS 5, 6

   Play the above game, but this time matching the *Numbers 0–10* with the *Numbers 0–10 in Words* Cards (Activity Masters 5 and 6).

Expansion activity levels are indicated through a three-star system:

✶ **Below-level** activities, for students who need extra support and some re-teaching of skills and content to master basic objectives

✶✶ **At-level** activities, for students who are performing well in class and can benefit from reinforcement

✶✶✶ **Above-level** activities, for students who want and deserve opportunities for enrichment and greater challenge

LESSON OBJECTIVE

Focus

Introduce yourself

Vocabulary

Hello.
Hi.
My name is _____.
I'm _____.
Nice to meet you.

GETTING READY

5–10 MINUTES

Introduce expressions for greetings and introductions.

1. Walk around the room and introduce yourself to students: "Hello. My name is _____."

2. Choose one student. Have this student introduce himself or herself to you: "Hello. My name is _____." You respond: "Hi. I'm _____. Nice to meet you." Have each student introduce himself or herself to you.

3. Walk around the room and introduce yourself again to students: "Hello. My name is _____." Students respond: "Hi. I'm _____. Nice to meet you." You respond: "Nice to meet you, too."

THE MODEL CONVERSATION

10 MINUTES

1. **SETTING THE SCENE:** Have students look at the model photograph. Set the scene: "These people are meeting for the first time."

2. **LISTENING:** With books closed, have students listen to the model conversation—presented by you, by a pair of students, or on the audio program. Check students' understanding of the situation and the vocabulary.

3. **CLASS PRACTICE:** With books still closed, model each line, and have the whole class practice in unison.

4. **READING:** With books open, have students follow along as two students present the model.

5. **PAIR PRACTICE:** In pairs, have students practice the model conversation.

THE CONVERSATION EXERCISES

10–20 MINUTES

1. **THE SKELETAL DIALOG:** Write the "skeletal dialog" on the board. Fill in information about you and a student in the class to show students how the guided conversation method works. Have that student come to the front of the class and stand next to you. Act out the conversation with the student and shake hands. Do the same with a few other students, using the skeletal framework on the board.

> A. Hello. My name is <u>Nancy Miller</u>.
> B. Hi. I'm <u>Manuel Gomez</u>.
>   Nice to meet you.
> A. Nice to meet you, *too*.

2. **EXERCISE PRACTICE:** (optional) Have pairs of students simultaneously practice the conversation, using their own first and last names.

3. **EXERCISE PRESENTATIONS:** Call on pairs of students to present their conversations to the class.

LANGUAGE IN *MOTION*

10 MINUTES

Have students walk around the classroom, introducing themselves to each other. (For larger classes, you can set a time limit or a limit on how many people students should introduce themselves to.)

MEMORY GAME

10 MINUTES

Have students stand in a circle for this activity. Student 1 says his or her name—for example: "Victor Silva." Student 2 repeats what Student 1 said and adds his or her name—for example: "Victor Silva. Rosa Fernandez." Continue around the room in this fashion, with each student repeating what the previous student said and adding his or her name. (*Note*: If the class is large, you can divide students into groups.)

NAMES AND THE ALPHABET

10 MINUTES

Point out how in the example, a student named Carlos circled the letters in his first name and then printed his name three times. Have students do this with their first names and their last names. Circulate around the classroom, helping students if necessary. After students have completed the activity, have them compare what they have written with a partner.

EXPANSION

1. **Alphabetize!** ★

   ACTIVITY MASTERS 1, 2

   a. Make copies of Activity Masters 1 and 2 and cut them into cards.

   b. Have students work in pairs. Give each pair a set of cards, and have them work together to place the letters in alphabetical order.

   c. Have Student A close his or her eyes. Have Student B take away several letters from the alphabet, leaving the "holes" visible. Have Student A open his or her eyes and identify the letters that are missing. As Student A names the letters, Student B replaces them.

   d. Have the students continue the game, taking turns.

2. **Beanbag Toss** ★

   Have students stand in a circle. Say a student's name and throw a beanbag to that student (Student 1). Student 1 says the name of another student and throws the beanbag to that student. Continue around the circle until all students have been identified.

LESSON OBJECTIVE

FOCUS

The alphabet
Spell your name

VOCABULARY

Letters of the alphabet

GETTING READY
5–10 MINUTES

1. Review the alphabet.

   a. Write the letters of the alphabet on the board. Point to each letter, and have the class say its name.

   b. Point to individual letters. Call on individual students to say the names.

2. Spelling names.

   a. Ask a student what his or her *first name* is: "What's your first name?" Then ask: "How do you spell it?" After the student responds, continue asking other students.

   b. Ask a student what his or her *last name* is: "What's your last name?" Then ask: "How do you spell it?" Ask other students.

THE MODEL CONVERSATION
10 MINUTES

1. **SETTING THE SCENE:** Have students look at the model photograph. Set the scene: "One person is asking the other for some information."

2. **LISTENING:** With books closed, have students listen to the model conversation—presented by you, by a pair of students, or on the audio program. Check students' understanding of the situation and the vocabulary.

3. **CLASS PRACTICE:** With books still closed, model each line, and have the whole class practice in unison.

4. **READING:** With books open, have students follow along as two students present the model.

5. **PAIR PRACTICE:** In pairs, have students practice the model conversation.

THE CONVERSATION EXERCISES
10–20 MINUTES

1. **THE SKELETAL DIALOG:** Write the "skeletal dialog" on the board. Fill in a replacement to show students how the guided conversation method works. Call on a few pairs of students to practice the dialog, using the skeletal framework on the board.

> A. What's your last name?
> B. Park.
> A. How do you spell it?
> B. P-A-R-K.

2. **EXERCISE PRACTICE:** (optional) Have pairs of students simultaneously practice conversations in which they spell their last names.

3. **EXERCISE PRESENTATIONS:** Call on pairs of students to present their conversations to the class.

LISTENING
5–10 MINUTES

Listen and circle.

1. A. What's your last name?
   B. Phan.
   A. How do you spell it?
   B. P-H-A-N.

2. A. What's your last name?
   B. Black.
   A. How do you spell it?
   B. B-L-A-C-K.

3. A. What's your last name?
   B. Clayton.
   A. How do you spell it?
   B. C-L-A-Y-T-O-N.

4. A. What's your last name?
   B. Green.
   A. How do you spell it?
   B. G-R-E-E-N.

5. A. What's your last name?
   B. Kramer.
   A. How do you spell it?
   B. K-R-A-M-E-R.

6. A. What's your last name?
   B. Sanchez.
   A. How do you spell it?
   B. S-A-N-C-H-E-Z.

Answers

1. P-H-A-N
2. B-L-A-C-K
3. C-L-A-Y-T-O-N
4. G-R-E-E-N
5. K-R-A-M-E-R
6. S-A-N-C-H-E-Z

MISSING LETTERS
5–10 MINUTES

Explain that in this activity there are some letters that are missing from the alphabet. First, students need to write in the missing letters, and then they use those letters to spell a word from the lesson. In the example, the letters A, E, M, and N are missing. These missing letters spell the word *NAME*. Have students complete the activity, and then compare answers with a partner.

Answers

A L S T   (LAST)
F I R S T   (FIRST)

LANGUAGE IN *MOTION*
10 MINUTES

1. Have students walk around the classroom. Each student asks another student for his or her first and last names and their spellings and then writes the information on the chart.

    What's your first name?
    How do you spell it?
    What's your last name?
    How do you spell it?

2. Have students report what they found out. Call on students to tell you the names and spellings of the students they interviewed.

EXPANSION

1. Letters of the Alphabet ★
ACTIVITY MASTERS 1, 2 OR 3, 4

a. Make copies of Activity Masters 1 and 2 or Activity Masters 3 and 4, and cut them into cards.

b. Have students work in pairs. Give each pair a set of cards out of order, and tell them to place the cards face-down in a pile. Have students take turns picking up an alphabet card, showing it to their partner, and saying the letter.

2. Alphabetize! ★
ACTIVITY MASTERS 1, 2

a. Make copies of Activity Masters 1 and 2 and cut them into cards.

b. Have students work in pairs. Give each pair a set of cards, and have them work together to place the letters in alphabetical order.

c. Have Student A close his or her eyes. Have Student B take away several letters from the alphabet, leaving the "holes" visible. Have Student A open his or her eyes and identify the letters that are missing. As Student A names the letters, Student B replaces them.

d. Have the students continue the game, taking turns.

3. Stand In Order: Letters ★★
ACTIVITY MASTERS 1, 2 OR 3, 4

Select a random sample of the alphabet cards. Give one letter of the alphabet to each student, and have students arrange themselves in a line alphabetically.

4. Game: What's the Name? ★★
Note: Use the first names of students in the class for this activity.

a. Write a series of lines on the board to represent the letters in a student's name. For example: *Rosa*

b. Have students take turns guessing the letters in the name.

c. Write in the correct letters when students give them. Write the incorrect letters in a separate area of the board for student reference.

d. The first student to guess the name is the winner.

5. Spelling Names ★★
a. Write a list of names on the board. For example:

John	Alice	Robert	Larry	Walter
Jim	Ann	Roger	Louise	William
Jeff	Albert	Rita	Lucy	Wendy

b. Have students practice spelling these names, first chorally, then individually.

6. Name Dictation ★★
Dictate a name from the list in the previous activity for students to write down. Continue with other names from the list. Have students compare their answers.

(continued)

UNIT 1   **7**

7. Stand in Order: Names ★★

a. Have students write their first names in large print on a piece of paper.

b. Have students stand up, hold their names in front of them so everyone can see, and arrange themselves in alphabetical order.

c. When everyone is in order, have students call out the first letter of their names and then the names themselves. For example:

> Student 1: A—Alicia
> Student 2: C—Carlos
> Student 3: D—David
> Student 4: G—Gina

8. The Name Game ★★

Divide the class into two teams. Call out common English names—both male names (*David, Joseph, William*) and female names (*Ann, Margaret, Susan*). Have team members take turns identifying whether a name is for a male or a female. A team gets one point for each name correctly identified.

9. Class Discussion: Names in My Country ★★★

As a class, in pairs, or in small groups, have students talk about names in their countries.

> What are common first names for boys?
> What are common first names for girls?
> Do children have their parents' names?

LESSON OBJECTIVE

FOCUS

Numbers 0–10
Telephone numbers

VOCABULARY

Numbers 0–10

GETTING READY — 10 MINUTES

1. Review numbers 0–10, using your own visuals or the numbers on student book page 8. Point to a number and call on individual students to say it.

2. Introduce *telephone number*.

   a. Using a prop or visual, introduce the word *telephone*.

   b. Write a telephone number on the board. For example:

   273-9854

   c. Say: "This is my telephone number: two seven three–nine eight five four."

   d. Tell students that phone numbers are always pronounced with a pause after the third number.

   e. Have students repeat the number on the board.

   f. Write other numbers on the board, and have students practice saying them.

THE MODEL CONVERSATION — 10 MINUTES

1. **SETTING THE SCENE:** Have students look at the model photograph. Set the scene: "One person is asking the other for some information."

2. **LISTENING:** With books closed, have students listen to the model conversation—presented by you, by a pair of students, or on the audio program. Check students' understanding of the situation and the vocabulary.

3. **CLASS PRACTICE:** With books still closed, model each line, and have the whole class practice in unison.

4. **READING:** With books open, have students follow along as two students present the model.

5. **PAIR PRACTICE:** In pairs, have students practice the model conversation.

THE CONVERSATION EXERCISES — 10–20 MINUTES

1. **THE SKELETAL DIALOG:** Write the "skeletal dialog" on the board. Fill in the replacement with any telephone number you wish to show students how the guided conversation method works. Call on a few pairs of students to practice the dialog, using the skeletal framework on the board.

   A. What's your telephone number?
   B. 273–9854.
   A. Is that 273–9854?
   B. Yes. That's correct.

2. **EXERCISE PRACTICE:** (optional) Have pairs of students simultaneously practice the conversation, using any telephone numbers they wish.

3. **EXERCISE PRESENTATIONS:** Call on pairs of students to present their conversations to the class.

LANGUAGE IN *MOTION* — 10 MINUTES

Have students walk around the classroom, asking six students their telephone numbers. Have students fill in the chart on student book page 8 and then report to the class what they found out. (*Note*: Students can use their real phone numbers or make up any phone number they wish.)

MISSING NUMBERS — 5 MINUTES

There are three sets of numbers from 0–10 with numbers that are missing. Have students fill in the missing numbers and then compare answers with a partner.

Answers

4, 7, 9
2, 5, 8, 10
1, 2, 3, 4, 6, 7, 8, 9

LISTENING

Listen and circle.

1. A. What's your telephone number?
   B. 249–1115.
   A. Is that 249–1115?
   B. Yes. That's correct.

2. A. What's your telephone number?
   B. 463–9221.
   A. Is that 463–9221?
   B. Yes. That's correct.

3. A. What's your telephone number?
   B. 948–6137.
   A. Is that 948–6137?
   B. Yes. That's correct.

4. A. What's your telephone number?
   B. 671–2098.
   A. Is that 671–2098?
   B. Yes. That's correct.

5. A. What's your telephone number?
   B. 728–0303.
   A. Is that 728–0303?
   B. Yes. That's correct.

6. A. What's your telephone number?
   B. 837–1284.
   A. Is that 837–1284?
   B. Yes. That's correct.

Answers

1. 249–1115
2. 463–9221
3. 948–6137
4. 671–2098
5. 728–0303
6. 837–1284

MATCHING

Have students complete the activity and then compare answers with a partner.

Answers

1. 4   4. 8
2. 9   5. 7
3. 1   6. 3

COMMUNITY CONNECTIONS

1. Provide students with telephone books or copies of the page in your city or town's telephone book that provides this information.

2. Have students do the activity individually, in pairs, or in small groups and then report back to the class.

3. For homework, encourage students to call directory assistance to ask for these telephone numbers.

4. Write the following on the board, and have students fill in the numbers:

Police: _____

Fire: _____

Ambulance: _____

Poison Control Center: _____

EXPANSION

1. Circle Counting (Variation 1) ★

Have students sit in a circle. (For larger classes, have students sit in two circles.) Student 1 starts counting: "One." Student 2 continues: "Two." Students continue counting around the circle, stopping at ten.

Circle Counting (Variation 2) ★★

Have students go around the circle, counting backwards.

Circle Counting (Variation 3) ★★

Have students count around the circle, using odd numbers only.

Circle Counting (Variation 4) ★★

Have students count around the circle, using even numbers only.

2. Number Cards ★

Divide the class into pairs and give each student ten blank cards. Tell students to write an Arabic number on one side and the word on the other side. Have the pairs drill each other, using these cards. One partner shows the other an Arabic number, for example, and the partner says or writes the word. Then reverse roles.

3. Stand in Order: Numbers ★
ACTIVITY MASTER 5

Make a copy of Activity Master 5 and cut it into cards. Give each student a card, and have students stand up and arrange themselves in order, according to the number they have.

4. Number Match: Numbers and Words ★
ACTIVITY MASTERS 5, 6

Make a copy of Activity Masters 5 and 6 and cut them into cards. Distribute the cards to students, and have them walk around the room, trying to find other classmates who have the same number.

5. Number Dictation ★★

Divide the class into pairs. Have Student A choose a telephone number from the Listening exercise on student book page 9 and dictate it to Student B, who writes it down. Have Student A check Student B's answer. Then reverse roles.

6. Sorry. Wrong Number! ★★★

a. Write the following on the board:

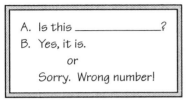

```
A. Is this _____?
B. Yes, it is.
        or
   Sorry. Wrong number!
```

b. For each of the numbered items in the Listening exercise on student book page 9, tell each student to write down one of the telephone numbers—either the number in the left column or the number in the right column.

c. Divide the class into pairs. Using the model on the board, have Student A "call" Student B and ask: "Is this (249–1115)?" Student B answers: "Yes, it is," if that student had chosen 249–1115, or "Sorry. Wrong number!" if that student had chosen 245–1119.

d. Continue with the remaining five sets of telephone numbers. Then reverse roles.

LESSON OBJECTIVE

Focus
Addresses
Numbers 1–10

Vocabulary
Street
Road
Avenue

GETTING READY
5–10 MINUTES

1. Review numbers 1–10.
2. Write the school's address on the board. Say: "This is the address of our school." Call on individual students to read the address.

MODEL CONVERSATION I
10 MINUTES

1. **SETTING THE SCENE:** Have students look at the model photograph. Set the scene: "One person is asking the other for information."

2. **LISTENING:** With books closed, have students listen to the model conversation—presented by you, by a pair of students, or on the audio program. Check students' understanding of the situation and the vocabulary.

3. **CLASS PRACTICE:** With books still closed, model each line, and have the whole class practice in unison.

4. **READING:** With books open, have students follow along as two students present the model.

5. **PAIR PRACTICE:** In pairs, have students practice the model conversation.

THE CONVERSATION EXERCISES
10–20 MINUTES

1. Write the abbreviations for Street, Road, and Avenue on the board, and then write the full words. For example:

```
St.  = Street
Rd.  = Road
Ave. = Avenue
```

2. **THE SKELETAL DIALOG:** Write the "skeletal dialog" on the board. Fill in the replacement

from Exercise 1 to show students how the guided conversation method works. Call on a few pairs of students to practice Exercise 1, using the skeletal framework on the board.

```
A. What's your address?
B. 4 Main Street.
A. 4 Main Street?
B. Yes. That's right.
```

3. **EXERCISE PRACTICE:** (optional) Have pairs of students simultaneously practice all the exercises.

4. **EXERCISE PRESENTATIONS:** Call on pairs of students to present their conversations to the class.

MODEL CONVERSATION II
10 MINUTES

1. **SETTING THE SCENE:** Have students look at the model photograph. Set the scene: "One person is asking the other for information."

2. **LISTENING:** With books closed, have students listen to the model conversation—presented by you, by a pair of students, or on the audio program. Check students' understanding of the situation and the vocabulary.

3. **CLASS PRACTICE:** With books still closed, model each line, and have the whole class practice in unison.

4. **READING:** With books open, have students follow along as two students present the model.

5. **PAIR PRACTICE:** In pairs, have students practice the model conversation.

THE CONVERSATION EXERCISES
10–20 MINUTES

1. **THE SKELETAL DIALOG:** Write the "skeletal dialog" on the board. Fill in the replacement from Exercise 1 to show students how the guided conversation method works. Call on a few pairs of students to practice Exercise 1, using the skeletal framework on the board.

```
A. My apartment number is 2A.
B. Did you say 2H?
A. No. 2A.
```

2. **EXERCISE PRACTICE:** (optional) Have pairs of students simultaneously practice all the exercises.

3. **EXERCISE PRESENTATIONS:** Call on pairs of students to present their conversations to the class.

PRONUNCIATION
5 MINUTES

In pairs, small groups, or as a class, have students practice these pairs of numbers, either individually or chorally.

LISTENING
5–10 MINUTES

Circle the apartment number you hear.

1. A. What's your apartment number?
   B. 6D.
   A. 6D?
   B. Yes. That's right.
2. A. What's your apartment number?
   B. 9J.
   A. 9J?
   B. Yes. That's right.
3. A. What's your apartment number?
   B. 1E.
   A. Did you say 1E?
   B. Yes. That's right.
4. A. What's your apartment number?
   B. 10K.
   A. Did you say 10K?
   B. Yes. That's correct.
5. A. What's your apartment number?
   B. 2D.
   A. 2D?
   B. Yes.
6. A. What's your apartment number?
   B. 8C.
   A. 8C?
   B. Yes. That's right.
7. A. What's your apartment number?
   B. 3E.
   A. Did you say 3E?
   B. Yes. That's right.

Answers

1. 6D	3. 1E	5. 2D	7. 3E
2. 9J	4. 10K	6. 8C	

FORM INFORMATION
5 MINUTES

Have students complete the activity and compare answers with a partner. Write the abbreviation for your state on the board if it is not included in the list on student book page 11.

FILL OUT THE FORM
10 MINUTES

Have students complete the form and compare answers with a partner.

EXPANSION

1. **Number Dictation** ★
   a. Dictate number and letter combinations. For example:

1A	7W	5C
3H	4N	10B

   b. Have students write what they hear and then compare their answers in pairs.
   c. Read the numbers again so students have an opportunity to correct themselves.

2. **Spelling** ★★
   In pairs or small groups, have students spell the names of their state, city, and street.

3. **Class Directory** ★★★
   a. Tell students that each of them is going to make a Class Directory—a list of all the names, addresses, and telephone numbers of everyone in the class.
   b. Have students make three columns on a piece of paper and write the following at the top of each column:

<u>Name</u>	<u>Address</u>	<u>Telephone Number</u>

   c. Have students fill out their directory by walking around the room and asking each other:

   What's your name?
   How do you spell it?
   What's your address?
   What's your telephone number?

   Variation: If there is concern about students giving out personal information, have them make up an address and phone number to give to each other.

4. **Interview** ★★★
   Make a form like the one on student book page 11 and give one copy to each student. Have students, working in pairs, take turns interviewing each other, asking the questions and filling in the information on the form.

LESSON OBJECTIVE

FOCUS

Family members

VOCABULARY

aunt	granddaughter	niece
brother	grandfather	sister
cousin	grandmother	son
daughter	mother	uncle
father	nephew	wife
grandson		

GETTING READY
10 MINUTES

Introduce vocabulary for family members.

1. Use your own visuals or draw a family tree on the board. For example:

2. Explain that Carla and Pablo are married. Carla is the *wife* and Pablo is the *husband*.

3. Ask students: "Who is the husband?" and "Who is the wife?"

4. Explain that Susanna and Samuel are Carla and Pablo's children. Carla is their *mother* and Pablo is their *father*. Susanna is Carla and Pablo's *daughter* and Samuel is their *son*.

5. Ask students: "Who is the mother?" and "Who is the father?", "Who is the daughter?" and "Who is the son?"

6. Explain that Anna and Henry are Carla's mother and father. Anna is Susanna and Samuel's *grandmother* and Henry is their *grandfather*.

7. Ask students: "Who is the grandmother?" and "Who is the grandfather?"

THE MODEL CONVERSATIONS
10 MINUTES

There are two model conversations. Introduce and practice the first model before going on to the second. For each model:

1. **SETTING THE SCENE:** Have students look at the model photograph. Set the scene:

   Model 1: "Someone is introducing his wife to a friend."
   Model 2: "Someone is introducing her husband to a friend."

2. **LISTENING:** With books closed, have students listen to the model conversation—presented by you, by a pair of students, or on the audio program. Check students' understanding of the situation and the vocabulary.

3. **CLASS PRACTICE:** With books still closed, model each line, and have the whole class practice in unison.

4. **READING:** With books open, have students follow along as two students present the model.

5. **PAIR PRACTICE:** In pairs, have students practice the model conversation.

THE CONVERSATION EXERCISES
10 MINUTES

1. **THE SKELETAL DIALOG:** Write the "skeletal dialog" on the board. Fill in the replacement from Exercise 1 to show students how the guided conversation method works. Call on a few pairs of students to practice Exercise 1, using the skeletal framework on the board.

   > A. This is my <u>mother</u>.
   > B. Nice to meet you.
   > C. Nice to meet you, too.

2. **VOCABULARY PRESENTATION:** Present the new vocabulary words in the exercises by reviewing the family tree you drew on the board. Then point to the photograph of each person in the book, say the word, and have the class repeat it chorally and individually. Check students' understanding and pronunciation of the vocabulary.

3. **EXERCISE PRACTICE:** (optional) Have pairs of students simultaneously practice all the exercises.

4. **EXERCISE PRESENTATIONS:** Call on pairs of students to present their conversations to the class.

A FAMILY TREE

Have students complete the sentences based on the family tree diagram and compare answers with a partner, a small group, or the whole class.

Answers

1. wife
2. husband
3. daughter
4. mother
5. father
6. brother
7. sister
8. grandmother
9. grandfather

MORE FAMILY VOCABULARY

1. Draw an extended family tree on the board. For example:

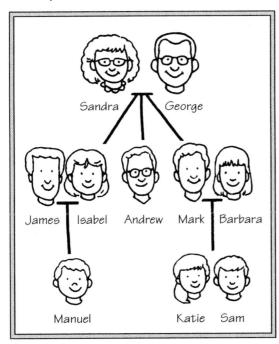

2. Explain that Sandra and George are married. They have three grown children (Isabel, Andrew, and Mark). The daughter Isabel is married to James, and they have one child. His name is Manuel. Mark and Barbara are married. They have two children—Katie and Sam.

3. Draw lines between relations on the family tree and explain the relationship. For example:

    Katie is Isabel's niece.
    Isabel is Katie's aunt.

In this manner, introduce the vocabulary on student book page 13—*aunt, uncle, niece, nephew, cousin, granddaughter,* and *grandson.*

YOUR FAMILY MEMBERS

Have students write their responses and share their responses with a partner, a small group, or the whole class.

LANGUAGE IN *MOTION*

1. Have students bring to class photographs of family members.

2. Write the following on the board:

    > Who is this?
    > What's his name?
    > What's her name?

Tell students to use *his* for men and boys and *her* for women and girls.

3. Have students walk around the classroom, asking questions about classmates' family members. (For larger classes, you can set a time limit or a limit on how many people students should ask.)

E X P A N S I O N

1. **He or She?** ✶

    a. Have students make two columns on a piece of paper and write <u>he</u> on the top of one column and <u>she</u> at the top of the other.

    b. Dictate family member words. For example:

mother	grandfather
father	granddaughter
daughter	grandson
son	aunt
sister	uncle
brother	niece
grandmother	nephew

    c. Have students write the words in the correct category. For example:

<u>he</u>	<u>she</u>
father	mother
grandson	daughter

    d. Have students compare their answers in pairs or write a master list on the board so students can check their spelling.

(continued)

2. Families ✷✷

a. Divide the class into groups. Each group is a *family*. Tell students to decide *who* is *who* in the family. One student is the mother; another is the father. There should be three generations.

b. Once they have decided who the people are, they should go *visit* another family.

c. The *father* or *mother* of the family introduces all the family members. For example: "This is my daughter Kim. This is my sister Gina."

d. Have all the *families* in the class visit each other and introduce their family members to each other.

3. My Family ✷✷✷

a. Have students fold a piece of paper in half lengthwise and then open up the paper.

b. On the left side, tell them to write a list of family members, and on the right side, the first names of these family members. For example:

mother	Marie
father	Joseph
sister	Carol
brother	Tom

c. Tell students to fold their paper lengthwise again and hand it to a partner (Student B) so that the partner sees only the person's name. For example:

Marie
Joseph
Carol
Tom

d. Student B asks about the first name on the list. For example: "Who is Marie?" Student A answers: "She's my mother."

e. Student B continues to ask about each name on the list.

f. Then reverse roles, where Student A asks and Student B answers.

4. Class Discussion: Family Words ✷✷✷

As a class, in pairs, or in small groups, have students tell common ways in their language of referring to close family members. For example, in English:

mother:	mom/mommy/mum/mummy/ma
father:	dad/daddy/papa/pa/abba
grandmother:	grandma/grammie/granny/nana/nona
grandfather:	grandpa/gramps/grampie

5. Family Tree Game ✷✷✷

Make statements about the family tree on student book page 13. Have students decide if the statements are true or false. If a statement is false, have students correct it. For example:

Frank is Maria's husband. [True.]
David is Frank's nephew. [False. David is Frank's son.]

6. Your Family ✷✷✷

a. Have students draw their family tree.

b. Divide the class into pairs. Student A shows his or her family tree to Student B and explains the family relationships. For example: "This is my mother. Her name is Maya."

c. Student B then writes as many sentences as he or she can about Student A's family.

d. Then have students reverse roles.

LESSON OBJECTIVE

FOCUS

Numbers 0–10

VOCABULARY

How old . . . ?

GETTING READY
5–10 MINUTES

1. Review numbers 1–10.
2. Introduce the questions in the model conversation.

   a. Draw a figure of a small child on the board. Say to the class: "This is my *daughter* (*niece, grandchild*). She's *5* (*2, 7, 9*) years old." Write on the board:

   > Who is this?
   > How old is she?

   b. Have a student ask you the questions and you answer.

THE MODEL CONVERSATIONS
10 MINUTES

There are two model conversations. Introduce and practice the first model before going on to the second. For each model:

1. **SETTING THE SCENE:** Have students look at the model photograph. Set the scene:

   Model 1: "Someone is showing a photograph to a friend."
   Model 2: "Someone is showing a photograph to a friend."

2. **LISTENING:** With books closed, have students listen to the model conversation—presented by you, by a pair of students, or on the audio program. Check students' understanding of the situation and the vocabulary.

3. **CLASS PRACTICE:** With books still closed, model each line, and have the whole class practice in unison.

4. **READING:** With books open, have students follow along as two students present the model.

5. **PAIR PRACTICE:** In pairs, have students practice the model conversation.

THE CONVERSATION EXERCISES
10–20 MINUTES

1. **THE SKELETAL DIALOG:** Write the "skeletal dialog" on the board. Fill in the replacement from Exercise 1 to show students how the guided conversation method works. Call on a few pairs of·students to practice Exercise 1, using the skeletal framework on the board.

   > A. Who is this?
   > B. This is my <u>sister</u>.
   > A. How old is <u>she</u>?
   > B. <u>She</u>'s <u>8</u> years old.

2. **VOCABULARY PRESENTATION:** Present the vocabulary words in the exercises. Point to the photograph of each person, say the word, and have the class repeat it chorally and individually. Check students' understanding and pronunciation of the vocabulary.

3. **EXERCISE PRACTICE:** (optional) Have pairs of students simultaneously practice all the exercises.

4. **EXERCISE PRESENTATIONS:** Call on pairs of students to present their conversations to the class.

NUMBERS
5 MINUTES

Have students write the numbers and compare answers with a partner, a small group, or the whole class.

Answers

7	9	4	8
2	5	3	6
0	10	1	

EXPANSION

1. **Disappearing Dialog** ✮

   Write the model conversation on the board and ask for two student volunteers to read the conversation. Erase a few of the words from the dialog, and have two different students read the conversation. Erase more words and call on two more students to read the conversation. Continue erasing words and calling on pairs of students until everyone has had a turn and the dialog has *disappeared*.

(continued)

2. Whose Family Is It? ✶✶

a. Have each student write two or three sentences about his or her family. For example:

> My son is two years old.
> His name is Fernando.

b. Make a master list of the sentences and distribute copies to students in the class. Have students guess who wrote the statements.

LANGUAGE EXPERIENCE JOURNAL

Have students draw their family trees, then write stories about their families. Depending on your students' writing abilities, either have them write in their journal or dictate their story for you to write. Then students should read what they have written to a classmate. If time permits, you may also want to write a response in each student's journal, sharing your own opinions and experiences as well as reacting to what the student has written.

Different Cultures, Different Ways
10 MINUTES

Have students first work in pairs or small groups, reacting to the photographs and responding to the questions. Then have students share with the class what they have talked about.

Students may not have the language to express what they would like to say. Encourage them to pantomime or bring in photos of people greeting each other in their culture.

PUT IT TOGETHER
15–20 MINUTES

In this activity, students talk with each other to find out the personal information necessary to complete the form.

1. Divide the class into pairs: Student A and Student B.
2. Tell all the Student A's to look at Part A of the activity on student book page 15. Tell all the Student B's to look at Part B on page 16.
3. Have everybody look at the first item on the form: *First Name.*
   a. In Student B's form, above *First,* it says, *Cathy.* Therefore, when Student A asks: "What's the person's first name?", Student B answers: "Cathy."
   b. Ask all the Student B's: " What's the person's first name?" Have all the Student B's respond in unison: "Cathy."
   c. Have all the Student A's look at their form. On their form above *Last,* it says, *Kwan.* Therefore, when Student B asks: "What's her last name?", Student A answers: "Kwan."
   d. Ask all the Student A's: "What's her last name?" Have all the Student A's respond in unison: "Kwan."
4. The Student A and Student B pairs are now ready to continue the activity with the rest of the application form.
5. When the pairs have completed their forms, have them check each other's answers.

VOCABULARY FOUNDATIONS
5–10 MINUTES

Have students review the list of words they have learned in this unit. Encourage students to get a small notebook where they can write down vocabulary that is new for them. If students have personal copies of dictionaries or picture dictionaries, have them look up these words in the dictionary and highlight them with a marker. Encourage them to look at their notebooks or dictionaries frequently to review what they have learned.

For additional practice, have students do one or more of the following activities.

1. **Taking Notes** ✮

   In their vocabulary notebooks or on a piece of paper, have students write all the words in one column. In a second column, have them write notes, draw pictures, or write the word in a sentence that will help them remember the meaning of the words.

2. **Spelling Game** ✮✮

   Divide the class into pairs. One partner reads a word and the other partner spells it.

3. **Categories** ✮✮

   In their personal vocabulary notebooks or on a separate piece of paper, have students write lists of the following:

   male family members
   female family members

4. **Alphabetical Order** ✮✮

   Have pairs of students work together to put in alphabetical order the list of family members in the second column of Vocabulary Foundations. Call on a pair to read their list, and have the class decide whether or not the order is correct.

LANGUAGE SKILL FOUNDATIONS
10–15 MINUTES

Explain to students that this is a list of skills they have learned in the unit. Students should become familiar with the vocabulary of describing their skills, but they don't need to master all the terms. For each speaking skill on the list, read the skill aloud to students, and have them demonstrate it. For example:

Teacher: I can introduce myself.
Students: Hello. My name is . . . .

(If students don't understand the vocabulary of a particular speaking skill, give them a concrete example rather than a description or explanation, and then have students practice your example and others.)

(continued)

Have students put a check next to each skill if they feel they have learned it. Use this information to determine which lessons you may want to review or reinforce for the entire class or for particular students. The Getting Ready and Expansion activities for this unit and the CD-ROM's Activity Bank of supplemental worksheets are excellent resources for additional practice. It may also be helpful to have stronger students or, if available, a classroom aide or volunteer, work with students who need more practice.

Talk About It! ▶▶▶   (Page 17)   20–30 MINUTES

(Page 17 is also available as a transparency.)

Use the scenes in this illustration to review the vocabulary and conversations in the unit. Have students first work in pairs or small groups to talk about the illustration and answer the questions posed at the bottom of the page. Then discuss as a class.

For additional motivating practice, students will enjoy doing one or more of the following activities.

This activity reviews Unit 1 vocabulary:

1. **The Longest List** ✲

   a. Divide the class into pairs or small groups. Have the pairs or groups make a list of all the family members they see in the scenes. Tell students to cover the list of words on student book page 16 with a piece of paper so they don't refer to that list. (Set a five-minute time limit for this activity.)

   b. Tell students to stop when the five minutes are up. Ask students to count the number of items on their lists. Who has the longest list?

   c. Check students' answers by calling on students to hold up their book, point to the person in the illustration, and say the family member word. Write each word on the board, and have students check their spelling.

These activities review Unit 1 conversations and grammar:

2. **Who Is It?** ✲✲

   a. Have students look at the transparency or the illustration on student book page 17.

   b. Say a phrase from a possible conversation in one of the scenes on page 17, and have students point to the character in the

illustration to identify who is speaking. For example:

> Teacher: Nice to meet you.
> Students: [*Point to the man shaking hands.*]
>
> Teacher: What's your address?
> Students: [*Point to the woman at the desk writing.*]
>
> Teacher: This is my wife.
> Students: [*Point to the man in the coffee shop.*]

Variation: Divide the class into pairs. One student says a line and the other points to the appropriate character. Then reverse roles.

3. **What Are They Doing?** ✲✲

   Have students look at the transparency or the illustration on student book page 17. Describe what a character is doing in one of the scenes, and have students point to the character in the illustration to identify it. For example:

> Teacher: He's bowing.
> Students: [*Point to one of the men who is bowing.*]
>
> Teacher: She's filling out a form.
> Students: [*Point to the woman at the desk.*]
>
> Teacher: He's introducing himself.
> Students: [*Point to the man waving to his new neighbors.*]

4. **What Are They Saying?** ✲✲

   a. Have pairs or small groups of students look at the transparency or the illustration on student book page 17.

   b. Point to one of the scenes in the illustration, and have the students in each pair or group work together to create a conversation between those characters.

   c. Call on students to present their conversations to the class.

   d. One at a time, point to other scenes on page 17 until students have created and presented conversations about all the scenes on the page.

Variation 1: Have pairs or small groups of students create a conversation based on one of the scenes, present it to the class, and the other students point to the appropriate scene in the book or on the transparency.

Variation 2: Have students write out the conversations they created for each scene.

UNIT 2 — THE CLASSROOM

LESSONS & UNIT ACTIVITIES	OBJECTIVES	TEXT	TEACHER'S GUIDE
Vocabulary Preview	Classroom objects	18–19	22
LESSON 1 Is this your pen?	Classroom objects	20–21	23–24
LESSON 2 Where's the bookshelf?	Classroom objects	22–23	25–27
LESSON 3 What's on your desk?	Classroom objects	24–25	28–30
LESSON 4 Classroom Actions	Classroom actions • Giving & following instructions	26–27	31–32
LESSON 5 NUMBERS: How many . . . ?	Numbers 11–19	28	33–34
Language Experience Journal	Writing about your classroom	28	34
Different Cultures / Different Ways	Classrooms around the world	29	35
Put It Together	Information Gap / Teamwork activity	29–30	35
Vocabulary Foundations / Language Skill Foundations	Review & skills checklist	30	35–36
Talk About It!	Review, conversations, activities, & games	31	36–37

UNIT RESOURCES

Audio Program:
Audio CD 1: Tracks 21–33
Audio Cassette 1A

Workbooks:
Activity Workbook
Literacy Workbook

Lesson Planner CD-ROM:
Activity Masters 7–11
Activity Bank Unit 2 Worksheets

Vocabulary Photo Cards: 1–31

Transparency: Color Overhead for Unit 2, page 31

PREVIEW
5 MINUTES

Activate students' prior knowledge of classroom vocabulary by doing either or both of the following:

1. Have students look around the classroom and brainstorm the classroom words they already know and write them on the board.

2. Have students look at the photographs on student book pages 18 and 19 while they cover the words at the bottom of the page. Have students identify the words they already know.

PRESENT
10–15 MINUTES

Using the photographs on student book pages 18 and 19 or the actual items in your classroom, point to each item or say its number, say the word, and have the class repeat it chorally and individually. (You can also play the audio program.) Check students' understanding and pronunciation of the vocabulary.

PRACTICE
10 MINUTES

As a class, in pairs, or in small groups, have students practice the vocabulary in either or both of the following ways:

• Say or write a word, and have students point to the item in their books or in the classroom, or tell the number.

• Point to a photograph in the book or in the classroom, or give the number, and have students say the word.

SPELLING PRACTICE
5–10 MINUTES

Say a word, and have students spell it aloud or write it. Or point to an item in the classroom or in the student book, and have students write the word. You can also spell a portion of a word on the board, and have students come to the board to complete it.

EXPANSION

1. **Tell and Show** ★
   PHOTO CARDS 1–21 (TWO SETS)

   a. Divide the class into pairs. Distribute all the Photo Cards randomly so every pair receives at least four or five cards.

   b. Have Student A in each pair select a Photo Card and tell Student B the classroom object. Have Student B point to the item on student book page 18 or 19.

   c. As the pairs finish using their Photo Cards, have them trade their sets with another pair and then continue the activity. Have students reverse roles each time they get a new set of cards.

2. **Match Game** ★
   PHOTO CARDS 1–21 (TWO SETS)

   a. Choose duplicate copies of any Photo Cards 1–21 and distribute them randomly, one to each student.

   b. Have students look at their card and identify the classroom object. Then have students circulate around the room, saying the name of the object on their card until they find their match. Make sure students don't show their cards to their classmates since this is a listening and speaking exercise.

   c. When students have found their match, have them compare their cards and come show you. Then give each student another Photo Card to keep the game going. Continue until students have found all the matches.

LESSON OBJECTIVE

Focus
Classroom objects

VOCABULARY
book
calculator
eraser
notebook
pen
pencil
ruler

GETTING READY

5–10 MINUTES

Use your own visuals, the photographs on student book page 20, or the objects themselves to practice the following classroom items: *book, calculator, eraser, notebook, pen, pencil,* and *ruler.* Say each word, and have the class repeat it chorally and individually. Check students' understanding and pronunciation of the vocabulary.

THE MODEL CONVERSATIONS

10 MINUTES

There are two model conversations. Introduce and practice the first model before going on to the second. For each model:

1. **SETTING THE SCENE:** Have students look at the model photograph. Set the scene:

   Model 1: "Two students are talking in class."
   Model 2: "Two students are talking in class."

2. **LISTENING:** With books closed, have students listen to the model conversation—presented by you, by a pair of students, or on the audio program. Check students' understanding of the situation and the vocabulary.

3. **CLASS PRACTICE:** With books still closed, model each line, and have the whole class practice in unison.

4. **READING:** With books open, have students follow along as two students present the model.

5. **PAIR PRACTICE:** In pairs, have students practice the model conversation.

THE CONVERSATION EXERCISES

10–20 MINUTES

1. **THE SKELETAL DIALOG:** Write the "skeletal dialog" on the board. Fill in the replacement from Exercise 1 to show students how the guided conversation method works. Call on a few pairs of students to practice Exercise 1, using the skeletal framework on the board.

   Model 1:

   > A. Is this your <u>pencil</u>?
   > B. Yes, it is. Thank you.

   Model 2:

   > A. Is this your <u>pencil</u>?
   > B. No, it isn't.

2. **VOCABULARY PRESENTATION:** Present the vocabulary words in the exercises. Point to the photograph of each item, say the word, and have the class repeat it chorally and individually. Check students' understanding and pronunciation of the vocabulary.

3. **EXERCISE PRACTICE:** (optional) Have pairs of students simultaneously practice all the exercises.

4. **EXERCISE PRESENTATIONS:** Call on pairs of students to present their conversations to the class.

MATCHING

5–10 MINUTES

Have students complete the activity and then compare answers with a partner.

Answers

1. pen
2. ruler
3. book
4. pencil
5. eraser
6. calculator
7. notebook

EXPANSION

1. Concentration ★

PHOTO CARDS 1–7 (TWO SETS)

a. Shuffle the cards and place them face-down in two rows of 7 each.

b. Divide the class into two teams. The object of the game is for students to find the matching cards and identify the vocabulary item. Both teams should be able to see the cards, since *concentrating* on their location is an important part of playing the game.

c. A student from Team 1 turns over two cards, and if they match, the student must identify the item. If the student correctly identifies the item, that team keeps the cards, and the student takes another turn. If they don't match or if the student isn't able to correctly identify the item, the student turns them face-down, and a member of Team 2 takes a turn.

d. The game continues until all the cards have been matched. The team with the most correct *matches* wins the game.

Variation:
PHOTO CARDS 1–7
ACTIVITY MASTER 7

Have the class play with one set of Photo Cards and one set of Word Cards.

2. Drawing Game ★★

ACTIVITY MASTER 7

You will need either an hourglass or a watch with a second hand for timing the following activity.

a. Make two copies of Activity Master 7. Cut them into cards and place the two sets of cards in two piles on a table or desk in the front of the classroom. Also, have a pad of paper and pencil next to each pile.

b. Divide the class into two teams. Have each team sit together in a different part of the room.

c. When you say: "Go!", a person from each team picks a card from the pile and draws the object. The rest of the team then guesses what the object is.

d. When a team correctly guesses the object, another team member picks a card and draws the object on that card.

e. Continue until each team has guessed all of the objects in their pile.

The team that guesses the objects in the shortest time wins the game.

3. Lost and Found ★★

a. Collect a similar item from all students—for example: a pen. Place the pens in a pile in the middle of the room.

b. Ask a student: "Is this your pen?" If the student says: "Yes it is", give it back to him or her. If he or she says: "No, it isn't", ask another student.

c. Once all the items have been returned, collect a different item. Ask a student to take your place and have that student ask: "Is this your _____?"

4. Memory Game ★★

a. Collect one item from each student. Tell students that the object of the game is to remember who the items belong to.

b. Ask the class about each item. For example: "Is this Mario's eraser?" Students answer: "Yes, it is" or "No, it isn't."

c. When the answer is *yes*, the item goes back to that student.

5. Is This Your . . . ? ★★★

Have students, working in pairs, put various items that belong to them on a common desk. Tell them to pick up items and ask and answer the question: "Is this your _____?" For example:

A. Is this your pen?
B. Yes, it is. Thank you. Is this your pencil?
A. No, it isn't.

LESSON OBJECTIVE

Focus

Classroom objects

VOCABULARY

board
bookshelf
bulletin board
chalk
computer
desk
globe
map
overhead projector
TV

GETTING READY

5–10 MINUTES

Use your own visuals, the photographs on page 22 of the student book, or the objects themselves, to practice the following classroom items: *board, bookshelf, bulletin board, chalk, computer, desk, globe, map, overhead projector,* and *TV.* Say each word, and have the class repeat it chorally and individually. Check students' understanding and pronunciation of the vocabulary.

THE MODEL CONVERSATION

10 MINUTES

1. **SETTING THE SCENE:** Have students look at the model photograph. Set the scene: "Two students are talking in class."

2. **LISTENING:** With books closed, have students listen to the model conversation—presented by you, by a pair of students, or on the audio program. Check students' understanding of the situation and the vocabulary.

3. **CLASS PRACTICE:** With books still closed, model each line, and have the whole class practice in unison.

4. **READING:** With books open, have students follow along as two students present the model.

5. **PAIR PRACTICE:** In pairs, have students practice the model conversation.

THE CONVERSATION EXERCISES

10–20 MINUTES

1. **THE SKELETAL DIALOG:** Write the "skeletal dialog" on the board. Fill in the replacement from Exercise 1 to show students how the guided conversation method works. Call on a few pairs of students to practice Exercise 1, using the skeletal framework on the board.

> A. Where's the <u>desk</u>?
> B. Over there.

2. **VOCABULARY PRESENTATION:** Present the vocabulary words in the exercises. Point to the photograph of each item, say the word, and have the class repeat it chorally and individually. Check students' understanding and pronunciation of the vocabulary.

3. **EXERCISE PRACTICE:** (optional) Have pairs of students simultaneously practice all the exercises.

4. **EXERCISE PRESENTATIONS:** Call on pairs of students to present their conversations to the class.

LISTENING

5–10 MINUTES

Listen and write the number under the correct picture.

1. A. Is this your pencil?
   B. Yes. Thank you.
2. A. Is this your book?
   B. Yes. Thank you.
3. A. Is this your pen?
   B. Yes. Thank you.
4. A. Where's the bookshelf?
   B. Over there.
5. A. Is this your notebook?
   B. Yes. Thank you.

Answers

3   1   4   2   5

GRAMMAR

10 MINUTES

1. Introduce *on* and *next to* by demonstrating with classroom objects.

   a. Place an eraser on a book and say: "The eraser is *on* the book." Have students repeat chorally and individually.

b. Place a book on the desk and say: "The book is *on* the desk." Have students repeat chorally and individually.

c. Place a pen next to the book and say: "The pen is *next to* the book." Have students repeat chorally and individually.

d. Place a pencil next to the pen and say: "The pencil is *next to* the pen." Have students repeat chorally and individually.

2. Practice the model sentences. Ask students: "Where's the computer?" Call on students to read the answer: "The computer is on the table." Do the same for the map.

CIRCLE THE CORRECT ANSWER

5 MINUTES

Have students choose the correct preposition based on the illustration and then compare answers with a partner.

Answers

1. on
2. next to
3. next to
4. on

EXPANSION

1. **Concentration** ★
   PHOTO CARDS 1–18 (TWO SETS)

   a. Choose duplicate copies of any nine Photo Cards 1–18. Shuffle the cards and place them face-down in three rows of 6 each.

   b. Divide the class into two teams. The object of the game is for students to find the matching cards and identify the vocabulary item. Both teams should be able to see the cards, since *concentrating* on their location is an important part of playing the game.

   c. A student from Team 1 turns over two cards and if they match, the student must identify the item. If the student correctly identifies the item, that team keeps the cards, and the student takes another turn. If they don't match or if the student isn't able to correctly identify the item, the student turns them face-down, and a member of Team 2 takes a turn.

   d. The game continues until all the cards have been matched. The team with the most correct *matches* wins the game.

Variation:
PHOTO CARDS 1–18

Any matching Word Cards from Activity Masters 7 and 8

Have the class play with one set of Photo Cards and one set of Word Cards.

2. **Clap in Rhythm** ★
   Object: Once a clapping rhythm is established, the students must continue naming different classroom objects.

   a. Have students sit in a circle.

   b. Establish a steady, even beat: one-two-three-four, one-two-three-four, etc., by having students clap their hands to their laps twice, and then clap their hands together twice. Repeat throughout the game, maintaining the same rhythm.

   c. The object is for each student in turn to name a different word *each time their hands are clapped together*. Nothing is said when students clap their hands on their laps.

   Note: The beat never stops! If a student misses a beat, he or she can either wait for the next beat or pass to the next student.

3. **Dictation Game** ★★
   a. In large print on a piece of paper, write a list of seven to nine vocabulary words from student book pages 20–23. For example:

   ```
   desk
   map
   pencil
   globe
   computer
   book
   eraser
   ```

   b. Divide the class into pairs—Student A and Student B. Have all the Student A's come outside the classroom with you. Show them the list of words, and have them spend a few minutes looking at it and trying to remember the words.

   c. Have the Student A's return to the classroom and give them three minutes to dictate what they remembered from the list to their Student B partners. The pair that has written the most words wins the game.

   d. For correction, have each pair call out one word on their list. Write that word on the board so students can check their spelling.

e. Repeat the game with a new list for Student B's to dictate to their Student A partners.

4. Where Is It? ★★

a. Write on the board:

> A. Where's the _____?
> B. Over there.
> { It's next to the _____.
> { It's on the _____.

b. Have students, working in pairs, ask and answer questions about objects in the classroom. For example:

> A. Where's the map?
> B. Over there. It's next to the bulletin board.

> A. Where's the computer?
> B. Over there. It's on the table.

5. Guessing Game ★★★

a. Tell students to choose an object in the classroom, and have them write two or three sentences about the location of the object. For example:

> It's on the bookshelf.
> It's next to the map.

b. Have students read their sentences aloud as the class listens and tries to guess the object.

6. Where Are My Things? ★★★

a. Write on the board:

> A. Where's the _____?
> B. Over there.
> { It's next to the _____.
> { It's on the _____.

b. Have students place a few of their things somewhere in the classroom. Then have pairs ask and answer questions about the location of the objects.

LESSON OBJECTIVE

Focus

Classroom objects

Vocabulary

book–books
eraser–erasers
pencil–pencils
pen–pens
ruler–rulers

GETTING READY
10 MINUTES

1. Introduce *a* and *an*.

   a. Put the following items on your desk: a pencil, a pen, a book, and a ruler. Point to each item and say: "a pencil," "a pen," and so on. Have students repeat chorally and individually.

   b. Put an eraser on your desk. Point and say: "an eraser." If there's an overhead projector in your classroom, say: "an overhead projector." Have students repeat chorally and individually.

   c. Write two columns on the board:

   d. Have students tell you words to write under each column. Explain that words starting with *a, e, i, o,* or *u* should be listed under the <u>an</u> column.

2. Introduce *there's*.

   a. Place single items on your desk—a pencil, a pen, a book, a ruler, and an eraser.

   b. Point to each individual item and model sentences such as: "There's a pen on my desk. There's a pencil on my desk." Have students repeat each sentence chorally and individually.

   c. Place single items on students' desks and ask students to make sentences about the items. For example: "There's a pen on my desk."

THE CONVERSATION EXERCISES
10–20 MINUTES

1. **THE MODEL SENTENCES:** With books closed, have students listen to the model sentences—presented by you, by a pair of students, or on the audio program.

2. **THE SKELETAL DIALOG:** Write the "skeletal dialog" on the board. Fill in the replacement from Exercise 1 to show students how the guided conversation method works. Call on a few pairs of students to practice Exercise 1, using the skeletal framework on the board.

   > A. What's on your desk?
   > B. There's <u>a pen</u> on my desk.

3. **VOCABULARY PRESENTATION:** Present the vocabulary words in the exercises. Point to the illustration of each item, say the word, and have the class repeat it chorally and individually. Check students' understanding and pronunciation of the vocabulary.

4. **EXERCISE PRACTICE:** (optional) Have pairs of students simultaneously practice all the exercises.

5. **EXERCISE PRESENTATIONS:** Call on pairs of students to present their conversations to the class.

GETTING READY
10 MINUTES

1. Introduce noun plurals.

   a. Collect the following items from students: some pens, pencils, erasers, and rulers. Hold up a pen and say: "a pen." Then hold up another pen and say: "two pens."

   b. Continue with other items you have collected—pencil/pencils, book/books, notebook/notebooks, eraser/erasers.

   c. Say a singular or plural form, and have students hold up one hand if they hear a singular and two hands if they hear a plural.

   d. Say a singular form (for example: *book*), and have students tell you the plural (*books*).

   e. Say a plural form (for example: *pens*), and have students tell you the singular (*pen*).

2. Introduce *there are.*

   a. Group multiple items on your desk—a few pens, pencils, books, erasers, and rulers.

   b. Point to the items and model sentences such as: "There are pens on my desk. There are pencils on my desk." Have students repeat each sentence chorally and individually.

   c. Place multiple items on students' desks and ask students to make sentences about the items. For example: "There are pens on my desk."

THE CONVERSATION EXERCISES
10–20 MINUTES

1. **THE MODEL SENTENCES:** With books closed, have students listen to the model sentences—presented by you, by a pair of students, or on the audio program.

2. **THE SKELETAL DIALOG:** Write the "skeletal dialog" on the board. Fill in the replacement from Exercise 1 to show students how the guided conversation method works. Call on a few pairs of students to practice Exercise 1, using the skeletal framework on the board.

   > A. What's on your desk?
   > B. There are <u>pens</u> on my desk.

3. **VOCABULARY PRESENTATION:** Present the vocabulary words in the exercises. Point to the illustration of each item, say the word, and have the class repeat it chorally and individually. Check students' understanding and pronunciation of the vocabulary.

4. **EXERCISE PRACTICE:** (optional) Have pairs of students simultaneously practice all the exercises.

5. **EXERCISE PRESENTATIONS:** Call on pairs of students to present their conversations to the class.

GRAMMAR
5 MINUTES

Have students complete the sentences, and then compare answers with a partner.

Answers

1. a
2. are
3. a
4. an
5. are
6. There's
7. There are
8. There's
9. There are
10. There are

MEMORY GAME
10 MINUTES

Have students stand in a circle for this activity. Student 1 says a sentence with a classroom item— for example: "In my classroom there's a teacher." Student 2 repeats what Student 1 said and adds another classroom item—for example: "In my classroom there's a teacher and a globe." Continue around the room in this fashion, with each student repeating what the previous student said and adding another classroom item. (*Note:* If the class is large, you can divide students into groups.)

COMMUNITY CONNECTIONS
10–15 MINUTES

Have students do the activity individually, in pairs, or in small groups, and then report back to the class. If you wish, you can make a master list on the board of all the different things that students found in their classroom visits.

EXPANSION

1. **Make a List!** ★

   a. In pairs or small groups, have students make a list of all the objects they see in their classroom. For example:

desks	a globe
a map	a computer
pencils	notebooks
pens	a board

   b. Compare students' lists and make a master list on the board.

2. **Up and Down!** ★★

   a. Have all the students sit down. Tell each student to say a sentence about what there is in the classroom. After a student has given a sentence, that student stands up.

   b. When all the students are standing up, the activity continues. But this time, after a student says a sentence, that student sits down. The activity stops when all the students are seated again.

3. **Remembering** ★★

   a. Write the following on the board:

      > There's a _____.
      > There's an _____.
      > There are _____.

(continued)

b. Arrange some individual items and groupings of items on your desk—for example: a pen, a few pencils, an eraser, some notebooks.

c. Tell students to look very carefully at the items for a few minutes because they have to remember everything they see.

d. Cover the items and have students either write about or tell what's on your desk, using the skeletal framework on the board.

4. True or False? (Variation 1) ★★

Call on students to take turns reading the sentences in the exercise on student book page 25. Students must say if the sentence is *true* or *false* about their own classroom.

5. True or False? (Variation 2) ★★★

Have each student write six sentences starting with *There's* or *There are* about objects in the classroom. Tell them that three sentences must be true and three must be false. Call on students to read their sentences to the class. The class decides if the sentence is true or false.

LESSON OBJECTIVE

FOCUS

Classroom actions
Giving & following instructions

VOCABULARY

Stand up.
Go to the board.
Write your name.
Erase your name.
Sit down.
Take out your book.
Open your book.
Raise your hand.
Close your book.
Put away your book.

VOCABULARY PRESENTATION   5–10 MINUTES

1. Use your own visuals, the photographs on student book page 26, or use pantomime and gestures to introduce the classroom actions. Model the pronunciation of each sentence. Have students repeat each one chorally and individually. (You can also play the audio program.)

2. In pairs or in small groups, have students point to each photograph and practice saying the sentence.

3. In pairs or small groups, have students look at each photograph, cover the sentence, and see if they can remember the sentence without looking at it.

MATCHING   5 MINUTES

Have students complete the activity, and then compare answers with a partner.

Answers

1. down.
2. up.
3. your name.
4. your book.
5. the door.
6. your name.
7. your pen.
8. your hand.

LISTENING   5 MINUTES

Listen and write the number under the correct picture.

1. Go to the board.
2. Write your name.
3. Take out your book.
4. Raise your hand.
5. Open your book.
6. Erase your name.

Answers

3	6	1
4	2	5

LANGUAGE IN *MOTION*   10 MINUTES

Have pairs of students take turns giving and following instructions.

Variation: This activity can be done in small groups or as a class, with students taking turns giving and following instructions.

E X P A N S I O N

1. Concentration ★

PHOTO CARDS 22–31 (TWO SETS)

a. Choose duplicate copies of any nine Photo Cards 22–31. Shuffle the cards and place them face-down in three rows of 6 each.

b. Divide the class into two teams. The object of the game is for students to find the matching cards and identify the vocabulary item. Both teams should be able to see the cards, since *concentrating* on their location is an important part of playing the game.

c. A student from Team 1 turns over two cards, and if they match, the student must identify the item. If the student correctly identifies the item, that team keeps the cards, and the student takes another turn. If they don't match or if the student isn't able to correctly identify the item, the student turns them face-down, and a member of Team 2 takes a turn.

d. The game continues until all the cards have been matched. The team with the most correct *matches* wins the game.

Variation:
PHOTO CARDS 22–31
ACTIVITY MASTER 9

Have the class play with one set of Photo Cards and one set of Word Cards.

(continued)

2. Follow the Command ★

Give instructions from the lesson, and call on students to carry them out.

3. "The Teacher Says" ★★

a. Tell the whole class to stand up. Give an instruction, and have the whole class follow it.

b. Explain to students that from now on they should only follow the instruction if you say: "The teacher says . . . " If you don't say: "The teacher says . . . " and a student follows the instruction, that student sits down and is *out* of the game.

c. Give instructions—some with "The teacher says . . ." and some without. The game continues until nobody is left standing.

Variation: Have individual students lead the activity stating their own name. For example: "Carlos says, 'Put away your books.'"

4. Miming Game ★★

Have students take turns choosing a classroom action and pantomiming it. The class must then guess what the action is.

Variation: This can be done as a game with two competing teams.

5. Finish the Sentence! ★★

Divide the class into two teams. Begin sentences, and have students from each team take turns finishing them with appropriate words from the lesson. For example:

Stand . . . *up.*
Go to . . . *the board.*
Write . . . *your name/the date.*
Erase . . . *the answer/your name.*
Take out . . . *your book/your pen/your pencil.*
Open . . . *your book.*
Raise . . . *your hand.*
Close . . . *your book/the door.*
Put away . . . *your book/your pen/your pencil.*

The team with the most correctly completed sentences wins.

6. Other Instructions ★★★

a. Tell students that as a teacher you tell them to do many things, not just the instructions listed on page 26. Ask what these other instructions are.

b. Write their list on the board. Possibilities include:

> Please listen.
> Please be quiet.
> Find a partner.
> Come over here.

c. Ask students what other instructions might be useful for them in your classroom. Possibilities include:

Please speak English.
Please speak more slowly.
Please repeat that.

d. Point out that *please* is used to make an instruction more polite.

LESSON OBJECTIVE

FOCUS

Numbers 11–19

VOCABULARY

Numbers 11–19

GETTING READY
5–10 MINUTES

Introduce numbers 11–19, using your own visuals or the numbers on student book page 28. Point to a number and call on individual students to say it. (You can also play the audio program.)

THE MODEL CONVERSATION
5–10 MINUTES

1. **SETTING THE SCENE:** Have students look at the model photograph. Set the scene: "Two students are talking on break."

2. **LISTENING:** With books closed, have students listen to the model conversation—presented by you, by a pair of students, or on the audio program. Check students' understanding of the situation and the vocabulary.

3. **CLASS PRACTICE:** With books still closed, model each line, and have the whole class practice in unison.

4. **READING:** With books open, have students follow along as two students present the model.

5. **PAIR PRACTICE:** In pairs, have students practice the model conversation.

THE CONVERSATION EXERCISES
10 MINUTES

1. **THE SKELETAL DIALOG:** Write the "skeletal dialog" on the board. Fill in the replacement, using a number between 12–19 to show students how the guided conversation method works. Call on a few pairs of students to practice the dialog, using the skeletal framework on the board.

> A. How many students are there in your English class?
> B. Twelve.

2. **EXERCISE PRACTICE:** (optional) Have pairs of students simultaneously practice conversations using numbers 11–19.

3. **EXERCISE PRESENTATIONS:** Call on pairs of students to present their conversations to the class.

NUMBERS
5–10 MINUTES

Have students complete the activity and then compare answers with a partner.

Answers

15	11	14	19
18	16	12	13

YOUR CLASSROOM INVENTORY
10 MINUTES

1. Explain that *inventory* answers the question "how many."

2. Write the following "skeletal dialog" on the board:

> A. How many _____ are there in our classroom?
> B. _____.

Fill in the replacement with *boards* and call on a few pairs of students to practice the dialog, using the skeletal framework.

> A. How many boards are there in our classroom?
> B. Two.

3. Write the answer on the board. Have students copy the answer in their student books.

> 2 boards

4. Call on a pair of students to model the next conversation (*bulletin boards*). Write their answer on the board, and have students copy it in their student books.

5. Have pairs of students simultaneously do the rest of the exercises.

6. Call on pairs of students to present their conversations and answers to the class. If there is disagreement about the answers, ask a student to stand up and count aloud the number of that item in the room to *prove* the answer.

EXPANSION

1. Circle Counting (Variation 1) ✶

Have students sit in a circle. (For larger classes, have students sit in two circles.) Student 1 starts counting: "One." Student 2 continues: "Two." Students continue counting around the circle, stopping at 19.

Circle Counting (Variation 2) ✶✶

Have students go around the circle, counting backwards from 19.

Circle Counting (Variation 3) ✶✶

Have students count around the circle, using odd numbers only.

Circle Counting (Variation 4) ✶✶

Have students count around the circle, using even numbers only.

2. Number Cards ✶

Divide the class into pairs and give each student nine blank cards. Tell students to write an Arabic number on one side and the word on the other side. Have the pairs drill each other, using these cards. One partner shows the other an Arabic number, for example, and the partner says or writes the word. Then reverse roles.

3. Stand in Order: Numbers ✶

ACTIVITY MASTER 10

Make a copy of Activity Master 10 and cut it into cards. Give each student a card, and have students stand up and arrange themselves in order, according to the number they have.

4. Number Match: Numbers and Words ✶

ACTIVITY MASTERS 10, 11

Make a copy of Activity Masters 10 and 11 and cut them into cards. Distribute the cards to students, and have them walk around the room, trying to find other classmates who have the same number.

5. Number Dictation ✶✶

Divide the class into pairs. Have Student A choose a number from student book page 28 and dictate it to Student B, who writes it down. Have Student A check Student B's answer. Then reverse roles.

LANGUAGE EXPERIENCE JOURNAL

Have students write about their classroom. Depending on your students' writing abilities, either have them write in their journal or dictate their story for you to write. Then students should read what they have written to a classmate. If time permits, you may also want to write a response in each student's journal, sharing your own opinions and experiences as well as reacting to what the student has written.

Different Cultures / Different Ways
10 MINUTES

Have students first work in pairs or small groups, reacting to the photographs and responding to the questions. Then have students share with the class what they have talked about.

PUT IT TOGETHER
15–20 MINUTES

In this activity, students talk with each other to find out what items are in the two different classrooms.

1. Divide the class into pairs: Student A and Student B.

2. Tell all the Student A's to look at Part A of the activity on page 29. Tell all the Student B's to look at Part B on page 30.

3. Have everybody look at the first item on the list: *bulletin board.*

   a. In Student B's list, next to *bulletin board,* it says, *Yes.* Therefore, when Student A asks: "Is there a bulletin board in your classroom?", Student B answers: "Yes, there is."

   b. Ask all the Student B's: "Is there a bulletin board in your classroom?" Have all the Student B's respond in unison: "Yes, there is."

   c. Have all the Student A's look at their list. In their list next to *bulletin board,* it says, *No.* Therefore, when Student B asks: "Is there a bulletin board in your classroom?", Student A answers: "No, there isn't."

   d. Ask all the Student A's: "Is there a bulletin board in your classroom?" Have all the Student A's respond in unison: "No, there isn't."

4. The Student A and Student B pairs are now ready to continue the activity with the rest of the items on their lists.

5. When the pairs have completed the activity, have them check each other's answers.

VOCABULARY FOUNDATIONS
5–10 MINUTES

Have students review the list of words they have learned in this unit. Encourage students to get a small notebook where they can write down vocabulary that is new for them. If students have personal copies of dictionaries or picture dictionaries, have them look up these words in the dictionary and highlight them with a marker. Encourage them to

look at their notebooks or dictionaries frequently to review what they have learned.

For additional practice, have students do one or more of the following activities.

1. **Taking Notes** ★

   In their vocabulary notebooks or on a piece of paper, have students write all the words in one column. In a second column, have them write notes, draw pictures, or write the word in a sentence that will help them remember the meaning of the words.

2. **Spelling Game** ★★

   Divide the class into pairs. One partner reads a word and the other partner spells it.

3. **Categories** ★★

   In their personal vocabulary notebooks or on a separate piece of paper, have students write lists of the following:

   small classroom objects
   large classroom objects
   classroom actions

4. **Alphabetical Order** ★★

   Have pairs of students work together to put in alphabetical order the list of classroom actions in the second column of Vocabulary Foundations. Call on a pair to read their list, and have the class decide whether or not the order is correct.

LANGUAGE SKILL FOUNDATIONS
10–15 MINUTES

Explain to students that this is a list of skills they have learned in the unit. Students should become familiar with the vocabulary of describing their skills, but they don't need to master all the terms. For each speaking skill on the list, read the skill aloud to students, and have them demonstrate it. For example:

Teacher: I can ask about someone's possessions.
Students: Is this your pen?

(If students don't understand the vocabulary of a particular speaking skill, give them a concrete example rather than a description or explanation, and then have students practice your example and others.)

Have students put a check next to each skill if they feel they have learned it. Use this information to determine which lessons you may want to review or reinforce for the entire class or for particular students. The Getting Ready and Expansion activities for this unit and the CD-ROM's Activity Bank of supplemental worksheets are excellent resources for additional practice. It may also be helpful to have stronger students or, if available, a classroom aide or volunteer, work with students who need more practice.

Talk About It! ▶▶▶ (Page 31) 20–30 MINUTES

(Page 31 is also available as a transparency.)

Use this scene to review the vocabulary and conversations in the unit. Have students first work in pairs or small groups to talk about the illustration and answer the questions posed at the bottom of the page. Then discuss as a class.

For additional motivating practice, students will enjoy doing one or more of the following activities.

These activities review Unit 2 vocabulary:

1. **The Longest List** ✶
   a. Divide the class into pairs or small groups. Have the pairs or groups make a list of all the objects they see in the scene. Tell students to cover the list of words on student book page 30 with a piece of paper so they don't refer to that list. (Set a five-minute time limit for this activity.)
   b. Tell students to stop when the five minutes are up. Ask students to count the number of items on their lists. Who has the longest list?
   c. Check students' answers by calling on students to name items on their lists. Write the words on the board, and have students check their spelling.

2. **Remember the Words!** ✶✶
   a. Tell students to spend two minutes looking carefully at the classroom scene on student book page 31.
   b. Have students close their books and write down all the classroom objects they remember from the illustration.
   c. Have students compare notes with a partner, and then look at the illustration again to see how well they remembered the classroom objects.

These activities review Unit 2 conversations and grammar:

3. **English in Action** ✶✶
   Call out various classroom actions from this unit and have students point to the character in the scene who is performing that action. For example:

   Teacher: Stand up.
   Students: [*Point to the female student standing up.*]

   Teacher: Open your book.
   Students: [*Point to the male student opening his book.*]

   Teacher: Put away your book.
   Students: [*Point to the male student putting away his book.*]

   Teacher: Erase your name on the board.
   Students: [*Point to the female student erasing the board.*]

   Variation: Have students work in pairs. One student calls out a classroom action and the other points to the person in the scene who is doing that action. Then reverse roles.

4. **Where Is It? (Version 1)** ✶✶
   Have students look at the transparency or the illustration on student book page 31 and answer questions about the location of objects in the classroom scene. For example:

   A. Where's the globe?
   B. It's on the bookshelf.

   A. Where's the map?
   B. It's next to the bulletin board.

   Variation: Do the activity in pairs or in small groups, with students asking as well as answering the questions. You can also do this as a game with competing teams.

5. **Where Is It? (Version 2)** ✶✶✶
   Divide the class into teams. Have each team prepare ten questions about the location of items in the illustration. Each team takes a turn asking the other team a question. The team with the most correct answers wins the game.

6. Do You Remember? ✪✪✪

Tell students to spend two minutes looking carefully at the illustration on student book page 31. Have students close their books. Ask students questions about the scene. For example:

How many students are there?
How many desks are there?
How many notebooks are there?
How many overhead projectors are there?

Is there a clock?
Is there a bookshelf?
Is there a screen?
Is there a calculator?
Is there a pen?

The following activity requires a preview of the present continuous tense, which is introduced in the next unit.

7. What Are They Doing? ✪✪✪

a. Write the following on the board:

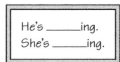

He's _____ing.
She's _____ing.

b. Tell a male student to raise his hand. Then tell the class: "He's raising his hand." Have students repeat. Tell another male student to stand up. Then tell the class: "He's standing up." Have students repeat. Then do the same with a female student ("She's raising her hand. She's standing up.").

c. In pairs, have students talk about what the characters in the scene are doing. One student points to a person and the other describes what he or she is doing. Then reverse roles.

Variation: One student describes what someone in the scene is doing and the other student points to that person.

UNIT 3 | EVERYDAY ACTIVITIES & WEATHER

LESSONS & UNIT ACTIVITIES	OBJECTIVES	TEXT	TEACHER'S GUIDE
Vocabulary Preview	Everyday activities	32–33	39
LESSON 1 What do you do every day?	Everyday activities	34–35	40–42
LESSON 2 What are you doing?	Everyday activities	36–37	43–44
LESSON 3 Every day or right now?	Everyday activities	38–39	45–47
LESSON 4 What's the weather?	Weather • Reading a map	40–41	48–49
LESSON 5 NUMBERS: How old are you?	Numbers 20–100	42	50–51
Language Experience Journal	Writing about what you do every day	42	51
Different Cultures / Different Ways	Household chores	43	52
Put It Together	Information Gap / Teamwork activity	43–44	52
Vocabulary Foundations / Language Skill Foundations	Review & skills checklist	44	52–53
Talk About It!	Review, conversations, activities, & games	45	53–54

UNIT RESOURCES

Audio Program:
Audio CD 1: Tracks 34–50
Audio Cassette 1B

Workbooks:
Activity Workbook
Literacy Workbook

Lesson Planner CD-ROM:
Activity Masters 12–21
Activity Bank Unit 3 Worksheets

Vocabulary Photo Cards: 32–67

Transparency: Color Overhead for Unit 3, page 45

PREVIEW
5 MINUTES

Activate students' prior knowledge of everyday activities vocabulary by doing either or both of the following:

1. Brainstorm with students the words for everyday activities they already know and write them on the board.

2. Have students look at the photographs on student book pages 32 and 33 while they cover the words at the bottom of the page. Have students identify the words they already know.

PRESENT
10–15 MINUTES

Using the photographs on student book pages 32 and 33, point to each item or say its number, say the phrase, and have the class repeat it chorally and individually. (You can also play the audio program.) Check students' understanding and pronunciation of the vocabulary.

PRACTICE
10 MINUTES

As a class, in pairs, or in small groups, have students practice the vocabulary in either or both of the following ways:

- Say or write a phrase, and have students point to the item in their books or tell the number.

- Point to a photograph in the student book or give the number, and have students say the phrase.

SPELLING PRACTICE
5–10 MINUTES

Say a word or phrase, and have students spell it aloud or write it. Or point to an item in the student book, and have students write the word or phrase. You can also spell a portion of a word or phrase on the board, and have students come to the board to complete it.

EXPANSION

1. **Tell and Show** ★
   PHOTO CARDS 32–60 (TWO SETS)

   a. Divide the class into pairs. Distribute all the Photo Cards randomly so every pair receives at least four or five cards.

   b. Have Student A in each pair select a Photo Card and tell Student B the daily activity. Have Student B point to the item on student book page 32 or 33.

   c. As the pairs finish using their Photo Cards, have them trade their sets with another pair and then continue the activity. Have students reverse roles each time they get a new set of cards.

2. **Match Game** ★
   PHOTO CARDS 32–60 (TWO SETS)

   a. Choose duplicate copies of any Photo Cards 32–60 and distribute them randomly, one to each student.

   b. Have students look at their card and identify the daily activity. Then have students circulate around the room, saying the daily activity on their card until they find their match. Make sure students don't show their cards to their classmates since this is a listening and speaking exercise.

   c. When students have found their match, have them compare their cards and come show you. Then give each student another Photo Card to keep the game going. Continue until students have found all the matches.

LESSON OBJECTIVE

Focus
Everyday activities

Vocabulary

brush my teeth	get up
comb my hair	go to bed
come home	go to school
cook dinner	go to work
eat breakfast	read
eat lunch	take a shower
get dressed	watch TV
get undressed	

GETTING READY
5–10 MINUTES

Introduce the concept of *every day*.

1. Bring a calendar to class. Point to all the days on the calendar and say:

   Every day I get up.
   Every day I take a shower.
   Every day I brush my teeth.

2. Ask students: "What do you do every day?" Indicate that they should use phrases from student book page 32 as their answers.

THE MODEL CONVERSATION
10 MINUTES

1. **SETTING THE SCENE:** Have students look at the model photograph. Set the scene: "Two friends are talking."

2. **LISTENING:** With books closed, have students listen to the model conversation—presented by you, by a pair of students, or on the audio program. Check students' understanding of the situation and the vocabulary.

3. **CLASS PRACTICE:** With books still closed, model each line, and have the whole class practice in unison.

4. **READING:** With books open, have students follow along as two students present the model.

5. **PAIR PRACTICE:** In pairs, have students practice the model conversation.

THE CONVERSATION EXERCISES
10–20 MINUTES

1. **THE SKELETAL DIALOG:** Write the "skeletal dialog" on the board. Fill in the replacement from items 1–3 on page 32 to show students how the guided conversation method works. Call on a few pairs of students to practice the dialog, using the skeletal framework on the board.

   A. What do you do every day?
   B. I <u>get up</u>, I <u>take a shower</u>, and I <u>brush my teeth</u>.

2. **VOCABULARY PRESENTATION:** Present the vocabulary words on student book page 32. Point to the photograph of each item, say the word, and have the class repeat it chorally and individually. Check students' understanding and pronunciation of the vocabulary.

3. **EXERCISE PRACTICE:** (optional) Have pairs of students simultaneously practice the conversation, using any words they wish from student book page 32.

4. **EXERCISE PRESENTATIONS:** Call on pairs of students to present their conversations to the class.

MEMORY GAME
10 MINUTES

Have students stand in a circle for this activity. Student 1 says an everyday activity that he or she does—for example: "Every day I get up." Student 2 repeats what Student 1 said and adds another everyday activity—for example: "Every day I get up and I take a shower." Continue around the room in this fashion, with each student repeating what the previous student said and adding another everyday activity. (*Note:* If the class is large, you can divide students into groups.)

MATCHING
5 MINUTES

Have students complete the activity and then compare answers with a partner.

Answers

1. TV	5. my hair
2. my teeth	6. breakfast
3. dressed	7. to work
4. a shower	8. undressed

LISTENING

5–10 MINUTES

Listen and write the number under the correct picture.

1. Every day I brush my teeth.
2. Every day I read.
3. Every day I cook dinner.
4. Every day I go to work.
5. Every day I go to bed.

Answers

3   1   5   2   4

WHAT'S THE ORDER?

10 MINUTES

Have students number each set of activities in chronological order and then compare answers with a partner or in small groups.

Answers

1. 3	3. 3	5. 3
2	2	2
1	1	1
2. 3	4. 2	6. 1
1	3	3
2	1	2

EXPANSION

1. Concentration ★

PHOTO CARDS 32–46 (TWO SETS)

a. Choose duplicate copies of any nine Photo Cards 32–46. Shuffle the cards and place them face-down in three rows of 6 each.

b. Divide the class into two teams. The object of the game is for students to find the matching cards and identify the vocabulary item. Both teams should be able to see the cards, since *concentrating* on their location is an important part of playing the game.

c. A student from Team 1 turns over two cards, and if they match, the student must identify the item. If the student correctly identifies the item, that team keeps the cards, and the student takes another turn. If they don't match or if the student isn't able to correctly identify the item, the student turns them face-down, and a member of Team 2 takes a turn.

d. The game continues until all the cards have been matched. The team with the most correct *matches* wins the game.

Variation:
PHOTO CARDS 32–46
ACTIVITY MASTER 12

Have the class play with one set of Photo Cards and one set of Word Cards.

2. Chain Game: Every Day ★★

Begin the chain: "Every day I get up in the morning and take a shower," and have students continue it. For example:

Teacher: Every day I get up in the morning and take a shower.

Student 1: Every day I get up in the morning, take a shower, and brush my teeth.

Student 2: Every day I get up in the morning, take a shower, brush my teeth, and comb my hair.

Etc.

3. "After That!" ★★

Have students sit in a circle. You start by saying: "I get up." Student 1 continues by telling an activity that might come *after that*. For example: "After I get up, I take a shower." Student 2 continues with another activity that might come *after that*. For example: "After I take a shower, I comb my hair." Continue around the circle until a student finally says: "I go to bed."

4. "Before That!" ★★

Students are still in the circle. You start by saying: "I go to bed." Student 1 continues by telling an activity that might come *before that*. For example: "Before I go to bed, I get undressed." Student 2 continues with another activity that might come *before that*. For example: "Before I get undressed, I read." Continue around the circle until a student finally says: "I get up."

5. Finish the Sentence! ★★

a. Write the following verbs on the board:

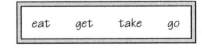

b. Start a sentence that begins with one of these verbs, and have students say phrases that can follow. For example:

I eat . . . *breakfast*.
I go . . . *to work*.

c. Either you or student volunteers write the phrase on the board under the appropriate verb.

6. Scrambled Phrase Game ★★★

ACTIVITY MASTER 13

a. Divide the class into groups of four. Make a copy of Activity Master 13 for each group. Cut the Activity Masters into cards and place them in two piles—one for verbs and the other for object phrases. Distribute the two sets of cards to each group.

b. Have students take turns picking up one card from each pile and reading the phrase to the group. For example:

The group decides if the phrase makes sense or doesn't make sense.

c. After all the cards have been picked, have the group lay out all the cards and put together all the phrase combinations that make sense.

7. Morning, Afternoon, or Evening? ★★★

a. Draw three columns on the board and write In the morning at the top of the left column, In the afternoon at the top of the middle column, and In the evening at the top of the right column.

b. Have students tell activities they do during each part of the day. Either you or student volunteers write the activity under the appropriate column. For example:

In the morning	In the afternoon	In the evening
I get up	I read	I watch TV

8. Listen and Number ★★★

Divide the class into pairs, and have students look at the pictures on student book page 32. Student A chooses six daily activities and tells a story beginning with the phrase, "Every day I . . ." Student B listens to the story and numbers the pictures in the order he or she hears them in Student A's story. Then reverse roles.

9. Story Dictation Game ★★★

a. Write the following story in large print on a piece of paper and make copies for half the students in the class:

> Every day I get up.
> I take a shower.
> I get dressed.
> I comb my hair.
> I eat breakfast.
> I go to work.

b. Divide the class into pairs. Give a copy of the story to each Student A to dictate to his or her partner.

c. Reverse roles, using the following story:

> Every day I go to school.
> I come home.
> I cook dinner.
> I read.
> I get undressed.
> I go to bed.

LESSON OBJECTIVE

Focus
Everyday activities

VOCABULARY

cleaning	making lunch
doing the laundry	making dinner
exercising	playing basketball
feeding the baby	playing the guitar
ironing	studying
listening to music	walking the dog
making breakfast	washing the dishes

GETTING READY
10–15 MINUTES

Introduce the concept of the present continuous tense.

1. Draw two columns on the board. At the top of the left column, write <u>Every Day</u>, and at the top of the right column, write <u>Now</u>.

2. Say several everyday activities in the simple present tense and write them in the appropriate column. Then mime the same actions and say: "Right now I'm (playing the guitar)." Write the present continuous form in the appropriate column. Continue with the other verbs. For example:

<u>Every Day</u>	<u>Now</u>
I play the guitar.	I'm playing the guitar.
I study English.	I'm studying English.
I wash the dishes.	I'm washing the dishes.

THE MODEL CONVERSATION
10–20 MINUTES

1. **SETTING THE SCENE:** Have students look at the model photographs. Set the scene: "Two friends are talking on the phone."

2. **LISTENING:** With books closed, have students listen to the model conversation—presented by you, by a pair of students, or on the audio program. Check students' understanding of the situation and the vocabulary.

3. **CLASS PRACTICE:** With books still closed, model each line, and have the whole class practice in unison.

4. **READING:** With books open, have students follow along as two students present the model.

5. **PAIR PRACTICE:** In pairs, have students practice the model conversation.

THE CONVERSATION EXERCISES
10–20 MINUTES

1. **THE SKELETAL DIALOG:** Write the "skeletal dialog" on the board. Fill in replacements to show students how the guided conversation method works. Call on a few pairs of students to practice the dialog, using the skeletal framework on the board.

> A. Hi! What are you doing?
> B. I'm <u>studying</u>. How about you?
> A. I'm <u>exercising</u>.

2. **VOCABULARY PRESENTATION:** Present the vocabulary words in the exercises. Point to the photograph of each item, say the word, and have the class repeat it chorally and individually. Check students' understanding and pronunciation of the vocabulary.

3. **EXERCISE PRACTICE:** (optional) Have pairs of students simultaneously practice all the exercises.

4. **EXERCISE PRESENTATIONS:** Call on pairs of students to present their conversations to the class.

MATCHING
5 MINUTES

Have students complete the activity and then compare answers with a partner.

Answers

1. music.	5. dinner.
2. lunch.	6. dishes.
3. the house.	7. TV.
4. baby.	8. guitar.

LISTENING
5–10 MINUTES

Listen and write the number under the correct picture.

1. A. What are you doing?
   B. I'm ironing.
2. A. What are you doing?
   B. I'm exercising.
3. A. What are you doing?
   B. I'm watching TV.

4. A. What are you doing?
   B. I'm washing the dishes.
5. A. What are you doing?
   B. I'm feeding the baby.
6. A. What are you doing?
   B. I'm listening to music.
7. A. What are you doing?
   B. I'm making dinner.
8. A. What are you doing?
   B. I'm eating lunch.

Answers

3	7	2	4
1	6	8	5

LANGUAGE IN *MOTION* 10 MINUTES

Have students take turns pantomiming activities for others to guess. Have them choose their activities from student book page 33 or hand them one of the Photo Cards 47–60 with an activity depicted on it.

EXPANSION

1. **Concentration** ★

   PHOTO CARDS 47–60 (TWO SETS)

   a. Choose duplicate copies of any nine Photo Cards 47–60. Shuffle the cards and place them face-down in three rows of 6 each.

   b. Divide the class into two teams. The object of the game is for students to find the matching cards and identify the vocabulary item. Both teams should be able to see the cards, since *concentrating* on their location is an important part of playing the game.

   c. A student from Team 1 turns over two cards, and if they match, the student must identify the item. If the student correctly identifies the item, that team keeps the cards, and the student takes another turn. If they don't match or if the student isn't able to correctly identify the item, the student turns them face-down, and a member of Team 2 takes a turn.

   d. The game continues until all the cards have been matched. The team with the most correct *matches* wins the game.

Variation:
PHOTO CARDS 47–60
ACTIVITY MASTER 14

Have the class play with one set of Photo Cards and one set of Word Cards.

2. **What Are You Doing?** ★★

   PHOTO CARDS 32–60

   Give a Photo Card to each student. Call one student to the front of the class to mime the action on his or her card. Other students say what he or she is doing, for example: "taking a shower."

3. **Alphabetical Order** ★★

   Have pairs of students work together to put in alphabetical order the ten activities depicted in the photographs on student book page 36. Call on a pair to read their list, and have the class decide whether or not the order is correct.

4. **Scrambled Phrase Game** ★★★

   ACTIVITY MASTER 15

   a. Divide the class into groups of four. Make a copy of Activity Master 15 for each group. Cut the Activity Masters into cards and place them in two piles—one for verbs and the other for object phrases. Distribute the two sets of cards to each group.

   b. Have students take turns picking up one card from each pile and reading the phrase to the group. For example:

making		basketball

   The group decides if the phrase makes sense or doesn't make sense.

   c. After all the cards have been picked, have the group lay out all the cards and put together all the phrase combinations that make sense.

5. **Magazine Photos** ★★★

   Bring in magazine photos that show people involved in everyday activities. As a class, in pairs, or in small groups, have students describe what's happening in the photos.

LESSON OBJECTIVE

FOCUS

Everyday activities

VOCABULARY

clean	making
cleaning	play
make	playing

GETTING READY

10 MINUTES

Contrast *every day* and *right now.*

1. Draw on the board a calendar for the week. Draw an arrow to today and write down that moment's actual time—for example: 9:30. Next to the arrow, write <u>right now</u>. Draw a circle around the whole week and above it write <u>every day</u>.

2. Make two columns on the board: <u>Every Day</u> and <u>Right Now</u>.

3. Ask students: "What do you do every day?" Write their answers in the <u>Every Day</u> column on the board. For example:

> <u>Every Day</u>
> I make breakfast.
> I eat lunch.
> I clean the house.

4. Using the list on the board, ask students: "Are you making breakfast right now? Are you eating lunch right now?" Students answer: "No."

5. Ask students: "What are you doing right now?" Write their answers on the board. Answers should include:

> <u>Right Now</u>
> I'm sitting in the classroom.
> I'm listening to the teacher.

6. Write the following on the board:

> I read.   I'm reading.

7. Draw an arrow from the *'m* contraction to the *-ing*. Explain to students that the *'m* and *-ing* go together.

THE MODEL CONVERSATION

10 MINUTES

1. **SETTING THE SCENE:** Have students look at the model photograph. Ask: "What do you see in his hands?" (A book.) "What is he doing?" (He's reading.) Set the scene: "This person and a friend are talking."

2. **LISTENING:** With books closed, have students listen to the model conversation—presented by you, by a pair of students, or on the audio program. Check students' understanding of the situation and the vocabulary.

3. **CLASS PRACTICE:** With books still closed, model each line, and have the whole class practice in unison.

4. **READING:** With books open, have students follow along as two students present the model.

5. **PAIR PRACTICE:** In pairs, have students practice the model conversation.

THE CONVERSATION EXERCISES

10 MINUTES

1. **THE SKELETAL DIALOG:** Write the "skeletal dialog" on the board. Fill in the replacement from Exercise 1 to show students how the guided conversation method works. Call on a few pairs of students to practice Exercise 1, using the skeletal framework on the board.

> A. What do you do every day?
> B. I <u>clean</u>.
> A. What are you doing right now?
> B. I'm <u>cleaning</u>.

2. **VOCABULARY PRESENTATION:** Present the vocabulary words in the exercises. Point to the photograph of each item, say the words, and have the class repeat them chorally and individually. Check students' understanding and pronunciation of the vocabulary.

3. **EXERCISE PRACTICE:** (optional) Have pairs of students simultaneously practice all the exercises.

4. **EXERCISE PRESENTATIONS:** Call on pairs of students to present their conversations to the class.

LISTENING

10 MINUTES

Listen and circle the correct words.

1. I study.
2. I'm eating dinner.
3. I exercise.
4. I'm combing my hair.
5. I'm listening to music.
6. I go to work.
7. I read.
8. I'm making lunch.

Answers

1. every day
2. right now
3. every day
4. right now
5. right now
6. every day
7. every day
8. right now

GRAMMAR

10 MINUTES

Have students circle the correct word and compare answers with a partner, a small group, or the whole class.

Answers

1. study
2. eating
3. go
4. doing
5. make
6. playing
7. feeding
8. read
9. ironing
10. listening

GRAMMAR

15–20 MINUTES

1. Review verbs in the first-person singular of the simple present tense, using student book pages 32 and 33 or Photo Cards 32–60.

   a. Point to a visual and tell about every day. For example: "Every day I make breakfast."

   b. Point to other visuals and have students make similar sentences. For example:

      Every day I study.
      Every day I make dinner.
      Every day I clean.
      Every day I wash the dishes.

2. Introduce the third-person singular of the present tense.

   a. Write on the board:

   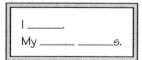

3. Introduce the third-person singular of the present tense.

   b. Also write the following verbs on the board:

cook	– cooks
eat	– eats
make	– makes
walk	– walks

   c. Make sentences such as the following, emphasizing the pronunciation of the final third-person [s]:

      I cook.
      My son cooks.

      I make breakfast.
      My husband makes breakfast.

      Have students practice sentences with these verbs.

   d. Write the following verbs on the board:

clean	– cleans
comb	– combs
feed	– feeds
iron	– irons
listen	– listens
play	– plays
read	– reads

   e. Make sentences such as the following, emphasizing the pronunciation of the final third-person [z]:

      I clean.
      My husband cleans.

      I listen to music.
      My daughter listens to music.

      Have students practice sentences with these verbs.

   f. Write the following verbs on the board:

brush	– brushes
exercise	– exercises
wash	– washes
watch	– watches

   g. Make sentences such as the following, emphasizing the pronunciation of the final third-person [ɪs]:

      I exercise.
      My wife exercises.

      I watch TV.
      My son watches TV.

Have students practice sentences with these verbs.

Note: Point out that the *-es* in *goes* does not add a syllable to the verb. The *-es* is a spelling convention—*s* never follows *o* in English.

3. Have students circle the correct word in the Grammar exercise and compare answers with a partner, a small group, or the whole class.

Answers

1. brush
2. cleans
3. washes
4. eat
5. plays
6. exercises
7. go
8. cooks
9. comb
10. watches

EXPANSION

1. Listen and Write ★

Divide the class into pairs. Say the following sentences, and have students write them. Then have the pairs check each other's sentences.

I read.	I eat.
I'm reading.	I'm playing.
I'm cooking.	I'm ironing.
I clean.	I watch TV.

2. Making Sentences ★★

ACTIVITY MASTER 16

Divide the class into pairs. Make enough copies of Activity Master 16 for half the class. Cut them into cards, and distribute one set to each pair of students. Have students take turns picking up a prompt and then saying the complete sentence.

Variation: Students can write their complete sentences and then compare their answers with other pairs.

3. Category Dictation ★★★

a. Have students make two columns on a piece of paper. Have them write Every Day at the top of the left column and Right Now at the top of the right column.

b. Dictate sentences from the lesson, and have students write them in the appropriate column. For example:

Every Day	Right Now
My father cooks dinner.	I'm ironing.
I study.	My brother is eating lunch.

c. After students have written down a sentence, write the sentence on the board so students can correct their work.

4. Every Day or Right Now? ★★★

a. Have students write four sentences—two with present continuous verbs and two with simple present.

b. In small groups, have students take turns reading their sentences aloud, and have the group members say: "Every day" or "Right now," depending on the sentence. For example:

Student: I come home.
Group members: Every day.

Student: I'm studying.
Group members: Right now.

5. Magazine Photos ★★★

a. Bring in photographs from magazines.

b. Write the following questions on the board:

> What is the person doing now?
> What do you think? What does he/she
> do every day?

c. Have students respond in pairs, small groups, or as a class.

LESSON OBJECTIVE

Focus

Weather
Reading a map

VOCABULARY

cloudy	raining
cold	snowing
foggy	sunny
hot	

GETTING READY
5–10 MINUTES

Activate students' prior knowledge of weather words. Have students look out the window.

Ask: "What's the weather?" Write students' answers on the board. Alternatively, show the class Photo Cards 61–67. Have students identify the weather vocabulary they already know.

THE MODEL CONVERSATION
5–10 MINUTES

1. **SETTING THE SCENE:** Have students look at the model photographs. Set the scene: "Two friends are talking on the phone."

2. **LISTENING:** With books closed, have students listen to the model conversation—presented by you, by a pair of students, or on the audio program. Check students' understanding of the situation and the vocabulary.

3. **CLASS PRACTICE:** With books still closed, model each line, and have the whole class practice in unison.

4. **READING:** With books open, have students follow along as two students present the model.

5. **PAIR PRACTICE:** In pairs, have students practice the model conversation.

THE CONVERSATION EXERCISES
10–20 MINUTES

1. **THE SKELETAL DIALOG:** Write the "skeletal dialog" on the board. Fill in the replacement from Exercise 1 to show students how the guided conversation method works. Call on a few pairs of students to practice Exercise 1, using the skeletal framework on the board.

> A. What's the weather?
> B. It's cloudy.

2. **VOCABULARY PRESENTATION:** Present the vocabulary words in the exercises. Point to the photograph of each item, say the phrase, and have the class repeat it chorally and individually. Check students' understanding and pronunciation of the vocabulary.

3. **EXERCISE PRACTICE:** (optional) Have pairs of students simultaneously practice all the exercises.

4. **EXERCISE PRESENTATIONS:** Call on pairs of students to present their conversations to the class.

What's the weather where YOU live?

In the same pairs, have students ask and answer the question.

LISTENING
5–10 MINUTES

Listen and write the number under the correct picture.

1. A. What's the weather?
   B. It's cold.

2. A. What's the weather?
   B. It's cloudy.

3. A. What's the weather?
   B. It's snowing.

4. A. What's the weather?
   B. It's foggy.

5. A. What's the weather?
   B. It's hot.

Answers

4   2   1   3   5

WEATHER MAP

GETTING READY
5 MINUTES

1. Introduce the weather icons in the upper right corner of the weather map. Point to each icon and say the type of weather. Have students repeat chorally and individually.

2. For students' reference, write the following on the board:

$$85°–90° = hot$$
$$20° = cold$$

THE CONVERSATION EXERCISES
10–20 MINUTES

1. **THE SKELETAL DIALOG:** Write the "skeletal dialog" on the board. Fill in the replacement with information from the weather map to show students how the guided conversation method works. Call on a few pairs of students to practice the dialog, using the skeletal framework on the board.

> A. What's the weather today in <u>Chicago</u>?
> B. It's <u>snowing</u>.

2. **VOCABULARY PRESENTATION:** Say each city name on the weather map, and have the class repeat it chorally and individually. Check students' pronunciation of the words.

3. **EXERCISE PRACTICE:** (optional) Have pairs of students simultaneously practice conversations about the other cities on the map.

4. **EXERCISE PRESENTATIONS:** Call on pairs of students to present their conversations to the class.

5. **LISTENING AND SPEAKING PRACTICE:** Questions about the weather map are also on the audio program.

COMMUNITY CONNECTIONS
10 MINUTES

Bring multiple newspapers to class, or have students bring newspapers to class. Individually, in pairs, or in small groups, have students complete the chart in the book by looking in a newspaper for the weather in any cities they wish. Have students report back to the class.

EXPANSION

1. **Concentration** ★

   PHOTO CARDS 61–67 (TWO SETS)

   a. Shuffle the cards and place them face-down in two rows of 7 each.

   b. Divide the class into two teams. The object of the game is for students to find the matching cards and identify the vocabulary item. Both teams should be able to see the cards, since *concentrating* on their location is an important part of playing the game.

c. A student from Team 1 turns over two cards, and if they match, the student must identify the item. If the student correctly identifies the item, that team keeps the cards, and the student takes another turn. If they don't match or if the student isn't able to correctly identify the item, the student turns them face-down, and a member of Team 2 takes a turn.

d. The game continues until all the cards have been matched. The team with the most correct *matches* wins the game.

Variation:
PHOTO CARDS 61–67
ACTIVITY MASTER 17

Have the class play with one set of Photo Cards and one set of Word Cards.

2. **Scrambled Words** ★★

   a. Choose words from the lesson, and write them on the board or on a card with the letters scrambled out of order. For example:

   b. Have students take turns guessing what the word is. [sunny]

Variation 1: Do the activity in pairs or small groups, with students taking turns scrambling words for others to guess.

Variation 2: Do the activity as a class game with competing teams.

LESSON OBJECTIVE

FOCUS

Numbers 20–100

VOCABULARY

Numbers 20–100

GETTING READY 5–10 MINUTES

Introduce numbers 20–100, using your own visuals or the numbers on student book page 42. Point to a number and call on individual students to say it. (You can also play the audio program.)

THE CONVERSATION EXERCISES 10–15 MINUTES

1. **THE SKELETAL DIALOGS:** Write the "skeletal dialogs" on the board. Fill in the replacement for the first model with "20" and the second model with "21" to show students how the guided conversation method works. Call on a few pairs of students to practice the dialogs, using the skeletal frameworks on the board. (The models are also on the audio program.)

> A. How old are you?
> B. I'm 20 years old.
>
> A. What's your address?
> B. 21 Main Street.

2. **EXERCISE PRACTICE:** (optional) Have pairs of students simultaneously practice conversations, using any numbers they wish between 20 and 100.

3. **EXERCISE PRESENTATIONS:** Call on pairs of students to present their conversations to the class.

NUMBERS 10 MINUTES

Have students complete the activity and then compare answers with a partner.

Answers

30	24	41	82
50	26	67	75

TEMPERATURES 10 MINUTES

1. Write the following "skeletal dialog" on the board:

> A. What's the temperature in _____?
> B. It's _____ degrees.

2. Ask about the temperature in Chicago (*What's the temperature in Chicago?*). Have students look at the map on student book page 41, tell you the temperature (20), and complete the dialog (*It's 20 degrees.*).

3. Call on a few pairs of students to practice the dialog, using the skeletal framework on the board and the temperatures on the map on student book page 41.

4. Have pairs of students simultaneously practice the conversation while reading the weather map.

5. Call on pairs of students to present their conversations and answers to the class. If there is disagreement about the answers, ask a student to point to the city on the map to *prove* the answer.

6. For listening and speaking practice, questions about the map on student book page 41 are also on the audio program.

EXPANSION

1. **Circle Counting (Variation 1)** ★

Have students sit in a circle. (For larger classes, have students sit in two circles.) Student 1 starts counting by tens: "Ten." Student 2 continues: "Twenty." Students continue counting around the circle, stopping at 100.

Circle Counting (Variation 2) ★★

Have students go around the circle, counting backwards by ones from 100. For example:

Student 1: 100
Student 2: 99
Student 3: 98

Circle Counting (Variation 3) ★★

Have students count around the circle, using odd numbers only.

Circle Counting (Variation 4) ★★

Have students count around the circle, using even numbers only.

2. Number Cards ★

Divide the class into pairs and give each student nine blank cards. Tell students to write the Arabic number (20, 30, 40, 50, 60, 70, 80, 90, 100) on one side and the word on the other side. Have the pairs drill each other, using these cards. One partner shows the other an Arabic number and the partner says or writes the word. Then reverse roles.

3. Stand in Order: Numbers ★

ACTIVITY MASTER 18

Make a copy of Activity Master 18 and cut it into cards. Give each student a card, and have students stand up and arrange themselves in order, according to the number they have.

4. Number Match: Numbers and Words ★

ACTIVITY MASTERS 18, 19

Make a copy of Activity Masters 18 and 19 and cut them into cards. Distribute the cards to students, and have them walk around the room, trying to find other classmates who have the same number.

5. Number Dictation ★★

Divide the class into pairs. Have Student A choose a number between 1 and 100 and dictate it to Student B, who writes it down. Have Student A check Student B's answer. Then reverse roles.

6. Number Contrast ★★

Pronunciation Note: Numbers ending in *-teen* stress that last syllable. Numbers ending in *-y* don't.

a. Write the following table on the board:

A	B
13	30
14	40
15	50
16	60
17	70
18	80
19	90

b. Call out a number, and have the class tell you whether it is an A number or a B number. For example:

Teacher: Fourteen.
Class: A.

Teacher: Eighty.
Class: B.

c. Once students have demonstrated they hear the difference between these numbers, have students take turns calling out a number, and have the class identify whether it is an A or B number.

7. What's the Temperature? ★★★

a. Bring in multiple copies of a current weather map from a newspaper or the Internet.

b. Write the following "skeletal dialog" on the board:

A. What's the temperature in _____?
B. It's _____ degrees.

c. Have pairs of students practice the conversation while reading their weather map.

d. Call on pairs of students to present their conversations and answers to the class.

8. Information Gap ★★★

ACTIVITY MASTER 20

a. Make multiple copies of Activity Master 20 and cut them in half (Table A and Table B).

b. Divide the class into pairs. Give each partner a different table—A or B. Have students share their information and fill in their tables. For example:

Student A: What's the temperature in Miami?
Student B: It's 95 degrees.

c. When the students have finished completing their tables, have them look at their partner's tables to make sure they have written the information correctly.

LANGUAGE EXPERIENCE JOURNAL

Have students write about their daily activities. Depending on your students' writing abilities, either have them write in their journal or dictate their story for you to write. Then students should read what they have written to a classmate. If time permits, you may also want to write a response in each student's journal, sharing your own opinions and experiences as well as reacting to what the student has written.

Different Cultures/ *Different Ways*
10 MINUTES

Have students first work in pairs or small groups, reacting to the photographs and responding to the questions. Then have students share with the class what they have talked about.

PUT IT TOGETHER
15–20 MINUTES

In this activity, students talk with each other to find out what they do every day.

1. Divide the class into pairs: Student A and Student B.

2. Tell all the Student A's to look at Part A of the activity on page 43. Tell all the Student B's to look at Part B on page 44.

3. Have students look at the *You* column and put a check mark by the activities they do every day.

4. Then, have everybody look at the first item on the list: *clean*.

    a. Have all the Student B's look at their lists. Explain that if there is a check mark next to *clean*, they answer: "Yes, I do," when Student A asks: "Do you clean the house every day?" If there is no check mark next to *clean*, they answer: "No, I don't."

    b. Ask one Student B: "Do you clean the house every day?" After he or she answers, ask one more Student B in order to show how the activity works.

    c. Have all the Student A's look at their lists. Explain that if there is a check mark next to *clean*, they answer: "Yes, I do," when Student B asks: "Do you clean the house every day?" If there is no check mark next to *clean*, they answer: "No, I don't."

    d. Ask one Student A: "Do you clean the house every day?" After he or she answers, ask one more Student A in order to show how the activity works.

5. The Student A and Student B pairs are now ready to continue the activity with the rest of the words on their lists.

6. When the pairs have completed the activity, have them check each other's answers.

VOCABULARY FOUNDATIONS
5–10 MINUTES

Have students review the list of words they have learned in this unit. Encourage students to get a small notebook where they can write down vocabulary that is new for them. If students have personal copies of dictionaries or picture dictionaries, have them look up these words in the dictionary and highlight them with a marker. Encourage them to look at their notebooks or dictionaries frequently to review what they have learned.

For additional practice, have students do one or more of the following activities.

1. **Taking Notes** ✭

    In their vocabulary notebooks or on a piece of paper, have students write all the words in one column. In a second column, have them write notes, draw pictures, or write the word in a sentence that will help them remember the meaning of the words.

2. **Beanbag Toss** ✭

    Have students stand in a circle and toss a beanbag back and forth. The student to whom the beanbag is tossed must name a word from the unit. Continue until everyone has had a turn.

3. **Spelling Game** ✭✭

    Divide the class into pairs. One partner reads a word and the other partner spells it.

4. **Miming Game** ✭✭
    PHOTO CARDS 32–60

    Place the cards on a desk or table in front of the room. Have students take turns coming to the front of the room, picking a card, and pantomiming the action on the card. The class tries to guess the action.

    Variation: Do the activity as a game with teams. Set a 30-second time limit for each turn. If the team can't guess the action within the time limit, the card is returned to the pile and the other team takes its turn with a new card.

5. **Finish the Sentence!** ✭✭

    Begin a sentence with one of the verbs in Vocabulary Foundations, and have students finish the sentence. For example:

    > I eat . . . *breakfast.*
    > I feed . . . *the baby.*

I go . . . *to school/to work/to bed.*
I listen . . . *to music.*
I play . . . *basketball/the guitar.*
I wash . . . *the dishes.*
I do . . . *the laundry.*
I comb . . *my hair.*
I cook . . . *breakfast/lunch/dinner.*
I make . . . *breakfast/lunch/dinner.*

6. Category Dictation ★★★

a. Have students make three columns on a piece of paper:

> sports activities
> activities in the home
> weather

b. Dictate words from the unit, and have students write them in the appropriate column. Make sure all students have covered the vocabulary items on student book page 44 with a piece of paper so they don't refer to that list.

c. As a class, in pairs, or in small groups, have students check their work.

7. Match Game ★★★

Activity Master 21

a. Make a copy of Activity Master 21, cut it into cards, and distribute the cards randomly, one to each student.

b. Have students memorize the question or response on their card and leave their cards on their desks. Then have students circulate around the room, saying their lines until they find their match.

c. When all the pairs have been matched, have students say their question and answer for the whole class.

8. Scrambled Phrase Game ★★★

Activity Masters 13, 15

a. Divide the class into groups of four. Make a copy of Activity Masters 13 and 15 for each group. Cut the Activity Masters into cards and place them in two piles—one for verbs and the other for object phrases. Distribute the two sets of cards to each group.

b. Have students take turns picking up one card from each pile and reading the phrase to the group. For example:

wash	breakfast

The group decides if the phrase makes sense or doesn't make sense.

c. After all the cards have been picked, have the group lay out all the cards and put together all the phrase combinations that make sense.

LANGUAGE SKILL FOUNDATIONS   10–15 MINUTES

Explain to students that this is a list of skills they have learned in the unit. Students should become familiar with the vocabulary of describing their skills, but they don't need to master all the terms. For each speaking skill on the list, read the skill aloud to students and have them demonstrate it. For example:

> Teacher: I can ask about other people's daily activities.
> Students: What do you do every day?

(If students don't understand the vocabulary of a particular speaking skill, give them a concrete example rather than a description or explanation, and then have students practice your example and others.)

Have students put a check next to each skill if they feel they have learned it. Use this information to determine which lessons you may want to review or reinforce for the entire class or for particular students. The Getting Ready and Expansion activities for this unit and the CD-ROM's Activity Bank of supplemental worksheets are excellent resources for additional practice. It may also be helpful to have stronger students or, if available, a classroom aide or volunteer, work with students who need more practice.

Talk About It! ▶▶▶   (Page 45)   20–30 MINUTES

(Page 45 is also available as a transparency.)

Use the scenes in this illustration to review the vocabulary and conversations in the unit. Have students first work in pairs or small groups to talk about the illustration and answer the question posed at the bottom of the page. Then discuss as a class.

For additional motivating practice, students will enjoy doing one or more of the following activities.

These activities review Unit 3 vocabulary:

1. The Longest List ★

a. Write the following on the board:

> Everyday Activities
> brush my teeth
> comb my hair

(continued)

b. Divide the class into pairs or small groups. Have the pairs or groups make a list of all the everyday activities they see in the scenes. Tell students to cover the list of words on student book page 44 with a piece of paper so they don't refer to that list. (Set a five-minute time limit for this activity.)

c. Tell students to stop when the five minutes are up. Ask students to count the number of items on their lists. Who has the longest list?

d. Check students' answers by calling on students to name items on their lists. Write the words on the board, and have students check their spelling.

2. Remember the Words! ★★

a. Tell students to spend two minutes looking carefully at the scenes on student book page 45.

b. Have students close their books and write down all the everyday activities they remember from the illustration.

c. Have students compare notes with a partner and then look at the scenes again to see how well they remembered the vocabulary of this unit.

These activities review Unit 3 conversations and grammar:

3. Who Is It? (Simple Present) ★★

a. Write the following question on the board:

> What do you do every day?

b. Have students look at the transparency or the illustration on student book page 45.

c. Say a sentence, and have students point to a character in the illustration to identify who is speaking. For example:

Teacher: I walk the dog.
Students: [*Point to the man walking the dog.*]

Teacher: I take a shower.
Students: [*Point to the woman taking a shower.*]

Teacher: I make dinner.
Students: [*Point to the man cutting vegetables.*]

Variation: Divide the class into pairs. One student says a line and the other points to the appropriate character. Then reverse roles.

4. Who Is It? (Present Continuous) ★★

a. Write the following question on the board:

> What are you doing right now?

b. Have students look at the transparency or the illustration on student book page 45.

c. Say a sentence, and have students point to a character in the illustration to identify who is speaking. For example:

Teacher: I'm watching TV.
Students: [*Point to the woman watching TV.*]

Teacher: I'm studying.
Students: [*Point to the girl studying.*]

Teacher: I'm feeding the baby.
Students: [*Point to the man feeding the baby.*]

Variation: Divide the class into pairs. One student says a line and the other points to the appropriate character. Then reverse roles.

5. What Are They Doing? ★★

Call out various everyday activities from this unit, and have students point to the character in the illustration who is performing that action. For example:

Teacher: This person is getting up.
Students: [*Point to the man getting up.*]

Teacher: This person is going to school.
Students: [*Point to the boy going to school.*]

Teacher: This person is watching TV.
Students: [*Point to the woman watching TV.*]

Teacher: This person is studying.
Students: [*Point to the woman studying.*]

Variation: Have students work in pairs. One student calls out an everyday activity and the other points to the person in the illustration who is doing that action. Then reverse roles.

UNIT 4 | NUMBERS, TIME, CALENDAR, MONEY

UNIT RESOURCES

Audio Program:
Audio CD 2: Tracks 2–29
Audio Cassette 2A

Workbooks:
Activity Workbook
Literacy Workbook

Lesson Planner CD-ROM:
Activity Masters 5, 6, 10, 11, 18, 19, 22–39
Activity Bank Unit 4 Worksheets

Vocabulary Photo Cards: 68–76

Transparency: Color Overhead for Unit 4, page 63

UNIT 4 VOCABULARY PREVIEW

NUMBERS 1–100 (PAGE 46)

REVIEW THE NUMBERS 5–10 MINUTES

Review the numbers 1–100 in one or more of the following ways:

1. Count together with the class from 1–100.
   Variation: Everybody clap their hands while counting.

2. Have students sit in a circle, with Student 1 beginning with "one," Student 2 continuing with "two," and so forth around the circle, continuing up to 100.

3. Review the pronunciation of *-teen* vs. *-ty*.
   a. Write the following on the board:

13	30
14	40
15	50
16	60
17	70
18	80
19	90

   b. Have students practice the pronunciation of *-teen* vs. *-ty* chorally and individually.

4. Play the number list on the audio program. Check students' pronunciation of the numbers.

DAYS OF THE WEEK (PAGE 47)

PREVIEW DAYS OF THE WEEK 5 MINUTES

Activate students' prior knowledge of the days of the week. Have students tell you the days of the week they know. As they tell you each day, write the full word on the board with only the first letter capitalized. (*Note*: Write the days in chronological order, leaving room for missing days.)

PRESENT DAYS OF THE WEEK 5 MINUTES

Complete the days of the week on the board, filling in any days students didn't brainstorm before. Next to each day of the week, write the capitalized abbreviation of the word, just as they are written in the calendar on student book page 47. For example:

Sunday	SUN
Monday	MON
Tuesday	TUE
Wednesday	WED
Thursday	THU
Friday	FRI
Saturday	SAT

Using the calendar on student book page 47, your words on the board, or an actual calendar in your classroom, point to each day or say its number, say the word, and have the class repeat it chorally and individually. (You can also play the audio program.) Check students' understanding and pronunciation of the vocabulary.

PRACTICE DAYS OF THE WEEK 5 MINUTES

As a class, in pairs, or in small groups, have students practice the vocabulary in either or both of the following ways:

- Say or write the full word for a day of the week, and have students point to the day in the calendar in their books or tell the number.
- Point to a day of the week in the calendar in the book or give the number, and have students say the word.

DAYS OF THE WEEK SPELLING PRACTICE 5 MINUTES

Say a day of the week, and have students spell it aloud or write it. Or point to a day of the week on your calendar or the calendar in the student book, and have students write the word. Make sure students capitalize the first letter. You can also spell a portion of a word on the board, and have students come to the board to complete it.

MONTHS OF THE YEAR (PAGE 47)

PREVIEW MONTHS OF THE YEAR 5 MINUTES

Activate students' prior knowledge of the months of the year. Have students tell you the months of the year they know. As they tell you each month, write the whole word on the board with only the first letter capitalized. (*Note*: Write the months in chronological order, leaving room for missing months.)

PRESENT MONTHS OF THE YEAR — 5–10 MINUTES

Complete the months of the year on the board, filling in any month students didn't brainstorm before. Next to each month, write the capitalized abbreviation of the word, just as they are written in the calendar on student book page 47. For example:

January	JAN
February	FEB
March	MAR
April	APR
May	MAY
June	JUN
July	JUL
August	AUG
September	SEP
October	OCT
November	NOV
December	DEC

Using the calendar on student book page 47, your words on the board, or an actual calendar in your classroom, point to each month or say its number, say the word, and have the class repeat it chorally and individually. (You can also play the audio program.) Check students' understanding and pronunciation of the vocabulary.

PRACTICE MONTHS OF THE YEAR — 5 MINUTES

As a class, in pairs, or in small groups, have students practice the vocabulary in either or both of the following ways:

- Say or write the full word for a month, and have students point to the month in the calendar in their books or tell the number.
- Point to a month in the calendar in the book or give the number, and have students say the word.

MONTHS OF THE YEAR PRACTICE SPELLING — 5 MINUTES

Say a month, and have students spell it aloud or write it. Or point to a month in the student book, and have students write the word. Make sure students capitalize the first letter. You can also spell a portion of a word on the board, and have students come to the board to complete it.

COINS AND CURRENCY (PAGE 47)

PREVIEW COINS AND CURRENCY — 5 MINUTES

Activate students' prior knowledge of coins and currency. Have students reach in their pockets and pull out coins and dollar bills, show them to the class, and tell the name of each one. As they tell you each word, write it on the board.

PRESENT COINS AND CURRENCY — 5 MINUTES

Using the photographs on student book page 47 or the actual items from your pockets, point to each item or say the number, say the word, and have the class repeat it chorally and individually. (You can also play the audio program.) Check students' understanding and pronunciation of the vocabulary.

PRACTICE COINS AND CURRENCY — 5 MINUTES

As a class, in pairs, or in small groups, have students practice the vocabulary in either or both of the following ways:

- Say or write a word, and have students point to the actual coin on their desks, or the item in their books, or tell the number.
- Point to a photograph in the book or show the class a coin, or give the number, and have students say the word.

COINS AND CURRENCY SPELLING PRACTICE — 5 MINUTES

Say a word, and have students spell it aloud or write it. Or show students a coin or bill, or point to one in the student book, and have students write the word. You can also spell a portion of a word on the board, and have students come to the board to complete it.

EXPANSION

1. **Concentration** ✷

   ACTIVITY MASTERS 5 AND 6, 10 AND 11, 18 AND 19, OR 22, OR 23

   a. Divide the class into pairs. Make multiple copies of one of the above sets of Activity Masters, cut them into cards, and give each pair one set of cards. Have students shuffle the cards and place them face-down in four rows of 5 each.

(continued)

b. The object of the game is for students to find the matching cards. Both students should be able to see the cards, since *concentrating* on their location is an important part of playing the game.

c. Student A turns over two cards, and if they match, the student must identify the item. If the student correctly identifies the item, he or she keeps the cards, and the student takes another turn. If they don't match or if the student isn't able to correctly identify the item, the student turns them face-down, and Student B takes a turn.

d. The game continues until all the cards have been matched. The student with the most correct *matches* wins the game.

2. Match Game ✭

ACTIVITY MASTERS 5 AND 6, 10 AND 11, 18 AND 19, OR 22, OR 23

a. Make duplicate copies of the above sets of Activity Masters, cut them into cards, and distribute them randomly, one to each student.

b. Have students look at their card and identify the word. Then have students circulate around the room, saying the word on their card until they find their match. Make sure students don't show their cards to their classmates since this is a listening and speaking exercise.

c. When students have found their match, have them compare their cards and come show you.

3. True or False? ✭✭

PHOTO CARDS 68–73

Show students Photo Cards of coins and currency, or show the actual items from your own pockets. Make a false statement about the item, and have students correct it. For example:

Teacher: [*showing the class a dollar bill or Photo Card 73*] This is a nickel.
Students: No. It's a dollar bill.

Teacher: [*showing the class a penny or Photo Card 68*] This is a quarter.
Students: No. It's a penny.

LESSON OBJECTIVE

FOCUS

Numbers 1–100 review
Addition
Saying large numbers

VOCABULARY

Numbers 1–100

GETTING READY

5–10
MINUTES

Review numbers 1–100 in one or more of the following ways:

- Have students sit in a circle, with Student 1 beginning with "one," Student 2 continuing with "two," and so forth around the circle.
- Have students go around the circle, counting backwards.
- Have students go around the circle, using odd numbers only.
- Have students go around the circle, using even numbers only.
- Dictate a series of numbers to students—for example: "1–50–22–34–43–9–15." Have students write down what you say, and then read the numbers back to you.

THE MODEL CONVERSATION

10
MINUTES

1. **SETTING THE SCENE:** Have students look at the model photograph. Set the scene: "A teacher is asking a student a question."

2. **LISTENING:** With books closed, have students listen to the model conversation—presented by you, by a pair of students, or on the audio program. Check students' understanding of the situation and the vocabulary.

3. **CLASS PRACTICE:** With books still closed, model each line, and have the whole class practice in unison.

4. **READING:** With books open, have students follow along as two students present the model.

5. **PAIR PRACTICE:** In pairs, have students practice the model conversation.

THE CONVERSATION EXERCISES

10–20
MINUTES

1. **THE SKELETAL DIALOG:** Write the "skeletal dialog" on the board. Fill in the replacement from Exercise 1 to show students how the guided conversation method works. Call on a few pairs of students to practice Exercise 1, using the skeletal framework on the board.

> A. How much is <u>seven</u> plus <u>three</u>?
> B. <u>Seven</u> plus <u>three</u> is <u>ten</u>.

2. **EXERCISE PRACTICE:** (optional) Have pairs of students simultaneously practice all the exercises.

3. **EXERCISE PRESENTATIONS:** Call on pairs of students to present their conversations to the class.

LANGUAGE IN *MOTION*

10
MINUTES

Have students walk around the classroom, asking each other addition problems. (For larger classes, you can set a time limit or a limit on how many people students should ask.)

PRONUNCIATION

10
MINUTES

1. Read the numbers aloud, and have students repeat after you chorally and individually. (You can also play the audio program.)

2. In pairs, have students take turns pronouncing the numbers. Circulate to listen in on their pronunciation and to provide feedback as necessary.

LISTENING

5–10
MINUTES

Circle the number you hear.

1. There are eight people in the room.
2. There are twenty books on the bookshelf.
3. There are thirteen students in the class.
4. There are forty desks in the classroom.
5. My address is sixteen Pond Road.
6. There are seven people in my family.
7. There are fifty classrooms in the school.
8. The temperature is ninety degrees.

Answers

1.	8	5.	16
2.	20	6.	7
3.	13	7.	50
4.	40	8.	90

SAYING LARGE NUMBERS & ROOM NUMBERS

GETTING READY 5–10 MINUTES

1. Write some three-digit numbers on the board and draw a slash between the first and second digit. Read the first few examples to the class. Then invite students to read the remaining examples. For example:

```
2/63      4/35
7/14      6/58
1/26      9/42
```

Teacher: two sixty-three
Teacher: seven fourteen
Teacher: one twenty-six
Student 1: four thirty-five
Student 2: six fifty-eight
Student 3: nine forty-two

2. Repeat the above process with four digit numbers. For example:

```
27/63      42/30
79/14      61/80
10/16      90/40
```

Teacher: twenty-seven sixty-three
Teacher: seventy-nine fourteen
Teacher: ten sixteen
Student 1: forty-two thirty
Student 2: sixty-one eighty
Student 3: ninety forty

3. Remind students that *zero* is "oh" in telephone numbers and addresses. Write three and four digit numbers with zeroes. Invite students to come to the board to draw the slash to separate the digits, and then read the number aloud. For example:

2/03—Student 1: two oh three
61/09—Student 2: sixty-one oh nine
13/40—Student 3: thirteen forty
13/04—Student 4: thirteen oh four

MODEL SENTENCES 10 MINUTES

1. **SETTING THE SCENE:** Set the scene: "People are giving personal information."

2. **LISTENING:** With books closed, have students listen to the model sentences—presented by you, by several students, or on the audio program.

3. **CLASS PRACTICE:** With books still closed, model each sentence, and have the whole class practice in unison.

4. **READING:** With books open, have students follow along as three students present the model sentences.

5. **PAIR PRACTICE:** In pairs, have students practice the model sentences.

THE EXERCISES 10 MINUTES

Have students do the activity individually, in pairs, or as a class. (You can also play the audio program.)

LISTENING 5–10 MINUTES

Write the number you hear.

1. My address is fourteen Main Street.
2. My address is seventy Pond Street.
3. My address is twenty-nine Center Street.
4. My address is thirty-four eleven Central Avenue.
5. My address is eighteen thirty-six Washington Street.
6. My apartment number is two thirty-four.
7. My apartment number is three nineteen.
8. My apartment number is four oh eight.
9. My English class is in Room one twenty-three.
10. My English class is in Room two thirteen.
11. My address is fifteen oh nine Main Street.
12. My address is thirty-two oh seven Central Avenue.

Answers

1.	14	5.	1836	9.	123
2.	70	6.	234	10.	213
3.	29	7.	319	11.	1509
4.	3411	8.	408	12.	3207

EXPANSION

1. **Math Problem Dictation** ★

   Dictate simple addition problems. For example:

   three plus five
   nine plus seven
   fifteen plus four

   After dictating the problems, have students solve them and compare their answers in pairs.

2. Listen for the Numbers ✶✶

a. Read the following sentences, and have students write down the number they hear:

> There are 17 people in the room.
> There are 30 books on the bookshelf.
> There are 18 students in the class.
> There are 15 desks in the classroom.
> There are 19 classrooms in the school.
> The temperature in Miami is 70 degrees.
> The temperature in Portland is 50 degrees.
> My address is 162 Main Street.
> My address is 1028 Main Street.
> My address is 403 Washington Avenue.
> My address is 8210 Center Street.

b. Have pairs of students check each others' answers.

3. Large Number Concentration ✶✶
ACTIVITY MASTER 24

Note: There are two sets of cards on Activity Master 24. Depending on the ability of the students in your class, you can give all 20 cards to each pair, or you can have the pairs do the activity twice—first with the top 10 cards, then with the bottom 10 cards.

a. Divide the class into pairs. Make multiple copies of Activity Master 24, cut them into cards, and give each pair one set of cards. Have students shuffle the cards and place them face-down in two rows of 10 each (or two rows of 5 each if you do the simplified version of the activity).

b. The object of the game is for students to find the matching cards. Both students should be able to see the cards, since *concentrating* on their location is an important part of playing the game.

c. Student A turns over two cards, and if they match, the student must identify the number. If the student correctly identifies the number, he or she keeps the cards, and the student takes another turn. If they don't match or if the student isn't able to correctly identify the number, the student turns them face-down, and Student B takes a turn.

d. The game continues until all the cards have been matched. The student with the most correct *matches* wins the game.

4. Large Number Match Game ✶✶
ACTIVITY MASTER 24

a. Make a copy of Activity Master 24, cut it into cards, and distribute the cards randomly, one to each student.

b. Have students circulate around the room, saying their numbers until they find their match. Make sure students don't show their cards to their classmates since this is a listening and speaking exercise.

c. When students have found their match, have them compare their cards and come show you.

5. Addition Match Game ✶✶
ACTIVITY MASTER 25

a. Make a copy of Activity Master 25, cut it into cards, and distribute the cards randomly, one to each student.

b. Have students memorize their addition problems or answers and leave their cards on their desks. Then have students circulate around the room, saying their lines until they find their match.

c. When all the pairs have been matched, have students say their addition problem for the whole class.

6. Math Whiz! ✶✶

a. Invite two students to come to the front of the class. Give an addition problem—for example: "How much is thirty plus nineteen?"

b. The first student to answer correctly remains standing. The other person returns to his or her seat and is replaced by a different student.

c. Continue the activity, with the student who answers first remaining in the game. The student who has remained standing the longest is the class *math whiz.*

7. Tic Tac Arithmetic ✶✶✶
ACTIVITY MASTER 26

a. Duplicate Activity Master 26 and give one copy to each student. Have students fill in the grid with any nine numbers from 1–50.

b. Make up simple addition problems, and have students cross out the answer if it is any of the numbers they have written down. Have them call out the answer to check for accuracy.

c. The first student to cross out three numbers in a straight line—either vertically, horizontally, or diagonally—wins the game.

LESSON OBJECTIVE

Focus
Time

Vocabulary
o'clock
time

GETTING READY
10–15 MINUTES

Introduce time expressions for hours.

1. Using a large clock or clock face with movable hands to display the time, point to the numbers on the clock and say:

   It's one o'clock.
   It's two o'clock.

   Have students repeat each time expression chorally and individually.

2. Using the same approach as above, introduce the time expressions for quarter and half hours:

   It's one fifteen.
   It's two fifteen.

   It's one thirty.
   It's two thirty.

   It's one forty-five.
   It's two forty-five.

   Set the clock at various times and ask individual students: "What time is it?"

3. You can also play the model sentences on the audio program.

THE MODEL CONVERSATION
10–20 MINUTES

1. **SETTING THE SCENE:** Have students look at the model photograph. Set the scene: "Two friends are talking."

2. **LISTENING:** With books closed, have students listen to the model conversation—presented by you, by a pair of students, or on the audio program. Check students' understanding of the situation and the vocabulary.

3. **CLASS PRACTICE:** With books still closed, model each line, and have the whole class practice in unison.

4. **READING:** With books open, have students follow along as two students present the model.

5. **PAIR PRACTICE:** In pairs, have students practice the model conversation.

THE CONVERSATION EXERCISES
10–20 MINUTES

1. **THE SKELETAL DIALOG:** Write the "skeletal dialog" on the board. Fill in the replacement from Exercise 1 to show students how the guided conversation method works. Call on a few pairs of students to practice Exercise 1, using the skeletal framework on the board.

   > A. What time is it?
   > B. It's <u>two o'clock</u>.

2. **EXERCISE PRACTICE:** (optional) Have pairs of students simultaneously practice all the exercises.

3. **EXERCISE PRESENTATIONS:** Call on pairs of students to present their conversations to the class.

READING A CLOCK
5 MINUTES

Have students circle the correct times and then compare answers with a partner.

Answers

1. ten o'clock
2. eight thirty
3. two fifteen
4. eleven forty-five
5. twelve o'clock

LISTENING
5–10 MINUTES

Circle the time you hear.

1. A. What time is it?
   B. It's eight o'clock.
2. A. What time is it?
   B. It's nine o'clock.
3. A. What time is it?
   B. It's eleven o'clock.
4. A. What time is it?
   B. It's ten thirty.
5. A. What time is it?
   B. It's four o'clock.

6. A. What time is it?
   B. It's two thirty.

7. A. What time is it?
   B. It's three fifteen.

8. A. What time is it?
   B. It's five forty-five.

Answers

1. 8:00	5. 4:00
2. 9:00	6. 2:30
3. 11:00	7. 3:15
4. 10:30	8. 5:45

WRITING TIMES

5 MINUTES

Have students write the times on the clocks and then compare answers with a partner.

Answers

9:00   5:30   11:15   4:45   6:00

EXPANSION

1. Listen and Write ✶

Divide the class into pairs. Call out times and have students write the times in digital form (for example: *8:15, 11:00*). Have pairs check each other's times and compare answers.

2. Listen and Draw ✶✶

ACTIVITY MASTER 27

a. Make copies of Activity Master 27 and distribute one or two to each student.

b. Divide the class into pairs. Call out times and have students draw the hands on their clocks.

c. Have pairs check each other's clocks and compare answers. Circulate to answer any questions students may have.

Variation: Make another set of cards and distribute to students. This time, have students take turns calling out times for the rest of the class to draw. Ask for a student volunteer to come stay at the board and draw each of the times as students call them out. Have everybody compare clocks.

3. Pair Interviews ✶✶

ACTIVITY MASTER 28

Make multiple copies of Activity Master 28 and distribute one to each student. In pairs, have students interview one another about their daily schedules. Have the pairs report back to the class. For example:

Jose gets up at 6:30.
He eats breakfast at 7:00.

4. Countdown ✶✶

Object: Students count down from twelve midnight to twelve noon, in fifteen-minute intervals.

Have students sit in a circle. Student 1 begins: "12:00 midnight." Student 2 continues: "11:45." Students continue around the circle, counting down to 12 noon (48 turns). For example:

Student 1: 12:00 midnight
Student 2: 11:45
Student 3: 11:30
Student 4: 11:15
Student 5: 11:00

5. Time Around the World ✶✶✶

a. Get a map indicating time differences throughout the world. (If you have access to the *Word by Word* Picture Dictionary, there is a Time Zone map on p. 172.)

b. Practice talking about what time it is in various places. For example:

   A. It's 3:00 P.M. here. What time is it in London?
   B. It's 8:00 P.M.

   A. It's now 1 P.M. Wednesday. What time is it in Tokyo?
   B. It's 2:00 A.M. Thursday.

LESSON OBJECTIVE

Focus

Days of the Week

Vocabulary

Monday	Friday
Tuesday	Saturday
Wednesday	Sunday
Thursday	

GETTING READY
5–10 MINUTES

Review the days of the week.

1. Using the calendar on student book page 47, say a day, and have students repeat it chorally and individually.

2. Write the sequence of days on the board:

Sunday	Thursday
Monday	Friday
Tuesday	Saturday
Wednesday	

Erase one day out of the sequence, and when students tell you what it is, write it back in. Continue with other days.

THE MODEL CONVERSATION
10 MINUTES

1. **SETTING THE SCENE:** Have students look at the model photographs. Set the scene: "Someone is calling a doctor's office and making an appointment."

2. **LISTENING:** With books closed, have students listen to the model conversation—presented by you, by a pair of students, or on the audio program. Check students' understanding of the situation and the vocabulary.

3. **CLASS PRACTICE:** With books still closed, model each line, and have the whole class practice in unison.

4. **READING:** With books open, have students follow along as two students present the model.

5. **PAIR PRACTICE:** In pairs, have students practice the model conversation.

THE CONVERSATION EXERCISES
10–20 MINUTES

1. **THE SKELETAL DIALOG:** Write the "skeletal dialog" on the board. Fill in the replacement from Exercise 1 to show students how the guided conversation method works. Call on a few pairs of students to practice Exercise 1, using the skeletal framework on the board.

> A. Can you come in on <u>Tuesday</u> at <u>4:00</u>?
> B. On <u>Tuesday</u> at <u>4:00</u>? Yes, I can.

2. **EXERCISE PRACTICE:** (optional) Have pairs of students simultaneously practice all the exercises.

3. **EXERCISE PRESENTATIONS:** Call on pairs of students to present their conversations to the class.

MISSING DAYS
5–10 MINUTES

Explain that in every set of three days, the day in the middle is missing. Have students fill in the missing days and then compare answers with a partner.

Answers

1. Tuesday	4. Monday
2. Thursday	5. Wednesday
3. Saturday	6. Friday

ABBREVIATIONS
5 MINUTES

Have students write the days of the week and then compare their answers in pairs.

Answers

1. Sunday	5. Thursday
2. Monday	6. Friday
3. Tuesday	7. Saturday
4. Wednesday	

LISTENING
5–10 MINUTES

Circle the day you hear.

1. I clean my apartment on Friday.
2. I do the laundry on Monday.
3. I play basketball on Saturday.
4. I go to school on Tuesday.
5. My daughter plays the guitar on Sunday.
6. My son washes the dishes on Wednesday.

7. We watch TV on Friday.

8. My grandmother cooks dinner on Thursday.

Answers

1. Friday
2. Monday
3. Saturday
4. Tuesday
5. Sunday
6. Wednesday
7. Friday
8. Thursday

LISTENING

5–10 MINUTES

Write the time you hear on the correct day.

1. A. Can you come in on Wednesday at three o'clock?
   B. On Wednesday at three o'clock? Yes, I can.

2. A. Can you come in on Friday at ten o'clock?
   B. On Friday at ten o'clock? Yes, I can.

3. A. Can you come in on Monday at nine thirty?
   B. On Monday at nine thirty? Yes, I can.

4. A. Can you come in on Thursday at two fifteen?
   B. On Thursday at two fifteen? Yes, I can.

5. A. Can you come in on Tuesday at one forty-five?
   B. On Tuesday at one forty-five? Yes, I can.

6. A. Can you play basketball on Saturday at eleven thirty?
   B. On Saturday at eleven thirty? Yes, I can.

7. A. Can you come for dinner on Sunday at six o'clock?
   B. On Sunday at six o'clock? Yes, I can. Thank you.

Answers

SUN	MON	TUE	WED	THU	FRI	SAT
6:00	9:30	1:45	3:00	2:15	10:00	11:30

EXPANSION

1. The Next Day ★

Have students sit in a circle. Student 1 says a day of the week. The student to the right says the next day. Have students continue around the circle until it is Student 1's turn again.

2. Concentration ★
ACTIVITY MASTER 22

a. Divide the class into pairs. Make copies of Activity Master 22, cut them into cards, and give each pair one set of cards. Have students shuffle the cards and place them face-down in two rows of 7 each.

b. The object of the game is for students to find the matching cards. Both students should be able to see the cards, since *concentrating* on their location is an important part of playing the game.

c. Student A turns over two cards, and if they match, the student must identify the item. If the student correctly identifies the item, he or she keeps the cards, and the student takes another turn. If they don't match or if the student isn't able to correctly identify the item, the student turns them face-down, and Student B takes a turn.

d. The game continues until all the cards have been matched. The student with the most correct *matches* wins the game.

3. My Favorite Day ★★

a. Ask students to write down their favorite days of the week. Then have students walk around the room, asking each other: "What's your favorite day of the week?"

b. All students who have the same favorite day should stand together in a group. Once the groups are formed, have students sit down and ask each other: "Why is (*Saturday*) your favorite day of the week? What do you do on (*Saturday*)?"

c. Have the groups report back to the class.

4. Listen for the Times ★★
ACTIVITY MASTER 29

a. Make copies of Activity Master 29 and distribute one to each student.

b. Read the following sentences, and have students write down the time they hear on the correct day:

    Can you come in on Monday at 10:30?
    Can you come in on Thursday at 3:45?
    Can you come in on Wednesday at 9:00?
    Can you come in on Friday at 8:30?
    Can you come in on Tuesday at 2:15?

c. Write the answer on the board after each sentence so students can check their answers.

5. Weekly Schedules ★★★
ACTIVITY MASTER 29

a. Make copies of Activity Master 29 and distribute one to each student.

b. Have each student fill in the calendar with activities he or she does on each day, including the time.

(continued)

c. Divide the class into pairs, and have students talk about their schedules with their partners.

6. Role Play: Scheduling an Appointment ★★★

a. Write on the board:

> A. Can you come in on _____ at _____?
> B. On _____ at _____? Yes, I can.
>   or
> B. On _____ at _____? No, I can't.

b. Divide the class into pairs. One member of the pair works in a doctor's office. The other is calling to make an appointment.

c. The receptionist at the doctor's office asks, for example: "Can you come in on Thursday at 2:00?" The person calling checks his or her actual schedule from Activity 4 and answers: "Yes, I can," if he or she is free at that time, or: "No, I can't," if he or she is busy.

d. Have the pairs reverse roles.

LESSON OBJECTIVE

Focus

Ordinal numbers

Vocabulary

Ordinal numbers: 1st–100th

GETTING READY
5–10 MINUTES

1. Introduce the concept of ordinal numbers.

   a. Have all the students stand in line.

   b. Identify each person by order in line and by name: "The *first* person is (*Marisa*). The second person is (*Carlos*). The *third* person is (*Julia*). The *fourth* person is (*Augustin*)," and so on.

2. Say an ordinal number, have students repeat it, and write it on the board—both in its abbreviated and full form. For example:

1st	first
2nd	second
3rd	third

3. Practice the pronunciation of the suffixes *-th* and *-ieth*.

   a. Write the following list on the board:

4th	– 40th
5th	– 50th
6th	– 60th
7th	– 70th
8th	– 80th
9th	– 90th

   b. Have students practice the pronunciation of *-th* vs. *-ieth* chorally and individually.

   c. You can also have students listen to the ordinal numbers on the audio program.

THE MODEL CONVERSATION
10 MINUTES

1. **SETTING THE SCENE:** Have students look at the model photograph. Set the scene: "Two new neighbors are talking."

2. **LISTENING:** With books closed, have students listen to the model conversation—presented by you, by a pair of students, or on the audio program. Check students' understanding of the situation and the vocabulary.

3. **CLASS PRACTICE:** With books still closed, model each line, and have the whole class practice in unison.

4. **READING:** With books open, have students follow along as two students present the model.

5. **PAIR PRACTICE:** In pairs, have students practice the model conversation.

THE CONVERSATION EXERCISES
10 MINUTES

1. **THE SKELETAL DIALOG:** Write the "skeletal dialog" on the board. Fill in the replacement with a different ordinal number to show students how the guided conversation method works. Call on a few pairs of students to practice the dialog, using the framework on the board.

   > A. What floor do you live on?
   > B. I live on the <u>fifth</u> floor.

2. **EXERCISE PRACTICE:** (optional) Have pairs of students simultaneously practice the conversation, using any ordinal numbers they wish.

3. **EXERCISE PRESENTATIONS:** Call on pairs of students to present their conversations to the class.

MATCHING
5 MINUTES

Have students complete the activity and then compare answers with a partner.

Answers

1.	7th	6.	14th
2.	16th	7.	4th
3.	2nd	8.	40th
4.	60th	9.	44th
5.	20th	10.	41st

NUMBERS

10 MINUTES

Have students write the ordinal numbers and then compare answers with a partner.

Answers

3rd	15th	16th	42nd
1st	5th	60th	29th
2nd	50th	6th	81st
10th	55th	66th	33rd

LISTENING

5–10 MINUTES

Circle the number you hear.

1. A. What floor do you live on?
    B. I live on the seventeenth floor.
    A. The seventeenth floor?
    B. Yes. That's right.

2. A. What floor do you live on?
    B. I live on the second floor.
    A. The second floor?
    B. Yes. That's right.

3. A. What floor do you live on?
    B. I'm on the thirteenth floor.
    A. The thirteenth floor?
    B. Yes. That's right.

4. A. Where is your apartment?
    B. It's on the fifteenth floor.
    A. The fifteenth floor?
    B. Yes. That's correct.

5. A. I live on the twelfth floor.
    B. The twelfth floor?
    A. Yes.

6. A. Where is the English classroom?
    B. It's on the third floor.
    A. The third floor?
    B. Yes.

7. A. Is this the twenty-first floor?
    B. Yes. It's the twenty-first floor.
    A. Thank you.

8. A. Is this the fortieth floor?
    B. Yes. It's the fortieth floor.
    A. Thank you.

9. A. Do you live on fifty-seventh Street?
    B. Yes. My apartment is on fifty-seventh Street.

10. A. Does your sister live on ninety-seventh Street?
    B. Yes. Her apartment is on ninety-seventh Street.

11. A. Excuse me. Is this thirty-fifth Street?
    B. Yes. This is thirty-fifth Street.

12. A. Excuse me. Is this nineteenth Street?
    B. Yes. This is nineteenth Street.

Answers

1. 17th		7. 21st
2. 2nd		8. 40th
3. 13th		9. 57th
4. 15th		10. 97th
5. 12th		11. 35th
6. 3rd		12. 19th

EXPANSION

1. **Circle Counting (Variation 1)** ✮

    Have students sit in a circle. (For larger classes, have students sit in two circles.) Student 1 starts counting: "First." Student 2 continues: "Second." Students continue counting around the circle, stopping at thirtieth.

    Circle Counting (Variation 2) ✮✮

    Have students go around the circle, counting backwards from 100th.

    Circle Counting (Variation 3) ✮✮

    Have students count around the circle, using odd numbers only.

    Circle Counting (Variation 4) ✮✮

    Have students count around the circle, using even numbers only.

2. **Ordinal Number Practice** ✮

    As a class, in pairs, or in small groups, have students practice the ordinal numbers in either or both of the following ways:

    - Say an ordinal number, and have students write it in its -st / -th form.
    - Write an ordinal number in its –st / -th form or in words, and have students say it.

3. **Stand in Order** ✮
    ACTIVITY MASTERS 30, 31, OR 32

    Make copies of any of the above Activity Masters and cut them into cards. Give each student a card with an ordinal number in full form written on it. The numbers should not be in succession. Also, some should be omitted to make the activity more fun. Have students say their numbers aloud and arrange themselves in a line from the lowest to the highest number.

    Variation: Divide the class into two teams. Have them compete to stand in order first.

4. Large Number Match Game ✴✴

ACTIVITY MASTERS 30, 31, OR 32

a. Make a copy of Activity Masters 30, 31, or 32, cut it into cards, and distribute the cards randomly, one to each student.

b. Have students circulate around the room, saying their numbers until they find their match. Make sure students don't show their cards to their classmates since this is a listening and speaking exercise.

c. When students have found their match, have them compare their cards and come show you.

5. Who Is First? ✴✴

Have half the class leave the room and re-enter one by one. The other half then takes turns announcing the arrival of each student. For example:

The first person is Alice.
The second person is Juan.
The third person is Louisa.

6. Spelling Names ✴✴✴

Say a name for students to spell—for example: "Marie." Students in turn tell you how to spell it. For example:

Student 1: The first letter is *M*.
Student 2: The second letter is *a*.
Etc.

7. Guess the Name ✴✴✴

a. Choose a name without telling students what it is—for example: *Antonio*.

b. Tell students how many letters the name has, and have them put that number of blanks on a piece of paper. For example:

c. Tell students the position of a letter and what the letter is. For example: "The seventh letter is o."

d. Continue with the remaining letters.

e. The first student to guess the name is the winner.

8. Information Gap ✴✴✴

ACTIVITY MASTER 33

a. Make multiple copies of Activity Master 33 and cut them in half (A and B).

b. Divide the class into pairs. Give one partner the A sheet and the other partner the B sheet. Explain that all the Smith family relatives live in the same apartment building. Have students complete their charts by asking their partners the question: "Who lives on the (*first*) floor?"

LESSON OBJECTIVE

Focus

Months of the year
Dates

Vocabulary

January	July
February	August
March	September
April	October
May	November
June	December

GETTING READY   5–10 MINUTES

Introduce months of the year.

1. Use the calendar at the top of student book page 56 to present months of the year. Say each month, and have the class repeat it chorally and individually. Check students' understanding and pronunciation of the vocabulary. (You can also have students listen to the audio program.)

2. For further practice, write a series of months on the board. For example:

> January
> February
> March
> April
> May

Erase one of the months and ask students to tell you the name of the missing month. Continue with another list on the board.

THE MODEL CONVERSATIONS   5–10 MINUTES

There are two model conversations. Introduce and practice the first model before going on to the second. For each model:

1. **SETTING THE SCENE:** Have students look at the model photograph. Set the scene:

   Model 1: "A customer is talking to a teller at the bank."
   Model 2: "Two co-workers are talking."

2. **LISTENING:** With books closed, have students listen to the model conversation—presented by you, by a pair of students, or on the audio program. Check students' understanding of the situation and the vocabulary.

3. **CLASS PRACTICE:** With books still closed, model each line, and have the whole class practice in unison.

4. **READING:** With books open, have students follow along as two students present the model.

5. **PAIR PRACTICE:** In pairs, have students practice the model conversation.

THE CONVERSATION EXERCISES   10 MINUTES

1. **THE SKELETAL DIALOG:** Write the "skeletal dialog" on the board. Fill in the replacement with different months (and ordinal numbers) to show students how the guided conversation method works. Call on a few pairs of students to practice the dialog, using the skeletal framework on the board.

   Model 1:

   > A. What month is it?
   > B. It's <u>December</u>.
   > A. Thanks.

   Model 2:

   > A. What's the <u>third</u> month of the year?
   > B. <u>March</u>.

2. **EXERCISE PRACTICE:** (optional) Have pairs of students simultaneously practice conversations, using any months they wish.

3. **EXERCISE PRESENTATIONS:** Call on pairs of students to present their conversations to the class.

ABBREVIATIONS   10 MINUTES

Have students write the month that corresponds to each abbreviation and then compare their answers in pairs.

Answers

January	July
February	August
March	September
April	October
May	November
June	December

HOW TO SAY A DATE

GETTING READY   5–10 MINUTES

Show how to say a date.

1. Write several dates on the board and say them to the class. Have students repeat chorally.

2. Write other dates on the board and call on students to say them. For example:

```
December 3
August 12
November 16
January 25
```

THE MODEL CONVERSATIONS   10 MINUTES

There are two model conversations. Introduce and practice the first model before going on to the second. For each model:

1. **SETTING THE SCENE:** Set the scene: "Two friends are talking."

2. **LISTENING:** With books closed, have students listen to the model conversation—presented by you, by a pair of students, or on the audio program. Check students' understanding of the vocabulary.

3. **CLASS PRACTICE:** With books still closed, model each line, and have the whole class practice in unison.

4. **READING:** With books open, have students follow along as two students present the model.

5. **PAIR PRACTICE:** In pairs, have students practice the model conversation.

Note: When writing a date, the convention is to write it with cardinal numbers even though it's pronounced as an ordinal number. For example: June 1, 2010 is spoken: "June first, two thousand ten."

THE CONVERSATION EXERCISES   10 MINUTES

1. **THE SKELETAL DIALOG:** Write the "skeletal dialog" on the board. Fill in a replacement to show students how the guided conversation

method works. Call on a few pairs of students to practice the dialog, using the skeletal framework on the board.

Model 1:

```
A. When is your birthday?
B. My birthday is September 21st.
```

Model 2:

```
A. What's today's date?
B. It's July 17th, two thousand nine.
```

2. **EXERCISE PRACTICE:** (optional) Have pairs of students simultaneously practice the conversations with any dates they wish.

3. **EXERCISE PRESENTATIONS:** Call on pairs of students to present their conversations to the class.

LISTENING   5–10 MINUTES

Circle the date you hear.

1. A. What's today's date?
   B. It's April sixteenth.
   A. April sixteenth?
   B. Yes. That's right.

2. A. What's today's date?
   B. It's November twelfth.
   A. November twelfth?
   B. Yes. That's right.

3. A. What's today's date?
   B. It's September third.
   A. September third?
   B. Yes. That's correct.

4. A. When is your birthday?
   B. My birthday is June seventh.
   A. June seventh?
   B. Yes.

5. A. When is your birthday?
   B. My birthday is August twenty-first.
   A. August twenty-first?
   B. Yes.

6. A. What's today's date?
   B. It's March second.
   A. March second?
   B. Yes.

7. A. What's the date today?
   B. Today is July tenth.
   A. July tenth?
   B. Yes.

UNIT 4   **71**

8. A. When is your birthday?
   B. My birthday is October thirty-first.
   A. October thirty-first?
   B. Yes.

9. A. Is your birthday November first?
   B. Yes. It's November first.

10. A. Is today January twentieth?
    B. Yes. It's January twentieth.

Answers

1. April 16	6. MAR 2
2. November 12	7. JUL 10
3. September 3	8. OCT 31
4. June 7	9. NOV 1
5. August 21	10. JAN 20

EXPANSION

1. Month Counting (Variation 1) ★

Have students sit in two circles. Student 1 starts naming the months of the year: "January." Student 2 continues: "February." Students continue around the circle, stopping at December.

Month Counting (Variation 2) ★★

Have students go around the circle, naming the months of the year backwards from December.

2. Stand in Line ★

ACTIVITY MASTER 23

Make a copy of Activity Master 23, cut it into cards, and give each student a card. Use either the full word form or the abbreviated form on the Activity Master. Have students line themselves up in chronological order.

3. Concentration ★

ACTIVITY MASTERS 34 AND/OR 35

Note: You can use the Activity Masters separately (and do the activity twice) or combine both Activity Masters.

a. Divide the class into groups of four. Make a copy of the Activity Masters for each group and cut them into cards. Then divide each group into two teams—Team A and Team B. Give each group a set of cards, and have them shuffle the cards and place them face-down in rows. Tell students that the object of the game is to find cards that match.

b. A student from Team A turns over two cards, and if they match, that team keeps the cards. If the cards don't match, the student turns them face-down, and a member of Team B takes a turn.

c. The play continues until all the cards have been matched. The team with the most correct *matches* wins the game.

4. Months of the Year Run ★★

a. Divide the class into teams of four students and give each team one piece of chalk.

b. Have the team stand at least five feet from the board. Have one student from each team run up to the board, write the month *January*, and return to the group, passing the chalk to another team member.

c. The next team member runs to the board and writes the month *February*.

There can be only one member of each team at the board at one time. The first team that writes all the months of the year in correct order and form wins.

5. Month Dictation ★★

Divide the class into pairs. Have Student A choose a month from student book page 56 and dictate it to Student B, who writes down the month. Have Student A check Student B's answer. Then reverse roles.

6. Spring, Summer, Fall, or Winter? ★★

a. Have students make four columns on a piece of paper.

b. Dictate the four seasons: *spring, summer, fall,* and *winter,* and have students write each at the top of one of the columns.

c. Dictate the months of the year in random order, and have students write the words in a seasonal column. For example:

spring	summer	fall	winter
April	August	October	December

d. Have students compare their answers. Some transitional months may be considered belonging to two different categories.

7. My Favorite Month ★★

a. Ask students to write down their favorite month of the year. Then have students walk around the room asking each other: "What's your favorite month of the year?"

b. All students who have the same favorite month should stand together in a group. Once the groups are formed, have students sit down and ask each other: "Why is (*June*) your favorite month?"

c. Have the groups report back to the class.

8. Match Game ★★

ACTIVITY MASTER 36

a. Make a copy of Activity Master 36, cut it into cards, and distribute them randomly, one to each student.

b. Have students look at their card and identify the date. Then have students circulate around the room, saying the date on their cards until they find their match. Make sure students don't show their cards to their classmates since this is a listening and speaking exercise.

c. When students have found their match, have them compare their cards and come show you.

9. True or False? ★★

Make various statements about the months of the year, and have students correct it if it is false. For example:

Teacher: January is the third month of the year.
Student 1: No. January is the first month of the year.

Teacher: June is the sixth month of the year.
Student 2: Yes, that's right.

10. Holidays ★★★

a. Have students brainstorm a list of holidays. Write them on the board.

b. As a class, in pairs, or in small groups, have students tell the dates of these holidays.

For example:

Valentine's Day	February 14
Memorial Day	Last Monday of May
Independence Day	July 4
Labor Day	First Monday of September
Veteran's Day	November 11
Thanksgiving	Fourth Thursday of November
Christmas	December 25
New Year's Day	January 1

LESSON OBJECTIVE

Focus

Coins & currency
Adding amounts

VOCABULARY

bill	half dollar
cents	nickel
dime	penny
dollar	quarter

GETTING READY

5–10
MINUTES

1. Introduce money vocabulary.

   a. Use your own money, Photo Cards 68–76, or the photographs at the top of student book page 58, to introduce money vocabulary: *a penny, a nickel, a dime, a quarter, a half-dollar, a dollar bill, a five-dollar bill, a ten-dollar bill,* and *a twenty-dollar bill.* Say each phrase, and have the class repeat it chorally and individually. Check students' understanding and pronunciation of the vocabulary. (You can also have students listen to the audio program.)

   b. For each coin or bill, write the amount on the board. For example:

   Say the amount of money for each coin or bill, and have students repeat chorally and individually. For example:

   > a penny–one cent
   > a nickel–five cents

   c. Have pairs of students practice saying the names of coins and currency and their respective amounts. One student names the coin or bill and the other tells the amount of money. For example:

   > Student 1: a penny
   > Student 2: one cent

2. Introduce the phrase *I just found.* Look for a specific item among your belongings. Tell students: "I'm looking for my pen." When you find it, say: "I just found my pen!"

THE MODEL CONVERSATIONS

10
MINUTES

There are two model conversations. Introduce and practice the first model before going on to the second. For each model:

1. **SETTING THE SCENE:** Have students look at the model photograph. Set the scene: "Someone just found some money."

2. **LISTENING:** With books closed, have students listen to the model conversation—presented by you, by a pair of students, or on the audio program. Check students' understanding of the situation and the vocabulary.

3. **CLASS PRACTICE:** With books still closed, model each line, and have the whole class practice in unison.

4. **READING:** With books open, have students follow along as two students present the model.

5. **PAIR PRACTICE:** In pairs, have students practice the model conversation.

THE CONVERSATION EXERCISES

10
MINUTES

1. **THE SKELETAL DIALOG:** Write the "skeletal dialog" on the board. Fill in the replacement with a different coin or bill to show students how the guided conversation method works. Call on a few pairs of students to practice the dialog, using the skeletal framework on the board.

   Model 1:

   > A. Look! I just found <u>a penny</u>!
   > B. <u>One cent</u>?
   > A. Yes.

   Model 2:

   > A. Look! I just found a <u>20-dollar bill</u>!
   > B. <u>Twenty dollars</u>?
   > A. Yes.

2. **EXERCISE PRACTICE:** (optional) Have pairs of students simultaneously practice conversations, using any money they wish.

3. **EXERCISE PRESENTATIONS:** Call on pairs of students to present their conversations to the class.

COIN VALUES

5 MINUTES

Have students complete the exercise individually and then compare answers with a partner.

Answers

25¢   10¢   15¢   31¢

LISTENING

5–10 MINUTES

Write the number under the correct picture.

1. A. I just found two dollars and twenty-five cents!
   B. Two dollars and twenty-five cents?
   A. Yes.

2. A. I just found a five-dollar bill!
   B. Five dollars?
   A. Yes.

3. A. I just found a fifty-dollar bill!
   B. Fifty dollars?
   A. Yes.

4. A. Do you have any money?
   B. Yes. I have a dollar bill and ten cents.
   A. A dollar and ten cents?
   B. Yes.

5. A. Do you have any change?
   B. I have fifty-two cents.
   A. Fifty-two cents?
   B. Yes.

6. A. I just found thirty-five dollars!
   B. Thirty-five dollars?
   A. Yes.

Answers

4	2	3
1	6	5

LISTENING

5–10 MINUTES

Circle the amount you hear.

1. five cents
2. twenty dollars
3. fifty cents
4. one dollar
5. thirty-five dollars
6. ten cents
7. seventy-five cents
8. one hundred dollars

Answers

1. 5¢	5. $35.00
2. $20.00	6. 10¢
3. 50¢	7. 75¢
4. $1.00	8. $100.00

LANGUAGE IN *MOTION*

10 MINUTES

Have students walk around the classroom asking each other addition problems with coins. (For larger classes, you can set a time limit or a limit on how many people students should ask.) Have students tell some of the coin problems they heard.

EXPANSION

1. Currency Concentration ★

PHOTO CARDS 68–76 (TWO SETS)

a. Choose duplicate copies of Photo Cards 68–76. Shuffle the cards and place them face-down in three rows of 6 each.

b. Divide the class into two teams. The object of the game is for students to find the matching cards and identify the money. Both teams should be able to see the cards, since *concentrating* on their location is an important part of playing the game.

c. A student from Team 1 turns over two cards, and if they match, the student must identify the item. If the student correctly identifies the item, that team keeps the cards, and the student takes another turn. If they don't match or if the student isn't able to correctly identify the item, the student turns them face-down, and a member of Team 2 takes a turn.

d. The game continues until all the cards have been matched. The team with the most correct *matches* wins the game.

Variation:
PHOTO CARDS 68–76
ACTIVITY MASTER 37

Have the class play with one set of Photo Cards and one set of Word Cards.

2. What's in the Bag? ★

Put some real coins in a paper bag. Have one student at a time reach into the bag, pick up a coin, and identify it without looking at it.

Variation: This activity may also be done as a game, with two teams competing against each other to see how many players identify the coins correctly.

3. Money Match Game ★★

ACTIVITY MASTER 38

a. Make a copy of Activity Master 38, cut it into cards, and distribute the cards randomly, one to each student.

(continued)

b. Have students circulate around the room, saying what's on their card until they find their match. Make sure students don't show their cards to their classmates since this is a listening and speaking exercise.

c. When students have found their match, have them compare their cards and come show you.

4. "Penny Jar" ★★

Bring in a large jar and collect students' pennies in the jar. Have each student look at the jar and estimate how many pennies are in the jar. Count the pennies and ask students how much money that represents.

5. Money Game: What's the Total? ★★★

a. Put some coins into several envelopes. Number the envelopes and put them on your desk.

b. Divide the class into several teams. Tell a member of each team to come up to your desk and take an envelope.

c. The students in each team then take the *money* out of their envelope, add it up, write the number of the envelope and the amount of money on a separate sheet of paper, return the envelope, and pick up another.

d. The first team to add up the money in all the envelopes and have the correct total, wins the game.

6. Empty Your Pockets! ★★★

Have students empty their pockets or coin purses and count how much change they have. Ask students: "How many nickels do you have? How many quarters?", and so on.

7. Making Change ★★★

a. Write several money amounts on the board.

b. In pairs or small groups, have students break down the amount into change in as many ways as possible. For example:

5 quarters
4 quarters, two dimes, and a nickel
12 dimes and 1 nickel
2 half dollars and 1 quarter

c. Have the class compare answers.

DATES

5–10 MINUTES

Have students write the important dates in their lives and then share their answers with a partner, in small groups, or with the entire class.

COMMUNITY CONNECTIONS

10 MINUTES

Have students complete the sentences individually, in pairs, or in small groups, and then report back to the class.

MEMORY GAME

10 MINUTES

Have students walk around the classroom. Student 1 asks Student 2 when his or her birthday is: "When is your birthday?" Student 2 answers with his or her birthday—for example: "My birthday is April 10th." Have students continue walking around, asking others when their birthdays are. Then have students stand in a circle. Each student says all the birthdays he or she remembers—for example: "Maya's birthday is October 2nd. Victoria's birthday is December 15th." (For larger classes, you can set a time limit or a limit on how many people students should ask.)

EXPANSION

1. Pair Conversations ✮

In pairs, have students ask and answer the questions listed in the Language Experience Journal activity. Circulate to listen to student conversations and help as necessary.

Note: This is a good way to warm up students for journal writing. For students who are insecure about writing, it's helpful to first talk about the topic before sitting down to write about it.

2. Guess Who! ✮✮

Play this game after doing the *Dates* exercise.

a. Have students copy and complete these sentences on a piece of paper:

> My birthday is _____ .
> My favorite holiday is _____ .
> My 1st day in this country was _____ .

b. Collect the papers and mix them up. Read each paper aloud to the class, and have students guess who the person is.

3. Scrambled Sentences ✮✮

Write the following scrambled sentences on the board, and have students write each sentence in the correct order.

> Monday / I / to / to / from / work / on / go / 5:00 P.M. / 8:00 A.M.
>
> goes / She / to / on / school / Tuesday / from / 9 P.M. / to / 6 P.M.
>
> get / You / up / 5:00 A.M. / on / at / Saturday
>
> on / to / at / go / bed / 9:30 P.M. / Wednesday /They /
>
> dinner / Saturday / eat / at / We / 8:00 / on
>
> to / 7 A.M. / They / work / 11 P.M. / to / go / from

LANGUAGE EXPERIENCE JOURNAL

See Expansion Activity 1 above for a warm-up activity before having students write or dictate their stories.

Have students write about their daily schedules. Depending on your students' writing abilities, either have them write in their journal or dictate their story for you to write. Then students should read what they have written to a classmate. If time permits, you may also want to write a response in each student's journal, sharing your own opinions and experiences as well as reacting to what the student has written.

Different Cultures *Different Ways* **10** MINUTES

Have students first work in pairs or small groups, reacting to the photographs and responding to the questions. Then have students share with the class what they have talked about.

PUT IT TOGETHER **15–20** MINUTES

In this activity, students talk with each other to find out information about a train schedule.

1. Divide the class into pairs: Student A and Student B.

2. Tell all the Student A's to look at Part A of the activity on student book page 61. Tell all the Student B's to look at Part B on page 62.

3. Have everybody look at the first item on the schedule: *Chicago.*

   a. In Student B's list, under the second column, it says, *4:30.* Therefore, when Student A asks: "What time does the train to Chicago leave?", Student B answers: "It leaves at 4:30."

   b. Ask all the Student B's: "What time does the train to Chicago leave?" Have all the Student B's respond in unison: "It leaves at 4:30."

4. Have everybody look at the second item on the schedule: *Los Angeles.*

   a. Have all the Student A's look at their list. In their list under the second column, it says, *5:00.* Therefore, when Student B asks: "What time does the train to Los Angeles leave?", Student A answers: "It leaves at 5:00."

   b. Ask all the Student A's: "What time does the train to Los Angeles leave?" Have all the Student A's respond in unison: "It leaves at 5:00."

5. The Student A and Student B pairs are now ready to continue the activity with the rest of the items on their schedules.

6. When the pairs have completed the activity, have them check each other's answers.

VOCABULARY FOUNDATIONS **5–10** MINUTES

Have students review the list of words they have learned in this unit. Encourage students to get a small notebook where they can write down vocabulary that is new for them. If students have personal copies of dictionaries or picture dictionaries, have them look up these words in the dictionary and highlight them with a marker. Encourage them to look at their notebooks or dictionaries frequently to review what they have learned.

For additional practice, have students do one or more of the following activities.

1. **Taking Notes** ✰

   In their vocabulary notebooks or on a piece of paper, have students write all the words in one column. In a second column, have them write notes, draw pictures, or write the word in a sentence that will help them remember the meaning of the words.

2. **Spelling Game** ✰✰

   Divide the class into pairs. One partner reads a word and the other partner spells it.

3. **Category Dictation** ✰✰✰

   a. Have students make three columns on a piece of paper:

      months of the year
      days of the week
      money

   b. Dictate words from Vocabulary Foundations and have students write them in the appropriate column. Make sure all students have covered the vocabulary items on student book page 62 with a piece of paper so they don't refer to that list.

   c. As a class, in pairs, or in small groups, have students check their work.

4. **Alphabetical Order** ✰✰✰

   Have pairs of students work together to put in alphabetical order the months of the year, the days of the week, and the coins and currency that are listed in Vocabulary Foundations. Call on a different pair to read each list, and have the class decide whether or not the order is correct.

5. **Match Game** ✰✰✰
   ACTIVITY MASTER 39

   a. Make a copy of Activity Master 39, cut it into cards, and distribute the cards randomly, one to each student.

b. Have students memorize the question or response on their card and leave their cards on their desks. Then have students circulate around the room, saying their lines until they find their match.

c. When students have found their match, have them compare their cards and come show you.

LANGUAGE SKILL FOUNDATIONS
10–15 MINUTES

Explain to students that this is a list of skills they have learned in the unit. Students should become familiar with the vocabulary of describing their skills, but they don't need to master all the terms. For each speaking skill on the list, read the skill aloud to students and have them demonstrate it. For example:

Teacher: I can say addition problems.
Students: Nine plus six is fifteen.

(If students don't understand the vocabulary of a particular speaking skill, give them a concrete example rather than a description or explanation, and then have students practice your example and others.)

Have students put a check next to each skill if they feel they have learned it. Use this information to determine which lessons you may want to review or reinforce for the entire class or for particular students. The Getting Ready and Expansion activities for this unit and the CD-ROM's Activity Bank of supplemental worksheets are excellent resources for additional practice. It may also be helpful to have stronger students or, if available, a classroom aide or volunteer, work with students who need more practice.

Talk About It! ▶▶▶ (Page 63)
20–30 MINUTES

(Page 63 is also available as a transparency.)

Use the scenes in this illustration to review the vocabulary and conversations in the unit. Have students first work in pairs or small groups to talk about the illustration and answer the questions posed at the bottom of the page. Then discuss as a class.

For additional motivating practice, students will enjoy doing one or more of the following activities.

This activity reviews Unit 4 vocabulary:

1. **Remember the Numbers!** ✯
   a. Tell students to spend two minutes looking carefully at the scenes on student book page 63.

   b. Have students close their books and write down all the numbers they remember from the illustration.

   c. Have students compare notes with a partner and then look at the scenes again to see how well they remembered the numbers.

These activities review Unit 4 conversations and grammar:

2. **Who Is It?** ✯✯
   a. Have students look at the transparency or the illustration on student book page 63.

   b. Say a sentence, and have students point to a character in the illustration to identify who is speaking. For example:

   Teacher: What's today's date?
   Students: [*Point to the man writing a check.*]

   Teacher: What floor do you live on?
   Students: [*Point to the woman in the elevator.*]

   Teacher: What's your address?
   Students: [*Point to the woman at the desk interviewing someone.*]

   Variation: Divide the class into pairs. One student says a line and the other points to the appropriate character. Then reverse roles.

3. **What Are They Saying?** ✯✯✯
   a. Have pairs of students look at the transparency or the illustration on student book page 63.

   b. Have them choose one of the scenes and write a conversation between the two characters. Circulate to help students and answer questions.

   c. Have students present their conversations to the class. Have the class listen and identify which characters in the illustration the students are portraying in their conversation.

UNIT 5 | HOME

LESSONS & UNIT ACTIVITIES	OBJECTIVES	TEXT	TEACHER'S GUIDE
Vocabulary Preview	Types of housing • Rooms in the home • Home appliances & features • Furniture	64–65	81–82
LESSON 1 Tell me about the apartment.	Rooms in the home	66–67	83–84
LESSON 2 Is there a refrigerator in the kitchen?	Home appliances & features	68–69	85–86
LESSON 3 Where do you want this table?	Rooms & furniture • Types of housing	70–71	87–88
LESSON 4 NUMBERS	Cardinal & ordinal numbers review	72	89
Language Experience Journal	Writing about your home	72	89
Different Cultures / Different Ways	Homes around the world	73	90
Put It Together	Information Gap / Teamwork activity	73–74	90
Vocabulary Foundations / Language Skill Foundations	Review & skills checklist	74	90–91
Talk About It!	Review, conversations, activities, & games	75	91–92

UNIT RESOURCES

Audio Program:
Audio CD 2: Tracks 30–39
Audio Cassette 2B

Workbooks:
Activity Workbook
Literacy Workbook

Lesson Planner CD-ROM:
Activity Masters 40–44
Activity Bank Unit 5 Worksheets

Vocabulary Photo Cards: 77–97

Transparency: Color Overhead for Unit 5, page 75

TYPES OF HOUSING AND ROOMS IN THE HOME (PAGE 64)

PREVIEW
5 MINUTES

Activate students' prior knowledge of the vocabulary. Have students tell you types of housing they already know. (Prompt them by asking: "Do you live in a house? Do you live in an apartment building?") Then have students tell you the rooms of the home they know. As they tell you the rooms, write them on the board.

PRESENT
5–10 MINUTES

Using the photographs on student book page 64, point to each photo or say its number, say the word, and have the class repeat it chorally and individually. (You can also play the audio program.) Check students' understanding and pronunciation of the vocabulary.

PRACTICE
5 MINUTES

As a class, in pairs, or in small groups, have students practice the vocabulary in either or both of the following ways:

- Say or write a word, and have students point to the item in their books or tell the number.
- Point to a photograph in the book or give the number, and have students say the word.

SPELLING PRACTICE
5 MINUTES

Say a word, and have students spell it aloud or write it. Or point to a photo in the student book, and have students write the word. You can also spell a portion of a word on the board, and have students come to the board to complete it.

HOME APPLIANCES & FEATURES AND FURNITURE (PAGE 65)

PREVIEW
5 MINUTES

Activate students' prior knowledge of the vocabulary. Have students tell you words for home appliances, furniture, and other parts of the home they already know. As they tell you the words, write them on the board.

PRESENT
5–10 MINUTES

Using the photographs on student book page 65, point to each photo or say its number, say the word, and have the class repeat it chorally and individually. (You can also play the audio program.) Check students' understanding and pronunciation of the vocabulary.

PRACTICE
5 MINUTES

As a class, in pairs, or in small groups, have students practice the vocabulary in either or both of the following ways:

- Say or write a word, and have students point to the item in their books or tell the number.
- Point to a photograph in the book or give the number, and have students say the word.

SPELLING PRACTICE
5 MINUTES

Say a word, and have students spell it aloud or write it. Or point to a photo in the student book, and have students write the word. You can also spell a portion of a word on the board, and have students come to the board to complete it.

EXPANSION

1. **Tell and Show** ★
   PHOTO CARDS 77–97 (TWO SETS)

   a. Divide the class into pairs. Distribute all the Photo Cards randomly so every pair receives at least four or five cards.

   b. Have Student A in each pair select a Photo Card and tell Student B the room in the home or furniture or appliance item. Have Student B point to the item on student book page 64 or 65.

   c. As the pairs finish using their Photo Cards, have them trade their sets with another pair and then continue the activity. Have students reverse roles each time they get a new set of cards.

2. **Match Game** ★
   PHOTO CARDS 77–97 (TWO SETS)

   a. Choose duplicate copies of any Photo Cards 77–97 and distribute them randomly, one to each student.

(continued)

b. Have students look at their card and identify the room in the home or furniture or appliance item. Then have students circulate around the room, saying the name of the object on their card until they find their match. Make sure students don't show their cards to their classmates since this is a listening and speaking exercise.

c. When students have found their match, have them compare their cards and come show you. Then give each student another Photo Card to keep the game going. Continue until students have found all the matches.

3. True or False? ★★
PHOTO CARDS 77–97

Show students various Photo Cards. Make a false statement about the item, and have students correct it. For example:

Teacher: [*showing the class Photo Card 77*] This is a kitchen.
Students: No. It's a living room.

Teacher: [*showing the class Photo Card 88*] This is a fireplace.
Students: No. It's a stove.

LESSON OBJECTIVE

Focus
Rooms in the home

VOCABULARY

apartment	large
balcony	living room
bathroom	nice
bedroom	patio
dining room	small
kitchen	

GETTING READY
5–10 MINUTES

1. Introduce the verb *have*.

   a. Show students items that belong to you—for example: "I have a pen. I have a book."

   b. Write the forms of the verb *have* on the board, and have students repeat after you:

   > I have
   > You have
   > We have
   > They have
   >
   > He has
   > She has
   > It has

2. Using your own visuals or the photos on student book page 66, point out the features of an apartment. For example:

   > The apartment has a living room.
   > The apartment has a patio.

THE MODEL CONVERSATION
10 MINUTES

1. **SETTING THE SCENE:** Have students look at the model photographs. Set the scene: "This woman is looking for a place to live. She's talking to a realtor."

2. **LISTENING:** With books closed, have students listen to the model conversation—presented by you, by a pair of students, or on the audio program. Check students' understanding of the situation and the vocabulary.

3. **CLASS PRACTICE:** With books still closed, model each line, and have the whole class practice in unison.

4. **READING:** With books open, have students follow along as two students present the model.

5. **PAIR PRACTICE:** In pairs, have students practice the model conversation.

THE CONVERSATION EXERCISES
10–20 MINUTES

1. **THE SKELETAL DIALOG:** Write the "skeletal dialog" on the board. Fill in the replacement from Exercise 1 to show students how the guided conversation method works. Call on a few pairs of students to practice Exercise 1, using the skeletal framework on the board.

   > A. Tell me about the apartment.
   > B. It has a very nice <u>kitchen</u>.

2. **VOCABULARY PRESENTATION:** Present the vocabulary words in the exercises. Point to the photograph of each item, say the word, and have the class repeat it chorally and individually. Check students' understanding and pronunciation of the vocabulary.

3. **EXERCISE PRACTICE:** (optional) Have pairs of students simultaneously practice all the exercises.

4. **EXERCISE PRESENTATIONS:** Call on pairs of students to present their conversations to the class.

WRITING
10 MINUTES

Have students complete the sentences and then compare their answers in pairs or as a class.

Answers

1. living room	4. dining room
2. bathroom	5. bedroom
3. kitchen	6. balcony

LISTENING
5–10 MINUTES

Listen and write the number under the correct picture.

1. A. Tell me about the apartment.
   B. It has a very nice bathroom.

2. A. Please tell me about the apartment.
   B. It has a very nice living room.

3. A. Tell me about the apartment.
   B. It has a very large kitchen.

4. A. Is there a dining room in the apartment?
    B. Yes, there is.
5. A. Please tell me about the bedroom.
    B. It's very large.

Answers

3   5   1   2   4

LANGUAGE IN *MOTION*   **10** MINUTES

Have students walk around the classroom, asking each other about their classmates' homes—for example: "How many bedrooms are there where you live? How many bathrooms are there?" (For larger classes, you can set a time limit or a limit on how many people students should ask.)

E X P A N S I O N

1. Concentration ★

PHOTO CARDS 77–83 (TWO SETS)

a. Shuffle the cards and place them face-down in two rows of 7 each.

b. Divide the class into two teams. The object of the game is for students to find the matching cards and identify the vocabulary item. Both teams should be able to see the cards, since *concentrating* on their location is an important part of playing the game.

c. A student from Team 1 turns over two cards, and if they match, the student must identify the item. If the student correctly identifies the item, that team keeps the cards, and the student takes another turn. If they don't match or if the student isn't able to correctly identify the item, the student turns them face-down, and a member of Team 2 takes a turn.

d. The game continues until all the cards have been matched. The team with the most correct *matches* wins the game.

Variation:
PHOTO CARDS 77–83
ACTIVITY MASTER 40

Have the class play with one set of Photo Cards and one set of Word Cards.

2. What Can You Do There? ★★

Divide the class into pairs or small groups. Have students choose a room of the home and make a list of things you can do in that room. For example:

[*kitchen*]
make dinner
wash the dishes

3. Magazine Photos ★★★

Bring in magazine photos of the interiors of houses and apartments. As a class, in pairs, or in small groups, have students describe the photos.

4. Guessing Game ★★★

Write the names of rooms of the house on separate cards or use Photo Cards 77–83. Have a student select a card and say an action that goes with that room—for example: "I eat dinner here." Other students guess what the room is.

5. My Home ★★★

a. Draw a floor plan of your house or apartment on the board. Talk about its features. For example:

My apartment has a very nice living room.
My apartment has a very small kitchen.

b. Have students draw floor plans of their own houses or apartments and in pairs, describe their diagrams. For example:

My apartment has a balcony.

6. My Dream Home ★★★

Have students draw their dream house or apartment. In pairs or small groups, have students show each other their drawings and tell about them. For example:

My dream house has two bathrooms.
My dream house has a balcony and a patio.

Help students with additional vocabulary they may need.

LESSON OBJECTIVE

FOCUS
Home appliances & features

VOCABULARY
closet
fireplace
refrigerator
shower
stove
window

GETTING READY
10–15 MINUTES

Introduce *there is.*

1. Write the following on the board:

> A. Is there a _____ in the _____?
> B. Yes, there is.

2. Point to objects in the classroom and ask questions such as the following:

> Is there a book in the classroom?
> Is there a pen in the classroom?

Students answer: "Yes, there is."

THE MODEL CONVERSATION
10 MINUTES

1. **SETTING THE SCENE:** Have students look at the model photograph. Set the scene: "This woman is asking a realtor about an apartment."

2. **LISTENING:** With books closed, have students listen to the model conversation—presented by you, by a pair of students, or on the audio program. Check students' understanding of the situation and the vocabulary.

3. **CLASS PRACTICE:** With books still closed, model each line, and have the whole class practice in unison.

4. **READING:** With books open, have students follow along as two students present the model.

5. **PAIR PRACTICE:** In pairs, have students practice the model conversation.

THE CONVERSATION EXERCISES
10–15 MINUTES

1. **THE SKELETAL DIALOG:** Write the "skeletal dialog" on the board. Fill in the replacement from Exercise 1 to show students how the guided conversation method works. Call on a few pairs of students to practice Exercise 1, using the skeletal framework on the board.

> A. Is there a <u>shower</u> in the <u>bathroom</u>?
> B. Yes, there is.

2. **VOCABULARY PRESENTATION:** Present the vocabulary words in the exercises. Point to the photograph of each item, say the home appliance or feature and the corresponding room, and have the class repeat them chorally and individually. Check students' understanding and pronunciation of the vocabulary.

3. **EXERCISE PRACTICE:** (optional) Have pairs of students simultaneously practice all the exercises.

4. **EXERCISE PRESENTATIONS:** Call on pairs of students to present their conversations to the class.

LISTENING
5–10 MINUTES

Listen and write the number under the correct picture.

1. A. Is there a shower in the bathroom?
   B. Yes, there is.
2. A. Is there a stove in the kitchen?
   B. Yes, there is.
3. A. Is there a closet in the bedroom?
   B. Yes, there is.
4. A. Is there a fireplace in the living room?
   B. Yes, there is.
5. A. Is there a window in the dining room?
   B. Yes, there is.

Answers

4 2 5 1 3

FINISH THE SENTENCE
5 MINUTES

Have students complete the sentences based on the illustrations and then compare answers with a partner.

Answers

1. bathroom
2. bedroom
3. kitchen
4. living room

IN YOUR HOME
5–10 MINUTES

Have students write the names of the rooms where they do the activities and then compare answers with a partner.

LANGUAGE IN *MOTION*
10 MINUTES

Have students look at student book pages 32 and 33 for ideas of actions to mime. Have students take turns standing in the front of the classroom and miming a home activity. Other students guess what room of the house the student is in and what the person is doing.

EXPANSION

1. Concentration ★
PHOTO CARDS 84–89 (TWO SETS)

a. Shuffle the cards and place them face-down in three rows of 4 each.

b. Divide the class into two teams. The object of the game is for students to find the matching cards and identify the vocabulary item. Both teams should be able to see the cards, since *concentrating* on their location is an important part of playing the game.

c. A student from Team 1 turns over two cards, and if they match, the student must identify the item. If the student correctly identifies the item, that team keeps the cards, and the student takes another turn. If they don't match or if the student isn't able to correctly identify the item, the student turns them face-down, and a member of Team 2 takes a turn.

d. The game continues until all the cards have been matched. The team with the most correct *matches* wins the game.

Variation:
PHOTO CARDS 84–89
ACTIVITY MASTER 41

Have the class play with one set of Photo Cards and one set of Word Cards.

2. Pair Interviews ★★
ACTIVITY MASTER 42

a. Make multiple copies of Activity Master 42 and distribute one to each student.

b. Write on the board the two possible responses to the questions:

> Yes, there is.
> No, there isn't.

c. In pairs, have students interview one another about their homes and then report back to the class. For example:

> There's a refrigerator in Miguel's kitchen.
> There's a window in his kitchen.

3. Finish the Sentence! ★★
Divide the class into two teams. Begin sentences such as the following, and have students from each team take turns finishing them with appropriate words from the lesson. For example:

> I put food in the . . . *refrigerator.*
> I put my clothes in a . . . *closet.*
> I have a fire in my . . . *fireplace.*
> I cook on the . . . *stove.*
> I look out my . . . *window.*
> I sleep in my . . . *bedroom.*
> I take a shower in my . . . *shower/bathroom.*
> I cook in my . . . *kitchen.*

The team with the most correctly completed sentences wins the game.

4. Magazine Photos ★★★
Bring in magazine photos of the interiors of houses and apartments. As a class, in pairs, or in small groups, have students describe the photos.

5. My Dream Home ★★★
Have students draw their dream houses or apartments. In pairs or small groups, have students show each other their drawings and tell about them. For example:

> In my dream house, there's a closet in every room.
> In my dream house, there's a fireplace in the bedroom.

Help students with additional vocabulary they may need.

LESSON OBJECTIVE

Focus

Rooms & furniture
Types of housing

VOCABULARY

bed	apartment building
chair	dormitory
lamp	duplex
rug	house
sofa	mobile home
table	shelter

GETTING READY

5–10 MINUTES

Introduce the action *put*.

1. Using classroom objects, hand one student an item and say: "Put it over there." (Indicate another area of the classroom.) The student places the item there.

2. Have students place other classroom items where you indicate.

THE MODEL CONVERSATION

10 MINUTES

1. **SETTING THE SCENE:** Have students look at the model photograph. Set the scene: "The furniture movers are talking to someone who is moving into a new apartment."

2. **LISTENING:** With books closed, have students listen to the model conversation—presented by you, by a pair of students, or on the audio program. Check students' understanding of the situation and the vocabulary.

3. **CLASS PRACTICE:** With books still closed, model each line, and have the whole class practice in unison.

4. **READING:** With books open, have students follow along as two students present the model.

5. **PAIR PRACTICE:** In pairs, have students practice the model conversation.

THE CONVERSATION EXERCISES

10 MINUTES

1. **THE SKELETAL DIALOG:** Write the "skeletal dialog" on the board. Fill in the replacement from Exercise 1 to show students how the guided conversation method works. Call on

a few pairs of students to practice Exercise 1, using the skeletal framework on the board.

> A. Where do you want this <u>sofa</u>?
> B. Put it in the <u>living room</u>.

2. **VOCABULARY PRESENTATION:** Present the vocabulary words in the exercises. Point to the photograph of each item, say the word, and have the class repeat it chorally and individually. Check students' understanding and pronunciation of the vocabulary.

3. **EXERCISE PRACTICE:** (optional) Have pairs of students simultaneously practice all the exercises.

4. **EXERCISE PRESENTATIONS:** Call on pairs of students to present their conversations to the class.

MEMORY GAME

5–10 MINUTES

Have students stand in a circle for this activity. Student 1 says a furniture item he or she has and where it is located—for example: "In my house, there's a table in the kitchen."

Student 2 repeats what Student 1 said and adds another furniture item—for example: "In my house, there's table in the kitchen and a bed in the bedroom." Continue around the room in this fashion, with each student repeating what the previous student said and adding another furniture item. (*Note:* If the class is large, you can divide students into groups.)

COMMUNITY CONNECTIONS

5–10 MINUTES

Practice the vocabulary words. Point to the photograph of each type of housing, say the word, and have the class repeat it chorally and individually. Check students' understanding and pronunciation of the vocabulary. Next, have students, working individually, in pairs, or in small groups, talk about the types of housing in their community and then report back to the class.

EXPANSION

1. **Concentration**
   PHOTO CARDS 91–96 (TWO SETS)

   a. Shuffle the cards and place them face-down in three rows of 4 each.

(continued)

b. Divide the class into two teams. The object of the game is for students to find the matching cards and identify the vocabulary item. Both teams should be able to see the cards, since *concentrating* on their location is an important part of playing the game.

c. A student from Team 1 turns over two cards, and if they match, the student must identify the item. If the student correctly identifies the item, that team keeps the cards, and the student takes another turn. If they don't match or if the student isn't able to correctly identify the item, the student turns them face-down, and a member of Team 2 takes a turn.

d. The game continues until all the cards have been matched. The team with the most correct *matches* wins the game.

Variation:
Photo Cards 91–96
Activity Master 43

Have the class play with one set of Photo Cards and one set of Word Cards.

2. Drawing Game ✭✭
Activity Masters 41, 43

You will need either an hourglass or a watch with a second hand for timing the following activity.

a. Make two copies of Activity Masters 41 and 43. Cut them into cards and place the two sets of cards in two piles on a table or desk in the front of the classroom. Also, have a pad of paper and pencil next to each pile.

b. Divide the class into two teams. Have each team sit together in a different part of the room.

c. When you say: "Go!", a person from each team picks a card from the pile and draws the object. The rest of the team then guesses what the object is.

d. When a team correctly guesses the object, another team member picks a card and draws the object on that card.

e. Continue until each team has guessed all of the objects in their pile.

The team that guesses all the objects in the shortest time wins the game.

3. Alphabetical Order ✭✭
Activity Master 43

Make multiple copies of Activity Master 43 and cut them into cards. Divide the class into pairs and give one set of cards to each pair. Have students work together to put the cards in alphabetical order. The first pair to finish alphabetizing the words can write their list on the board. Go over the answers with the class.

4. Associations ✭✭
Divide the class into small groups. Call out a room of the home, and have the groups write down as many associations as they can think of. For example:

> kitchen: [stove/refrigerator/table/chairs/
>   cabinets]
> living room: [sofa/lamp/fireplace/chairs/rug]

5. True or False? ✭✭
Make statements about the apartment in the Finish the Sentence exercise on student book page 69. Students must decide if the statements are true or false. If a statement is false, have students correct it. For example:

> There's a bed in the bedroom. [True.]
> There's a lamp in the bedroom. [True.]
> There's a sofa in the bedroom. [False. There's a sofa in the living room.]
> There's a stove in the bathroom. [False. There's a stove in the kitchen.]
> There's a shower in the bathroom. [True.]
> There's a refrigerator in the kitchen. [True.]
> There's a fireplace in the kitchen. [False. There's a fireplace in the living room.]

6. Telephone ✭✭
a. Have students sit in a circle or semicircle. Make up two sentences, using the new vocabulary in this lesson, and whisper them to Student 1. For example:

> John lives in a dormitory. There's a table, a lamp, a bed, and a closet in his room.

b. The first student whispers what he or she heard to the second student, who whispers it to the third student, and so forth. When the message gets to the last student, that person says it aloud. Is it the same message you started with?

Give each student in the class a chance to start his or her own message.

7. Magazine Photos ✭✭✭
Bring in magazine photos of houses or apartments and distribute to students. In pairs or small groups, have students write sentences describing the photos. Have students hold up the photos and read their sentences to the class.

LESSON OBJECTIVE

Focus

Cardinal & ordinal numbers review

READING

GETTING READY
5–10 MINUTES

1. Explain the expressions *There's and There are.*
   a. Write the following on the board:

   > There is → There's
   > There are
   > There's a stove in the kitchen.
   > There's a refrigerator in the kitchen.
   > There are chairs in the kitchen.

   b. Explain that *There's* is an abbreviated form of *There is*. *There's* is used when there is only one thing (a stove, a refrigerator). *There are* is used when there are more things (chairs, cabinets).

2. Introduce the new words *bathtub* and *cabinet*. Point to the items in the illustration on student book page 72. You can also use Photo Cards 90 and 97.

MY APARTMENT
10–15 MINUTES

1. Have students cover the text and listen and point to the illustrations as you read or play the story on the audio program.

2. Read or play the story again, as students read along.

3. In pairs or in small groups, have students read the story to each other.

Answers

1. Three.
2. 12th Street.
3. Six.
4. Second floor.
5. Four.
6. Two.
7. Four.

EXPANSION

1. **Listen for the Numbers** ★
   Read the story to students again, this time with their books closed. Have students write down all the numbers they hear. Have students compare their answers. If some students missed numbers, have the class listen again.

   Answers

12th	4
3	3
2nd	2
6	4
4	1st

2. **Retell the Story** ★★
   Divide the class into pairs. Have students cover the text and then point to the pictures as they retell the story to their partners.

3. **Dictation Game** ★★
   a. Write down 4–5 sentences from the story in large print on a large piece of paper. For example:

   > There are four rooms in my apartment.
   > There are three windows in the living room.
   > There are two closets in the bedroom.
   > There's a stove, there's a refrigerator, and there are four cabinets in the kitchen.

   b. Put the paper on the far side of the room or out in the hallway.

   c. Divide the class into pairs. One student from each pair runs to read the story and then returns to dictate the story to their partner. The runner may go back and forth as many times as necessary. The first pair to finish the story wins.

LANGUAGE EXPERIENCE JOURNAL

Have students write about their homes. Depending on your students' writing abilities, either have them write in their journal or dictate their story for you to write. Then students should read what they have written to a classmate. If time permits, you may also want to write a response in each student's journal, sharing your own opinions and experiences as well as reacting to what the student has written.

Different Cultures Different Ways

5–10 MINUTES

Have students first work in pairs or small groups, reacting to the photographs and responding to the questions. Then have students share with the class what they have talked about.

PUT IT TOGETHER

15–20 MINUTES

In this activity, students talk with each other to find out information about an apartment.

1. Divide the class into pairs: Student A and Student B.

2. Tell all the Student A's to look at Part A of the activity on page 73. Tell all the Student B's to look at Part B on page 74.

3. Have everybody look at the first item on the list: *refrigerator in the kitchen.*

   a. In Student B's list, in the second column, it says, *Yes.* Therefore, when Student A asks: "Is there a refrigerator in the kitchen?", Student B answers: "Yes, there is."

   b. Ask all the Student B's: "Is there a refrigerator in the kitchen?" Have all the Student B's respond in unison: "Yes, there is."

4. Have everybody look at the second item on the list: *shower in the bathroom.*

   a. Have all the Student A's look at their list. In their list in the second column, it says, *Yes.* Therefore, when Student B asks: "Is there a shower in the bathroom?", Student A answers: "Yes, there is."

   b. Ask all the Student A's: "Is there a shower in the bathroom?" Have all the Student A's respond in unison: "Yes, there is."

5. The Student A and Student B pairs are now ready to continue the activity with the rest of the information on their lists.

6. When the pairs have completed the activity, have them check each other's answers.

VOCABULARY FOUNDATIONS

5–10 MINUTES

Have students review the list of words they have learned in this unit. Encourage students to get a small notebook where they can write down vocabulary that is new for them. If students have personal copies of dictionaries or picture dictionaries, have them look up these words in the dictionary and highlight them with a marker.

Encourage them to look at their notebooks or dictionaries frequently to review what they have learned.

For additional practice, have students do one or more of the following activities.

1. **Taking Notes** ★

   In their vocabulary notebooks or on a piece of paper, have students write all the words in one column. In a second column, have them write notes, draw pictures, or write the word in a sentence that will help them remember the meaning of the words.

2. **Guess the Word!** ★★

   a. Divide the class into two teams. Choose a vocabulary word from the unit, and on the board write a blank for each letter in the word. For example: *shower*

   b. Give students a clue about the word. For example: "You use this in the bathroom." The team that guesses the word gets one point. The team with the most points wins the guessing game.

3. **Theme Matching Game** ★★★
   ACTIVITY MASTER 44

   a. Make a copy of Activity Master 44, cut it into cards, and give one to each student. Half of the cards are theme headings and half of the cards are lists of items that belong under those theme headings.

   b. Have students walk around the room, telling each other the items on their cards until they find their match. When all the pairs have been matched, have them say the items on their cards for the whole class.

4. **Category Dictation** ★★★

   a. Have students make three columns on a piece of paper:

      rooms
      types of housing
      furniture

   b. Dictate words from Vocabulary Foundations, and have students write them in the appropriate column. Make sure all students have covered the vocabulary items on student book page 74 with a piece of paper so they don't refer to that list.

c. As a class, in pairs, or in small groups, have students check their work.

LANGUAGE SKILL FOUNDATIONS

Explain to students that this is a list of skills they have learned in the unit. Students should become familiar with the vocabulary of describing their skills, but they don't need to master all the terms. For each speaking skill on the list, read the skill aloud to students, and have them demonstrate it. For example:

Teacher: I can ask about an apartment.
Students: Tell me about the apartment.

(If students don't understand the vocabulary of a particular speaking skill, give them a concrete example rather than a description or explanation, and then have students practice your example and others.)

Have students put a check next to each skill if they feel they have learned it. Use this information to determine which lessons you may want to review or reinforce for the entire class or for particular students. The Getting Ready and Expansion activities for this unit and the CD-ROM's Activity Bank of supplemental worksheets are excellent resources for additional practice. It may also be helpful to have stronger students or, if available, a classroom aide or volunteer, work with students who need more practice.

Talk About It! ▶ ▶ ▶   (Page 75)
20–30 MINUTES

(Page 75 is also available as a transparency.)

Use the scenes in this illustration to review the vocabulary, conversations, and grammar in the unit. Have students first work in pairs or small groups to talk about the illustration and answer the questions posed at the bottom of the page. Then discuss as a class.

For additional motivating practice, students will enjoy doing one or more of the following activities.

The following activities review Unit 5 vocabulary:

1. The Longest List ★
a. Divide the class into pairs or small groups. Have the pairs or groups make a list of all the places in the home and objects they see in the scene. Tell students to cover the list of words on student book page 74 with a piece of paper so they don't refer to that

list. (Set a five-minute time limit for this activity.)

b. Tell students to stop when the five minutes are up. Ask students to count the number of items on their lists. Who has the longest list?

c. Check students' answers by calling on students to name items on their lists. Write the words on the board, and have students check their spelling.

2. Remember the Actions! ★★
a. Tell students to spend two minutes looking carefully at the home scene on student book page 75.

b. Have students close their books and write down every action they remember from the illustration. For example:

exercising
setting the table
watching TV
reading the paper
making dinner
studying
brushing teeth
getting dressed

c. Have students compare notes with a partner and then look at the scene again to see how well they remembered what people are doing.

The following activities review Unit 5 conversations and grammar:

3. True or False? ★★
Make statements about the scene on student book page 75, and have students decide if the statements are true or false. If a statement is false, have students correct it. For example:

There are two bedrooms. [True.]
There are three windows in the kitchen. [False. There's one window.]

Variation: Do the activity as a game with competing teams.

4. Where Are They? ★★
In pairs, have students talk about where the characters in the illustration are. One student points to a character and the other describes where he or she is. Then reverse roles.

Variation: One student describes where a character is and the other student points to that person.

(continued)

5. Class Story ★★

a. Have students look at the scene on student book page 75. Ask questions about the scene to help them imagine a storyline. For example:

> Who are they? What are their names?
> Do they all live together?
> What time of day is it?
> What are they doing?

b. Have students dictate the story to you as you write it on the board. Ask them how to spell various words as they're dictating the story to you. Also, ask the class to point out any grammar errors they find in the story.

Variation: As a review of the vocabulary, erase all the unit vocabulary from the story, and have students come to the board and fill in the words.

6. Who Is It? ★★★

a. Divide the class into pairs. Have each pair choose one character in the illustration and write two sentences describing that person. For example:

> [*the grandmother*]
> She's on the patio.
> She's exercising.

b. Have the pairs read their sentences to the class and see if students can guess which character is being described.

7. Do You Remember? ★★★

Tell students to spend two minutes looking carefully at the illustration on student book page 75. Then have students close their books. Ask students questions about the illustration. For example:

> How many rooms are there?
> How many chairs are there?
> How many tables are there?
> How many beds are there?
>
> Is there a fireplace in the living room?
> Is there a lamp in the living room?
> Is there a bathtub in the bathroom?
> Is there a cat in the dining room?
> Is there a rug in the mother's bedroom?

UNIT 6 COMMUNITY

LESSONS & UNIT ACTIVITIES	OBJECTIVES	TEXT	TEACHER'S GUIDE
Vocabulary Preview	Places in the community	76–77	94
LESSON 1 Where are you going?	Places in the community	78–79	95–97
LESSON 2 Where's the post office?	Places in the community	80–81	98–100
LESSON 3 Where's the bank?	Asking for & giving location	82–83	101–103
LESSON 4 NUMBERS: On 12th Street	Ordinal numbers	84	104–105
Language Experience Journal	Writing about your neighborhood	84	105
Different Cultures / Different Ways	Shopping in different communities and countries	85	106
Put It Together	Information Gap / Teamwork activity	85–86	106
Vocabulary Foundations / Language Skill Foundations	Review & skills checklist	86	106–107
Talk About It!	Review, conversations, activities, & games	87	107–108

UNIT RESOURCES

Audio Program:
Audio CD 2: Tracks 40–52
Audio Cassette 2B

Workbooks:
Activity Workbook
Literacy Workbook

Lesson Planner CD-ROM:
Activity Masters 45–50
Activity Bank Unit 6 Worksheets
Vocabulary Photo Cards: 98–115
Transparency: Color Overhead for Unit 6, page 87

PREVIEW — 5 MINUTES

Activate students' prior knowledge of community vocabulary by doing either or both of the following:

1. Have students brainstorm places in their community and write them on the board.

2. Have students look at the photographs on student book pages 76 and 77 while they cover the words at the bottom of the page. Have students identify the words they already know.

PRESENT — 10 MINUTES

Using the photographs on student book pages 76 and 77, point to each item or say its number, say the word, and have the class repeat it chorally and individually. (You can also play the audio program.) Check students' understanding and pronunciation of the vocabulary.

PRACTICE — 10 MINUTES

As a class, in pairs, or in small groups, have students practice the vocabulary in either or both of the following ways:

* Say or write a word, and have students point to the item in their books or tell the number.
* Point to a photograph in the book or give the number, and have students say the word.

SPELLING PRACTICE — 5 MINUTES

Say a word, and have students spell it aloud or write it. Or point to an item in the student book, and have students write the word. You can also spell a portion of a word on the board, and have students come to the board to complete it.

EXPANSION

1. Tell and Show ★
PHOTO CARDS 98–115 (TWO SETS)

a. Divide the class into pairs. Distribute all the Photo Cards randomly so every pair receives at least four or five cards.

b. Have Student A in each pair select a Photo Card and tell Student B the place. Have Student B point to the place on student book page 76 or 77.

c. As the pairs finish using their Photo Cards, have them trade their sets with another pair and then continue the activity. Have students reverse roles each time they get a new set of cards.

2. Match Game ★
PHOTO CARDS 98–115 (TWO SETS)

a. Choose duplicate copies of any Photo Cards 98–115 and distribute them randomly, one to each student.

b. Have students look at their card and identify the place in the community. Then have students circulate around the room, saying the name of the place on their card until they find their match. Make sure students don't show their cards to their classmates since this is a listening and speaking exercise.

c. When students have found their match, have them compare their cards and come show you. Then give each student another Photo Card to keep the game going. Continue until students have found all the matches.

3. True or False? ★★
PHOTO CARDS 98–115

Show students various Photo Cards. Make a false statement about the place, and have students correct it. For example:

Teacher: [showing the class Photo Card 107] This is a gas station.
Students: No. It's a post office.

Teacher: [showing the class Photo Card 113] This is a bakery.
Students: No. It's a movie theater.

LESSON OBJECTIVE

FOCUS

Places in the community

VOCABULARY

bakery
bank
bus station
clinic
drug store
gas station
grocery store
laundromat
library

GETTING READY
5–10 MINUTES

Use your own visuals or the photos on student book page 78 to introduce the following vocabulary: *laundromat, bank, clinic, bakery, library, gas station, bus station, drug store,* and *grocery store.* Say each word, and have the class repeat it chorally and individually. Check students' understanding and pronunciation of the vocabulary.

THE MODEL CONVERSATION
10 MINUTES

1. **SETTING THE SCENE:** Have students look at the model photographs. Set the scene: "Two friends are talking."

2. **LISTENING:** With books closed, have students listen to the model conversation—presented by you, by a pair of students, or on the audio program. Check students' understanding of the situation and the vocabulary.

3. **CLASS PRACTICE:** With books still closed, model each line, and have the whole class practice in unison.

4. **READING:** With books open, have students follow along as two students present the model.

5. **PAIR PRACTICE:** In pairs, have students practice the model conversation.

THE CONVERSATION EXERCISES
10–20 MINUTES

1. **THE SKELETAL DIALOG:** Write the "skeletal dialog" on the board. Fill in the replacement from Exercise 1 to show students how the

guided conversation method works. Call on a few pairs of students to practice Exercise 1, using the skeletal framework on the board.

> A. Where are you going?
> B. I'm going to the <u>bank</u>.

2. **VOCABULARY PRESENTATION:** Present the vocabulary words in the exercises. Point to the photograph of each item, say the word, and have the class repeat it chorally and individually. Check students' understanding and pronunciation of the vocabulary.

3. **EXERCISE PRACTICE:** (optional) Have pairs of students simultaneously practice all the exercises.

4. **EXERCISE PRESENTATIONS:** Call on pairs of students to present their conversations to the class.

LISTENING
5–10 MINUTES

Listen and write the number under the correct picture.

1. A. Where are you going?
   B. I'm going to the library.
2. A. Where are you going?
   B. I'm going to the bus station.
3. A. Where are you going?
   B. I'm going to the laundromat.
4. A. Where are you going?
   B. I'm going to the gas station.
5. A. Where are you going?
   B. I'm going to the bank.

Answers

2   5   1   4   3

CLOZE READING
5–10 MINUTES

Explain that a "cloze reading" is a story with words missing. Tell students that their task is to write the correct words in the blanks based on the illustrations above. Have students complete the activity and then compare answers with a partner.

Answers

1. laundromat
2. bank
3. library
4. drug store
5. gas station

MISSING LETTERS

Point out that there are letters missing in these words and students have to figure out what those missing letters are and write them in the blanks. Have students fill in the missing letters and then compare answers with a partner.

Answers

1. clinic
2. park
3. bakery
4. laundromat
5. drug store
6. bus station

EXPANSION

1. Concentration ★

PHOTO CARDS 98–106 (TWO SETS)

a. Shuffle the cards and place them face-down in three rows of 6 each.

b. Divide the class into two teams. The object of the game is for students to find the matching cards and identify the vocabulary item. Both teams should be able to see the cards, since *concentrating* on their location is an important part of playing the game.

c. A student from Team 1 turns over two cards, and if they match, the student must identify the item. If the student correctly identifies the item, that team keeps the cards, and the student takes another turn. If they don't match or if the student isn't able to correctly identify the item, the student turns them face-down, and a member of Team 2 takes a turn.

d. The game continues until all the cards have been matched. The team with the most correct *matches* wins the game.

Variation:
PHOTO CARDS 98–106
ACTIVITY MASTER 45

Have the class play with one set of Photo Cards and one set of Word Cards.

2. Alphabetical Order ★★

Have pairs of students work together to put in alphabetical order the places on student book page 78. Call on a pair to read their list, and have the class decide whether or not the order is correct.

3. Memory Game ★★

Begin the activity by saying: "Today I'm going to the bank." Student 1 repeats what you said and adds another place—for example: "Today I'm going to the bank and the library." Student 2 repeats what you and Student 1 said and adds another place—for example: "Today I'm going to the bank, the library, and the laundromat." Continue around the room in this fashion, with each student repeating what the previous student said and adding another place. Do the activity again, beginning and ending with different students.

4. More Missing Letters ★★

a. Divide the class into two teams. Draw a series of blanks on the board to represent the letters in a word from student book page 78.

b. Have students from each team take turns calling out letters. If the letter is correct, put it in the appropriate blank and give the team one point. If the letter is incorrect, put it on a list to the side. The team that gets the most points wins the game.

5. What Can You Do There? ★★

a. Divide the class into pairs or small groups. Have students make a list of the places in the community on student book page 78, and for each place, write an activity they can do there. For example:

laundromat—do the laundry
grocery store—buy food

b. Call on pairs to present their list to the class and compare everybody's ideas. Write a master list of ideas on the board, and have students copy the words into their notebooks.

6. Association Game ★★

Divide the class into several teams. Call out a place from student book page 78. Have the students in each team work together to see how many words they can associate with that place. For example:

library: [books/read/study/relax]

The team with the most correct items wins.

7. Names of Places in Our Community ✷✷

Call out one of the places around town on student book page 78—for example: "Bank." Have students tell the names of banks in their community. Write the names on the board. For example:

```
Bank
National Bank
Union Bank
Bay Bank
```

8. Clues! ✷✷✷

a. Have one student leave the classroom for a few minutes.

b. Call out one of the places on student book page 78, and have the class think of different activities they do there. Students can either say or write their answers. For example:

> [*library*]
> I study there.
> I read magazines.
> I relax.

c. The student then returns to the classroom, listens as others read or say their clues, and tries to guess the place.

Variation: This activity can be done as a game with competing teams. The team whose members guess the words with the fewest number of clues wins the game.

9. Ranking ✷✷✷

a. Have students look at the vocabulary on student book page 78 and choose the five places they visit the most. Have students rank these items from one to five, with one being the place they visit the most. For example:

1. grocery store
2. bank
3. gas station
4. drug store
5. laundromat

b. As a class, in pairs, or in small groups, have students compare their lists.

10. Class Directory ✷✷✷

Have everybody in the class supply the names and addresses of places in the community from student book page 78 they are familiar with and recommend. Compile the information and create a class directory.

LESSON OBJECTIVE

FOCUS

Places in the community

VOCABULARY

department store
hospital
movie theater
park
post office
restaurant
shopping mall
supermarket
train station
on

GETTING READY

5 MINUTES

Use your own visuals or the photos on student book page 80 to introduce the following vocabulary items: *post office, supermarket, hospital, park, restaurant, shopping mall, movie theater, train station,* and *department store.* Say each word, and have the class repeat it chorally and individually. Check students' understanding and pronunciation of the vocabulary.

THE MODEL CONVERSATIONS

10 MINUTES

1. **SETTING THE SCENE:** Have students look at the model photographs. Set the scene: "Two people on the street are talking."

2. **LISTENING:** With books closed, have students listen to the model conversation—presented by you, by a pair of students, or on the audio program. Check students' understanding of the situation and the vocabulary.

3. **CLASS PRACTICE:** With books still closed, model each line, and have the whole class practice in unison.

4. **READING:** With books open, have students follow along as two students present the model.

5. **PAIR PRACTICE:** In pairs, have students practice the model conversation.

THE CONVERSATION EXERCISES

10–15 MINUTES

1. **THE SKELETAL DIALOG:** Write the "skeletal dialog" on the board. Fill in the replacement from Exercise 1 to show students how the guided conversation method works. Call on a few pairs of students to practice Exercise 1, using the skeletal framework on the board. Encourage students to name streets in their community.

> A. Excuse me. Where's the <u>supermarket</u>?
> B. It's on (<u>Central Avenue</u>).

2. **VOCABULARY PRESENTATION:** Present the vocabulary words in the exercises. Point to the photograph of each item, say the word, and have the class repeat it chorally and individually. Check students' understanding and pronunciation of the vocabulary.

3. **EXERCISE PRACTICE:** (optional) Have pairs of students simultaneously practice all the exercises.

4. **EXERCISE PRESENTATIONS:** Call on pairs of students to present their conversations to the class.

LISTENING

5–10 MINUTES

Listen and write the number under the correct picture.

1. A. Excuse me. Where's the train station?
   B. It's on Central Avenue.
   A. Thanks.
2. A. Excuse me. Where's the movie theater?
   B. It's on Main Street.
   A. Thanks.
3. A. Excuse me. Where's the park?
   B. It's on Lake Street.
   A. Thank you.
4. A. Excuse me. Where's the post office?
   B. It's on Walker Avenue.
   A. Thanks.
5. A. Excuse me. Where's the hospital?
   B. It's on River Road.
   A. Thanks.

Answers

3 1 5 2 4

CLOZE READING

10 MINUTES

Tell students that their task is to write the correct words in the blanks based on the illustrations above. Have students complete the activity and then compare answers with a partner.

Answers
1. post office
2. supermarket
3. shopping mall
4. restaurant

LANGUAGE IN *MOTION*

10 MINUTES

Have students take turns standing in the front of the classroom and miming an activity in the community. Other students try to guess the action and the place.

E X P A N S I O N

1. Concentration ★

PHOTO CARDS 107–115 (TWO SETS)

a. Shuffle the cards and place them face-down in three rows of 6 each.

b. Divide the class into two teams. The object of the game is for students to find the matching cards and identify the vocabulary item. Both teams should be able to see the cards, since *concentrating* on their location is an important part of playing the game.

c. A student from Team 1 turns over two cards, and if they match, the student must identify the item. If the student correctly identifies the item, that team keeps the cards, and the student takes another turn. If they don't match or if the student isn't able to correctly identify the item, the student turns them face-down, and a member of Team 2 takes a turn.

d. The game continues until all the cards have been matched. The team with the most correct *matches* wins the game.

Variation:
PHOTO CARDS 107–115
ACTIVITY MASTER 46

Have the class play with one set of Photo Cards and one set of Word Cards.

2. Memory Game ★★

Begin the activity by saying: "Today I'm going to the post office." Student 1 repeats what you said and adds another place—for example: "Today I'm going to the post office and the train station."

Student 2 repeats what you and Student 1 said and adds another place—for example: "Today I'm going to the post office, the train station, and the hospital." Continue around the room in this fashion, with each student repeating what the previous student said and adding another place. Do the activity again, beginning and ending with different students.

3. Missing Letters ★★

a. Divide the class into two teams. Draw a series of blanks on the board to represent the letters in a word from student book page 80.

b. Have students from each team take turns calling out letters. If the letter is correct, put it in the appropriate blank and give the team one point. If the letter is incorrect, put it on a list to the side. The team that gets the most points wins the game.

4. What Can You Do There? ★★

a. Divide the class into pairs or small groups. Have students make a list of the places in the community on student book page 80, and for each place, write an activity they can do there. For example:

supermarket—buy food
hospital—see a doctor

b. Call on pairs to present their list to the class and compare everybody's ideas. Write a master list of ideas on the board, and have students copy the words in their notebooks.

5. Association Game ★★

Divide the class into several teams. Call out a place from student book page 80. Have the students in each group work together to see how many words they can associate with that place. For example:

hospital: [doctors/nurses/sick/visit]

The team with the most correct items wins.

6. Names of Places in Our Community ★★

Call out one of the places around town on student book page 80—for example: "Park." Have students tell the names of parks in their community. Write the names on the board. For example:

Park
Central Park
Riverside Park
Washington Park

(continued)

7. Community Maps ✪✪✪

Draw a simple map of the area around your school, writing in the names of streets and buildings. Either put it on the board or make copies to give to each student. Have students ask and answer questions with *on* about the locations of buildings. For example:

> A. Where's the Stop 'n Save Supermarket?
> B. It's on Park Street.

8. Clues! ✪✪✪

a. Have one student leave the classroom for a few minutes.

b. Call out one of the places on student book page 80, and have the class think of different activities they do there. Students can either say or write their answers. For example:

> [*movie theater*]
> I watch a movie there.
> I eat popcorn.
> I relax.

c. The student then returns to the classroom, listens as others read or say their clues, and tries to guess the place.

Variation: This activity can be done as a game with competing teams. The team whose members guess the words with the fewest number of clues wins the game.

9. Ranking ✪✪✪

a. Have students look at the vocabulary on student book page 80 and choose the five places they visit the most. Have students rank these items from one to five, with one being the place they visit most often. For example:

> 1. supermarket
> 2. park
> 3. restaurant
> 4. department store
> 5. train station

b. As a class, in pairs, or in small groups, have students compare their lists.

10. Class Directory ✪✪✪

Have everybody in the class supply the names and addresses of places around town from student book page 80 they are familiar with and recommend. Compile the information and create a class directory.

LESSON OBJECTIVE

Focus

Asking for & giving location

Vocabulary

next to
across from
between

PAGE 82 CONVERSATIONS AND EXERCISES

GETTING READY
5 MINUTES

1. Invite a student up to the front of the class. Stand next to the student and say: "Next to. I am next to (Angela)." Write the phrase *next to* on the board.

2. Then step back from the student, face the student, and say: "Across from. I am across from (Angela)." Write the phrase *across from* on the board.

THE MODEL CONVERSATION
10 MINUTES

There are two model conversations. Introduce and practice the first model before going on to the second. For each model:

1. **SETTING THE SCENE:** Have students look at the model photograph. Set the scene: "Two people on the street are talking."

2. **LISTENING:** With books closed, have students listen to the model conversation—presented by you, by a pair of students, or on the audio program. Check students' understanding of the situation and the vocabulary.

3. **CLASS PRACTICE:** With books still closed, model each line, and have the whole class practice in unison.

4. **READING:** With books open, have students follow along as two students present the model.

THE CONVERSATION EXERCISES
10 MINUTES

1. **THE SKELETAL DIALOG:** Write the "skeletal dialog" on the board. Fill in the replacement from Exercise 1 to show students how the guided conversation method works. Call on

a few pairs of students to practice Exercise 1, using the skeletal framework on the board.

> A. Where's the <u>drug store</u>?
> B. The <u>drug store</u> is next to the <u>supermarket</u>.

2. **VOCABULARY PRESENTATION:** Present the vocabulary words in the exercises. Point to the illustrations, say the names of the places, and have the class repeat them chorally and individually. Check students' understanding and pronunciation of the vocabulary.

3. **EXERCISE PRACTICE:** (optional) Have pairs of students simultaneously practice all the exercises.

4. **EXERCISE PRESENTATIONS:** Call on pairs of students to present their conversations to the class.

5. **PAIR PRACTICE:** In pairs, have students practice the model conversation.

PAGE 83 CONVERSATIONS AND EXERCISES

GETTING READY
5 MINUTES

Invite two students up to the front of the class. Stand between the two students and say: "Between. I am between (Ana) and (Pablo)." Write the preposition *between* on the board.

THE MODEL CONVERSATION
10 MINUTES

1. **SETTING THE SCENE:** Have students look at the model photograph. Set the scene: "Two people on the street are talking."

2. **LISTENING:** With books closed, have students listen to the model conversation—presented by you, by a pair of students, or on the audio program. Check students' understanding of the situation and the vocabulary.

3. **CLASS PRACTICE:** With books still closed, model each line, and have the whole class practice in unison.

4. **READING:** With books open, have students follow along as two students present the model.

5. **PAIR PRACTICE:** In pairs, have students practice the model conversation.

THE CONVERSATION EXERCISES
10 MINUTES

1. **THE SKELETAL DIALOG:** Write the "skeletal dialog" on the board. Fill in the replacement from Exercise 1 to show students how the guided conversation method works. Call on a few pairs of students to practice Exercise 1, using the skeletal framework on the board.

> A. Where's the bank?
> B. The bank is between the bakery and the drug store.

2. **VOCABULARY PRESENTATION:** Present the vocabulary words in the exercises. Point to the illustrations, say the names of the places, and have the class repeat them chorally and individually. Check students' understanding and pronunciation of the vocabulary.

3. **EXERCISE PRACTICE:** (optional) Have pairs of students simultaneously practice all the exercises.

4. **EXERCISE PRESENTATIONS:** Call on pairs of students to present their conversations to the class.

LANGUAGE IN *MOTION*
10 MINUTES

Have students walk around the classroom, asking one another about the six places in the chart at the bottom of student book page 83—for example: "Is there a bank in your neighborhood?" Students respond by saying either: "No, there isn't" or: "Yes, there is." If a student responds: "Yes, there is," write that student's name next to that place in the chart. Students should ask for the spelling of a person's name if they aren't sure how to spell it. For example:

A. Is there a bank in your neighborhood?
B. Yes, there is.

A. How do you spell your name?
B. R-A-H-A-L.

EXPANSION

1. Guess the Word! ★
a. Divide the class into two teams. Choose a vocabulary word from the lesson, and on the board write a blank for each letter in the word. For example: *library*

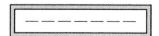

b. Give students a clue about the word. For example: "You read books here." The team that guesses the word gets a point. The team with the most points wins the game.

2. Telephone ★★
a. Have students sit in a circle or semicircle. Make up two sentences, using the prepositions in this lesson and whisper them to Student 1. For example:

> The school is on Central Avenue. It's next to the park and across from the bank.

b. The first student whispers what he or she heard to the second student, who whispers it to the third student, and so forth. When the message gets to the last student, that person says it aloud. Is it the same message you started with?

Give each student in the class a chance to start his or her own message.

3. Listen and Draw ★★
ACTIVITY MASTERS 47, 48

a. Make a copy of Activity Masters 47 and 48 for all the students in your class.

b. Divide the class into pairs. Have all the students fold the sheet in half so they only see the A or B section. Have the B Students read the sentences aloud as the A Students listen and complete the map.

c. After the pairs complete Activity Master 47, have them compare their maps with another pair of students. Then have students reverse roles for Activity Master 48.

Variation: To simplify this activity, pairs can work individually or together to read the sentences *and* complete the maps.

4. Community Maps ★★★
Draw a simple map of the area around your school, writing in the names of streets and buildings. Either put it on the board or make copies to give to each student. Have students ask and answer questions about the locations of buildings, using the prepositions *on*, *next to*, *between*, and *across from*. For example:

A. Where's the parking lot?
B. It's on River Street, next to the school.

5. Guessing Game ★★★

a. Write the following on the board:

> It's on _____.
> It's next to _____.
> It's across from _____.
> It's between _____ and _____.

b. Have students choose a building in their community and write three sentences describing its location.

c. Have students read their sentences to the class without saying what the building is. The class then identifies the building. For example:

Student 1: It's on Main Street.
　　　　　 It's next to the supermarket.
　　　　　 It's across from the gas station.
Student 2: The library.
Student 1: That's right.

6. My Neighborhood ★★★

Have students draw maps of their neighborhoods, writing in the names of streets and buildings. Divide the class into pairs. Have the pairs show their maps to each other and describe the locations of buildings.

LESSON OBJECTIVE

FOCUS
Ordinal numbers

VOCABULARY
nearby

GETTING READY

Explain that *nearby* means *in the area* or *close by*.

THE MODEL CONVERSATION ⏱ 10 MINUTES

1. **SETTING THE SCENE:** Have students look at the model photograph. Set the scene: "Two people on the street are talking."

2. **LISTENING:** With books closed, have students listen to the model conversation—presented by you, by a pair of students, or on the audio program. Check students' understanding of the situation and the vocabulary.

3. **CLASS PRACTICE:** With books still closed, model each line, and have the whole class practice in unison.

4. **READING:** With books open, have students follow along as two students present the model.

5. **PAIR PRACTICE:** In pairs, have students practice the model conversation.

THE CONVERSATION EXERCISES ⏱ 10 MINUTES

1. **THE SKELETAL DIALOG:** Write the "skeletal dialog" on the board. Fill in the replacement from Exercise 1 to show students how the guided conversation method works. Call on a few pairs of students to practice Exercise 1, using the skeletal framework on the board.

> A. Excuse me. Is there a <u>laundromat</u> nearby?
> B. Yes. There's a <u>laundromat</u> on <u>51st Street</u>.
> A. Thank you.

2. **VOCABULARY PRESENTATION:** Present the vocabulary words in the exercises. Point to the illustrations, say the names of the places and the street names, and have the class repeat them chorally and individually. Check students'

understanding and pronunciation of the vocabulary.

3. **EXERCISE PRACTICE:** (optional) Have pairs of students simultaneously practice all the exercises.

4. **EXERCISE PRESENTATIONS:** Call on pairs of students to present their conversations to the class.

COMMUNITY CONNECTIONS ⏱ 10–15 MINUTES

Have students do the activity individually, in pairs, or in small groups, and then report back to the class.

EXPANSION

1. **Listen for the Numbers** ★★
   a. Read the following sentences, and have students write down the number they hear:

   There's a drug store on 15th Street.
   There's a clinic on 2nd Avenue.
   There's a post office on 10th Street.
   There's a library on 3rd Avenue.
   There's a bank on 81st Street.
   There's a supermarket on 75th Street.
   There's a laundromat on 4th Avenue.
   There's a grocery store on 14th Street.
   There's a restaurant on 5th Avenue.
   There's a bus station on 42nd Street.

   b. Have pairs of students check each other's answers.

2. **Telephone Books** ★★
   a. Bring to class telephone books for students to use. In pairs, have students find the telephone numbers for the community locations they listed in the Community Connections activity on student book page 84.

   b. Have the class create a master list of all the places and telephone numbers students filled in for the Community Connections activity.

3. **Information Gap** ★★
   ACTIVITY MASTER 49

   a. Make multiple copies of Activity Master 49 and cut them in half (Table A and Table B).

   b. Divide the class into pairs. Give each partner a different table—A or B. Have students share their information and fill in their tables. For example:

Student A: Is there a bakery nearby?
Student B: Yes. There's a bakery on 1st Street.

c. When the pairs have finished completing their tables, have them look at their partner's tables to make sure they have written the information correctly.

4. Scavenger Hunt ★★★

a. Make a list of specific community businesses and locations in your town that you think would be useful for students to know about. Give each student a copy of the list. For example:

Central Bank
Public Library
City Hall
Chinese-American Cultural Center
Main Street Health Clinic

b. Have students find out the addresses, phone numbers, and exact locations of each item on your list and report back to the class.

LANGUAGE EXPERIENCE JOURNAL

Have students write about their neighborhoods. Depending on your students' writing abilities, either have them write in their journal or dictate their story for you to write. Then students should read what they have written to a classmate. If time permits, you may also want to write a response in each student's journal, sharing your own opinions and experiences as well as reacting to what the student has written.

Different Cultures/Different Ways 10 MINUTES

Have students first work in pairs or small groups, reacting to the photographs and responding to the questions. Then have students share with the class what they have talked about.

PUT IT TOGETHER 15–20 MINUTES

In this activity, students talk with each other to find out the locations of places on their maps.

1. Divide the class into pairs: Student A and Student B.

2. Tell all the Student A's to look at Part A of the activity on student book page 85. Tell all the Student B's to look at Part B on page 86.

3. Point to the gas station on the map and ask: "What's across from the department store?"

    a. In Student B's map, there is a gas station across from the department store. Therefore, when Student A asks: "What's across from the department store?", Student B answers: "The gas station."

    b. Ask all the Student B's: "What's across from the department store?" Have all the Student B's respond in unison: "The gas station."

4. Have Student B's identify a blank building on their map and phrase the question. For example, "What's next to the bus station?"

    a. In Student A's map, there's a supermarket next to the bus station. Therefore, when Student B asks: "What's next to the bus station?", Student A answers: "The supermarket."

    b. Ask all the Student A's: "What's next to the bus station?" Have all the Student A's respond in unison: "The supermarket."

5. The Student A and Student B pairs are now ready to continue the activity with the rest of the map.

6. When the pairs have completed the activity, have them check each other's answers.

VOCABULARY FOUNDATIONS 5–10 MINUTES

Have students review the list of words they have learned in this unit. Encourage students to get a small notebook where they can write down vocabulary that is new for them. If students have personal copies of dictionaries or picture dictionaries, have them look up these words in the dictionary and highlight them with a marker. Encourage them to look at their notebooks or dictionaries frequently to review what they have learned.

For additional practice, have students do one or more of the following activities.

1. **Taking Notes** ★

    In their vocabulary notebooks or on a piece of paper, have students write all the words in one column. In a second column, have them write notes, draw pictures, or write the word in a sentence that will help them remember the meaning of the words.

2. **Guess the Word!** ★

    a. Divide the class into two teams. Choose a vocabulary word from the lesson, and on the board write a blank for each letter in the word. For example: *bakery*

    b. Give students a clue about the word. For example: "You buy bread here." The team that guesses the word gets one point. The team with the most points wins the game.

3. **Finish the Sentence!** ★★

    Divide the class into two teams. Begin sentences, and have students from each team take turns finishing them with appropriate words from the unit. For example:

    I buy bread at the . . . *bakery.*
    I put my money in a . . . *bank.*
    I get a bus at the . . . *bus station.*
    I see a doctor at the . . . *clinic/hospital.*
    I get medicine at the . . . *drug store.*
    I buy gas for my car at the . . . *gas station.*
    I do my laundry at the . . . *laundromat.*
    I see movies at the . . . *movie theater.*
    I buy stamps at the . . . *post office.*
    I eat dinner at a . . . *restaurant.*
    I buy food at a . . . *grocery store/supermarket.*
    I get a train at the . . . *train station.*

    The team with the most correctly completed sentences wins the game.

4. **Category Dictation** ★★★

    a. Have students make four columns on a piece of paper:

        food places
        public places
        transportation places
        fun places

b. Dictate words from Vocabulary Foundations, and have students write them in the appropriate column. Make sure all students have covered the list of vocabulary items on student book page 86 with a piece of paper so they don't refer to that list.

c. As a class, in pairs, or in small groups, have students check their work.

5. Match Game ★★★

ACTIVITY MASTER 50

a. Make a copy of Activity Master 50, cut it into cards, and distribute the cards randomly, one to each student.

b. Have students memorize the question or response on their card. Then have students circulate around the room, saying their lines until they find their match. Make sure students don't show their cards to their classmates since this is a listening and speaking exercise.

c. When students have found their match, have them compare their cards and come show you.

LANGUAGE SKILL FOUNDATIONS   10–15 MINUTES

Explain to students that this is a list of skills they have learned in the unit. Students should become familiar with the vocabulary of describing their skills, but they don't need to master all the terms. For each speaking skill on the list, read the skill aloud to students and have them demonstrate it. For example:

Teacher: I can ask for the location of places.
Students: Excuse me. Where's the post office?

(If students don't understand the vocabulary of a particular speaking skill, give them a concrete example rather than a description or explanation, and then have students practice your example and others.)

Have students put a check next to each skill if they feel they have learned it. Use this information to determine which lessons you may want to review or reinforce for the entire class or for particular students. The Getting Ready and Expansion activities for this unit and the CD-ROM's Activity Bank of supplemental worksheets are excellent resources for additional practice. It may also be helpful to have stronger students or, if available, a classroom aide or volunteer, work with students who need more practice.

Talk About It! ▶▶▶   (Page 87)   20–30 MINUTES

(Page 87 is also available as a transparency.)

Use the scenes in this illustration to review the vocabulary, conversations, and grammar in the unit. Have students first work in pairs or small groups to talk about the illustration and answer the questions posed at the bottom of the page. Then discuss as a class.

For additional motivating practice, students will enjoy doing one or more of the following activities.

These activities review Unit 6 vocabulary:

1. Places in the Community ★
a. Divide the class into pairs or small teams. Have the pairs or groups make a list of all the places they see in the scenes on student book page 87. (Set a two-minute time limit for this.)

b. Tell students to stop when the two minutes are up. Have students tell you what they saw. For example:

park
drug store
bank
post office
supermarket
laundromat
restaurant
gas station

2. Remember the Actions! ★★
a. Tell students to spend two minutes looking carefully at the community scenes on student book page 87.

b. Have students close their books and write down every action they remember from the illustration. For example:

playing basketball
playing guitar
reading a book
buying medicine
putting money in the bank
buying stamps
buying food
doing laundry
eating

c. Have students compare notes with a partner and then look at the scenes again to see how well they remembered what people are doing.

(continued)

These activities review Unit 6 conversations and grammar:

3. What Are They Doing? ⭐⭐

a. Write the following on the board:

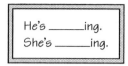

He's _____ing.
She's _____ing.

b. In pairs, have students talk about what the characters in the illustration are doing. One student points to a character and the other describes what he or she is doing. Then reverse roles.

Variation: One student describes what a character in the illustration is doing and the other student points to that person.

4. Where Are They? ⭐⭐

In pairs, have students talk about where the characters in the illustration are. One student points to a character and the other describes where he or she is. Then reverse roles.

Variation: One student describes where a character is and the other student points to that person.

5. Who Is It? ⭐⭐

a. Have students look at the transparency or the illustration on student book page 87.

b. Make statements about where someone is and what that person is doing, and have students point to a character in the illustration to identify who is speaking. For example:

    Teacher: I'm in the park. I'm playing the guitar.
    Students: [*Point to the man on the bench.*]

    Teacher: I'm in the supermarket. I'm buying food.
    Students: [*Point to the woman at the checkout counter.*]

Variation: Divide the class into pairs. One student makes a statement and the other points to the appropriate character. Then reverse roles.

6. Location! Location! ⭐⭐

Have students look at the illustration on student book page 87 and answer questions about the location of places in the illustration. For example:

    Teacher: Where's the post office?
    Student: It's between the drug store and the laundromat.

    Teacher: Where's the restaurant?
    Student: It's across from the gas station.

Variation: Do the activity in pairs or in small groups, with students asking as well as answering the questions. You can also do this as a game with competing teams.

7. Do You Remember? ⭐⭐⭐

Tell students to spend two minutes looking carefully at the illustration on student book page 87. Then have students close their books. Ask students questions about the illustration. For example:

    Where is the drug store?
    Where is the bank?
    Where is the post office?
    Where is the supermarket?
    Where is the laundromat?
    Where is the restaurant?
    Where is the gas station?

8. The "Write" Location! ⭐⭐⭐

a. Tell students to choose a place in the illustration on student book page 87. Have them write down two or three sentences about the location of the place. For example:

    [*the drug store*]
    It's across from the bank.
    It's next to the post office.
    It's across from the park.

b. Have students read their sentences aloud as the class listens and tries to guess the place.

Variation: This activity can be done in pairs or in small groups.

9. The "Write" Person! ⭐⭐⭐

a. Divide the class into pairs. Have each pair choose one character in the illustration on student book page 87 and write two sentences describing that person. For example:

    [*the girl in the park*]
    She's sitting.
    She's reading a book.

b. Have the pairs read their sentences to the class and see if students can guess who is being described.

LESSONS & UNIT ACTIVITIES	OBJECTIVES	TEXT	TEACHER'S GUIDE
Vocabulary Preview	Describing age • Describing height • Describing marital status • Describing hair and eye color	88–89	110
LESSON 1 She's young. He's tall.	Describing people: Age, Height	90–91	111–113
LESSON 2 She has brown hair. He has blue eyes.	Describing people: Hair color, Eye color, Height • Titles	92–93	114–116
LESSON 3 I'm single.	Describing marital status • Describing feelings	94–95	117–119
LESSON 4 Where are you from? What language do you speak?	Countries • Languages • Filling out a form	96–97	120–121
LESSON 5 NUMBERS	Indicating age, height, weight	98	122–123
Language Experience Journal	Writing about yourself	98	123
Different Cultures / Different Ways	Showing feelings in different cultures	99	124
Put It Together	Information Gap / Teamwork activity	99–100	124
Vocabulary Foundations / Language Skill Foundations	Review & skills checklist	100	124–125
Talk About It!	Review, conversations, activities, & games	101	125–126

UNIT RESOURCES

Audio Program:
Audio CD 3: Tracks 2–15
Audio Cassette 2B

Workbooks:
Activity Workbook
Literacy Workbook

Lesson Planner CD-ROM:
Activity Masters 51–60
Activity Bank Unit 7 Worksheets

Vocabulary Photo Cards: 116–136

Transparency: Color Overhead for Unit 7, page 101

AGE, HEIGHT, AND MARITAL STATUS (PAGE 88)

PREVIEW
5 MINUTES

Activate students' prior knowledge of words to describe people's age, height, and marital status by doing either or both of the following:

1. Have students brainstorm words and write them on the board.

2. Have students look at the photographs on student book page 88 while they cover the words at the bottom of the page. Have students identify the words they already know.

PRESENT
5–10 MINUTES

Using the photographs on student book page 88, point to each item or say its number, say the word, and have the class repeat it chorally and individually. (You can also play the audio program.) Check students' understanding and pronunciation of the vocabulary.

PRACTICE
5 MINUTES

As a class, in pairs, or in small groups, have students practice the vocabulary in either or both of the following ways:

- Say or write a word, and have students point to the item in their books or tell the number.
- Point to a photograph in the book or give the number, and have students say the word.

HAIR COLOR AND EYE COLOR (PAGE 89)

PREVIEW
5 MINUTES

Activate students' prior knowledge of words to describe hair color and eye color by doing either or both of the following:

1. Have students brainstorm words and write them on the board.

2. Have students look at the illustrations on student book page 89 while they cover the words at the bottom of the page. Have students identify the words they already know.

PRESENT
5–10 MINUTES

Using the illustrations on student book page 89, point to each item or say its number, say the word, and have the class repeat it chorally and

individually. (You can also play the audio program.) Check students' understanding and pronunciation of the vocabulary.

PRACTICE
5 MINUTES

As a class, in pairs, or in small groups, have students practice the vocabulary in either or both of the following ways:

- Say or write a word, and have students point to the item in their books or tell the number.
- Point to an illustration in the book or give the number, and have students say the word.

SPELLING PRACTICE
5 MINUTES

Say a word from student book page 88 or 89 and have students spell it aloud or write it. Or point to an item in the student book and have students write the word. You can also spell a portion of a word on the board and have students come to the board to complete it.

EXPANSION

1. **Match Game** ★

   PHOTO CARDS 116–121, 125–128 (TWO SETS)

   a. Choose duplicate copies of any Photo Cards 116–121, 125–128, and distribute them randomly, one to each student.

   b. Have students look at their card and identify the word. Then have students circulate around the room, saying their word until they find their match. Make sure students don't show their cards to their classmates since this is a listening and speaking exercise.

   c. When students have found their match, have them compare their cards and come show you.

2. **True or False?** ★★

   Make statements about the people on student book pages 88 and 89. If a statement is false, have students correct it. For example:

   Teacher: [*pointing to #1*] She's old.
   Student: False. She's young.

   Teacher: [*pointing to #20*] He has brown hair.
   Student: True.

LESSON OBJECTIVE

FOCUS

Describing people: Age, Height

VOCABULARY

young	tall
middle-aged	average height
old	short

GETTING READY
5–10 MINUTES

Use your own visuals or the photos on student book page 90 to practice the following vocabulary: *young, middle-aged, old, tall, average height,* and *short.* Say each word, and have the class repeat it chorally and individually. Check students' understanding and pronunciation of the vocabulary.

THE MODEL CONVERSATIONS
10 MINUTES

There are two model conversations. Introduce and practice the first model before going on to the second. For each model:

1. **SETTING THE SCENE:** Set the scene: "Two people are talking about the people in the photos."

2. **LISTENING:** With books closed, have students listen to the model conversation—presented by you, by a pair of students, or on the audio program. Check students' understanding of the situation and the vocabulary.

3. **CLASS PRACTICE:** With books still closed, model each line, and have the whole class practice in unison.

4. **READING:** With books open, have students follow along as two students present the model.

5. **PAIR PRACTICE:** In pairs, have students practice the model conversation.

THE CONVERSATION EXERCISES
10 MINUTES

1. **THE SKELETAL DIALOG:** Write the "skeletal dialog" on the board. Fill in the replacement from Exercise 1 to show students how the guided conversation method works. Call on a few pairs of students to practice Exercise 1, using the skeletal framework on the board.

Model 1:

> A. What's her age?
> B. She's <u>young</u>.

Model 2:

> A. What's his height?
> B. He's <u>tall</u>.

2. **VOCABULARY PRESENTATION:** Present the vocabulary words in the exercises. Point to the photograph of each item, say the word, and have the class repeat it chorally and individually. Check students' understanding and pronunciation of the vocabulary.

3. **EXERCISE PRACTICE:** (optional) Have pairs of students simultaneously practice all the exercises.

4. **EXERCISE PRESENTATIONS:** Call on pairs of students to present their conversations to the class.

GRAMMAR
10 MINUTES

1. Write the full conjugation of the verb *to be* on the board.

> I am
> She is
> He is
> It is
> We are
> You are
> They are

2. Then erase the first letter of the conjugated verb and insert an apostrophe where that letter was. Explain that since we use the verb *to be* a lot, we sometimes make it short so it's easier to say. The short form is called a *contraction.*

3. Point to and read the full forms and the contractions aloud. Have students repeat them chorally and individually. Give special attention to the pronunciation of *we're, you're,* and *they're.*

4. Have students write the sentences with contractions and then compare their answers in pairs. Call on individual students for their

answers, paying special attention to their pronunciation.

Answers

1. We're tall.
2. She's young.
3. I'm short.
4. They're old.
5. He's middle-aged.
6. You're average height.

CLOZE READING

10 MINUTES

Remind students that a "cloze reading" is a story with words missing. Tell students that their task is to write the correct words in the blanks based on the illustration. Have students complete the paragraph and then compare answers with a partner.

Option: This is a good opportunity to teach students how to check off items as they move through an exercise. Call on a student to read the example sentence. Have all students check off the word *old* in the box. Call on a student to read and complete the next sentence. Then have all students check off the word *middle-aged* in the box.

Answers

1. old
2. middle-aged
3. young
4. tall
5. average height

DESCRIBING YOUR FAMILY

10 MINUTES

1. Model the activity for the class. Copy the table on the board, and then fill in information about someone in *your* family, talking about that person as you write. For example:

   My sister is young. Her name is Elisa.
   My parents are middle-aged. Their names are David and Catherine Parker.

	Family Member	Name
young?	my sister	Elisa
middle-aged?	my parents	David and Catherine Parker

2. Have students work individually to complete the table. Circulate around the room, helping as necessary.

3. Have students compare their information in pairs.

EXPANSION

1. **Listen for the Verb** ★

   a. Write the conjugation of the verb *to be* on the board in both full and contracted forms. Write the letter *A* over the full forms and *B* over the contracted forms. For example:

A	B
I am	I'm
He is	He's
She is	She's
It is	It's
We are	We're
You are	You're
They are	They're

   b. Say sentences, using either the full form or the contracted form, and have students identify which form they hear. For example:

   Teacher: She's old.
   Students: B

   Teacher: We are young.
   Students: A

2. **Alphabetize!** ★

   ACTIVITY MASTER 51

   a. Make copies of Activity Master 51 and cut them into cards.

   b. Have students work in pairs. Give each pair a set of cards, and have them work together to place the words in alphabetical order.

   c. Have the first pair to complete the alphabetization write their list on the board. Go over the list with the class.

3. **Scrambled Words** ★

   a. Choose words from the lesson and write them on the board or on a card with the letters scrambled out of order. For example:

   g u n o y

   b. Have students take turns guessing what the word is. [young]

   Variation 1: Do the activity in pairs or small groups, with students taking turns scrambling words for others to guess.

   Variation 2: Do the activity as a class game with competing teams.

4. Descriptions ★★

a. Call out the name of a student—for example: "Marisa."

b. Have students describe that person. For example:

> She's young.
> She's tall.

5. Magazine Photos ★★★

Bring in magazine photos of people. Have students ask and answer questions about the people in the photos. For example:

A. What's her age?
B. She's middle-aged.

6. Draw, Write, and Read ★★★

Have students draw a picture of someone special. Then have them write a description to accompany the picture. Have students share their work in pairs, describing their pictures as they show them.

LESSON OBJECTIVE

Focus

Describing people: Hair color, Eye color, Height
Titles

VOCABULARY

black	eyes	hair
blond	gray	red
blue	green	white
brown		

PAGE 92 CONVERSATION AND EXERCISES

GETTING READY
5 MINUTES

Model the verb *have* by describing students' hair and eye color. Point to a female student and say: "Elena has (*black*) hair. She has (*brown*) eyes." Point to a male student and describe his hair and eye color.

THE MODEL CONVERSATIONS
10 MINUTES

There are two model conversations. Introduce and practice the first model before going on to the second. For each model:

1. **SETTING THE SCENE:** Set the scene: "Two people are talking about the people in the illustrations."

2. **LISTENING:** With books closed, have students listen to the model conversation—presented by you, by a pair of students, or on the audio program. Check students' understanding of the situation and the vocabulary.

3. **CLASS PRACTICE:** With books still closed, model each line, and have the whole class practice in unison.

4. **READING:** With books open, have students follow along as two students present the model.

5. **PAIR PRACTICE:** In pairs, have students practice the model conversation.

THE CONVERSATION EXERCISES
10–15 MINUTES

1. **THE SKELETAL DIALOG:** Write the "skeletal dialog" on the board. Fill in the replacement from Exercise 1 to show students how the guided conversation method works. Call on a few pairs of students to practice Exercise 1, using the skeletal framework on the board.

Model 1:

> A. What color hair *does she have?*
> B. She has <u>brown</u> hair.

Model 2:

> A. What color eyes *does he have?*
> B. He has <u>brown</u> eyes.

2. **VOCABULARY PRESENTATION:** Present the vocabulary words in the exercises. Point to the illustration of each item, say the word, and have the class repeat it chorally and individually. Check students' understanding and pronunciation of the vocabulary.

3. **EXERCISE PRACTICE:** (optional) Have pairs of students simultaneously practice all the exercises.

4. **EXERCISE PRESENTATIONS:** Call on pairs of students to present their conversations to the class.

GRAMMAR
10 MINUTES

1. Write the conjugation of the verb *have* on the board. Point to each form and say it aloud. Have students repeat chorally and individually.

2. Have students complete the sentences and then compare their answers in pairs. Call on individual students for their answers.

Answers

1. have
2. has
3. has
4. have
5. have
6. have

PAGE 93 CONVERSATION AND EXERCISES

GETTING READY
5 MINUTES

1. Introduce the phrase *Please give this to _____*. Hand a pen to a student and say: "Please give this to (*Mario*)" and gesture to the student (*Mario*). Have the student give the pen to (*Mario*). Repeat several times with other students until the class is familiar with the language.

2. Introduce the titles *Mr.*, *Mrs.*, and *Ms.* Explain that *Mr.* is for all men. *Ms.* is for all women, whether they are married or not. *Mrs.* is only for married women.

THE MODEL CONVERSATION
5–10 MINUTES

1. **SETTING THE SCENE:** Have students look at the model photograph. Set the scene: "Two people at work are talking."

2. **LISTENING:** With books closed, have students listen to the model conversation—presented by you, by a pair of students, or on the audio program. Check students' understanding of the situation and the vocabulary.

3. **CLASS PRACTICE:** With books still closed, model each line, and have the whole class practice in unison.

4. **READING:** With books open, have students follow along as two students present the model.

5. **PAIR PRACTICE:** In pairs, have students practice the model conversation.

THE CONVERSATION EXERCISES
10–15 MINUTES

1. **THE SKELETAL DIALOG:** Write the "skeletal dialog" on the board. Fill in the replacement from Exercise 1 to show students how the guided conversation method works. Call on a few pairs of students to practice Exercise 1, using the skeletal framework on the board.

> A. Please give this to <u>Ms. Potter</u>.
> B. What does she look like?
> A. <u>She's short, with red hair.</u>

2. **VOCABULARY PRESENTATION:** Present the sentences in the exercises. Point to the corresponding illustration for each sentence, say the sentence, and have the class repeat it chorally and individually. Check students' understanding and pronunciation of the vocabulary.

3. **EXERCISE PRACTICE:** (optional) Have pairs of students simultaneously practice all the exercises.

4. **EXERCISE PRESENTATIONS:** Call on pairs of students to present their conversations to the class.

LISTENING
5–10 MINUTES

Listen and write the number next to the correct picture.

1. A. What does he look like?
   B. He's short, with gray hair.
2. A. What does she look like?
   B. She's short, with black hair.
3. A. What does she look like?
   B. She's tall, with blond hair.
4. A. What does he look like?
   B. He's average height, with brown hair.
5. A. What does she look like?
   B. She's average height, with brown hair.

Answers

2   3   5   4   1

EXPANSION

1. **Listen and Point** ★
   Divide the class into pairs. Have Student A cover the sentences on student book page 93 and look just at the illustrations. Have Student B read sentences in random order. Student A must point to the appropriate illustration. Then reverse roles.

2. **Missing Letters** ★
   a. Divide the class into two teams. Draw a series of blanks on the board to represent the letters in a word from student book pages 92 and 93.
   b. Have students from each team take turns calling out letters. If the letter is correct, put it in the appropriate blank and give the team one point. If the letter is incorrect, put it on a list to the side. The team that gets the most points wins the game.

3. **Right or Wrong?** ★★
   Divide the class into pairs. Have students take turns making correct and incorrect statements about the people in the illustrations on student book pages 92 and 93. For example:

   A. [*pointing to an illustration*] She's tall.
   B. No. She's short. [*pointing to a different illustration*] He has blue eyes.
   A. Yes. He has blue eyes.   *(continued)*

4. True or False? ✶✶

a. Bring in a picture of a person and show it to the class for one minute.

b. Put the picture away and make several statements about the picture, using language from student book pages 92 and 93. The statements may be true or false. For example:

> Teacher: The man is tall.
> Student: That's true.
>
> Teacher: The man has white hair.
> Student: False. He has gray hair.

c. Students have to decide if the statements are true or false. If a statement is false, have students correct it. Then have students look at the picture to see if they were right.

Variation: This can be done as a dictation with a *True* column and a *False* column. Students have to write the statement in the appropriate column. At the end of the dictation, have students check the picture to see if they were correct.

5. Sentence Formation ✶✶✶

ACTIVITY MASTERS 51, 52

a. Divide the class into pairs. Make multiple copies of Activity Masters 51 and 52, cut them into cards, and give one set to every pair of students.

b. Have students take turns picking up a card and forming a sentence using the word. For example:

> A. [*picking up the card "black hair"*]
>   She has black hair.
> B. [*picking up the card "young"*]
>   He's young.

6. Who Is It? ✶✶✶

a. Ask students to write on a piece of paper three or more sentences that describe themselves. Students should not write their names on their papers. For example:

> I have brown eyes.
> I have black hair.
> I'm average height.

b. Collect the students' descriptions, read them to the class, and have the class guess who wrote them.

Variation: Write all the sets of adjectives submitted by the students on a sheet of paper and make copies for the class. Have students then guess who everybody is.

7. The "Write" Person! ✶✶✶

a. Have students choose another classmate and write two sentences describing that person. For example:

> She's middle-aged.
> She has red hair.

b. Have the pairs read their sentences to the class and see if students can guess who is being described.

LESSON OBJECTIVE

Focus

Describing marital status
Describing feelings

Vocabulary

divorced	afraid	sad
married	angry	sick
single	happy	thirsty
widowed	hungry	tired

PAGE 94 CONVERSATION AND EXERCISES

GETTING READY   5–10 MINUTES

Introduce the concept of *marital status*. Point to your ring finger and say: "I'm married" or "I'm single" (whichever is true). Use the photos on student book page 94 to introduce the following vocabulary: *married, divorced, widowed*, and *single*. Say each word, and have the class repeat it chorally and individually. Check students' understanding and pronunciation of the vocabulary.

THE MODEL CONVERSATION   10 MINUTES

1. **SETTING THE SCENE:** Have students look at the model photographs. Set the scene: "A person is filling out a form."

2. **LISTENING:** With books closed, have students listen to the model conversation—presented by you, by a pair of students, or on the audio program. Check students' understanding of the situation and the vocabulary.

3. **CLASS PRACTICE:** With books still closed, model each line, and have the whole class practice in unison.

4. **READING:** With books open, have students follow along as two students present the model.

THE CONVERSATION EXERCISES   10 MINUTES

1. **THE SKELETAL DIALOG:** Write the "skeletal dialog" on the board. Fill in the replacement from Exercise 1 to show students how the guided conversation method works. Call on a few pairs of students to practice Exercise 1, using the skeletal framework on the board.

A. What's your marital status?
B. I'm <u>married</u>.

2. **VOCABULARY PRESENTATION:** Present the vocabulary words in the exercises. Point to the photograph of each item, say the word, and have the class repeat it chorally and individually. Check students' understanding and pronunciation of the vocabulary.

3. **EXERCISE PRACTICE:** (optional) Have pairs of students simultaneously practice all the exercises.

4. **EXERCISE PRESENTATIONS:** Call on pairs of students to present their conversations to the class.

5. **PAIR PRACTICE:** In pairs, have students practice the model conversation.

GRAMMAR   10 MINUTES

Explain that students must complete the sentences with the words in the box. Call on individual students for the answers.

Option: This is a good opportunity to give students practice checking off items as they work through an exercise. Call on a student to read the example sentence. Have all students check off the phrase *He's* in the box. Call on a student to read and complete the next sentence. Then have all students check off the phrase *She's* in the box.

Answers

1. He's
2. She's
3. They're
4. We're
5. I'm

PAGE 95 CONVERSATION AND EXERCISES

GETTING READY   5 MINUTES

Use gestures or the photos on student book page 95 to introduce the following vocabulary: *hungry, thirsty, happy, sad, tired, angry, sick*, and *afraid*. Say each word, and have the class repeat it chorally and individually. Check students' understanding and pronunciation of the vocabulary.

THE MODEL CONVERSATION `5–10 MINUTES`

1. **SETTING THE SCENE:** Set the scene: "Two friends are talking."

2. **LISTENING:** With books closed, have students listen to the model conversation—presented by you, by a pair of students, or on the audio program. Check students' understanding of the situation and the vocabulary.

3. **CLASS PRACTICE:** With books still closed, model each line, and have the whole class practice in unison.

4. **READING:** With books open, have students follow along as two students present the model.

5. **PAIR PRACTICE:** In pairs, have students practice the model conversation.

THE CONVERSATION EXERCISES `10–15 MINUTES`

1. **THE SKELETAL DIALOG:** Write the "skeletal dialog" on the board. Fill in the replacement from Exercise 1 to show students how the guided conversation method works. Call on a few pairs of students to practice Exercise 1, using the skeletal framework on the board.

> A. Are you <u>hungry</u>?
> B. Yes. I'm very <u>hungry</u>.

2. **VOCABULARY PRESENTATION:** Present the vocabulary words in the exercises. Point to the photograph of each item, say the word, and have the class repeat it chorally and individually. Check students' understanding and pronunciation of the vocabulary.

3. **EXERCISE PRACTICE:** (optional) Have pairs of students simultaneously practice all the exercises.

4. **EXERCISE PRESENTATIONS:** Call on pairs of students to present their conversations to the class.

FINISH THE SENTENCE `10 MINUTES`

Read the example sentence to the class. Then have students connect the other sentences. Have them compare their answers in pairs. Call on individual students to check answers.

Answers

1. I eat.
2. I go to bed.
3. I drink water.
4. I go to the clinic.

LANGUAGE IN *MOTION* `10 MINUTES`

Have students take turns standing in the front of the classroom and pantomiming a feeling. Other students guess the feeling.

DESCRIBING PEOPLE YOU KNOW `15 MINUTES`

1. Model the activity for the class by reading through the sample answers. Then copy the columns of the table on the board and fill in information about people *you* know, talking as you write. For example:

> My friend is Chris. He's young. He's tall. He has brown hair. He has green eyes. He's married.

Name	Age	Height	Hair Color	Eye Color	Marital Status
Chris	young	tall	brown	green	married

2. Have students work individually to complete the table. Circulate around the room, helping students as necessary.

3. Have students share their information in pairs.

Option: For homework, have students write sentences about the people they described in the table. In the next class, have students submit their writing to you for correction.

EXPANSION

The following activities are about describing physical characteristics and marital status.

1. **Alphabetize!** ★
   ACTIVITY MASTER 53

   a. Divide the class into pairs. Make copies of Activity Master 53 and cut them into cards.

   b. Give each pair a set of cards, and have them work together to place the words in alphabetical order. Have the first pair to complete the alphabetization write their list on the board. Go over the list with the class.

2. **Telephone** ★★

   a. Have students sit in a circle or semicircle. Make up two sentences, using language from this lesson, and whisper them to Student 1. For example:

   > My brother is middle-aged and married.
   > He's short, with brown hair and blue eyes.

   b. The first student whispers what he or she heard to the second student, who whispers it to the third student, and so forth. When the message gets to the last student, that person says it aloud. Is it the same message you started with?

Give each student in the class a chance to start his or her own message.

3. Category Dictation ✷✷

a. Have students make two columns on a piece of paper. Have them write <u>He's</u> at the top of the left column and <u>He has</u> at the top of the right column.

b. Dictate the following words from Lessons 1–3: *young, short, red hair, blue eyes,* and *divorced.* Have students write the words in the appropriate column. For example:

He's	He has
young	red hair
short	blue eyes
divorced	

c. Have students compare their answers in pairs.

4. Information Gap ✷✷✷

ACTIVITY MASTER 54

a. Make multiple copies of Activity Master 54 and cut them in half (Table A and Table B).

b. Divide the class into pairs. Give each partner a different table—A or B. Have students share their information and fill in their tables. For example:

Student A: Ms. Rivera. What's her age?
Student B: She's young.

c. When the pairs have finished completing their tables, have them look at their partner's tables to make sure they have written the information correctly.

The following activities are about describing feelings.

5. Concentration ✷

PHOTO CARDS 129–136 (TWO SETS)

a. Shuffle the cards and place them face-down in four rows of 4 each.

b. Divide the class into two teams. The object of the game is for students to find the matching cards and identify the vocabulary item. Both teams should be able to see the cards, since *concentrating* on their location is an important part of playing the game.

c. A student from Team 1 turns over two cards, and if they match, the student must identify the item. If the student correctly identifies the item, that team keeps the cards, and the

student takes another turn. If they don't match, or if the student isn't able to correctly identify the item, the student turns them face-down, and a member of Team 2 takes a turn.

d. The game continues until all the cards have been matched. The team with the most correct *matches* wins the game.

Variation:
PHOTO CARDS 129–136
ACTIVITY MASTER 55

Have the class play with one set of Photo Cards and one set of Word Cards.

6. True or False? ✷✷

a. Find several magazine pictures of people and show each one to the class for one minute.

b. One at a time, put each picture away and make several statements about the picture, using adjectives from student book page 95. The statements may be true or false. For example:

The man is happy.
The woman is angry.

c. Students have to decide if the statements are true or false. If a statement is false, have students correct it. Then have students look at the picture to see if they were right.

7. Positive or Negative? ✷✷✷

a. Have students make three columns on a piece of paper. At the top of the left column, have them write <u>Positive</u>, at the top of the middle column, have them write <u>Neutral</u>, and at the top of the right column, have them write <u>Negative</u>. (Explain that the meaning of *neutral* is *not positive and not negative*.)

b. Dictate various feelings. For example:

thirsty	afraid
hungry	angry
happy	tired
sad	sick

c. Tell students to write the adjectives in one of the columns.

d. At the end of the dictation, have students compare their lists. There may be a variety of opinions.

8. Magazine Photos ✷✷✷

Bring in magazine photos of people expressing feelings. As a class, in pairs, or in small groups, have students describe the feelings.

UNIT 7 LESSON 4 WHERE ARE YOU FROM? WHAT LANGUAGE DO YOU SPEAK?

STUDENT BOOK
PAGES 96–97

LESSON OBJECTIVE

Focus

Countries
Languages
Filling out a form

Vocabulary

Brazil	Portuguese
China	Chinese
Greece	Greek
Haiti	Haitian
Japan	Japanese
Korea	Korean
Mexico	Spanish
Morocco	Arabic
Russia	Russian
Vietnam	Vietnamese

GETTING READY 5–10 MINUTES

Use the photos and flags on student book page 96 to introduce the lesson vocabulary. Say each word, and have the class repeat it chorally and individually. If you have a world map in your classroom, point to each country as you introduce it, or invite individual students to locate the country and show the class. Alternatively, have students refer to the World Map in the Appendix of the *Word By Word Basic* Picture Dictionary. Check students' understanding and pronunciation of the vocabulary.

THE MODEL CONVERSATIONS 10 MINUTES

There are two model conversations. Introduce and practice the first model before going on to the second. For each model:

1. **SETTING THE SCENE:** Have students look at the model photograph. Set the scene: "Two classmates are talking."

2. **LISTENING:** With books closed, have students listen to the model conversation—presented by you, by a pair of students, or on the audio program. Check students' understanding of the situation and the vocabulary.

3. **CLASS PRACTICE:** With books still closed, model each line, and have the whole class practice in unison.

4. **READING:** With books open, have students follow along as two students present the model.

5. **PAIR PRACTICE:** In pairs, have students practice the model conversation.

THE CONVERSATION EXERCISES 10 MINUTES

1. **THE SKELETAL DIALOG:** Write the "skeletal dialog" on the board. Fill in the replacement from Exercise 1 to show students how the guided conversation method works. Call on a few pairs of students to practice Exercise 1, using the skeletal framework on the board.

> A. Where are you from?
> B. I'm from <u>Korea</u>.
> A. What language do you speak?
> B. I speak <u>Korean</u>.

2. **VOCABULARY PRESENTATION:** Present the vocabulary words in the exercises. Point to the flags, say the names of the countries and languages, and have the class repeat them chorally and individually. Check students' understanding and pronunciation of the vocabulary.

3. **EXERCISE PRACTICE:** (optional) Have pairs of students simultaneously practice all the exercises.

4. **EXERCISE PRESENTATIONS:** Call on pairs of students to present their conversations to the class.

LANGUAGE IN *MOTION* 15 MINUTES

1. Write the names of countries and languages of students in your class that are not introduced on student book page 96. Say the words, and have the class repeat them chorally and individually.

2. Model the activity. With student books closed, write the table on the board and then interview one student, asking: "What's your name? Where are you from? What language do you speak?" When each student answers, also ask: "How do you spell that?"

3. Have students circulate around the classroom, each asking six other students the questions: *What's your name? Where are you from? What language do you speak?* and, if necessary,

How do you spell that? Have students complete the chart in the student book. Listen in on student conversations and provide help if necessary.

FILL OUT THE FORM

15 MINUTES

1. Go over the form with the class. Point to each section and explain what information the section requires. Model how to write in the grid. Draw an example of the grid for the address section on the board and show students how to print the school street address, leaving empty spaces between each word. Explain that *country of origin* means "where you are from."

2. Have students work individually to complete their forms. Circulate to answer questions.

Option: You may want to make some additional copies of the form for students who make multiple mistakes and may want to start over again on a clean form.

EXPANSION

1. Beanbag Toss ★

Have students stand in a circle. Say the name of a country and throw a beanbag to Student 1. Student 1 says the name of another country and throws the beanbag to another student. Continue around the circle until all students have mentioned a different country.

Variation: Play the same game with students naming languages instead.

2. Listening Contrast ★

a. Write the following categories on the board:

> Country
> Language

b. Call out a word from student book page 96, and have the class tell you whether it is a country or a language. For example:

> Teacher: Portuguese
> Students: Language
> Teacher: Russia
> Students: Country

3. Association Game ★★

a. Write five languages from student book page 96 on the board.

b. Divide the class into several teams. Have the students in each team work together to see how many countries they can associate with each language. For example:

> English: [England/Australia/United States/Singapore]
> Arabic: [Morocco/Egypt/Saudi Arabia/Jordan]
> Chinese: [China/Taiwan/Singapore]
> Portuguese: [Brazil/Portugal/Mozambique/Angola]
> Spanish: [Spain/Mexico/El Salvador/Chile]

c. Set a time limit for the game. When the time limit is up, call on the teams to read their list of associations to the class. The team with the most correct items wins.

Option: You can also list French and German as they also are internationally spoken languages.

4. Match Game ★★★

ACTIVITY MASTER 56

a. Make a copy of Activity Master 56, cut it into cards, and distribute the cards randomly, one to each student.

b. Have students memorize the question or response on their card. Then have students circulate around the room, saying their lines until they find their match. Make sure students don't show their cards to their classmates since this is a listening and speaking exercise.

c. When students have found their match, have them compare their cards and come show you.

LESSON OBJECTIVE

FOCUS

Indicating age, height, weight

VOCABULARY

thin
average weight
heavy
pounds
feet
inches

GETTING READY
5–10 MINUTES

Use the photos on student book page 98 to introduce the following vocabulary: *thin, average weight,* and *heavy.* Say each word, and have the class repeat it chorally and individually. Check students' understanding and pronunciation of the vocabulary.

MATCH THE SENTENCES
10 MINUTES

1. Explain the U.S. systems of measurements.

   • A pound is a little less than half a kilogram. If necessary, write the following conversion chart on the board:

Pounds	Kilograms
70	about 32
150	about 68
210	about 95

   • A foot is about .3 of a meter. There are twelve inches in a foot. If necessary, write the following conversion chart on the board:

Feet	Meters
5 feet	1.52 meters
5 feet six inches	1.68 meters
6 feet	1.83 meters

2. Read the example sentences aloud. (You can also play the audio program.) Have students work individually to match the sentences. Circulate around the classroom to answer

questions as necessary. Have students compare their answers in pairs.

Answers

1. He's thin.
2. He's average weight.
3. He's heavy.

1. He's young.
2. He's middle-aged.
3. He's old.

1. She's short.
2. She's tall.
3. She's average height.

WAYS TO SAY IT
10 MINUTES

1. Model the questions. With books closed, have students listen as you read aloud the model questions. Have students repeat after you chorally and individually. With books open, have the class follow along as various individual students read the questions.

2. Have students complete the information individually, and then ask and answer the questions in pairs. Circulate to answer questions as necessary.

Note: Questions about age and weight are personal. In social conversation, people do not ask one another about age or weight. These are typically questions for identification and health records.

EXPANSION

1. Concentration ★

PHOTO CARDS 116–128 (TWO SETS)

a. Shuffle the cards and place them face-down in four rows.

b. Divide the class into two teams. The object of the game is for students to find the matching cards and identify the vocabulary item. Both teams should be able to see the cards, since *concentrating* on their location is an important part of playing the game.

c. A student from Team 1 turns over two cards, and if they match, the student must identify the item. If the student correctly identifies the item, that team keeps the cards, and the student takes another turn. If they don't match or if the student isn't able to correctly identify the item, the student turns them face-down, and a member of Team 2 takes a turn.

d. The game continues until all the cards have been matched. The team with the most correct *matches* wins the game.

Variation:
PHOTO CARDS 116–128
ACTIVITY MASTERS 51, 53, 57

Have the class play with one set of Photo Cards and one set of Word Cards.

2. **Descriptions** ✶✶

a. Call out the name of a student—for example: "Fernando."

b. Have students describe that person. For example:

> He's middle-aged.
> He has black hair.
> He's thin.

3. **Magazine Photos** ✶✶✶

Bring in magazine photos of people. Have students ask and answer questions about the people in the photos. For example:

> A. What's her height?
> B. She's short.

4. **Match Game** ✶✶✶

ACTIVITY MASTER 58

a. Make a copy of Activity Master 58, cut it into cards, and distribute the cards randomly, one to each student.

b. Have students memorize the question or response on their card. Then have students circulate around the room, saying their lines until they find their match. Make sure students don't show their cards to their classmates since this is a listening and speaking exercise.

c. When students have found their match, have them compare their cards and come show you.

LANGUAGE EXPERIENCE JOURNAL

Have students write about themselves. Depending on your students' writing abilities, either have them write in their journal or dictate their story for you to write. Then students should read what they have written to a classmate. If time permits, you may also want to write a response in each student's journal, sharing your own opinions and experiences as well as reacting to what the student has written.

Different Cultures/ *Different Ways* | 10 MINUTES

Have students first work in pairs or small groups, reacting to the photographs and responding to the questions. Then have students share with the class what they have talked about.

PUT IT TOGETHER | 15–20 MINUTES

In this activity, students talk with each other to fill out a form.

1. Divide the class into pairs: Student A and Student B.
2. Tell all the Student A's to look at Part A of the activity on student book page 99. Tell all the Student B's to look at Part B on page 100.
3. Have everybody look at the first item on the form: *First* and *Last Name*.
   a. On Student B's form, above *Last,* it says, *Robles.* Therefore, when Student A asks: "What's the person's last name?", Student B answers: "Robles."
   b. Ask all the Student B's: "What's the person's last name?" Have all the Student B's respond in unison: "Robles."
   c. Have all the Student A's look at their form. On their form above *First,* it says, *Gloria.* Therefore, when Student B asks: "What's her first name?", Student A answers: "Gloria."
   d. Ask all the Student A's: "What's her first name?" Have all the Student A's respond in unison: "Gloria."
4. The Student A and Student B pairs are now ready to continue the activity with the rest of the application form.
5. When the pairs have completed their forms, have them check each other's answers.

VOCABULARY FOUNDATIONS | 5–10 MINUTES

Have students review the list of words they have learned in this unit. Encourage students to get a small notebook where they can write down vocabulary that is new for them. If students have personal copies of dictionaries or picture dictionaries, have them look up these words in the dictionary and highlight them with a marker. Encourage them to look at their notebooks or dictionaries frequently to review what they have learned.

For additional practice, have students do one or more of the following activities.

1. **Taking Notes** ✮
   In their vocabulary notebooks or on a piece of paper, have students write all the words in one column. In a second column, have them write notes, draw pictures, or write the word in a sentence that will help them remember the meaning of the words.

2. **Guess the Word!** ✮✮
   a. Divide the class into two teams. Choose a vocabulary word from the unit, and on the board write a blank for each letter in the word. For example: *hungry*

   b. Give students a clue about the word. For example: [*rubbing stomach*] "I need to eat." The team that guesses the word gets one point. The team with the most points wins the guessing game.

3. **Finish the Sentence!** ✮✮
   Divide the class into two teams. Begin sentences, and have students from each team take turns finishing them with appropriate words from the unit. For example:

   I drink water when I'm . . . *thirsty.*
   I eat when I'm . . . *hungry.*
   I go to bed when I'm . . . *tired.*
   I see a doctor when I'm . . . *sick.*
   Ms. Keller is 6 feet tall. She's . . . *tall.*
   Mr. Howard is 5 feet tall. He's . . . *short.*
   I'm from Brazil. I speak . . . *Portuguese.*
   She weighs 250 pounds. She's . . . *heavy.*
   Mr. Smith weighs 90 pounds. He's . . . *thin.*
   George is 50 years old. He's . . . *middle-aged.*
   Maria 18 years old. She's . . . *young.*
   Mrs. Harris is 86 years old. She's . . . *old.*

   The team with the most correctly completed sentences wins the game.

4. **Category Dictation** ✮✮✮
   a. Have students make three columns on a piece of paper:

      eye color
      hair color
      feelings

b. Dictate words from Vocabulary Foundations, and have students write them in the appropriate column. Make sure all students have covered the vocabulary items on student book page 100 with a piece of paper so they don't refer to that list.

c. As a class, in pairs, or in small groups, have students check their work.

5. Match Game: Questions and Answers ★★★

ACTIVITY MASTER 59

a. Make a copy of Activity Master 59, cut it into cards, and distribute the cards randomly, one to each student.

b. Have students memorize the question or response on their card and leave their cards on their desks. Then have students circulate around the room, saying their lines until they find their match. Make sure students don't show their cards to their classmates since this is a listening and speaking exercise.

c. When students have found their match, have them compare their cards and come show you. Then give each student another card to keep the game going. Continue until students have found all the matches.

LANGUAGE SKILL FOUNDATIONS   10–15 MINUTES

Explain to students that this is a list of skills they have learned in the unit. Students should become familiar with the vocabulary of describing their skills, but they don't need to master all the terms. For each speaking skill on the list, read the skill aloud to students and have them demonstrate it. For example:

Teacher: I can describe people by age.
Students: She's young. She's 14 years old.

(If students don't understand the vocabulary of a particular speaking skill, give them a concrete example rather than a description or explanation, and then have students practice your example and others.)

Have students put a check next to each skill if they feel they have learned it. Use this information to determine which lessons you may want to review or reinforce for the entire class or for particular students. The Getting Ready and Expansion activities for this unit and the CD-ROM's Activity Bank of supplemental worksheets are excellent

resources for additional practice. It may also be helpful to have stronger students or, if available, a classroom aide or volunteer, work with students who need more practice.

Talk About It! ▶ ▶ ▶   (Page 101)   20–30 MINUTES

(Page 101 is also available as a transparency.)

Use this scene to review the vocabulary, conversations, and grammar in the unit. Have students first work in pairs or small groups to talk about the illustration and answer the question posed at the bottom of the page. Then discuss as a class.

For additional motivating practice, students will enjoy doing one or more of the following activities.

These activities review Unit 7 vocabulary:

1. The Longest List ★

a. Point to a character in the park scene on student book page 101.

b. In pairs, have students write as many words as they can to describe that character. Tell students to cover the list of words on student book page 100 with a piece of paper so they don't refer to that list. (Set a two-minute time limit for this activity.)

c. Tell students to stop when the two minutes are up. Ask students to count the number of words used to describe the character. Who has the longest list? Continue the activity, choosing several more characters.

2. Remember the Feelings! ★★

a. Tell students to spend two minutes looking carefully at the park scene on student book page 101.

b. Have students close their books and write down all the feelings they remember from the illustration. For example:

angry
sick
afraid
happy
sad
hungry
thirsty
tired

c. Have students compare notes with a partner and then look at the illustration again to see how well they remembered how people are feeling.

(continued)

These activities review Unit 7 conversations and grammar:

3. Student Question and Answer ★★

ACTIVITY MASTER 60

a. Make multiple copies of Activity Master 60. Divide the class into pairs and give each pair a copy.

b. Have the pairs of students choose characters in the illustration on student book page 101. Have them ask and answer the questions about the people they chose. Circulate to help as necessary.

Note: Students may not be able to answer all the questions about every character.

4. Who Is It? ★★★

a. Have students look at the transparency or the illustration on student book page 101.

b. Make statements about a character in the illustration on student book page 101. The statement can tell what the person is doing, what the person looks like, and how the person is feeling. Have students point to the character to identify the person. For example:

[*the woman sitting alone on a bench*]
She's sitting on a bench.
She has gray hair.
She's widowed.
She's sad.

Variation: Divide the class into pairs. One student makes a statement and the other points to the appropriate character. Then reverse roles.

5. The "Write" Person! ★★★

ACTIVITY MASTER 60

a. Make multiple copies of Activity Master 60. Give each student a copy.

b. Have each student choose one character in the illustration on student book page 101 and write several sentences describing that person, using Activity Master 160 as a guide. For example:

[*the man with the hot dog*]
He's young. He's 25 years old.
He's tall. He's six feet tall.
He has brown hair.
He has blue eyes.
He's thin.
He's eating.
He feels sick.

c. In small groups, have students read their sentences and see if their classmates can guess who is being described.

UNIT 8 · FOOD

LESSONS & UNIT ACTIVITIES	OBJECTIVES	TEXT	TEACHER'S GUIDE
Vocabulary Preview	Common foods	102–103	128
LESSON 1 I'm looking for a cookie.	Food	104–105	129–131
LESSON 2 There isn't any more bread.	Food	106–107	132–134
LESSON 3 Excuse me. I'm looking for bananas.	Food	108–109	135–137
LESSON 4 What do we need?	Food containers & quantities	110–111	138–140
LESSON 5 I'd like a hamburger, please.	Ordering food in a restaurant	112–113	141–143
LESSON 6 NUMBERS: A quart of milk	Quantities & abbreviations	114	144–145
Language Experience Journal	Writing about your favorite food	114	145
Different Cultures / Different Ways	Eating in different cultures	115	146
Put It Together	Information Gap / Teamwork activity	115–116	146
Vocabulary Foundations / Language Skill Foundations	Review & skills checklist	116	146–147
Talk About It!	Review, conversations, activities, & games	117	148

UNIT RESOURCES

Audio Program:
Audio CD 3: Tracks 16–34
Audio Cassette 3A

Workbooks:
Activity Workbook
Literacy Workbook

Lesson Planner CD-ROM:
Activity Masters 26, 61–69
Activity Bank Unit 8 Worksheets

Vocabulary Photo Cards: 137–170

Transparency: Color Overhead for Unit 8, page 117

PREVIEW
5 MINUTES

Activate students' prior knowledge of food vocabulary by doing either or both of the following:

1. Have students brainstorm food items and write them on the board. You can ask students: "What foods do you have in your kitchen? What foods do you buy at the supermarket?"

2. Have students look at the photographs on student book pages 102 and 103 while they cover the words at the bottom of the page. Have students identify the words they already know.

PRESENT
10 MINUTES

Using the photographs on student book pages 102 and 103, point to each item or say its number, say the word, and have the class repeat it chorally and individually. (You can also play the audio program.) Check students' understanding and pronunciation of the vocabulary.

PRACTICE
10 MINUTES

As a class, in pairs, or in small groups, have students practice the vocabulary in either or both of the following ways:

- Say or write a word, and have students point to the item in their books or tell the number.
- Point to a photograph in the book or give the number, and have students say the word.

SPELLING PRACTICE
5 MINUTES

Say a word and have students spell it aloud or write it. Or point to an item in the student book, and have students write the word. You can also spell a portion of a word on the board, and have students come to the board to complete it.

EXPANSION

1. Tell and Show ★
PHOTO CARDS 137–156, 161–170 (TWO SETS)

a. Divide the class into pairs. Distribute all the Photo Cards randomly so every pair receives at least five or six cards.

b. Have Student A in each pair select a Photo Card and tell Student B the food item. Have Student B point to the food item on student book page 102 or 103.

c. As the pairs finish using their Photo Cards, have them trade their sets with another pair and then continue the activity. Have students reverse roles each time they get a new set of cards.

2. Match Game ★
PHOTO CARDS 137–156, 161–170 (TWO SETS)

a. Choose duplicate copies of any Photo Cards 137–156 and 161–170, and distribute them randomly, one to each student.

b. Have students look at their card and identify the food item. Then have students circulate around the room, saying the name of the food on their card until they find their match. Make sure students don't show their cards to their classmates since this is a listening and speaking exercise.

c. When students have found their match, have them compare their cards and come show you. Then give each student another Photo Card to keep the game going. Continue until students have found all the matches.

3. True or False? ★★
PHOTO CARDS 137–156, 161–170

Show students various Photo Cards. Make a false statement about the item, and have students correct it. For example:

Teacher: [*showing the class Photo Card 164*] This is a taco.
Students: No. It's a cheeseburger.

Teacher: [*showing the class Photo Card 151*] This is sugar.
Students: No. It's butter.

LESSON OBJECTIVE

FOCUS

Food

VOCABULARY

a banana	an apple
a carrot	an egg
a cookie	an onion
a peach	an orange
a potato	
a tomato	

GETTING READY
5–10 MINUTES

1. Review the indefinite article *a/an*, using Photo Cards 137–146, or the photos on student book page 104.

   a. Point to a food item, and have students repeat after you. For example, say: "a cookie," and have students repeat. Continue with: "a banana," "a carrot," "a tomato," "a potato," "a peach."

   b. Point to and say the following words, emphasizing the pronunciation of *an*: "an apple," "an egg," "an orange," "an onion."

2. Practice *a/an*.

   a. Make two columns on the board. At the top of one column, write <u>a</u>. At the top of the other column, write <u>an</u>.

   b. Have students tell you food items that go in each column.

   c. Ask students what the difference is between the groups of words. Help students, if necessary, by underlining the vowels at the beginning of *apple*, *egg*, *orange*, and *onion*.

3. Review noun plurals, using Photo Cards 137–146, or the photos on student book page 105.

   a. Elicit plural forms from students by holding up a Photo Card, and having students give the plural.

   b. Point out the pronunciation of the plural *-s*:

      [s] carrots
      [z] bananas, tomatoes, potatoes, apples, eggs, onions
      [ɪz] peaches, oranges

THE MODEL CONVERSATION
10 MINUTES

1. **SETTING THE SCENE:** Have students look at the model photograph. Set the scene: "A wife and husband are talking"

2. **LISTENING:** With books closed, have students listen to the model conversation—presented by you, by a pair of students, or on the audio program. Check students' understanding of the situation and the vocabulary.

3. **CLASS PRACTICE:** With books still closed, model each line, and have the whole class practice in unison.

4. **READING:** With books open, have students follow along as two students present the model.

5. **PAIR PRACTICE:** In pairs, have students practice the model conversation.

THE CONVERSATION EXERCISES
10–20 MINUTES

1. **THE SKELETAL DIALOG:** Write the "skeletal dialog" on the board. Fill in the replacement from Exercise 1 to show students how the guided conversation method works. Call on a few pairs of students to practice Exercise 1, using the skeletal framework on the board.

   > A. What are you looking for?
   > B. A <u>banana</u>.
   > A. Sorry. There aren't any more <u>bananas</u>.

2. **VOCABULARY PRESENTATION:** Present the vocabulary words in the exercises. Point to the photograph of each item, say the word, and have the class repeat it chorally and individually. Check students' understanding and pronunciation of the vocabulary.

3. **EXERCISE PRACTICE:** (optional) Have pairs of students simultaneously practice all the exercises.

4. **EXERCISE PRESENTATIONS:** Call on pairs of students to present their conversations to the class.

GRAMMAR
5–10 MINUTES

Have students work individually to circle the correct word and then compare answers with a partner. Then call on individual students for the answers, paying particular attention to their pronunciation of the plural nouns.

Answers

1. a cookie
2. bananas
3. eggs
4. an onion
5. peaches
6. an orange

LISTENING
5–10 MINUTES

Listen and write the number under the correct picture.

1. I'm looking for an apple.
2. I'm looking for apples.
3. There aren't any more oranges.
4. I'm looking for a banana.
5. I'm looking for an orange.
6. There aren't any more bananas.

Answers

4	1	5
3	6	2

EXPANSION

1. Concentration ★

PHOTO CARDS 137–146 (TWO SETS)

a. Shuffle the cards and place them face-down in four rows of 5 each.

b. Divide the class into two teams. The object of the game is for students to find the matching cards and identify the vocabulary item. Both teams should be able to see the cards, since *concentrating* on their location is an important part of playing the game.

c. A student from Team 1 turns over two cards, and if they match, the student must identify the item. If the student correctly identifies the item, that team keeps the cards, and the student takes another turn. If they don't match or if the student isn't able to correctly identify the item, the student turns them face-down, and a member of Team 2 takes a turn.

d. The game continues until all the cards have been matched. The team with the most correct *matches* wins the game.

Variation:
PHOTO CARDS 137–146
ACTIVITY MASTER 61

Have the class play with one set of Photo Cards and one set of Word Cards.

2. Scrambled Words ★

a. Choose words from the lesson and write them on the board or on a card with the letters scrambled out of order. For example:

attoop

b. Have students take turns guessing what the word is. [potato]

Variation 1: Do the activity in pairs or small groups, with students taking turns scrambling words for others to guess.

Variation 2: Do the activity as a class game with competing teams.

3. The Letter Game ★

Divide the class into two teams. Say: "I'm thinking of a food that starts with *b*." The first person to raise his or her hand and guess correctly (*banana*) wins a point for the team. Continue with the other letters of the alphabet.

4. Drawing Game ★★

ACTIVITY MASTER 61

You will need either an hourglass or a watch with a second hand for timing the following activity.

a. Make two copies of Activity Master 61, cut them into cards, and place the two sets of cards in two piles on a table or desk in the front of the classroom. Also, have a pad of paper and pencil next to each pile.

b. Divide the class into two teams. Have each team sit together in a different part of the room.

c. When you say: "Go!", a person from each team picks a card from the pile and draws the food item. The rest of the team then guesses what the food item is.

d. When a team correctly guesses the food item, another team member picks a card and draws the food item on that card.

e. Continue until each team has guessed all the food items in their pile.

The team that guesses the food items in the shortest time wins the game.

5. Dictation Game ★★

a. In large print on a piece of paper, write a list of seven vocabulary words from the lesson. For example:

an apple
an orange
a peach
a tomato
a carrot
bananas
eggs

b. Divide the class into pairs—Student A and Student B. Have all the Student A's come outside the classroom with you. Show them the list of words, and have them spend a few minutes looking at it and trying to remember the words.

c. Have the Student A's return to the classroom and give them three minutes to dictate what they remembered from the list to their Student B partners. The pair that has written the most words wins the game.

d. For correction, have each pair call out one word on their list. Write that word on the board so students can check their spelling.

e. Repeat the game with a new list for Student B's to dictate to their Student A partners.

6. Likes and Dislikes ✶✶

a. Have students take out a piece of paper and draw a line down the center of the page. At the top of the left column, have them write I like, and at the top of the right column, have them write I don't like.

b. Dictate various food items. For example:

> carrots
> cookies
> oranges
> onions
> potatoes

c. Have students write the food item in either the left or the right column, depending on whether they *like* or *don't like* it.

d. At the end of the dictation, have students compare their lists to see which foods people *like* and *don't like*.

7. Memory Game ✶✶

Begin the activity by saying: "There aren't any more bananas." Student 1 repeats what you said and adds another food—for example: "There aren't any more bananas or peaches." Student 2 repeats what you and Student 1 said and adds another food—for example: "There aren't any more bananas, peaches, or oranges." Continue around the room in this fashion, with each student repeating what the previous student said and adding another food. Do the activity again, beginning and ending with different students.

8. Category Dictation ✶✶

a. Have students make two columns on a piece of paper. Have them write Fruit at the top of the left column and Vegetable at the top of the right column.

b. Dictate words from the lesson, and have students write them in the appropriate column. For example:

Fruit	Vegetable
peach	onion
orange	potato

c. After students have written down a word, write it on the board so students can correct their work.

9. Ranking ✶✶✶

a. Have students look at the food items on student book page 104 and choose the five they eat most often. Have students then rank these items from one to five, with one being the food item they eat most often. For example:

1. cookie
2. banana
3. orange
4. potato
5. tomato

b. As a class, in pairs, or in small groups, have students compare their lists.

10. In My Country ✶✶✶

As a class, in pairs, or in small groups, have students tell about fruits and vegetables in their countries.

LESSON OBJECTIVE

Focus

Food

Vocabulary

bread	lettuce
butter	milk
cereal	soda
cheese	soup
ice cream	sugar

> A. What are you looking for?
> B. _Cheese_.
> A. Sorry. There isn't any more _cheese_.

GETTING READY
5 MINUTES

Use your own visuals or the photos on student book page 106 to introduce the following vocabulary items: *bread, cheese, milk, cereal, butter, sugar, lettuce, soup, soda,* and *ice cream*. Say each word, and have the class repeat it chorally and individually. Check students' understanding and pronunciation of the vocabulary.

THE MODEL CONVERSATION
10 MINUTES

1. **SETTING THE SCENE:** Have students look at the model photograph. Set the scene: "A wife and husband are talking."

2. **LISTENING:** With books closed, have students listen to the model conversation—presented by you, by a pair of students, or on the audio program. Check students' understanding of the situation and the vocabulary.

3. **CLASS PRACTICE:** With books still closed, model each line, and have the whole class practice in unison.

4. **READING:** With books open, have students follow along as two students present the model.

5. **PAIR PRACTICE:** In pairs, have students practice the model conversation.

THE CONVERSATION EXERCISES
10–15 MINUTES

1. **THE SKELETAL DIALOG:** Write the "skeletal dialog" on the board. Fill in the replacement from Exercise 1 to show students how the guided conversation method works. Call on a few pairs of students to practice Exercise 1, using the skeletal framework on the board.

2. **VOCABULARY PRESENTATION:** Present the vocabulary words in the exercises. Point to the photograph of each item, say the word, and have the class repeat it chorally and individually. Check students' understanding and pronunciation of the vocabulary.

3. **EXERCISE PRACTICE:** (optional) Have pairs of students simultaneously practice all the exercises.

4. **EXERCISE PRESENTATIONS:** Call on pairs of students to present their conversations to the class.

LISTENING
5–10 MINUTES

Listen and write the number under the correct picture.

1. There isn't any more cheese.
2. I'm looking for milk.
3. There isn't any more soda.
4. I'm looking for sugar.
5. There isn't any more lettuce.
6. I'm looking for bread.

Answers

3	5	2
4	1	6

GRAMMAR
20 MINUTES

1. Introduce the concept of *count* and *non-count* nouns.

   a. Make two columns on the board. At the top of the left column, put a row of short lines or dots, and count them aloud: "One, two, three, four, five." Ask students: "What are some foods we count?" Help them out by offering the first answer: "One banana, two bananas, three bananas, four bananas, five bananas." Elicit from students other food items they can count. Write the foods they suggest on the board.

   b. At the top of the right column, draw a circle or any graphic that symbolizes the concept of *wholeness* or an *entirety* to you. Tell students: "Some things we can't count. For example, we can't say: 'one milk, two milks, three milks.'" Have students look again at the food items on student book page 106. Tell them that none of these food items can be counted.

c. Call out any foods students know—for example: *bananas, carrots, milk, tomatoes, cheese, potatoes, peaches, sugar, apples, oranges,* and *soda.* Either you or a student volunteer should write the food words under the appropriate category on the board.

Count Nouns	Non-count Nouns
bananas	milk
carrots	cheese

2. Explain *there aren't* vs. *there isn't* by referring to the lists of count and non-count nouns you have on the board.

a. Start with the list of count nouns. Say: "There aren't any more bananas," emphasizing the plural *-s.* Then call on students to use each word in the list to make a sentence beginning with *There aren't.*

b. Now point to the non-count list. Start a sentence for students: "There isn't any more . . .," and have students complete it with the first item listed. Continue with other non-count foods.

3. Have students complete the exercise individually and then compare answers in pairs. Circulate to answer questions as necessary

Answers

1. isn't
2. aren't
3. isn't
4. aren't
5. aren't
6. isn't

FOOD IN YOUR HOME
10 MINUTES

Have students individually answer the questions and then ask and answer the questions in pairs. Circulate to answer questions as necessary.

EXPANSION

1. Concentration ★

PHOTO CARDS 147–156 (TWO SETS)

a. Shuffle the cards and place them face-down in four rows of 5 each.

b. Divide the class into two teams. The object of the game is for students to find the matching cards and identify the vocabulary item. Both teams should be able to see the cards, since *concentrating* on their location is an important part of playing the game.

c. A student from Team 1 turns over two cards, and if they match, the student must identify

the item. If the student correctly identifies the item, that team keeps the cards, and the student takes another turn. If they don't match or if the student isn't able to correctly identify the item, the student turns them face-down, and a member of Team 2 takes a turn.

d. The game continues until all the cards have been matched. The team with the most correct *matches* wins the game.

Variation:
PHOTO CARDS 147–156
ACTIVITY MASTER 62

Have the class play with one set of Photo Cards and one set of Word Cards.

2. Scrambled Words ★

a. Choose words from the lesson and write them on the board or on a card with the letters scrambled out of order. For example:

b. Have students take turns guessing what the word is. [sugar]

Variation 1: Do the activity in pairs or small groups, with students taking turns scrambling words for others to guess.

Variation 2: Do the activity as a class game with competing teams.

3. The Letter Game ★

Divide the class into two teams. Say: "I'm thinking of a food that starts with *l.*" The first person to raise his or her hand and guess correctly (*lettuce*) wins a point for the team. Continue with the other letters of the alphabet.

4. Dictation Game ★★

a. In large print on a piece of paper, write a recipe using words from student book pages 104 and 106. For example:

Cheese Pie	Salad
cheese	lettuce
milk	tomatoes
eggs	carrots
onions	onions

b. Divide the class into pairs—Student A and Student B. Have all the Student A's come outside the classroom with you. Show them the recipe, and have them spend a few minutes looking at it and trying to remember the words. *(continued)*

c. Have the Student A's return to the classroom and give them three minutes to dictate what they remembered from the recipe to their Student B partners. The pair that has written the complete recipe wins the game.

d. For correction, have each pair call out one word on their recipe. Write that word on the board so students can check their spelling.

e. Repeat the game with a new recipe for Student B's to dictate to their Student A partners.

5. Likes and Dislikes ★★

a. Have students take out a piece of paper and draw a line down the center of the page. At the top of the left column, have them write <u>I like</u>, and at the top of the right column, have them write <u>I don't like</u>.

b. Dictate various food items. For example:

cheese	cereal
bread	butter
soda	lettuce
ice cream	sugar
soup	milk

c. Have students write the food item in either the left or the right column, depending on whether they *like* or *don't like* it.

d. At the end of the dictation, have students compare their lists to see which foods people *like* and *don't like*.

6. Finish the Sentence! ★★

Divide the class into two teams. Begin sentences, and have members of each team take turns finishing them with any appropriate food item they wish. For example:

There isn't any . . . *milk.*
There aren't any . . . *bananas.*

The team with the most correctly completed sentences wins.

7. Memory Game ★★

Begin the activity by saying: "There isn't any more cheese." Student 1 repeats what you said and adds another food—for example: "There isn't any more cheese or bread." Student 2 repeats what you and Student 1 said and adds another food—for example: "There isn't any more cheese, bread, or butter." Continue around the room in this fashion, with each student repeating what the previous student said and adding another food. Do the activity again, beginning and ending with different students.

8. The Foods We Eat ★★

a. Write the following on the board:

I eat _____.
My husband/My wife/My friend eats _____.

b. As a class, in pairs, or in small groups, have students tell about foods they and their friends or family members eat.

9. Dialog Practice: Sorry! ★★★
ACTIVITY MASTERS 61, 62

a. Divide the class into pairs. Make copies of Activity Masters 61 and 62, cut them into cards, and give one set to each pair of students.

b. Write the following skeletal dialog on the board:

A. What are you looking for?
B. _____.
A. Sorry. There isn't any more _____.
   Sorry. There aren't any more _____.

c. Have the pairs take turns picking up a card and using the word as a prompt in the skeletal dialog. For example:

A. What are you looking for?
B. [*picks up a "cheese" card*] Cheese.
A. Sorry. There isn't any more cheese.

A. What are you looking for?
B. [*picks up a "banana" card*] A banana.
A. Sorry. There aren't any more bananas.

10. Ranking ★★★

a. Have students look at the food items on student book page 106 and choose the five they eat most often. Have students then rank these items from one to five, with one being the food item they eat most often. For example:

1. milk
2. lettuce
3. cereal
4. butter
5. soup

b. As a class, in pairs, or in small groups, have students compare their lists.

11. In My Kitchen ★★★

As a class, in pairs, or in small groups, have students tell about what they *don't* have in their kitchens right now. For example:

There isn't any milk.
There aren't any oranges.

LESSON OBJECTIVE

FOCUS

Food

VOCABULARY

aisle
baked goods
dairy
fruits & vegetables

GETTING READY
5 MINUTES

1. Draw on the board a simple map of a supermarket with three aisles. Put the names of count-noun food items in each aisle. For example:

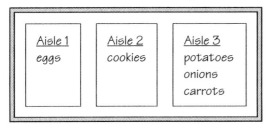

2. Explain to the class that this is a map of a supermarket. Ask about the location of foods in this *supermarket*. For example:

> Teacher: Where are the eggs?
> Student 1: In Aisle 1.
>
> Teacher: Where are the potatoes?
> Student 2: In Aisle 3.

Note: Don't erase the map. You will build on in it for the second model conversation.

MODEL CONVERSATION 1
10 MINUTES

1. **SETTING THE SCENE:** Have students look at the model photograph. Set the scene: "A customer is looking for something. She's talking to a supermarket clerk."

2. **LISTENING:** With books closed, have students listen to the model conversation—presented by you, by a pair of students, or on the audio program. Check students' understanding of the situation and the vocabulary.

3. **CLASS PRACTICE:** With books still closed, model each line, and have the whole class practice in unison.

4. **READING:** With books open, have students follow along as two students present the model.

5. **PAIR PRACTICE:** In pairs, have students practice the model conversation.

THE CONVERSATION EXERCISES
10 MINUTES

1. **THE SKELETAL DIALOG:** Write the "skeletal dialog" on the board. Fill in the replacement from Exercise 1 to show students how the guided conversation method works. Call on a few pairs of students to practice Exercise 1, using the skeletal framework on the board.

> A. Excuse me. I'm looking for <u>carrots</u>.
> B. <u>Carrots</u> are in Aisle 3.
> A. Thank you.

2. **VOCABULARY PRESENTATION:** Present the vocabulary words in the exercises. Point to the illustrations, say the names of the foods (1. carrots, 2. oranges, 3. apples), and have the class repeat them chorally and individually. Check students' understanding and pronunciation of the vocabulary.

3. **EXERCISE PRACTICE:** (optional) Have pairs of students simultaneously practice all the exercises.

4. **EXERCISE PRESENTATIONS:** Call on pairs of students to present their conversations to the class.

GETTING READY
5 MINUTES

1. Building on the same map as the previous Getting Ready, write in the names of non-count foods in each aisle. For example:

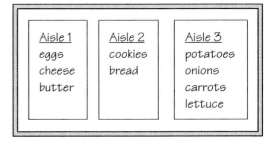

2. Ask students about the location of non-count foods in the supermarket. For example:

> Teacher: Where's the cheese?
> Student 1: In Aisle 1.
>
> Teacher: Where's the bread?
> Student 2: In Aisle 2.

MODEL CONVERSATION II

1. **SETTING THE SCENE:** Have students look at the model photograph. Set the scene: "A customer is looking for something. He's talking to a supermarket clerk."

2. **LISTENING:** With books closed, have students listen to the model conversation—presented by you, by a pair of students, or on the audio program. Check students' understanding of the situation and the vocabulary.

3. **CLASS PRACTICE:** With books still closed, model each line and have the whole class practice in unison.

4. **READING:** With books open, have students follow along as two students present the model.

5. **PAIR PRACTICE:** In pairs, have students practice the model conversation.

THE CONVERSATION EXERCISES

1. **THE SKELETAL DIALOG:** Write the "skeletal dialog" on the board. Fill in the replacement from Exercise 1 to show students how the guided conversation method works. Call on a few pairs of students to practice Exercise 1, using the skeletal framework on the board.

> A. Excuse me. I'm looking for <u>butter</u>.
> B. <u>Butter</u> is in Aisle 1.
> A. Thank you.

2. **VOCABULARY PRESENTATION:** Present the vocabulary words in the exercises. Point to the illustrations, say the names of the foods (1. butter, 2. cheese, 3. ice cream), and have the class repeat them chorally and individually. Check students' understanding and pronunciation of the vocabulary.

3. **EXERCISE PRACTICE:** (optional) Have pairs of students simultaneously practice all the exercises.

4. **EXERCISE PRESENTATIONS:** Call on pairs of students to present their conversations to the class.

GRAMMAR

Have students complete the sentences individually and then compare their answers in pairs.

Answers

1.	are	4.	are
2.	is	5.	is
3.	are	6.	is

CATEGORIES

1. Have students look at the illustrations of the three different supermarket sections. Say the names of the sections, and have students repeat them chorally and individually. Then have students spend time looking carefully at the foods depicted in the illustrations to see what foods are in each of the supermarket sections.

2. Tell students that their task is to sort the words into the correct categories. Point out the sample answer—*apples* are in the *Fruits & Vegetables* section. (*Note:* This is a good opportunity for students to practice checking off items as they move through an exercise. Have all the students check off the word *apples* in the box.) Call out the next word in the box (*bread*), and ask students: "Is bread a fruit? Is it a vegetable? Is it a baked good? Is it dairy?" When you hear the correct answer, tell all the students to write *bread* under *Baked Goods*. Have students complete the lists, and then compare answers with a partner.

Answers

Fruits & Vegetables

apples
lettuce
oranges

Baked Goods

bread
cookies

Dairy

butter
cheese
milk

MEMORY GAME

Have students stand in a circle for this activity. Student 1 says a food item he or she is looking for—for example: "I'm looking for milk." Student 2 repeats what Student 1 said and adds another food item—for example: "I'm looking for milk and bananas." Continue around the room in this fashion, with each student repeating what the previous student said and adding another food item. (*Note:* If the class is large, you can divide students into groups.)

EXPANSION

1. Disappearing Dialog ★

Write one of the two model conversations on the board and ask for two student volunteers to read the conversation. Erase a few of the words from the dialog, and have two different students read the conversation. Erase more words and call on two more students to read the conversation. Continue erasing words and calling on pairs of students until everyone has had a turn and the dialog has *disappeared*.

2. Finish the Dialog! ★★

a. Divide the class into two teams. Begin a dialog, and have members of each team take turns completing it with any aisle number they wish. For example:

Teacher: Excuse me. I'm looking for potatoes.
Student: Potatoes are in Aisle 3.

Teacher: Excuse me. I'm looking for milk.
Student: Milk is in Aisle 1.

b. The team with the most correctly completed dialogs wins.

3. Dialog Practice: Excuse me! ★★★
ACTIVITY MASTERS 61, 62

a. Divide the class into pairs. Make copies of Activity Masters 61 and 62, cut them into cards, and give one set to each pair of students.

b. Write the following skeletal dialog on the board:

```
A.  Excuse me. I'm looking for _____.
B.  _____ is/are in Aisle 2.
A.  Thank you.
```

c. Have the pairs take turns picking up a card and using the word as a prompt in the skeletal dialog. For example:

A. [*picking up a "sugar" card*] Excuse me. I'm looking for sugar.
B. Sugar is in Aisle 2.
A. Thank you.

A. [*picking up a "tomato" card*] Excuse me. I'm looking for tomatoes.
B. Tomatoes are in Aisle 2.
A. Thank you.

4. Information Gap ★★★
ACTIVITY MASTER 63

a. Make multiple copies of Activity Master 63 and cut them in half (Table A and Table B).

b. Divide the class into pairs. Give each partner a different table—A or B. Have students share their information and fill in their supermarket maps. For example:

A. I'm looking for cereal.
B. Cereal is in Aisle 2.

c. When the pairs have finished making their maps, have them look at their partners' maps to make sure they have written the information correctly.

LESSON OBJECTIVE

Focus
Food containers & quantities

VOCABULARY
bag
bottle
box
bunch
can
dozen
jar
loaf
pound
quart

mayonnaise

GETTING READY
10 MINUTES

Use your own visuals, the illustrations on student book page 110, or the actual items themselves to introduce the following new vocabulary: *box, bag, can, loaf, bunch, bottle, pound, jar, quart,* and *dozen.*

1. Write on the board:

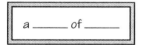

a _____ of _____

2. Hold up a visual or container, or point to the item in the student book, say the item, and have students repeat chorally and individually. Check students' understanding and pronunciation of the vocabulary.

3. Point out that with *dozen,* we say: "a dozen eggs," not "a dozen of eggs."

THE MODEL CONVERSATION
10 MINUTES

1. **SETTING THE SCENE:** Have students look at the model photograph. Set the scene: "A husband and wife are talking. He's going to the supermarket."

2. **LISTENING:** With books closed, have students listen to the model conversation—presented by you, by a pair of students, or on the audio program. Check students' understanding of the situation and the vocabulary.

3. **CLASS PRACTICE:** With books still closed, model each line, and have the whole class practice in unison.

4. **READING:** With books open, have students follow along as two students present the model.

5. **PAIR PRACTICE:** In pairs, have students practice the model conversation.

THE CONVERSATION EXERCISES
10 MINUTES

1. **THE SKELETAL DIALOG:** Write the "skeletal dialog" on the board. Fill in the replacement from Exercise 1 to show students how the guided conversation method works. Call on a few pairs of students to practice Exercise 1, using the skeletal framework on the board.

> A. What do we need at the supermarket?
> B. We need <u>a bag of sugar</u>.

2. **VOCABULARY PRESENTATION:** Present the vocabulary words in the exercises. Point to the illustrations, say the names of the food containers and quantities and have the class repeat them chorally and individually. Check students' understanding and pronunciation of the vocabulary.

3. **EXERCISE PRACTICE:** (optional) Have pairs of students simultaneously practice all the exercises.

4. **EXERCISE PRESENTATIONS:** Call on pairs of students to present their conversations to the class.

MATCHING
10 MINUTES

Have students match the containers and quantities with the foods and then compare their answers with a partner. Call on individual students to tell you the answers. Have them include "of" in their answers when possible. For example: *bottle of soda, bag of sugar,* and *dozen eggs.*

Answers

1. soda
2. sugar
3. eggs
4. mayonnaise
5. cheese
6. bread
7. cookies
8. soup
9. milk
10. bananas

LISTENING

10 MINUTES

Listen and write the number under the correct picture.

1. We need a jar of mayonnaise.
2. We need a bag of sugar.
3. We need a box of cookies.
4. I'm looking for a loaf of bread.
5. I'm looking for a can of soup.
6. We need a bunch of bananas.
7. We need a pound of cheese.
8. I'm looking for a dozen eggs.

Answers

3	6	8	2
5	1	4	7

MEMORY GAME

10 MINUTES

Have students stand in a circle for this activity. Student 1 says a food item needed from the supermarket—for example: "We need a loaf of bread." Student 2 repeats what Student 1 said and adds another food item—for example: "We need a loaf of bread and a can of soup." Continue around the room in this fashion, with each student repeating what the previous student said and adding another food item. (*Note*: If the class is large, you can divide students into groups.)

EXPANSION

1. True or False? ★

PHOTO CARDS 147–149, 152, 154–155, 157–160

Show students various Photo Cards. Make a false statement about the item, and have students correct it. For example:

Teacher: [*showing the class Photo Card 152*] This is a bottle of sugar.
Students: No. It's a bag of sugar.

Teacher: [*showing the class Photo Card 157*] This is a box of bread.
Students: No. It's a box of cookies.

2. Beanbag Toss ★

Have students sit or stand in a circle. Say the name of a food container or quantity and throw a beanbag to Student 1. Student 1 names another food item from student book page 110 and throws the beanbag to another student. Continue until everyone has had a turn.

3. Telephone ★

a. Have students sit in a circle or semicircle. Make up a sentence, using the new vocabulary in this lesson, and whisper it to Student 1. For example:

We need a box of cookies, a dozen eggs, and a quart of milk.

b. The first student whispers what he or she heard to the second student, who whispers it to the third student, and so forth. When the message gets to the last student, that person says it aloud. Is it the same message you started with?

Give each student in the class a chance to start his or her own message.

4. Name That Container! ★★

Call out the name of a container or quantity and have students repeat it, adding an appropriate noun. For example:

Teacher: bag
Students: a bag of sugar

Teacher: dozen
Students: a dozen eggs

Variation: Reverse the procedure. Call out the name of a food, and have students come up with the appropriate container or quantity. For example:

Teacher: sugar
Students: a bag of sugar

Teacher: eggs
Students: a dozen eggs

5. The Category Game ★★

Divide the class into teams. Call out the name of a container or quantity. Have each team write down as many supermarket items as they can think of that can be bought in that container or quantity. The team with the most correct items wins the game.

6. Dictation Game ★★

a. In large print on a piece of paper, write a list of six vocabulary words from the lesson. For example:

a jar of mayonnaise
a bag of sugar
a pound of cheese
a dozen eggs
a can of soup
a bunch of bananas

(continued)

b. Divide the class into pairs—Student A and Student B. Have all the Student A's come outside the classroom with you. Show them the list of words, and have them spend a few minutes looking at it and trying to remember the words.

c. Have the Student A's return to the classroom and give them three minutes to dictate what they remembered from the list to their Student B partners. The pair that has written the most words wins the game.

d. For correction, have each pair call out one word on their list. Write that word on the board so students can check their spelling.

e. Repeat the game with a new list for Student B's to dictate to their Student A partners.

7. Match Game ✷✷

PHOTO CARDS 147–150, 152, 154–155, 158–160
ACTIVITY MASTER 64

a. Make a copy of Activity Master 64 and cut it into cards. Select matching Photo Cards and distribute both Word Cards and Photo Cards randomly, one to each student.

b. Have students look at their card and identify the item. Then have students circulate around the room, saying their container and food item until they find their match. Make sure students don't show their cards to their classmates since this is a listening and speaking exercise.

c. When students have found their match, have them compare their cards and come show you.

8. Container Pictures ✷✷

Bring in pictures of supermarket items. As a class, in pairs, or in small groups, have students identify the items as you hold up the pictures—for example: a bag of sugar, a bunch of bananas, two cans of soup.

9. What Do You Need? ✷✷

a. In pairs, have students write a list of three food items they need at the supermarket.

b. Ask one pair of students: "What do you need at the supermarket?" The students answer according to what they have written down. For example: "We need a loaf of bread, a pound of cheese, and a bottle of soda."

10. Tic Tac Spell ✷✷✷

ACTIVITY MASTER 26

a. Write the following container and quantity words on the board:

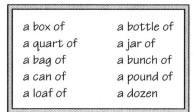

a box of	a bottle of
a quart of	a jar of
a bag of	a bunch of
a can of	a pound of
a loaf of	a dozen

b. Duplicate Activity Master 26 and give a copy to each student. Have students copy any nine container and quantity words into their grids.

c. One at a time, call out foods from the lesson. Tell students to identify the container or quantity that goes with that food. If they have that container or quantity on their grids, they should cross that box out.

d. The first person to cross out three words in a straight line—either vertically, horizontally, or diagonally—wins the game.

e. Have the winner call out the words to check the accuracy.

LESSON OBJECTIVE

Focus

Ordering food in a restaurant

Vocabulary

cheeseburger	lemonade
coffee	pizza
donut	sandwich
hamburger	taco
hot dog	tea

GETTING READY
5 MINUTES

Use your own visuals or the photos on student book page 112 to introduce the following new vocabulary: *hamburger, hot dog, sandwich, cheeseburger, taco, pizza, donut, lemonade, coffee,* and *tea.* Say each word, and have the class repeat it chorally and individually. Check students' understanding and pronunciation of the vocabulary.

THE MODEL CONVERSATION
10 MINUTES

1. **SETTING THE SCENE:** Have students look at the model photograph. Set the scene: "Someone is ordering food in a fast-food restaurant."

2. **LISTENING:** With books closed, have students listen to the model conversation—presented by you, by a pair of students, or on the audio program. Check students' understanding of the situation and the vocabulary.

3. **CLASS PRACTICE:** With books still closed, model each line, and have the whole class practice in unison.

4. **READING:** With books open, have students follow along as two students present the model.

5. **PAIR PRACTICE:** In pairs, have students practice the model conversation.

THE CONVERSATION EXERCISES
10 MINUTES

1. **THE SKELETAL DIALOG:** Write the "skeletal dialog" on the board. Fill in the replacement from Exercise 1 to show students how the guided conversation method works. Call on a few pairs of students to practice Exercise 1, using the skeletal framework on the board.

A. Can I help you?
B. Yes. I'd like <u>a hot dog</u>, please.

2. **VOCABULARY PRESENTATION:** Present the vocabulary words in the exercises. Point to the photograph of each item, say the word, and have the class repeat it chorally and individually. Check students' understanding and pronunciation of the vocabulary.

3. **EXERCISE PRACTICE:** (optional) Have pairs of students simultaneously practice all the exercises.

4. **EXERCISE PRESENTATIONS:** Call on pairs of students to present their conversations to the class.

LISTENING
5–10 MINUTES

Listen and write the number under the correct picture.

1. A. Can I help you?
   B. Yes. I'd like a hot dog, please.
2. A. Can I help you?
   B. Yes. I'd like a pizza, please.
3. A. May I help you?
   B. Yes. I'd like a taco, please.
4. A. May I help you?
   B. Yes, please. I'd like a sandwich.
5. A. Can I help you?
   B. Yes. I'd like lemonade, please.

Answers

4   1   3   5   2

MISSING LETTERS
5–10 MINUTES

Have students fill in the missing letters to complete each word. Have students read answers chorally. Then encourage individuals to go back and look at their words one more time to make sure they are correct. Students can then compare answers with a partner.

Answers

1. pizza
2. taco
3. sandwich
4. danish
5. coffee
6. lemonade
7. hot dog
8. cheeseburger

Model the activity. Make two grids on the board similar to the grids on student book page 113. Interview one student about food stores he or she goes to, and write that student's answers into the grid on the board. Then interview another student about fast-food restaurants, and write that student's answers into the second grid on the board. Have students work individually for at least five minutes completing the grids in their books. Have students discuss their answers in small groups, and then report back to the class.

EXPANSION

1. Concentration ✸

PHOTO CARDS 161–170 (TWO SETS)

a. Shuffle the cards and place them face-down in four rows of 5 each.

b. Divide the class into two teams. The object of the game is for students to find the matching cards and identify the vocabulary item. Both teams should be able to see the cards, since *concentrating* on their location is an important part of playing the game.

c. A student from Team 1 turns over two cards, and if they match, the student must identify the item. If the student correctly identifies the item, that team keeps the cards, and the student takes another turn. If they don't match or if the student isn't able to correctly identify the item, the student turns them face-down, and a member of Team 2 takes a turn.

d. The game continues until all the cards have been matched. The team with the most correct *matches* wins the game.

Variation:
PHOTO CARDS 161–170
ACTIVITY MASTER 65

Have the class play with one set of Photo Cards and one set of Word Cards.

2. Scrambled Words ✸

a. Choose words from the lesson and write them on the board or on a card with the letters scrambled out of order. For example:

    chainswd

b. Have students take turns guessing what the word is. [sandwich]

Variation 1: Do the activity in pairs or small groups, with students taking turns scrambling words for others to guess.

Variation 2: Do the activity as a class game with competing teams.

3. Drawing Game ✸✸

ACTIVITY MASTER 65

You will need either an hourglass or a watch with a second hand for timing the following activity.

a. Make two copies of Activity Master 65. Cut them into cards and place the two sets of cards in two piles on a table or desk in the front of the classroom. Also, have a pad of paper and pencil next to each pile.

b. Divide the class into two teams. Have each team sit together in a different part of the room.

c. When you say: "Go!", a person from each team picks a card from the pile and draws the object on the pad. The rest of the team then guesses what the object is.

d. When a team correctly guesses the object, another team member picks a card and draws the object on that card.

e. Continue until each team has guessed all of the objects in their pile.

The team that guesses the objects in the shortest time wins the game.

4. Dictation Game ✸✸

a. In large print on a piece of paper, write a list of seven food words from student book page 112. For example:

    a pizza
    a hamburger
    a donut
    coffee
    a taco
    a sandwich
    lemonade

b. Divide the class into pairs—Student A and Student B. Have all the Student A's come outside the classroom with you. Show them the list of words, and have them spend a few minutes looking at it and trying to remember the words.

c. Have the Student A's return to the classroom and give them three minutes to dictate what they remembered from the list to their Student B partners. The pair that has written the most words wins the game.

d. For correction, have each pair call out one word on their list. Write that word on the board so students can check their spelling.

e. Repeat the game with a new list for Student B's to dictate to their Student A partners.

5. Likes and Dislikes ✮✮

a. Have students take out a piece of paper and draw a line down the center of the page. At the top of the left column, have them write <u>I like</u>, and at the top of the right column, have them write <u>I don't like</u>.

b. Dictate various food items from student book page 112.

c. Have students write the food item in either the left or the right column, depending on whether they *like* or *don't like* them.

d. At the end of the dictation, have students compare their lists to see which foods people *like* and *don't like*.

6. Memory Game ✮✮

Begin the activity by saying: "I'd like a hamburger, please." Student 1 repeats what you said and adds another food—for example: "I'd like a hamburger and a donut, please." Student 2 repeats what you and Student 1 said and adds another food—for example: "I'd like a hamburger, a donut, and coffee, please." Continue around the room in this fashion, with each student repeating what the previous student said and adding another food. Do the activity again, beginning and ending with different students.

7. The Foods We Eat ✮✮

a. Write the following on the board:

> I eat _____.
> My son/My daughter/My friend eats
> _____.

b. As a class, in pairs, or in small groups, have students tell about foods from the lesson they and their friends or family members eat.

8. Ranking ✮✮✮

a. Have students look at the food items on student book page 112 and choose the five they eat most often. Have students then rank these items from one to five, with one being the food item they eat most often. For example:

1. sandwich
2. pizza
3. taco
4. hamburger
5. hot dog

b. As a class, in pairs, or in small groups, have students compare their lists.

9. Community Directory: Favorite Food Stores ✮✮✮

Compile the names of food stores that students recommended while doing the Community Connections activity and publish a class Community Directory of food stores. For each store, give its name and location.

10. Fast-Food Guide ✮✮✮

Compile the names of fast-food restaurants that students recommended while doing the Community Connections activity and publish a Fast-Food Guide. For each restaurant, give its name, location, and the specific food items that students recommend there.

LESSON OBJECTIVE

Focus

Quantities & abbreviations

Vocabulary

doz.
lb.
lbs.
qt.
qts.

GETTING READY
5–10 MINUTES

Point to the table on student book page 114 to introduce the following abbreviations: *doz., lb., lbs., qt.,* and *qts.* Point out that abbreviations almost always have a period. Say each full word, and have the class point to the abbreviation and repeat the word chorally and individually. Check students' understanding and pronunciation of the vocabulary.

THE MODEL CONVERSATIONS
10 MINUTES

There are two model conversations. Introduce and practice the first model before going on to the second. For each model:

1. **SETTING THE SCENE:** Set the scene: "Two family members or roommates are making a shopping list."

2. **LISTENING:** With books closed, have students listen to the model conversation—presented by you, by a pair of students, or on the audio program. Check students' understanding of the situation and the vocabulary.

3. **CLASS PRACTICE:** With books still closed, model each line, and have the whole class practice in unison.

4. **READING:** With books open, have students follow along as two students present the model.

5. **PAIR PRACTICE:** In pairs, have students practice the model conversation.

THE CONVERSATION EXERCISES
10–20 MINUTES

1. **THE SKELETAL DIALOG:** Write the "skeletal dialog" on the board. Fill in the replacement from Exercises 1 and 2 to show students how the guided conversation method works. Call

on a few pairs of students to practice the exercises, using the skeletal framework on the board.

Model 1:

> A. Please get <u>a pound of cheese</u>.
> B. <u>A pound of cheese</u>?
> A. Yes.

Model 2:

> A. Please get <u>two quarts of milk</u>.
> B. <u>Two quarts of milk</u>?
> A. Yes.

2. **VOCABULARY PRESENTATION:** Present the vocabulary words in the exercises. Point to each food item and its abbreviated form, say the food item, and have the class repeat it chorally and individually. Check students' understanding and pronunciation of the vocabulary.

3. **EXERCISE PRACTICE:** (optional) Have pairs of students simultaneously practice all the exercises.

4. **EXERCISE PRESENTATIONS:** Call on pairs of students to present their conversations to the class.

MAKE A SHOPPING LIST
10 MINUTES

Have students individually write up a shopping list of foods they need to get. Encourage them to use the abbreviations at the top of student book page 114. Have students then compare their lists in pairs.

EXPANSION

1. **Concentration** ★
   ACTIVITY MASTER 66

   a. Divide the class into pairs. Make multiple copies of Activity Master 66, cut them into cards, and give each pair of students one set of cards. Have students shuffle the cards and place them face-down in two rows of 7 each.

   b. The object of the game is for students to find the matching cards. Both students should be able to see the cards, since *concentrating* on their location is an important part of playing the game.

   c. Student A turns over two cards, and if they match, the student keeps the cards. If the cards don't match, the student turns them face-down and Student B takes a turn.

   d. The play continues until all the cards have been matched. The student with the most correct *matches* wins the game.

2. Listen and Write ★★

Divide the class into pairs. Say the following quantities of food, and have students write them in abbreviated forms. Then have the pairs check each other's abbreviations.

    a dozen eggs (1 doz. eggs)
    two quarts of milk (2 qts. milk)
    three pounds of apples (3 lbs. apples)
    half a dozen oranges (1/2 doz. oranges)
    a pound of cheese (1 lb. cheese)

3. Association Game ★★

   a. Write the following quantities on the board:

> a pound of
> a dozen
> a quart of

   b. Divide the class into several teams. Have the students in each team work together to see how many foods they can associate with each type of quantity. For example:

    a pound of: [cheese/butter/meat]
    a dozen: [eggs/apples/tomatoes]
    a quart of: [milk/lemonade/ice cream]

   c. Set a time limit for the game. When the time limit is up, call on the teams to read their list of associations to the class. The team with the most correct items wins.

4. Match Game: Shopping Lists ★★★
ACTIVITY MASTER 67

   a. Make a copy of Activity Master 67, cut it into cards, and distribute the cards randomly, one to each student.

   b. Have students look at their card and read the phrase or list. Then have students circulate around the room saying their lines or reading their lists until they find their match. Make sure students don't show their cards to their classmates since this is a listening and speaking exercise.

   c. When students have found their match, have them compare their cards and come show you.

LANGUAGE EXPERIENCE JOURNAL

Have students write about their favorite foods. Depending on your students' writing abilities, either have them write in their journal or dictate their story for you to write. Then students should read what they have written to a classmate. If time permits, you may also want to write a response in each student's journal, sharing your own opinions and experiences as well as reacting to what the student has written.

Different Cultures *Different Ways*   10 MINUTES

Have students first work in pairs or small groups, reacting to the photographs and responding to the questions. Then have students share with the class what they have talked about.

PUT IT TOGETHER   15–20 MINUTES

In this activity, students talk with each other to find out what foods each person has in his or her kitchen.

1. Divide the class into pairs: Student A and Student B.

2. Tell all the Student A's to look at Part A of the activity on student book page 115. Tell all the Student B's to look at Part B on page 116.

3. Have everybody look at the first item on the list: *milk.*

   a. In Student B's list, under *You*, it says, *Yes.* Therefore, when Student A asks: "Do you have milk?", Student B answers: "Yes. I have milk."

   b. Ask all the Student B's: "Do you have milk?" Have all the Student B's respond in unison: "Yes. I have milk."

   c. Have all the Student A's look at their list. In their list under *You*, it says, *No.* Therefore, when Student B asks: "Do you have milk?", Student A answers: "No. I don't have milk."

   d. Ask all the Student A's: "Do you have milk?" Have all the Student A's respond in unison: "No. I don't have milk."

4. The Student A and Student B pairs are now ready to continue the activity with the rest of the words on their lists.

5. When the pairs have completed the activity, have them check each other's answers.

VOCABULARY FOUNDATIONS   5–10 MINUTES

Have students review the list of words they have learned in this unit. Encourage students to get a small notebook where they can write down vocabulary that is new for them. If students have personal copies of dictionaries or picture dictionaries, have them look up these words in the dictionary and highlight them with a marker. Encourage them to look at their notebooks or dictionaries frequently to review what they have learned.

For additional practice, have students do one or more of the following activities.

1. **Taking Notes** ★

   In their vocabulary notebooks or on a piece of paper, have students write all the words in one column. In a second column, have them write notes, draw pictures, or write the word in a sentence that will help them remember the meaning of the words.

2. **Food Review** ★

   a. Write the following alphabet letters on the board:

   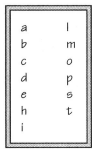

   b. Have students take turns calling out the names of foods that begin with each letter of the alphabet written on the board. Either you or a student volunteer can write the words on the board next to the appropriate letter of the alphabet. For example:

a – apple		l
b – banana		m – milk
c		o
d		p
e		s
h		t
i		

3. **Scrambled Words** ★

   a. Choose words from the unit and write them on the board or on a card with the letters scrambled out of order. For example:

   b. Have students take turns guessing what the word is. [cookie]

   Variation 1: Do the activity in pairs or small groups, with students taking turns scrambling words for others to guess.

Variation 2: Do the activity as a class game with competing teams.

4. **Telephone** ✷✷

   a. Have students sit in a circle or semicircle. Make up a sentence, using the new vocabulary in this unit, and whisper it to Student 1. For example:

   > We need to get a quart of milk, a jar of mayonnaise, and two pounds of carrots at the supermarket.

   b. The first student whispers what he or she heard to the second student, who whispers it to the third student, and so forth. When the message gets to the last student, that person says it aloud. Is it the same message you started with?

   Give each student in the class a chance to start his or her own message.

5. **Category Dictation** ✷✷

   a. Have students make four columns on a piece of paper:

   > fast food
   > dairy
   > fruits and vegetables
   > baked goods

   b. Dictate words from Vocabulary Foundations, and have students write them in the appropriate column. Make sure all students have covered the vocabulary items on student book page 116 with a piece of paper so they don't refer to that list.

   c. As a class, in pairs, or in small groups, have students check their work.

6. **Scrambled Sentences** ✷✷✷

   ACTIVITY MASTER 68

   Divide the class into pairs. Make enough copies of Activity Master 68 for half the class. Cut them into cards, and distribute a set to each pair of students. Have students take turns picking up a prompt and then saying the complete sentence.

   Variation: Students can write their complete sentences and compare their answers with other pairs.

7. **Match Game** ✷✷✷

   ACTIVITY MASTER 69

   a. Make a copy of Activity Master 69, cut it into cards, and distribute the cards randomly, one to each student.

   b. Have students memorize the question or response on their card and leave their cards on their desks. Then have students circulate around the room, saying their lines until they find their match.

   c. When students have found their match, have them compare their cards and come show you.

8. **Different Countries, Different Foods** ✷✷✷

   a. Write the following on the board:

   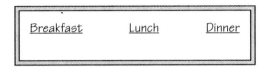

   b. Have students tell foods they typically eat for each of these meals. Either you or a student volunteer should write the food items on the board under the appropriate category.

   c. Compare similarities and differences in the foods that different students have for each of these meals.

LANGUAGE SKILL FOUNDATIONS 10–15 MINUTES

Explain to students that this is a list of skills they have learned in the unit. Students should become familiar with the vocabulary of describing their skills, but they don't need to master all the terms. For each speaking skill on the list, read the skill aloud to students, and have them demonstrate it. For example:

> Teacher: I can express food needs.
> Students: I'd like a hamburger, please.

(If students don't understand the vocabulary of a particular speaking skill, give them a concrete example rather than a description or explanation, and then have students practice your example and others.)

Have students put a check next to each skill if they feel they have learned it. Use this information to determine which lessons you may want to review or reinforce for the entire class or for particular students. The Getting Ready and Expansion activities for this unit and the CD-ROM's Activity Bank of supplemental worksheets are excellent resources for additional practice. It may also be helpful to have stronger students or, if available, a classroom aide or volunteer, work with students who need more practice.

(Page 117 is also available as a transparency.)

Use this scene to review the vocabulary, conversations, and grammar in the unit. Have students first work in pairs or small groups to talk about the illustration and answer the question posed at the bottom of the page. Then discuss as a class.

For additional motivating practice, students will enjoy doing one or more of the following activities.

These activities review Unit 8 vocabulary:

1. **Find the Foods!** ★

   Call out any of the following food items, and have students locate them in the illustration on student book page 117:

a bag of sugar	a bunch of bananas
a glass of lemonade	a can
a hot dog	a cheeseburger
a loaf of bread	a cup of coffee
an onion	a dozen eggs
a quart of milk	a hamburger
two apples	a jar of mayonnaise
two bags of potatoes	a pound of butter
three boxes of cookies	boxes of cereal
three donuts	cheese
three peaches	cookies
three pizzas	ice cream
four bottles of soda	lettuce
a bag of carrots	money
a box of tea	

   Variation: Copy this list and distribute it to pairs of students. Have students work with their partners to locate all the objects.

2. **The Longest List** ★★

   a. Call out a category of food. For example:

Dairy	Fruit	Drinks
Vegetables	Baked Goods	Fast Foods

   b. In pairs, have students write all the foods in that category they see in the scene on student book page 117. Tell students to cover the list of words on student book page 116 with a piece of paper so they don't refer to that list. (Set a one-minute time limit for this activity.)

   c. Tell students to stop after one minute. Ask students to count the number of foods they wrote for that category. Who has the longest list? Continue the activity, calling out other categories.

3. **Remember the Words!** ★★

   a. Tell students to spend two minutes looking carefully at the supermarket scene on student book page 117.

   b. Have students close their books and write down all the food items they remember from the illustration.

   c. Have students compare notes with a partner, and then look at the illustration again to see how well they remembered the food items.

This activity reviews Unit 8 conversations and grammar:

4. **What Are They Saying?** ★★★

   a. Have pairs or small groups of students look at the transparency or the illustration on student book page 117.

   b. Point to two characters in the scene, and have the students in each pair or group work together to create a conversation between those characters.

   c. Have students present their conversations to the class.

   d. One at a time, point to another two characters talking on page 117 until students have created and presented conversations between all the characters in the illustration.

   Variation 1: Have pairs or small groups of students create a conversation between a group of characters, present it to the class, and the other students point to the appropriate characters in the book or on the transparency.

   Variation 2: Have students write out the conversations they created for each scene.

This activity expands on Unit 8 vocabulary:

5. **Vocabulary Expansion** ★★★

   Write the following words on the board and have students identify these objects in the illustration on student book page 117 or on the overhead transparency.

Fast-food Counter	Check-out Counter
cups	bag
ketchup	bagger
mustard	basket
napkins	cart
	cash register
	cashier
	checkout
	receipt
	scanner

UNIT 9 CLOTHING, COLORS, & SHOPPING

LESSONS & UNIT ACTIVITIES	OBJECTIVES	TEXT	TEACHER'S GUIDE
Vocabulary Preview	Clothing • Accessories • Sizes	118–119	150
LESSON 1 I'm looking for a shirt.	Clothing	120–121	151–153
LESSON 2 I'm looking for a pair of shoes.	Clothing	122–123	154–156
LESSON 3 What's your favorite color?	Colors • Clothing	124–125	157–158
LESSON 4 What size?	Clothing sizes	126–127	159–161
LESSON 5 NUMBERS: What's the price?	Prices	128	162–163
Language Experience Journal	Writing about your favorite clothing	128	163
Different Cultures / Different Ways	Special clothing	129	164
Put It Together	Information Gap / Teamwork activity	129–130	164
Vocabulary Foundations / Language Skill Foundations	Review & skills checklist	130	164–165
Talk About It!	Review, conversations, activities, & games	131	165–166

UNIT RESOURCES

Audio Program:
Audio CD 3: Tracks 35–50
Audio Cassette 3A

Workbooks:
Activity Workbook
Literacy Workbook

Lesson Planner CD-ROM:
Activity Masters 70–77
Activity Bank Unit 9 Worksheets

Vocabulary Photo Cards: 171–190

Transparency: Color Overhead for Unit 9, page 131

PREVIEW
5 MINUTES

Activate students' prior knowledge of clothing vocabulary by doing any or all of the following:

1. Brainstorm with students the words for clothing they already know and write them on the board.

2. Have students look at the photographs on student book pages 118 and 119 while they cover the words at the bottom of the page. Have students identify the words they already know.

3. Have students look around at what their classmates are wearing and identify the clothing words they already know.

PRESENT
10–15 MINUTES

Using the photographs on student book pages 118 and 119, or the actual clothing students are wearing, point to each item, say the word, and have the class repeat it chorally and individually. (You can also play the audio program.) Check students' understanding and pronunciation of the vocabulary.

PRACTICE
10 MINUTES

As a class, in pairs, or in small groups, have students practice the vocabulary in either or both of the following ways:

- Say or write a word, and have students point to the item in their books, tell the number, or point to student wearing the clothing item.

- Point to a photograph in the student book, or give the number, or point to a clothing item a student is wearing, and have students say the word.

SPELLING PRACTICE
5–10 MINUTES

Say a word, and have students spell it aloud or write it. Or point to a clothing item in the student book or on a student and have students write the word. You can also spell a portion of a word on the board, and have students come to the board to complete it.

EXPANSION

1. Tell and Show ★
PHOTO CARDS 171–190 (TWO SETS)

a. Divide the class into pairs. Distribute all the Photo Cards randomly so each pair receives at least five or six cards.

b. Have Student A in each pair select a Photo Card and tell Student B the clothing item. Have Student B point to the item on student book page 118 or 119.

c. As the pairs finish using their Photo Cards, have them trade their sets with another pair and then continue the activity. Have students reverse roles each time they get a new set of cards.

2. Match Game ★
PHOTO CARDS 171–190 (TWO SETS)

a. Choose duplicate copies of any Photo Cards and distribute them randomly, one to each student.

b. Have students look at their card and identify the clothing item. Then have students circulate around the room, saying the clothing item on their card until they find their match. Make sure students don't show their cards to their classmates since this is a listening and speaking exercise.

c. When students have found their match, have them compare their cards and come show you. Then give each student another Photo Card to keep the game going. Continue until students have found all the matches.

3. What Am I Wearing? ★★

In pairs, have students make a list of what they are wearing. Then have each pair stand up and read their list to the class as they show their clothing items.

4. True or False? ★★
PHOTO CARDS 171–190

Show students various Photo Cards. Make a false statement about the item, and have students correct it. For example:

Teacher: [*showing the class Photo Card 172*] This is a blouse.
Students: No. It's a coat.

Teacher: [*showing the class Photo Card 182*] This is a watch.
Students: No. It's a necklace.

LESSON OBJECTIVE

Focus

Clothing

Vocabulary

belt
blouse
coat
dress
jacket
necklace
shirt
suit
sweater
tie
umbrella
watch

GETTING READY
5–10 MINUTES

1. Use your own visuals, the photos on student book page 120, or the actual items themselves to introduce the following clothing vocabulary: *shirt, coat, suit, belt, jacket, tie, sweater, umbrella, blouse, dress, watch,* and *necklace*.

2. Review noun plurals by naming a few items from student book page 120 and having students tell the plural form. Point out that the nouns *blouse, dress, watch,* and *necklace* add an extra syllable in their plural form (for example: blou/ses, dres/ses, wat/ches, and neck/la/ces).

THE MODEL CONVERSATION
10 MINUTES

1. **SETTING THE SCENE:** Have students look at the model photograph. Set the scene: "A customer is talking to a salesperson in a department store."

2. **LISTENING:** With books closed, have students listen to the model conversation—presented by you, by a pair of students, or on the audio program. Check students' understanding of the situation and the vocabulary.

3. **CLASS PRACTICE:** With books still closed, model each line, and have the whole class practice in unison.

4. **READING:** With books open, have students follow along as two students present the model.

5. **PAIR PRACTICE:** In pairs, have students practice the model conversation.

THE CONVERSATION EXERCISES
10–20 MINUTES

1. **THE SKELETAL DIALOG:** Write the "skeletal dialog" on the board. Fill in the replacement from Exercise 1 to show students how the guided conversation method works. Call on a few pairs of students to practice Exercise 1, using the skeletal framework on the board.

> A. I'm looking for a <u>coat</u>.
> B. <u>Coats</u> are over there.
> A. Thank you.

2. **VOCABULARY PRESENTATION:** Present the vocabulary words on student book page 120. Point to the photograph of each item, say the word, and have the class repeat it chorally and individually. Check students' understanding and pronunciation of the vocabulary.

3. **EXERCISE PRACTICE:** (optional) Have pairs of students simultaneously practice all the exercises.

4. **EXERCISE PRESENTATIONS:** Call on pairs of students to present their conversations to the class.

LISTENING
5–10 MINUTES

Listen and write the number under the correct picture.

1. A. I'm looking for a coat.
   B. Coats are over there.
   A. Thank you.

2. A. I'm looking for a blouse.
   B. Blouses are over there.
   A. Thank you.

3. A. I'm looking for a shirt.
   B. Shirts are over there.
   A. Thank you.

4. A. May I help you?
   B. Yes. I'm looking for a suit.
   A. Suits are over there.
   B. Thank you.

5. A. May I help you?
   B. Yes. I'm looking for a dress.
   A. Dresses are over there.
   B. Thanks.

Answers

5 3 2 1 4

ONE OR MORE?

Point out that the task is to choose a singular noun or a plural noun. Have students work individually to complete the exercise, and then compare answers in pairs.

Answers

1. ties
2. blouse
3. skirts
4. umbrella
5. sweaters
6. necklace

PRONUNCIATION

Model the pronunciation of the top word in each column. Have students identify which column (Column 1, 2, or 3) ends in an -*s* sound (Column 1), which column ends in a -*z* sound (Column 2), and which column ends in an -*es* syllable (Column 3). Explain to students that nouns ending in -*s*, -*sh*, -*x*, and some words that end in -*ch*, add an -*e*- before the plural -*s* suffix. For example: *dress—dresses*; *watch—watches*.

Have students work individually to write the nouns in the plural forms and then practice their pronunciation in pairs or as a class.

Answers

coats	sweaters	dresses
shirts	ties	watches
suits	umbrellas	blouses

GRAMMAR

Have students work individually to complete the exercise and then compare their answers in pairs.

Answers

1. dress
2. Belts
3. watch
4. Suits
5. jackets
6. tie
7. Blouses
8. coats

EXPANSION

1. Concentration ✸

PHOTO CARDS 171–182 (TWO SETS)

a. Choose duplicate copies of any nine Photo Cards 171–182. Shuffle the cards and place them face-down in two rows of 9 each.

b. Divide the class into two teams. The object of the game is for students to find the matching cards and identify the vocabulary item. Both teams should be able to see the cards, since *concentrating* on their location is an important part of playing the game.

c. A student from Team 1 turns over two cards, and if they match, the student must identify the item. If the student correctly identifies the item, that team keeps the cards, and the student takes another turn. If they don't match or if the student isn't able to correctly identify the item, the student turns them face-down, and a member of Team 2 takes a turn.

d. The game continues until all the cards have been matched. The team with the most correct *matches* wins the game.

Variation:
PHOTO CARDS 171–182
ACTIVITY MASTER 70

Have the class play with one set of Photo Cards and one set of Word Cards.

2. Clap in Rhythm ✸

Object: Once a clapping rhythm is established, the students must continue naming different clothing items.

a. Have students sit in a circle.

b. Establish a steady, even beat: one-two-three-four, one-two-three-four, etc., by having students clap their hands to their laps twice, and then clap their hands together twice. Repeat throughout the game, maintaining the same rhythm.

c. The object is for each student in turn to name a different word *each time their hands are clapped together*. Nothing is said when students clap their hands on their laps.

Note: The beat never stops! If a student misses a beat, he or she can either wait for the next beat or pass to the next student.

3. Listening Practice ✸

Say the following words in random order, and have students raise one hand if they hear a singular noun and two hands if they hear a plural noun.

shirt	shirts
coat	coats
suit	suits
belt	belts
jacket	jackets
tie	ties
sweater	sweaters
umbrella	umbrellas
blouse	blouses
dress	dresses
watch	watches
necklace	necklaces

4. Pronunciation Practice ★

In pairs, have students take turns reading aloud the singular or plural nouns from the One or More? and Pronunciation exercises on student book page 121. One student reads the words and the other points to the word he or she hears. Then have students reverse roles.

5. Alphabetical Order ★

ACTIVITY MASTER 70

Make multiple copies of Activity Master 70 and cut them into cards. Divide the class into pairs and give a set of cards to each pair. Have students work together to put the word cards in alphabetical order. Call on a pair to read their list, and have the class decide whether or not the order is correct.

6. Clothing Chain Game ★★

Begin the chain: "I'm looking for a coat," and have students continue it. For example:

    Teacher: I'm looking for a coat.
    Student 1: I'm looking for a coat and a belt.
    Student 2: I'm looking for a coat, a belt, and a watch.
    Etc.

7. Drawing Game ★★

ACTIVITY MASTER 70

You will need either an hourglass or a watch with a second hand for timing the following activity.

a. Make two copies of Activity Master 70. Cut them into cards and place the two sets of cards in two piles on a table or desk in the front of the classroom. Also, have a pad of paper and pencil next to each pile.

b. Divide the class into two teams. Have each team sit together in a different part of the room.

c. When you say: "Go!", a person from each team picks a card from the pile and draws the object. The rest of the team then guesses what the object is.

d. When a team correctly guesses the object, another team member picks a card and draws the object on that card.

e. Continue until each team has guessed all of the objects in their pile.

The team that guesses the objects in the shortest time wins the game.

8. For Men, Women, or Both? ★★★

a. Have students take out a piece of paper and draw two lines down the page. Have them write <u>Men</u> at the top of the left column, <u>Women</u> at the top of the middle column, and <u>Both</u> on the top of the right column.

b. Dictate various clothing words. For example:

    suit
    dress
    shirt
    tie
    blouse
    necklace

c. Have students write the clothing items in the appropriate columns. At the end of the dictation, have students compare their lists.

LESSON OBJECTIVE

Focus

Clothing

Vocabulary

gloves	pants	a pair of
jeans	shoes	
mittens	socks	
pajamas		

GETTING READY *5–10 MINUTES*

1. Use your own visuals, the photos on student book page 122, or the actual clothing items themselves to introduce the following words: *shoes, pants, socks, jeans, gloves, mittens,* and *pajamas.*

2. Introduce the phrase *a pair of.*

   a. Ask students which clothing items always come *in two's* or always have two equal parts. Generate a list on the board:

   > pants
   > socks
   > jeans
   > pajamas
   > gloves
   > mittens
   > shoes

   b. Model the first item: "a pair of pants." Have students say similar phrases for each of the items in the list.

THE MODEL CONVERSATION *10–20 MINUTES*

1. **SETTING THE SCENE:** Have students look at the model photograph. Set the scene: "A salesclerk and a customer are talking in a department store."

2. **LISTENING:** With books closed, have students listen to the model conversation—presented by you, by a pair of students, or on the audio program. Check students' understanding of the situation and the vocabulary.

3. **CLASS PRACTICE:** With books still closed, model each line, and have the whole class practice in unison.

4. **READING:** With books open, have students follow along as two students present the model.

5. **PAIR PRACTICE:** In pairs, have students practice the model conversation.

THE CONVERSATION EXERCISES *10–20 MINUTES*

1. **THE SKELETAL DIALOG:** Write the "skeletal dialog" on the board. Fill in the replacement from Exercise 1 to show students how the guided conversation method works. Call on a few pairs of students to practice Exercise 1, using the skeletal framework on the board.

   > A. May I help you?
   > B. Yes. I'm looking for a pair of <u>pants</u>.
   > A. <u>Pants</u> are over there.

2. **VOCABULARY PRESENTATION:** Present the vocabulary words in the exercises. Point to the photograph of each item, say the word, and have the class repeat it chorally and individually. Check students' understanding and pronunciation of the vocabulary.

3. **EXERCISE PRACTICE:** (optional) Have pairs of students simultaneously practice all the exercises.

4. **EXERCISE PRESENTATIONS:** Call on pairs of students to present their conversations to the class.

LISTENING *5–10 MINUTES*

Listen and write the number under the correct picture.

1. A. May I help you?
   B. Yes. I'm looking for a pair of pajamas.
2. A. May I help you?
   B. Yes. I'm looking for a pair of jeans.
3. A. May I help you?
   B. Yes. I'm looking for a pair of shoes.
4. A. May I help you?
   B. Yes. I'm looking for a pair of gloves.
5. A. May I help you?
   B. Yes. I'm looking for a pair of mittens.
6. A. May I help you?
   B. Yes, please. I'm looking for a pair of socks.
7. A. I'm looking for a suit.
   B. Suits are over there.

8. A. I'm looking for a pair of pants.
    B. Pants are over there.

Answers

8	1	6	3
4	7	2	5

MISSING LETTERS   10 MINUTES

Have students fill in the missing letters to complete each word. Have students read the answers chorally. Then encourage individuals to go back and look at their words one more time to make sure they are correct. Students can then compare answers with a partner.

MEMORY GAME   10 MINUTES

Have students stand in a circle for this activity. Student 1 says a clothing item he or she is looking for—for example: "I'm looking for a jacket." Student 2 repeats what Student 1 said and adds another clothing item—for example: "I'm looking for a jacket and a pair of socks." Continue around the room in this fashion, with each student repeating what the previous student said and adding another clothing item. (*Note:* If the class is large, you can divide students into groups.)

EXPANSION

1. **Listen and Point** ★

    Divide the class into pairs. Have Student A look at the photos in the Listening activity on student book page 123. Have Student B say the clothing items in random order. Student A must point to the appropriate photo. Then have the pairs reverse roles.

2. **Look Around!** ★

    Tell students to look around and describe all the clothing items they see that come in pairs.

3. **Disappearing Dialog** ★

    Write the model conversation on the board and ask for two student volunteers to read the conversation. Erase a few of the words from the dialog, and have two different students read the conversation. Erase more words and call on two more students to read the conversation. Continue erasing words and calling on pairs of students until everyone has had a turn and the dialog has *disappeared*.

4. **Concentration** ★

    PHOTO CARDS 184-190 (TWO SETS)

    a. Shuffle the cards and place them face-down in two rows of 7 each.

    b. Divide the class into two teams. The object of the game is for students to find the matching cards and identify the vocabulary item. Both teams should be able to see the cards, since *concentrating* on their location is an important part of playing the game.

    c. A student from Team 1 turns over two cards, and if they match, the student must identify the item. If the student correctly identifies the item, that team keeps the cards, and the student takes another turn. If they don't match or if the student isn't able to correctly identify the item, the student turns them face-down, and a member of Team 2 takes a turn.

    d. The game continues until all the cards have been matched. The team with the most correct *matches* wins the game.

    Variation:
    PHOTO CARDS 184–190
    ACTIVITY MASTER 71

    Have the class play with one set of Photo Cards and one set of Word Cards.

5. **Labeling Pictures** ★
    ACTIVITY MASTER 71

    a. Duplicate a copy of Activity Master 71 and cut it into cards.

    b. Bring in several pictures of items from this lesson. The pictures should be as clear and as large as possible.

    c. Distribute the cards randomly to the students and tell them to tape their cards next to a picture that features that item.

    d. As a class, review all of the items in the pictures.

    This activity can be a warm-up for students to then write a description about one of the pictures.

6. **Do You Remember?** ★★
    Bring to class a full-length magazine picture of a person. Tell students to spend two minutes looking carefully at the picture. Put the picture away, and ask students questions about the clothes the person in the picture is wearing. For example:

    Is she wearing a pair of pants?
    Is she wearing a pair of gloves?
    Is she wearing a jacket?
    Is she wearing a watch?

(continued)

7. Dictate the Picture Game ★★★

a. Bring to class a full-length magazine picture of a person wearing cold weather clothes.

b. Divide the class into pairs—Student A and Student B. Have all the Student A's come outside the classroom with you. Show them the picture, and have them spend a few minutes talking about what the person in the picture is wearing.

c. Have the Student A's return to the classroom and give them three minutes to dictate to their Student B partners what they remembered from the picture. The pair that has written the most clothing items wins the game.

d. For correction, have each pair call out one word on their list. Write that word on the board so students can check their spelling.

e. Repeat the game with a new picture for Student B's to dictate to their Student A partners.

8. Listen and Number ★★★

Divide the class into pairs, and have students look at the pictures on student book page 122. Student A chooses four clothing items and says: "I'm looking for (a pair of pants, a pair of socks, a pair of shoes, and a pair of pajamas)." Student B listens to the statement and numbers the pictures in the order that he or she hears them in Student A's statement. Then reverse roles.

LESSON OBJECTIVE

FOCUS

Colors
Clothing

VOCABULARY

black	gray	pink	white
blue	green	purple	yellow
brown	orange	red	

GETTING READY
5–10 MINUTES

Use your own visuals, the illustration on student book page 124, or the actual colors on clothing students are wearing to introduce the following colors: *red, pink, orange, yellow, green, blue, purple, black, white, gray,* and *brown.*

THE MODEL CONVERSATION
10 MINUTES

1. **SETTING THE SCENE:** Have students look at the model photograph. Set the scene: "Two friends are talking."

2. **LISTENING:** With books closed, have students listen to the model conversation—presented by you, by a pair of students, or on the audio program. Check students' understanding of the situation and the vocabulary.

3. **CLASS PRACTICE:** With books still closed, model each line, and have the whole class practice in unison.

4. **READING:** With books open, have students follow along as two students present the model.

5. **PAIR PRACTICE:** In pairs, have students practice the model conversation.

THE CONVERSATION EXERCISES
10 MINUTES

1. **THE SKELETAL DIALOG:** Write the "skeletal dialog" on the board. Fill in a replacement color to show students how the guided conversation method works. Call on a few pairs of students to practice the dialog, using the skeletal framework on the board.

> A. What's your favorite color?
> B. <u>Red</u>.

2. **VOCABULARY PRESENTATION:** Point to each color in the panel on the left side of the page, say the word, and have the class repeat it chorally and individually. Check students' understanding and pronunciation of the vocabulary.

3. **EXERCISE PRACTICE:** (optional) Have pairs of students simultaneously practice conversations.

4. **EXERCISE PRESENTATIONS:** Call on pairs of students to present their conversations to the class.

LANGUAGE IN *MOTION*
10 MINUTES

1. Have students walk around the classroom, asking each other about their favorite colors. (For larger classes, you can set a time limit or a limit on how many people students should ask.)

2. Have students report what they found out.

   a. Write the following on the board:

   > _____'s favorite color is _____.

   b. Call on students to tell you about students they interviewed. For example:

   > Michael's favorite color is red.
   > Carla's favorite color is purple.

WHAT ARE THEY WEARING?
10 MINUTES

Point out that the task is to identify the colors of the clothes. Have students work individually to complete the exercise and then compare answers in pairs.

Note: You may want to point out that the article *a* precedes singular nouns, but there is no article before plural nouns. For example: He's wearing *a* blue suit, *a* red tie, and brown shoes.

Answers

1. He's wearing a <u>blue</u> suit, a <u>red</u> tie, and <u>brown</u> shoes.
2. She's wearing a <u>pink</u> blouse, a <u>gray</u> skirt, and <u>black</u> shoes.
3. He's wearing a <u>yellow</u> sweater, <u>green</u> pants, and <u>white</u> shoes.

WHAT ARE YOU WEARING TODAY?
15 MINUTES

1. **THE SKELETAL DIALOG:** Write the "skeletal dialog" on the board. Fill in a replacement with colors and clothes to show students how

the conversation works. Call on a few pairs of students to practice the dialog, using the skeletal framework on the board.

> A. What are you wearing today?
> B. I'm wearing a white blouse, a gray skirt, and black shoes.

2. **CONVERSATION PRACTICE:** (optional) Have students circulate around the classroom, practicing the conversation with several other students.

3. **CONVERSATION PRESENTATIONS:** Ask several students: "What are you wearing today?"

GUESSING GAME
10 MINUTES

1. Point out the classroom scene that's depicted on student book page 125. The teacher is telling what someone in her class is wearing, and students guess who it is.

2. Model the activity by describing what a student in *your* class is wearing, and then have students guess who it is. For example: "This person is wearing a blue sweater, a white shirt, blue jeans, and black shoes."

3. Have students take turns describing what others in the class are wearing and see if classmates can guess who is being described.

EXPANSION

1. **Listen and Point** ★
   Divide the class into pairs. Have Student A look at the colors on student book page 124. Have Student B say the names of colors in random order. Student A must point to the appropriate color. Then have pairs reverse roles.

2. **Try to Remember!** ★★
   Have pairs of students sit back-to-back and tell the items of clothing the other is wearing. (Don't tell them what they're going to do until after they're seated back-to-back!)

3. **Magazine Pictures** ★★
   Bring in magazine pictures that show people wearing different clothes. As a class, in pairs, or in small groups, have students describe what the people in the pictures are wearing.

4. **Family Photos** ★★
   Have students bring in photos of their family members. In pairs or small groups, have students describe who is in the photo and what

each person is wearing. For example: "This is my sister. She's wearing a pink dress."

5. **Clothing Scavenger Hunt** ★★
   ACTIVITY MASTER 72

   a. Make multiple copies of Activity Master 72 and distribute one to every student.

   b. Have students walk around the classroom (or the school), find people who are wearing those items, and write their names to complete the sentences.

   c. The first student to match people with all the clothing items is the winner.

6. **Remember the Picture Game** ★★
   Show students a magazine picture or catalog page of clothing items for two to three minutes. Turn the picture over. Have students tell you what they remember, or have them write sentences.

7. **Dictate the Picture Game** ★★★

   a. Bring to class a full-length magazine picture of a person who is wearing colorful clothes.

   b. Divide the class into pairs—Student A and Student B. Have all the Student A's come outside the classroom with you. Show them the picture, and have them spend a few minutes talking about what the person in the picture is wearing and the clothing colors.

   c. Have the Student A's return to the classroom and give them three minutes to dictate to their Student B partners what they remembered from the picture. The pair that has written the most words (colors and clothing items) wins the game.

   d. For correction, have each pair call out a phrase on their list. Write that phrase on the board so students can check their spelling.

   e. Repeat the game with a new picture for Student B's to dictate to their Student A partners.

8. **A Fashion Show** ★★★
   Put on a fashion show! Have students describe each other's clothing as if they were modeling in a fashion show. For example: "Maria is wearing a blue blouse, red pants, and a black belt."

   Note: Prepare students by telling them to come to the next class wearing their most colorful clothes.

LESSON OBJECTIVE

Focus

Clothing sizes

Vocabulary

large
medium
size
small

GETTING READY   5–10 MINUTES

Introduce *size* vocabulary.

1. Draw and label three boxes on the board—one *small*, one *medium*, and one *large*:

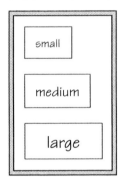

small

medium

large

2. Tell students that many articles of clothing come in these sizes—for example: gloves, sweaters, and jackets. Have students practice saying the size name.

3. Write on the board names of articles of clothing and some common sizes. For example:

Women's Clothes											
shirts, pants, dresses:	2	4	6	8	10	12	14	16			
shoes:	5	5½	6	6½	7	7½	8	8½	9	9½	10
Men's Clothes											
pants:	32	34	36	38	40	42	44	46			
shoes:	7	7½	8	8½	9	9½	10	10½	11	11½	12

Have students practice saying the size number.

THE MODEL CONVERSATION   5–10 MINUTES

1. **SETTING THE SCENE:** Have students look at the model photograph. Set the scene: "A customer and a salesperson are talking in a department store."

2. **LISTENING:** With books closed, have students listen to the model conversation—presented by you, by a pair of students, or on the audio program. Check students' understanding of the situation and the vocabulary.

3. **CLASS PRACTICE:** With books still closed, model each line, and have the whole class practice in unison.

4. **READING:** With books open, have students follow along as two students present the model.

5. **PAIR PRACTICE:** In pairs, have students practice the model conversation.

THE CONVERSATION EXERCISES   10–20 MINUTES

1. **THE SKELETAL DIALOG:** Write the "skeletal dialog" on the board. Fill in the replacement from Exercise 1 to show students how the guided conversation method works. Call on a few pairs of students to practice Exercise 1, using the skeletal framework on the board.

> A. I'm looking for a <u>sweater</u>.
> B. What size?
> A. <u>Medium</u>.

2. **VOCABULARY PRESENTATION:** Present the vocabulary words in the exercises. Point to the photograph of each item, say the size and clothing item, and have the class repeat it chorally and individually. Check students' understanding and pronunciation of the vocabulary.

3. **EXERCISE PRACTICE:** (optional) Have pairs of students simultaneously practice all the exercises.

4. **EXERCISE PRESENTATIONS:** Call on pairs of students to present their conversations to the class.

WHAT SIZE DO YOU WEAR? 10 MINUTES

1. **THE SKELETAL DIALOG:** Write the "skeletal dialog" on the board. Fill in a few replacements to show students how the conversation works. Call on a few pairs of students to practice the dialog, using the skeletal framework on the board.

> A. What size <u>shirt</u> do you wear?
> B. <u>Small</u>.
>
> A. What size <u>pants</u> do you wear?
> B. <u>Size 32</u>.

2. **VOCABULARY PRESENTATION:** Present the vocabulary words in the exercises. Point to the illustration of each item say the size and clothing item, and have the class repeat it chorally and individually. (Students have already learned small, medium, and large. Introduce size *extra-large*.) Check students' understanding and pronunciation of the vocabulary.

3. **EXERCISE PRACTICE:** (optional) Have pairs of students simultaneously practice conversations.

4. **EXERCISE PRESENTATIONS:** Call on pairs of students to present their conversations to the class.

PROBLEMS WITH CLOTHING 10 MINUTES

1. **INTRODUCE THE NEW VOCABULARY:** Point to each picture and say the phrase. Have students repeat them chorally and individually.

2. **WRITE THE CORRECT WORDS:** Read the first question, and then have students complete the conversation based on the illustration to the left of the skeletal dialog.

3. **PRACTICE THE CONVERSATION:** With books closed, model each line, and have the whole class practice in unison. Then, with books open, have students follow along as two students present the model. Finally, have students practice the model conversation in pairs.

4. **ADDITIONAL PRACTICE:** Have pairs of students create conversations about other clothing items with problems. Call on pairs to present their conversations to the class.

COMMUNITY CONNECTIONS 10 MINUTES

Explain that in the first column of the chart, students should write three different types of clothing items they bought. In the second column, they write the name of the store where they bought each item, and in the third column, they tell the location of each store. Have students complete the chart with their own information, and then meet in small groups to share their information.

EXPANSION

1. **Stand In Line!** ★
   a. Have students stand up and arrange themselves in a line according to shoe size. Students ask each other: "What size shoes do you wear?"

   b. Once students are arranged, have each student say his or her shoe size, starting with the smallest shoe size first.

   Variation: Once students are arranged, have them try to guess everybody's shoe size.

2. **My Personal Size Information** ★★
   ACTIVITY MASTER 73

   a. Make multiple copies of Activity Master 73 and distribute one to every student.

   b. Individually, have students complete the chart, using the measurement information at the bottom of the Activity Master to help them determine their sizes.

   Note: Bring several measuring tapes to class to help students determine their sizes.

3. **Size Scavenger Hunt** ★★
   ACTIVITY MASTER 74

   a. Make multiple copies of Activity Master 74 and distribute one to every student. Tell students that for this activity, they will ask people: "What size shirt do you wear?", "What size shoes do you wear?", etc.

b. Have students walk around the classroom (or the school), find people who wear those sizes, and write their names to complete the sentences.

c. The first student to match people with all the sizes is the winner.

4. **Ordering from a Catalog** ★★★

Bring in clothing catalogs and distribute them to students. Tell students they have to order a complete outfit for a spouse, child, or friend. Have students fill in the order form with the clothing description, size, color, and price information.

5. **Everybody Likes a Bargain!** ★★★

After students share their information in Community Connections, have them talk in their small groups about which stores have the best bargains (the lowest prices). As students report to the class, write a master list on the board of students' favorite bargain stores and their locations.

Variation: You can publish a *Clothing Shopping Guide* and distribute it to members of the class for their reference.

LESSON OBJECTIVE

FOCUS
Prices

VOCABULARY
price

GETTING READY
10 MINUTES

1. Review numbers 1–100 in one or more of the following ways:

   a. Count together with the class from 1 to 100.

      Variation: Everybody clap their hands while counting.

   b. Have students sit in a circle. Student 1 starts counting: "One." Student 2 continues: "Two," and so forth around the circle, continuing up to 100. (Students can also count by two's, three's, five's, or ten's. For example 2, 4, 6, 8, 10, 12 . . . .)

2. Write some dollar prices on the board. Read the first few examples to the class. Then invite students to read the remaining examples. For example:

   $14.00—fourteen dollars
   $25.00—twenty-five dollars
   $59.00—fifty-nine dollars
   $36.00—thirty-six dollars

3. Write some dollar and cent prices on the board. Read the first few examples to the class. Then invite students to read the remaining examples. For example:

   $14.50—fourteen fifty
   $25.45—twenty-five forty-five
   $59.99—fifty-nine ninety-nine
   $36.49—thirty-six forty-nine

THE MODEL CONVERSATIONS
10 MINUTES

There are two model conversations. Introduce and practice the first model before going on to the second. For each model:

1. **SETTING THE SCENE:** Have students look at the model illustration. Set the scene: "A customer is asking a salesclerk about the price of different items."

2. **LISTENING:** With books closed, have students listen to the model conversation—presented by you, by a pair of students, or on the audio program. Check students' understanding of the situation and the vocabulary.

3. **CLASS PRACTICE:** With books still closed, model each line, and have the whole class practice in unison.

4. **READING:** With books open, have students follow along as two students present the model.

5. **PAIR PRACTICE:** In pairs, have students practice the model conversation.

THE CONVERSATION EXERCISES
10–20 MINUTES

1. **THE SKELETAL DIALOG:** Write the "skeletal dialog" on the board. Fill in the replacement from Exercise 1 to show students how the guided conversation method works. Call on a few pairs of students to practice Exercise 1, using the skeletal framework on the board.

   > A. What's the price of the <u>dresses</u>?
   > B. <u>Forty-two dollars</u>.

2. **VOCABULARY PRESENTATION:** Present the vocabulary words on student book page 128. Point to the illustration of each item, say the name and price of each item, and have the class repeat them chorally and individually. Check students' understanding and pronunciation of the vocabulary.

3. **EXERCISE PRACTICE:** (optional) Have pairs of students simultaneously practice all the exercises.

4. **EXERCISE PRESENTATIONS:** Call on pairs of students to present their conversations to the class.

EXPANSION

1. **Stand in Order: Numbers** ✶
   ACTIVITY MASTER 75

   Make a copy of Activity Master 75 and cut it into cards. (*Note*: For this activity, use just the number cards in the left column of the Activity Master.) Give each student a *number* card, and have students stand up and arrange themselves in order, according to the number they have, starting from the lowest to the highest price.

2. Number Dictation ⭐

Divide the class into pairs. Have Student A choose a price on student book page 128 and dictate it to Student B, who writes it down. Have Student A check Student B's answer. Then reverse roles.

3. Price Concentration ⭐⭐
ACTIVITY MASTER 75

a. Divide the class into pairs. Make multiple copies of Activity Master 75, cut them into cards, and give each pair of students one set of cards. Have students shuffle the cards and place them face-down in four rows of 5 each.

b. The object of the game is for students to find the matching cards. Both students should be able to see the cards, since *concentrating* on their location is an important part of playing the game.

c. Student A turns over two cards, and if they match, the student keeps the cards. If the cards don't match, the student turns them face-down and Student B takes a turn.

d. The game continues until all the cards have been matched. The student with the most correct *matches* wins the game.

4. Listen for the Price ⭐⭐

a. Read the following sentences, and have students write down the price they hear:

> The shirts are $14.99.
> The pants are $55.00.
> The ties are $65.00.
> The socks are $1.99.
> The shoes are $88.50.
> The umbrellas are $10.50.
> The coats are $56.99.
> The necklaces are on sale for $99.99.
> The brown gloves are on sale for $40.75.
> The blue sweaters are on sale for $39.00.

b. Have pairs of students check each other's answers.

5. Price Match Game ⭐⭐
ACTIVITY MASTER 75

a. Make a copy of Activity Master 75, cut it into cards, and distribute the cards randomly, one to each student.

b. Have students look at their card and identify the price. Then have students circulate around the room saying the prices on their cards until they find their match. Make sure students don't show their cards to their classmates since this is a listening and speaking exercise.

c. When students have found their match, have them compare their cards and come

show you. Continue until students have found all the matches.

6. Information Gap ⭐⭐⭐
ACTIVITY MASTER 76

a. Make multiple copies of Activity Master 76 and cut them in half (Table A and Table B).

b. Divide the class into pairs. Give each partner a different table—A or B. Have students share their information and fill in their tables. For example:

> A. What's the price of the shirts?
> B. Sixteen ninety-nine.

c. When the pairs have finished completing their tables, have them look at their partner's tables to make sure they have written the information correctly.

7. Family Photos ⭐⭐⭐

Have students bring in photos that show special clothing from their countries, or have students bring in or wear clothing from their countries. In pairs, small groups, or as a class, have students talk about their photos and clothing. Encourage students to talk about what colors are typically worn and the differences between men's, women's, and children's clothing.

8. Special Events ⭐⭐⭐

a. Write the following special events on the board:

> weddings
> funerals
> New Year's Eve

b. As a class, in pairs, or in small groups, have students tell what they wear in their countries for these events.

LANGUAGE EXPERIENCE JOURNAL

Have students write about their favorite clothing item. Depending on your students' writing abilities, either have them write in their journal or dictate their story for you to write. Then students should read what they have written to a classmate. If time permits, you may also want to write a response in each student's journal, sharing your own opinions and experiences as well as reacting to what the student has written.

UNIT ACTIVITIES

Different Cultures *Different Ways* — 10 MINUTES

Have students first work in pairs or small groups, reacting to the photographs and responding to the questions. Then have students share with the class what they have talked about.

PUT IT TOGETHER — 15–20 MINUTES

In this activity, students talk with each other to find out what they do every day.

1. Review ordinal numbers 1st to 5th.
2. Divide the class into pairs: Student A and Student B.
3. Tell all the Student A's to look at Part A of the activity on page 129. Tell all the Student B's to look at Part B on page 130.
4. Have everybody look at the first item on the list: *Shoes.*
   a. Have all the Student B's look at their list. In Student B's list in the second column, it says, *1*. Therefore, when Student A asks: "Where are shoes?", Student B answers: "Shoes are on the first floor."
   b. Ask all the Student B's: "Where are shoes?" Have all the Student B's respond in unison: "Shoes are on the first floor."
5. Have everybody look at the second item on the list: *Coats.*
   a. Have all the Student A's look at their list. In their list in the second column, it says, *3*. Therefore, when Student B asks: "Where are coats?", Student A answers: "Coats are on the third floor."
   b. Ask all the Student A's: "Where are coats?" Have all the Student A's respond in unison: "Coats are on the third floor."
6. The Student A and Student B pairs are now ready to continue the activity with the rest of the words on their lists.
7. When the pairs have completed the activity, have them check each other's answers.

VOCABULARY FOUNDATIONS — 5–10 MINUTES

Have students review the list of words they have learned in this unit. Encourage students to get a small notebook where they can write down vocabulary that is new for them. If students have personal copies of dictionaries or picture dictionaries, have them look up these words in the dictionary and highlight them with a marker. Encourage them to look at their notebooks or dictionaries frequently to review what they have learned.

For additional practice, have students do one or more of the following activities.

1. **Taking Notes** ★
   In their vocabulary notebooks or on a piece of paper, have students write all the words in one column. In a second column, have them write notes, draw pictures, or write the word in a sentence that will help them remember the meaning of the words.

2. **Clap in Rhythm** ★
   Object: Once a clapping rhythm is established, the students must continue naming different clothing items.
   a. Have students sit in a circle.
   b. Establish a steady, even beat: one-two-three-four, one-two-three-four, etc., by having students clap their hands to their laps twice, and then clap their hands together twice. Repeat throughout the game, maintaining the same rhythm.
   c. The object is for each student in turn to name a different word from Unit 9 *each time their hands are clapped together*. Nothing is said when students clap their hands on their laps.

   Note: The beat never stops! If a student misses a beat, he or she can either wait for the next beat or pass to the next student.

3. **Scrambled Words** ★
   a. Choose words from the unit and write them on the board or on a card with the letters scrambled out of order. For example:

   ```
   neacckle
   ```

   b. Have students take turns guessing what the word is. [necklace]

   Variation 1: Do the activity in pairs or small groups, with students taking turns scrambling words for others to guess.

   Variation 2: Do the activity as a class game with competing teams.

4. Match Game ✶✶

ACTIVITY MASTER 77

a. Make a copy of Activity Master 77, cut it into cards, and distribute the cards randomly, one to each student.

b. Have students memorize the question or response on their card and leave their cards on their desks. Then have students circulate around the room, saying their lines until they find their match.

c. When students have found their match, have them compare their cards and come show you. Then give each student another card to keep the game going. Continue until students have found all the matches.

5. What Do You Wear? ✶✶✶

Ask students what they usually wear to a certain place. For example:

What do you wear to work?
What do you wear to church/temple/mosque?
What do you wear to a soccer game?
What do you wear to a wedding?

LANGUAGE SKILL FOUNDATIONS
10–15 MINUTES

Explain to students that this is a list of skills they have learned in the unit. Students should become familiar with the vocabulary of describing their skills, but they don't need to master all the terms. For each speaking skill on the list, read the skill aloud to students, and have them demonstrate it. For example:

Teacher: I can ask for clothing in the store.
Students: I'm looking for pants.

(If students don't understand the vocabulary of a particular speaking skill, give them a concrete example rather than a description or explanation, and then have students practice your example and others.)

Have students put a check next to each skill if they feel they have learned it. Use this information to determine which lessons you may want to review or reinforce for the entire class or for particular students. The Getting Ready and Expansion activities for this unit and the CD-ROM's Activity Bank of supplemental worksheets are excellent resources for additional practice. It may also be helpful to have stronger students or, if available, a classroom aide or volunteer, work with students who need more practice.

Talk About It! ▶▶▶ (Page 131)
20–30 MINUTES

(Page 131 is also available as a transparency.)

Use the scenes in this illustration to review the vocabulary and conversations in the unit. Have students first work in pairs or small groups to talk about the illustration and answer the question posed at the bottom of the page. Then discuss as a class.

For additional motivating practice, students will enjoy doing one or more of the following activities.

These activities review Unit 9 vocabulary:

1. Can You Find Them? ✶

Call out any of the following items, and have students locate them in the illustration on student book page 131:

a blue suit
a pink necklace
pink and green necklaces
green sweaters
blue shoes
green jackets
pink dresses
a yellow and blue tie
blue socks
green shoes
grey gloves
brown belts
yellow and blue jackets

Variation: Copy this list and hand it out to pairs of students. Have students work with their partners to locate all the objects.

2. The Longest List ✶

a. In pairs or small groups, have students make a list of all the clothing items they see in the illustration. Tell students to cover the list of words on student book page 130 with a piece of paper so they don't refer to that list. (Set a five-minute time limit for this activity.)

b. Tell students to stop when the five minutes are up. Ask students to count the number of items on their lists. Who has the longest list?

c. Check students' answers by calling on students to name items on their lists. Write the words on the board, and have students check their spelling.

Variation: ✶✶ To make this task more challenging, have students list the clothing items and their colors. For example: blue socks,

(continued)

purple shirts, green skirts, a blue suit, a pink necklace.

3. Remember the Words! ✷✷

a. Tell students to spend two minutes looking carefully at the illustration on student book page 131.

b. Have students close their books and write down all the clothing items and colors they remember from the illustration.

c. Have students compare notes with a partner, and then look at the illustration again to see how well they remembered the clothing items and colors of this unit.

These activities review Unit 9 conversations and grammar:

4. True or False? ✷✷

Make statements about the scenes on student book page 131, and have students decide if the statements are true or false. If a statement is false, have students correct it. For example:

Women's clothes are on the third floor. [True.]
Men's clothes are on the first floor. [False. Men's clothes are on the second floor.]
Men's pants are on sale. [True.]
Belts are $9.99. [False. They're $19.99.]

5. Who Is It? ✷✷

a. Have students look at the transparency or the illustration on student book page 131.

b. Describe a character in the illustration, and have students point to that person. For example:

Teacher: She's wearing an orange shirt, a red necklace, and gray pants.
Students: [*Point to the woman looking at necklaces.*]

Teacher: He's wearing a blue suit. It's too large for him.
Students: [*Point to the man looking in the mirror.*]

Teacher: She's wearing a purple shirt and blue pants.
Students: [*Point to the woman looking at shoes.*]

Variation: Divide the class into pairs. One student describes a character and the other points to the appropriate character in the illustration. Then reverse roles.

6. Questions and Answers ✷✷✷

a. Write the following questions on the board:

```
Where are the _____?
What's the price of the _____?
```

b. Divide the class into pairs. Have students take turns asking and answering questions about the clothing in the illustration. For example:

A. Where are the pants?
B. Over there [*pointing to the pants in the illustration*].

A. What's the price of the pants?
B. Thirty-seven fifty.

7. Do You Remember? ✷✷

Tell students to spend two minutes looking carefully at the illustration on student book page 131. Then have students close their books. Ask students questions about the illustration. For example:

What the price of the sweaters? [$32.50.]
What's the price of the belts? [$19.99.]
Are there watches? [Yes.]
What colors are the men's shirts? [Blue, pink, yellow, and green.]
How many customers are in the store? [Ten.]
What colors are the women's skirts? [Brown and green.]

Variation: Do the activity as a game with competing teams.

8. What Are They Saying? ✷✷✷

a. Have pairs of students look at the transparency or the illustration on student book page 131.

b. Have the students in each pair choose a character in one of the scenes and work together to create a conversation that the character might have with a salesclerk in the store. For example:

Salesclerk: May I help you?
Customer: Yes. I'm looking for shoes.
Salesclerk: What size?
Customer: Size ten.
Salesclerk: Size ten shoes are over there.

c. Call on the pairs to present their conversations to the class. Have other students listen and then identify the character in the book or transparency.

Variation: Have students write out the conversations they created for each scene.

UNIT 10   THE BANK & POST OFFICE

LESSONS & UNIT ACTIVITIES	OBJECTIVES	TEXT	TEACHER'S GUIDE
Vocabulary Preview	Bank items • Postal Items	132–133	168
LESSON 1 Where's the checkbook?	Bank	134–135	169–171
LESSON 2 I'm writing a check.	Checks	136–137	172–173
LESSON 3 I want to buy stamps.	Post office	138–139	174–175
LESSON 4 NUMBERS: Your change is $2.50.	Making change	140	176–177
Language Experience Journal	Writing about ways to save money	140	177
Different Cultures / Different Ways	Identifying bills and coins in different countries	141	178
Put It Together	Information Gap / Teamwork activity	141–142	178
Vocabulary Foundations / Language Skill Foundations	Review & skills checklist	142	178–179
Talk About It!	Review, conversations, activities, & games	143	179–180

UNIT RESOURCES

Audio Program:
    Audio CD 4: Tracks 2–11
    Audio Cassette 3B

Workbooks:
    Activity Workbook
    Literacy Workbook

Lesson Planner CD-ROM:
    Activity Masters 78–87
    Activity Bank Unit 10 Worksheets

Vocabulary Photo Cards: 191–202

Transparency: Color Overhead for Unit 10, page 143

PREVIEW 5 MINUTES

Activate students' prior knowledge of bank and post office vocabulary by doing any or all of the following:

1. Have students brainstorm bank and post office items and write them on the board.

2. Bring in the actual bank and post office items for students to identify.

3. Have students look at the photographs on student book pages 132 and 133 while they cover the words at the bottom of the page. Have students identify the words they already know.

PRESENT 10 MINUTES

Using the photographs on student book pages 132 and 133, or the actual bank and post office items themselves, point to each item, say the word, and have the class repeat it chorally and individually. (You can also play the audio program.) Check students' understanding and pronunciation of the vocabulary.

PRACTICE 10 MINUTES

As a class, in pairs, or in small groups, have students practice the vocabulary in either or both of the following ways:

• Say or write a word, and have students point to the item in their books or tell the number.

• Point to a photograph in the book or give the number, and have students say the word.

SPELLING PRACTICE 5 MINUTES

Say a word, and have students spell it aloud or write it. Or point to an item in the student book, and have students write the word. You can also spell a portion of a word on the board, and have students come to the board to complete it.

EXPANSION

1. Tell and Show ★

PHOTO CARDS 191–202

Place the Photo Cards in a pile at the front of the classroom. Have students take turns coming up the front of the class, selecting a Photo Card, and telling the class the item without showing the card. Have the rest of the students point to the item on student book page 132 or 133.

2. Listen and Point ★

Divide the class into pairs. Have Student A cover the words on student book pages 132 and 133 and look just at the photos. Have Student B read the words in random order. Student A must point to the appropriate photo. Then have pairs reverse roles.

3. Match Game ★

PHOTO CARDS 191–202 (TWO SETS)

a. Choose duplicate copies of any Photo Cards and distribute them randomly, one to each student.

b. Have students look at their card and identify the item. Then have students circulate around the room, saying the name of the item on their card until they find their match. Make sure students don't show their cards to their classmates since this is a listening and speaking exercise.

c. When students have found their match, have them compare their cards and come show you.

LESSON OBJECTIVE

FOCUS

Bank

VOCABULARY

ATM card
bank book
check
checkbook
credit card
deposit slip
withdrawal slip

GETTING READY
5 MINUTES

Use the photos on student book page 134, or the objects themselves to introduce the following vocabulary items: *checkbook, check, bank book, ATM card, credit card, deposit slip,* and *withdrawal slip.* Say each word, and have the class repeat it chorally and individually. Check students' understanding and pronunciation of the vocabulary.

THE MODEL CONVERSATION
10 MINUTES

1. **SETTING THE SCENE:** Have students look at the model photograph. Set the scene: "A wife and husband are talking."

2. **LISTENING:** With books closed, have students listen to the model conversation—presented by you, by a pair of students, or on the audio program. Check students' understanding of the situation and the vocabulary.

3. **CLASS PRACTICE:** With books still closed, model each line, and have the whole class practice in unison.

4. **READING:** With books open, have students follow along as two students present the model.

5. **PAIR PRACTICE:** In pairs, have students practice the model conversation.

THE CONVERSATION EXERCISES
10–20 MINUTES

1. **THE SKELETAL DIALOG:** Write the "skeletal dialog" on the board. Fill in the replacement from Exercise 1 to show students how the guided conversation method works. Call on a few pairs of students to practice Exercise 1, using the skeletal framework on the board.

> A. Where's the <u>check</u>?
> B. Here it is.

2. **VOCABULARY PRESENTATION:** Present the vocabulary words in the exercises. Point to the photograph of each item, say the word, and have the class repeat it chorally and individually. Check students' understanding and pronunciation of the vocabulary.

3. **EXERCISE PRACTICE:** (optional) Have pairs of students simultaneously practice all the exercises.

4. **EXERCISE PRESENTATIONS:** Call on pairs of students to present their conversations to the class.

LISTENING
5–10 MINUTES

Listen and write the number under the correct picture.

1. A. Where's the deposit slip?
   B. The deposit slip? Here it is.
2. A. Where's my ATM card?
   B. Your ATM card? Here it is.
3. A. Where's the check?
   B. The check is on the table.
4. A. Where's the withdrawal slip?
   B. The withdrawal slip? Here it is.
5. A. I'm looking for the checkbook.
   B. The checkbook is in the living room.
6. A. I'm looking for my credit card.
   B. I think your credit card is in the kitchen.

Answers

3	6	1
2	4	5

MATCHING
5 MINUTES

Have students complete the activity individually and then share their answers in pairs, small groups, or as a class.

Answers

1. checkbook.
2. deposit slip.
3. credit card.
4. withdrawal slip.
5. ATM card.

Model the activity. Make a chart on the board similar to the chart on student book page 135. Interview one student, using the questions in the speech bubbles, and write that student's answers in the chart. Then have each student interview four other students in the class and complete the chart in the book with those students' answers.

E X P A N S I O N

1. Concentration ★
PHOTO CARDS 191–197 (TWO SETS)

a. Shuffle the cards and place them face-down in two rows of 7 each.

b. Divide the class into two teams. The object of the game is for students to find the matching cards and identify the vocabulary item. Both teams should be able to see the cards, since *concentrating* on their location is an important part of playing the game.

c. A student from Team 1 turns over two cards, and if they match, the student must identify the item. If the student correctly identifies the item, that team keeps the cards, and the student takes another turn. If they don't match or if the student isn't able to correctly identify the item, the student turns them face-down, and a member of Team 2 takes a turn.

d. The game continues until all the cards have been matched. The team with the most correct *matches* wins the game.

Variation:
PHOTO CARDS 191–197
ACTIVITY MASTER 78

Have the class play with one set of Photo Cards and one set of Word Cards.

2. Scrambled Words ★
a. Choose words from the lesson and write them on the board or on a card with the letters scrambled out of order. For example:

```
stopedi  pils
```

b. Have students take turns guessing what the word is. [deposit slip]

Variation 1: Do the activity in pairs or small groups, with students taking turns scrambling words for others to guess.

Variation 2: Do the activity as a class game with competing teams.

3. Alphabetize! ★
ACTIVITY MASTER 78

a. Make copies of Activity Master 78 and cut them into cards.

b. Have students work in pairs. Give each pair a set of cards, and have them work together to place the words in alphabetical order.

c. Have the first pair to complete the alphabetization write their list on the board. Go over the list with the class.

4. Paper or Plastic? ★★
a. Have students make two columns on a piece of paper. Have them write Paper at the top of the left column and Plastic at the top of the right column.

b. Dictate words from the lesson, and have students write them in the appropriate column. For example:

Paper	Plastic
check	credit card
bank book	ATM card
deposit slip	

c. After students have written down a word, write it on the board so students can check their answers.

5. What Can You Do in a Bank? ★★
a. Divide the class into pairs or small groups. Have students make a list of all the things they can do in a bank. For example:

cash a check
make a deposit
take out money
apply for a loan
use an ATM machine

b. Compare students' lists and make a master list on the board.

6. A Trip to the Bank ★★
Have students go to a bank and do one or more of the following:

a. Copy down all the printed words and phrases they want to understand. Have a class discussion about the words that students report back.

b. Bring to class deposit and withdrawal slips and practice filling them out.

c. Find out the fees for different kinds of checking accounts and what the names for these accounts are and then report back to the class.

7. Using an ATM Machine ✮✮✮

If students have access to the Internet, have them visit a banking website that instructs them on how to use an ATM card (for example: www.beehive.org). Afterward, in class, review the ATM phrases and vocabulary. See if students can remember the steps in using an ATM machine.

8. Put in Order ✮✮✮

ACTIVITY MASTER 79

Divide the class into pairs. Make multiple copies of Activity Master 79, cut them into cards, and distribute a set to each pair. Have students read the cards and put the steps in order. To check their answers, have students take turns reading the steps aloud.

9. A Classroom Visitor ✮✮✮

Arrange with a local bank for a representative to speak to your class about basic checking and savings accounts. Have students prepare questions before the visit and make sure that each student has a prepared question to ask.

LESSON OBJECTIVE

Focus
Checks

GETTING READY
5 MINUTES

Using the check depicted below the model photograph, ask the following questions:

- What's the date? (June 15, 2009)
- Who is the check to? (Wilson's Department Store)
- How much is the check for? ($87.50)
- Who signed the check? (Marta Ramirez)

THE MODEL CONVERSATION
10 MINUTES

1. **SETTING THE SCENE:** Have students look at the model photograph. Set the scene: "A husband and wife are talking."

2. **LISTENING:** With books closed, have students listen to the model conversation—presented by you, by a pair of students, or on the audio program. Check students' understanding of the situation and the vocabulary.

3. **CLASS PRACTICE:** With books still closed, model each line, and have the whole class practice in unison.

4. **READING:** With books open, have students follow along as two students present the model.

5. **PAIR PRACTICE:** In pairs, have students practice the model conversation.

THE CONVERSATION EXERCISES
10–15 MINUTES

1. **THE SKELETAL DIALOG:** Write the "skeletal dialog" on the board. Fill in the replacement from Exercise 1 to show students how the guided conversation method works. Call on a few pairs of students to practice Exercise 1, using the skeletal framework on the board.

> A. What are you doing?
> B. I'm writing a check to <u>Dr. Harrison</u>.
> A. For how much?
> B. <u>$95.00</u>.

2. **VOCABULARY PRESENTATION:** Present the vocabulary words in the exercises. Point to the each check and ask: "Who is the check to?" and "How much is the check for?" Check students' understanding and pronunciation of the vocabulary.

3. **EXERCISE PRACTICE:** (optional) Have pairs of students simultaneously practice all the exercises.

4. **EXERCISE PRESENTATIONS:** Call on pairs of students to present their conversations to the class.

WRITING CHECKS
15 MINUTES

1. Using the check in Exercise 1, point out that the amount of the check is written in numbers *and* in words. To prepare students for doing the exercise, write on the board a few other check amounts in numbers and words.

2. Have students work individually to complete the checks and then compare their answers in pairs. Circulate around the classroom to check students' work.

EXPANSION

1. **Concentration** ★
ACTIVITY MASTER 80

   a. Divide the class into pairs. Make multiple copies of Activity Master 80, cut them into cards and give each pair of students one set of cards. Have students shuffle the cards and place them face-down in two rows of 4 each.

   b. The object of the game is for students to find the matching cards. Both students should be able to see the cards, since *concentrating* on their location is an important part of playing the game.

   c. Student A turns over two cards, and if they match, the student keeps the cards. If the cards don't match, the student turns them face-down, and Student B takes a turn.

   d. The play continues until all the cards have been matched. The student with the most correct *matches* wins the game.

2. Write Me a Check ✶✶

ACTIVITY MASTER 81

a. Make copies of Activity Master 81 and distribute one to each student.

b. Have each student use the blank check to write a check to another student in the class, for any amount that student wishes.

c. Write on the board the following skeletal dialog. As students are filling in their checks, circulate around the room, interviewing each student, using the skeletal conversation as a guide.

> Teacher: What are you doing?
> Student: I'm writing a check to _____?
> Teacher: For how much?
> Student: _____.

LESSON OBJECTIVE

FOCUS
Post office

VOCABULARY
air letter
money order
package
registered letter
stamps

buy
mail
send

GETTING READY
5 MINUTES

1. Use your own visuals, the objects themselves, or the photos on student book page 138 to introduce the following new vocabulary items: *stamps, package, registered letter, money order,* and *air letter.*

2. Explain that in a post office, the place where each postal clerk works is called a *window.*

THE MODEL CONVERSATION
10 MINUTES

1. **SETTING THE SCENE:** Have students look at the model photograph. Set the scene: "A customer is talking to a postal clerk in the post office."

2. **LISTENING:** With books closed, have students listen to the model conversation—presented by you, by a pair of students, or on the audio program. Check students' understanding of the situation and the vocabulary.

3. **CLASS PRACTICE:** With books still closed, model each line, and have the whole class practice in unison.

4. **READING:** With books open, have students follow along as two students present the model.

5. **PAIR PRACTICE:** In pairs, have students practice the model conversation.

THE CONVERSATION EXERCISES
10 MINUTES

1. **THE SKELETAL DIALOG:** Write the "skeletal dialog" on the board. Fill in the replacement from Exercise 1 to show students how the guided conversation method works. Call on

a few pairs of students to practice Exercise 1, using the skeletal framework on the board.

> A. I want to <u>mail a package</u>.
> B. You can <u>mail a package</u> at the next window.
> A. Thank you.

2. **VOCABULARY PRESENTATION:** Present the vocabulary words in the exercises. Point to the photographs, say the words, and have the class repeat them chorally and individually. Check students' understanding and pronunciation of the vocabulary.

3. **EXERCISE PRACTICE:** (optional) Have pairs of students simultaneously practice all the exercises.

4. **EXERCISE PRESENTATIONS:** Call on pairs of students to present their conversations to the class.

MATCHING
5 MINUTES

Tell students that their task is to match the post office windows to the post office items. Have them work individually to complete the exercise, and then compare answers in pairs.

Answers

2   1   5   3   4

AN ENVELOPE
10 MINUTES

1. Point to each part of the envelope on student book page 139 and introduce the new vocabulary: *mailing address* and *return address*.

2. Have students answer the questions individually and then compare answers in pairs or with the class.

Answers

Roberta Fernandez
977 Westwood Avenue, Los Angeles, CA 90024
Henry Wong
1415 Center Street, Boston, MA 02218

COMMUNITY CONNECTIONS

Have students go to a local post office and find out when that post office opens and closes. There is usually a sign that tells the post office hours. If not, they should ask a postal clerk. Have students complete the chart. In the next class, have students compare their information in small groups. Follow-up by asking the class: "Which post office is open the most hours?"

Note: It's also possible to obtain this information on the United States Postal Service website at www.USPS.com under the tab "locate a post office."

EXPANSION

1. Disappearing Dialog ✶

Write the model conversation on the board and ask for two student volunteers to read the conversation. Erase a few of the words from the dialog, and have two different students read the conversation. Erase more words and call on two more students to read it. Continue erasing words and calling on pairs of students until everyone has had a turn and the dialog has *disappeared*.

2. Concentration ✶

PHOTO CARDS 198–202 (TWO SETS)

a. Shuffle the cards and place them face-down in two rows of 5 each.

b. Divide the class into two teams. The object of the game is for students to find the matching cards and identify the vocabulary item. Both teams should be able to see the cards, since *concentrating* on their location is an important part of playing the game.

c. A student from Team 1 turns over two cards, and if they match, the student must identify the item. If the student correctly identifies the item, that team keeps the cards, and the student takes another turn. If they don't match or if the student isn't able to correctly identify the item, the student turns them face-down, and a member of Team 2 takes a turn.

d. The game continues until all the cards have been matched. The team with the most correct *matches* wins the game.

Variation:
PHOTO CARDS 198–202
ACTIVITY MASTER 82

Have the class play with one set of Photo Cards and one set of Word Cards.

3. What Can You Do? ✶

a. Divide the class into pairs or small groups. Have students make a list of all the things they can do at the post office. For example:

> buy stamps
> mail a letter
> buy an aerogramme
> mail an air letter
> send a package
> send a registered letter
> buy a money order

b. Compare students' lists and make a master list on the board.

4. Chain Game ✶✶

Have students sit in a circle. Begin the activity by saying: "At the post office, you can buy stamps." Student 1 repeats what you said and adds another post office action—for example: "At the post office you can buy stamps and mail packages." Student 2 repeats what you and Student 1 said and adds another post office action. Continue around the circle in this fashion, with each student repeating what the previous student said and adding another activity. Do the activity again, beginning and ending with different students.

5. Put in Order ✶✶

ACTIVITY MASTER 83

Divide the class into pairs. Make multiple copies of Activity Master 83, cut them into cards, and distribute one set to each pair. Have students read the cards and put the steps in order. To check their answers, have students take turns reading the steps aloud.

6. Information Gap: Reading an Envelope ✶✶✶

ACTIVITY MASTER 84

a. Make multiple copies of Activity Master 84 and cut them in half (Envelope A and Envelope B).

b. Divide the class into pairs. Give each partner a different envelope—A or B. Have students share their information and complete their envelopes. For example:

> A. What's the return address?
> B. 99 Central Avenue, Chicago, Illinois 60649
> A. How do you spell Illinois?
> B. I-L-L-I-N-O-I-S.

c. When students have finished completing their envelopes, have them look at their partner's envelopes to make sure they have written the information correctly.

7. Send Me a Letter! ✶✶✶

Give each student a piece of paper the size of an envelope. Dictate the information that goes on an envelope for students to write in the appropriate place.

8. Post Office Forms ✶✶✶

Get samples of different forms from the post office. Discuss the use of each and the information that is required on each. Have students practice filling them out.

LESSON OBJECTIVE

FOCUS

Making change

VOCABULARY

change

GETTING READY
5 MINUTES

Before introducing the model conversation, write the following on the board and refer to it as you introduce the model:

```
  $20.00
– $17.50
  $2.50
```

THE MODEL CONVERSATION
10 MINUTES

1. **SETTING THE SCENE:** Have students look at the model photograph. Set the scene: "A cashier and a customer are talking in a store."

2. **LISTENING:** With books closed, have students listen to the model conversation—presented by you, by a pair of students, or on the audio program. Check students' understanding of the situation and the vocabulary.

3. **CLASS PRACTICE:** With books still closed, model each line, and have the whole class practice in unison.

4. **READING:** With books open, have students follow along as two students present the model.

5. **PAIR PRACTICE:** In pairs, have students practice the model conversation.

THE CONVERSATION EXERCISES
10 MINUTES

1. For students weak in math skills, you can do one of the following:

   • Give students several minutes to work individually on the math problems, and then go over the answers with the class.

   • Write the problems and their answers on the board for students to copy into their books.

$40.00	$10.00	$5.00
– 36.00	– 8.50	– 3.20
$4.00	$1.50	$1.80
$50.00	$100.00	$60.00
– 42.40	– 94.80	– 56.90
$7.60	$5.20	$3.10

2. **THE SKELETAL DIALOG:** Write the "skeletal dialog" on the board. Fill in the replacement from Exercise 1 to show students how the guided conversation method works. Call on a few pairs of students to practice Exercise 1, using the skeletal framework on the board.

> A. That's <u>thirty-six dollars</u>.
> B. Here's <u>forty dollars</u>.
> A. Your change is <u>four dollars</u>.

3. **EXERCISE PRACTICE:** (optional) Have pairs of students simultaneously practice all the exercises.

4. **EXERCISE PRESENTATIONS:** Call on pairs of students to present their conversations to the class.

EXPANSION

1. **Listen for the Money** ☆

   a. Read the following sentences, and have students write down the amount of money they hear:

That's $42.00.	Your change is $9.15.
That's $40.02.	Your change is $9.50.
That's $3.16.	Your change is $8.26.
That's $3.60.	Your change is $18.36.
Here's $10.00.	Your change is $2.19.
Here's $8.00.	
Here's $12.00.	
Here's $75.00.	

   b. After dictating each item, write the number on the board so students can check their answers.

2. How Much Change? ★★

ACTIVITY MASTER 85

a. Write the following on the board:

> A. That's _____.
> B. Here's _____ dollars.
> A. Your change is _____.

b. Make multiple copies of Activity Master 85 and give one to each student. Have students work individually to complete the chart.

c. Have students compare their charts in pairs and then practice conversations, using the model on the board. Circulate to listen in on student conversations and provide feedback when necessary.

d. Call on pairs to present conversations to the class.

3. Dialog Match Game: Your Change Is . . . ★★

ACTIVITY MASTER 86

a. Make a copy of Activity Master 86, cut it into cards, and give each student a card.

b. Half the class will have dialog cards with a missing line for Speaker B. The other students have those missing Speaker B lines on their cards. Students with the dialogs should circulate around the room, saying their Speaker A lines. Students with the missing Speaker B lines should circulate around the room, saying their lines until they have found their matching dialog.

c. When students have found their matches, have them present their dialogs to the class.

4. Tips for Saving Money ★★★

a. Write the following list on the board:

> Groceries
> Clothes
> Babysitting
> Housing
> Medicine

b. In small groups, have students talk about how they save money on each of the items on the list.

c. Ask students to share their ideas with the class. Write their ideas on the board. For example:

> Groceries
> use coupons
> buy food on sale
>
> Medicine
> buy large amounts

LANGUAGE EXPERIENCE JOURNAL

Have students write about the ways they save money. Depending on your students' writing abilities, either have them write in their journal or dictate their story for you to write. Then students should read what they have written to a classmate. If time permits, you may also want to write a response in each student's journal, sharing your own opinions and experiences as well as reacting to what the student has written.

Different Cultures, *Different Ways* — 10 MINUTES

Have students first work in pairs or small groups, reacting to the photograph and responding to the questions. Then have students share with the class what they have talked about.

PUT IT TOGETHER — 15–20 MINUTES

In this activity, students talk with each other to find out the prices for items in a fast-food restaurant.

1. Divide the class into pairs: Student A and Student B.

2. Tell all the Student A's to look at Part A of the activity on page 141. Tell all the Student B's to look at Part B on page 142.

3. Have everybody look at the first item on the list: *A hot dog.*

   a. In Student B's list, next to *A hot dog,* it says, *$1.75.* Therefore, when Student A asks: "How much is a hot dog?", Student B answers: "A hot dog is $1.75."

   b. Ask all the Student B's: "How much is a hot dog?" Have all the Student B's respond in unison: "A hot dog is $1.75."

4. Have everybody look at the second item on the list: *A hamburger.*

   a. Have all the Student A's look at their list. In their list next to *A hamburger,* it says, *$2.25.* Therefore, when Student B asks: "How much is a hamburger?", Student A answers: "A hamburger is $2.25."

   b. Ask all the Student A's: "How much is hamburger?" Have all the Student A's respond in unison: "A hamburger is $2.25."

5. The Student A and Student B pairs are now ready to continue the activity with the rest of the words on their lists.

6. When the pairs have completed the activity, have them check each other's answers.

VOCABULARY FOUNDATIONS — 5–10 MINUTES

Have students review the list of words they have learned in this unit. Encourage students to get a small notebook where they can write down vocabulary that is new for them. If students have personal copies of dictionaries or picture dictionaries, have them look up these words in the dictionary and highlight them with a marker. Encourage them to look at their notebooks or

dictionaries frequently to review what they have learned.

For additional practice, have students do one or more of the following activities.

1. **Taking Notes** ✶

   In their vocabulary notebooks or on a piece of paper, have students write all the words in one column. In a second column, have them write notes, draw pictures, or write the word in a sentence that will help them remember the meaning of the words.

2. **Scrambled Words** ✶

   a. Choose words from the unit and write them on the board or on a card with the letters scrambled out of order. For example:

   b. Have students take turns guessing what the word is. [coins]

   Variation 1: Do the activity in pairs or small groups, with students taking turns scrambling words for others to guess.

   Variation 2: Do the activity as a class game with competing teams.

3. **Listen and Point** ✶

   To review the vocabulary on the list, have students return to the Vocabulary Preview on student book pages 132 and 133.

   Divide the class into pairs. Have Student A cover the words and look just at the photos. Have Student B read the words in random order. Student A must point to the appropriate photo. Then have pairs reverse roles.

4. **Category Dictation** ✶✶

   a. Have students make two columns on a piece of paper:

      bank
      post office

   b. Dictate words from Vocabulary Foundations, and have students write them in the appropriate column. Make sure all students have covered the vocabulary items on student book page 142 with a piece of paper so they don't refer to that list.

c. As a class, in pairs, or in small groups, have students check their work.

5. Mixed-Up Words ✷✷
ACTIVITY MASTER 87

a. Divide the class into groups of four. Make a copy of Activity Master 87 for each group. Cut the Activity Masters into cards, and place them in two piles (one pile for the wide cards and the other for the narrow cards).

b. Distribute the two sets of cards to each group. Have students take turns picking up one card from each pile and reading the two words to the group. For example:

withdrawal		letter

The group decides if the words fit together or not.

c. After all the cards have been picked, have the group lay out all the cards and put together all the word combinations that make sense.

6. Money Around the World ✷✷✷
Have students bring in coins and bills from their country. As a class, in pairs, or in small groups, have students talk about the people, the scenes, or the images represented on the money.

7. Class Discussion ✷✷✷
As a class, in pairs, or in small groups, have students discuss the following questions:

Are ATM machines common in your country?
Are credit cards common in your country?
How do you pay your bills? Do you write checks? Do you use money orders? Do you pay on the Internet? Do you pay at a store?

LANGUAGE SKILL FOUNDATIONS   10–15 MINUTES

Explain to students that this is a list of skills they have learned in the unit. Students should become familiar with the vocabulary of describing their skills, but they don't need to master all the terms. For each speaking skill on the list, read the skill aloud to students, and have them demonstrate it. For example:

Teacher: I can obtain post office services.
Students: I want to buy stamps.

(If students don't understand the vocabulary of a particular speaking skill, give them a concrete example rather than a description or explanation, and then have students practice your example and others.)

Have students put a check next to each skill if they feel they have learned it. Use this information to determine which lessons you may want to review or reinforce for the entire class or for particular students. The Getting Ready and Expansion activities for this unit and the CD-ROM's Activity Bank of supplemental worksheets are excellent resources for additional practice. It may also be helpful to have stronger students or, if available, a classroom aide or volunteer, work with students who need more practice.

Talk About It! ▶▶▶   (Page 143)   20–30 MINUTES

(Page 143 is also available as a transparency.)

Use the scenes in this illustration to review the vocabulary, conversations, and grammar in the unit. Have students first work in pairs or small groups to talk about the illustration and answer the questions posed at the bottom of the page. Then discuss as a class.

For additional motivating practice, students will enjoy doing one or more of the following activities.

These activities review Unit 10 vocabulary:

1. The Longest List ✷✷

a. In pairs, have students write all the things they see in the scenes on student book page 143. Tell students to cover the list of words on student book page 142 with a piece of paper so they don't refer to that list. (Set a three-minute time limit for this activity.)

b. Tell students to stop when the three minutes are up. Ask students to count the number of items on their lists. Who has the longest list?

c. Check students' answers by calling on students to name items on their lists. Write the words on the board, and have students check their spelling.

2. Do You Remember? ✷✷
Tell students to spend two minutes looking carefully at the scenes on student book page 143. Have students close their books and write down all the things they remember from the illustration. Have students compare notes with a partner and then look at the illustration again to see how well they remembered it.

3. True or False? ✶✶

Make statements about the characters in the scenes on student book page 143, and have students decide if the statements are true or false. If a statement is false, have students correct it. For example:

> This woman is making a deposit. [True.]
> This man is withdrawing $100. [False. He's withdrawing $50.]
> This women wants to mail a registered letter. [False. She wants to mail a package.]
> This woman is writing a check. [True.]

4. What Are They Saying? ✶✶✶

a. Have pairs or small groups of students look at the transparency or the illustration on student book page 143.

b. Point to two characters in one of the scenes, and have the students in each pair or group work together to create a conversation between those characters.

c. Call on students to present their conversations to the class.

d. One at a time, point to another two people talking on page 143 until students have created and presented conversations between all the characters in the illustration.

Variation 1: Have pairs or small groups of students create a conversation based on one of the scenes, present it to the class, and the other students point to the appropriate scene in the book or on the transparency.

Variation 2: Have students write out the conversations they created for each scene.

5. The "Write" Person! ✶✶✶

a. Divide the class into pairs. Have each pair choose one character in the illustration on student book page 143 and write two sentences about that person. For example:

> [*the woman taking money out of the ATM*]
> She's taking money out of the bank.
> She's next to an ATM.

b. Have the pairs read their sentences to the class and see if students can guess who is being described.

UNIT 11 HEALTH

LESSONS & UNIT ACTIVITIES	OBJECTIVES	TEXT	TEACHER'S GUIDE
Vocabulary Preview	Parts of the body • Ailments	144–145	182
LESSON 1 What's the matter?	Parts of the body • Ailments	146–147	183–185
LESSON 2 You should use cough syrup.	Medicine	148–149	186–188
LESSON 3 I want to make an appointment.	Making a doctor's appointment • Injuries • Medicine	150–151	189–191
LESSON 4 Exercise 30 minutes a day.	Medical advice • Staying healthy • Calling for an ambulance	152–153	192–194
LESSON 5 NUMBERS: One pill three times a day.	Dosages	154	195–197
Language Experience Journal	Writing about ailments and remedies	154	197
Different Cultures / Different Ways	Remedies in different cultures	155	198
Put It Together	Information Gap / Teamwork activity	155–156	198
Vocabulary Foundations / Language Skill Foundations	Review & skills checklist	156	198–199
Talk About It!	Review, conversations, activities, & games	157	199–200

UNIT RESOURCES

Audio Program:
  Audio CD 4: Tracks 12–28
  Audio Cassette 3B
Workbooks:
  Activity Workbook
  Literacy Workbook

Lesson Planner CD-ROM:
  Activity Masters 88–100
  Activity Bank Unit 11 Worksheets
Vocabulary Photo Cards: 203–223
Transparency: Color Overhead for Unit 11, page 157

PARTS OF THE BODY (PAGE 144)

PREVIEW 5 MINUTES

Activate students' prior knowledge of the vocabulary. Have students point to parts of the body and say the words they already know. As they tell you the words, write them on the board.

PRESENT 5–10 MINUTES

Using the photographs on student book page 144 or your own body, point to each part or say its number, say the word, and have the class repeat it chorally and individually. (You can also play the audio program.) Check students' understanding and pronunciation of the vocabulary.

PRACTICE 5 MINUTES

As a class, in pairs, or in small groups, have students practice the vocabulary in either or both of the following ways:

- Say or write a word, and have students point to the item in their books or tell the number.
- Point to the photograph in the book or on your own body, and have students say the word.

SPELLING PRACTICE 5 MINUTES

Say a word, and have students spell it aloud or write it. Or point to a body part in the student book or on your own body, and have students write the word. You can also spell a portion of a word on the board, and have students come to the board to complete it.

AILMENTS (PAGE 145)

PREVIEW 5 MINUTES

Activate students' prior knowledge. Have students tell you words for ailments they already know. As they tell you the words, write them on the board.

PRESENT 5–10 MINUTES

Using the photographs on student book page 145 or using mime to illustrate each ailment, point to each item or say its number, say the word, and have the class repeat it chorally and individually. (You can also play the audio program.)

PRACTICE 5 MINUTES

As a class, in pairs, or in small groups, have students practice the vocabulary in either or both of the following ways:

- Say or write a word, and have students point to the item in their books or tell the number.
- Point to a photograph in the book or give the number, and have students say the word.

SPELLING PRACTICE 5 MINUTES

Say a word, and have students spell it aloud or write it. Or mime an ailment, and have students write the word. You can also spell a portion of a word on the board, and have students come to the board to complete it.

EXPANSION

1. Touch and Tell ★
ACTIVITY MASTER 88

Make a copy of Activity Master 88, cut it into cards, and place them in a pile in the front of the classroom. Have students take turns coming up to the front of the class, picking a card from the pile, and pointing to that part of the body without showing the card to the class. The class then says what the part of the body is.

2. Miming Game ★
PHOTO CARDS 203–211

Place the cards on a desk or table in the front of the room. Have students take turns coming to the front of the room, picking a card, and pantomiming the ailment on the card. The class tries to guess the ailment.

Variation: Do the activity as a game with teams. Set a 30-second time limit for each turn. If the team can't guess the ailment within the time limit, the card is returned to the pile and the other team takes its turn with a new card.

3. True or False? ★★

Point to various body parts or mime ailments. Make a false statement about the body part or ailment, and have students correct it. For example:

Teacher: [*pointing to your head*] This is my foot.
Students: No. It's your head.

Teacher: [*miming a cough*] I have a backache.
Students: No. You have a cough.

LESSON OBJECTIVE

FOCUS

Parts of the body
Ailments

VOCABULARY

backache	headache
cold	sore throat
cough	stomachache
earache	toothache
fever	

GETTING READY
5 MINUTES

Use your own visuals, mime and gestures, or the photos on student book page 146 to introduce the following new vocabulary: *headache, stomachache, backache, earache, toothache, sore throat, cold, cough,* and *fever*.

THE MODEL CONVERSATION
10 MINUTES

1. **SETTING THE SCENE:** Have students look at the model photograph. Set the scene: "Two co-workers are talking."

2. **LISTENING:** With books closed, have students listen to the model conversation—presented by you, by a pair of students, or on the audio program. Check students' understanding of the situation and the vocabulary.

3. **CLASS PRACTICE:** With books still closed, model each line, and have the whole class practice in unison.

4. **READING:** With books open, have students follow along as two students present the model.

5. **PAIR PRACTICE:** In pairs, have students practice the model conversation.

THE CONVERSATION EXERCISES
10–20 MINUTES

1. **THE SKELETAL DIALOG:** Write the "skeletal dialog" on the board. Fill in the replacement from Exercise 1 to show students how the guided conversation method works. Call on a few pairs of students to practice Exercise 1, using the skeletal framework on the board.

> A. What's the matter?
> B. I have a <u>stomachache</u>.

2. **VOCABULARY PRESENTATION:** Present the vocabulary words in the exercises. Point to the photograph of each item, say the word, and have the class repeat it chorally and individually. Check students' understanding and pronunciation of the vocabulary.

3. **EXERCISE PRACTICE:** (optional) Have pairs of students simultaneously practice all the exercises.

4. **EXERCISE PRESENTATIONS:** Call on pairs of students to present their conversations to the class.

GRAMMAR
10–15 MINUTES

1. Write the following on the board:

> I have
> You have
> He has
> She has

2. Tell about an ailment, using the first-person subject pronoun. For example: "I have a headache."

3. Start a sentence with "You", and have a student complete it the same way. For example:

> Teacher: You . . .
> Student: You *have a headache.*

4. Continue with "He" and "She."

5. Do the same with different ailments from student book page 146.

6. Have students work individually to complete the sentences on student book page 147 and then compare answers with a partner. Then call on individual students for the answers.

Answers

1. has
2. have
3. has
4. have
5. have
6. has

LISTENING
5 MINUTES

Listen and write the number under the correct picture.

1. She has a headache.
2. He has a cold.

3. I have a backache.
4. He has a toothache.
5. She has a cough.

Answers

3   5   4   1   2

PARTS OF THE BODY | 10 MINUTES

1. **THE SKELETAL DIALOG:** Write the "skeletal dialog" on the board. Fill in a replacement to show students how the guided conversation method works. Call on a few pairs of students to practice the dialog, using the skeletal framework on the board. For example:

   > A. What's the matter?
   > B. My _neck_ hurts.

2. **CONVERSATION PRACTICE:** (optional) Have students circulate around the classroom, practicing the conversation with several other students.

3. **CONVERSATION PRESENTATION:** Call on pairs to present their conversations to the class. (Have Student B point to the body part that *hurts*.)

E X P A N S I O N

1. **Concentration** ★

   PHOTO CARDS 203–211 (TWO SETS)

   a. Shuffle the cards and place them face-down in three rows of 6 each.

   b. Divide the class into two teams. The object of the game is for students to find the matching cards and identify the ailment. Both teams should be able to see the cards, since *concentrating* on their location is an important part of playing the game.

   c. A student from Team 1 turns over two cards, and if they match, the student must identify the ailment—for example: "She has a toothache." If the student correctly identifies the item, that team keeps the cards, and the student takes another turn. If they don't match or if the student isn't able to correctly identify the item, the student turns them face-down, and a member of Team 2 takes a turn.

   d. The game continues until all the cards have been matched. The team with the most correct *matches* wins the game.

Variation:

PHOTO CARDS 203–211
ACTIVITY MASTER 89

Have the class play with one set of Photo Cards and one set of Word Cards.

2. **Scrambled Words** ★

   a. Choose words from the lesson and write them on the board or on a card with the letters scrambled out of order. For example:

   b. Have students take turns guessing what the word is. [hand]

   Variation 1: Do the activity in pairs or small groups, with students taking turns scrambling words for others to guess.

   Variation 2: Do the activity as a class game with competing teams.

3. **The Letter Game** ★

   Divide the class into two teams. Say: "I'm thinking of a body part that starts with *b*." The first person to raise his or her hand and guess correctly (*back*), wins a point for the team. Continue with the other letters of the alphabet.

4. **Mime the Ailment** ★

   ACTIVITY MASTER 88

   a. Write the following on the board:

   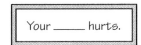

   b. Make a copy of Activity Master 88, cut it into cards, and put the cards in a pile on a table or desk in the front of the classroom.

   c. Have students take turns coming to the front of the room, picking a card, and miming that part of the body being *hurt*. The class guesses the student's problem—for example: "Your neck hurts.", "Your leg hurts."

   Variation: Do the activity as a game with teams. Set a 30-second time limit for each turn. If the team can't guess the ailment within the time limit, the card is returned to the pile and the other team takes its turn with a new card.

5. **Telephone** ★★

   a. Have students sit in a circle or semicircle. Make up a sentence, using the new vocabulary in this lesson, and whisper it to Student 1. For example:

> Jane has a fever, a sore throat, a headache, and her neck hurts.

b. The first student whispers what he or she heard to the second student, who whispers it to the third student, and so forth. When the message gets to the last student, that person says it aloud. Is it the same message you started with?

Give each student in the class a chance to start his or her own message.

6. Memory Game ★★

Begin the activity by saying: "I feel terrible. I have a headache." Student 1 repeats what you said and adds another ailment—for example: "I feel terrible. I have a headache and an earache." Student 2 repeats what you and Student 1 said and adds another ailment—for example: "I feel terrible. I have a headache, an earache, and a toothache." Continue around the room in this fashion, with each student repeating what the previous student said and adding another ailment. Do the activity again, beginning and ending with different students.

7. Category Dictation ★★

a. Have students make two columns on a piece of paper. Have them write I have at the top of the left column and My _____ hurts at the top of the right column.

b. Dictate words from the lesson, and have students write the words in the appropriate column. For example:

I have	My _____ hurts
a sore throat	ear
a cold	foot

c. After students have written down a word, write it on the board so students can correct their work.

8. Ranking ★★★

a. Have students look at the ailments on student book page 146 and choose the four ailments they have most often. Have students then rank these items from one to four, with one being the one they have most often. For example:

1. backache
2. sore throat
3. cough
4. cold

b. As a class, in pairs, or in small groups, have students compare their lists.

LESSON OBJECTIVE

Focus

Medicine

Vocabulary

aisle
antacid tablets
aspirin
cold medicine

cough syrup
ear drops
throat lozenges

GETTING READY
5 MINUTES

Introduce medicine vocabulary. Use your own visuals, the photos on student book page 148, or the actual objects themselves to introduce the following medicine items: *cough syrup, aspirin, ear drops, cold medicine, antacid tablets,* and *throat lozenges.* Tell students that these are things that people should use when they don't feel well.

THE MODEL CONVERSATION
10 MINUTES

1. **SETTING THE SCENE:** Have students look at the model photograph. Set the scene: "A wife and husband are talking."

2. **LISTENING:** With books closed, have students listen to the model conversation—presented by you, by a pair of students, or on the audio program. Check students' understanding of the situation and the vocabulary.

3. **CLASS PRACTICE:** With books still closed, model each line, and have the whole class practice in unison.

4. **READING:** With books open, have students follow along as two students present the model.

5. **PAIR PRACTICE:** In pairs, have students practice the model conversation.

THE CONVERSATION EXERCISES
10–15 MINUTES

1. **THE SKELETAL DIALOG:** Write the "skeletal dialog" on the board. Fill in the replacement from Exercise 1 to show students how the guided conversation method works. Call on a few pairs of students to practice Exercise 1, using the skeletal framework on the board.

> A. I have <u>a headache</u>. What should I do?
> B. You should use <u>aspirin</u>.

2. **VOCABULARY PRESENTATION:** Present the vocabulary words in the exercises. Point to the photograph of each item, say the word, and have the class repeat it chorally and individually. Check students' understanding and pronunciation of the vocabulary.

3. **EXERCISE PRACTICE:** (optional) Have pairs of students simultaneously practice all the exercises.

4. **EXERCISE PRESENTATIONS:** Call on pairs of students to present their conversations to the class.

LISTENING
5–10 MINUTES

Listen and write the number next to the correct medicine.

1. I have a cough. What should I use?
2. I have an earache. What should I use?
3. I have a stomachache. What should I use?
4. I have a sore throat. What should I use?
5. I have a headache. What should I use?

Answers

5 1 3 2 4

MATCHING
5–10 MINUTES

Have students match the two phrases and then compare their answers with a partner. Then call on individual students to tell you the answers.

Answers

1. ear drops.
2. cough syrup.
3. cold medicine.
4. antacid tablets.
5. throat lozenges.

WHERE CAN I FIND COUGH SYRUP?

THE MODEL CONVERSATION
10 MINUTES

1. Use your own visual or the illustration on student book page 149 to introduce the word *aisle.*

2. **SETTING THE SCENE:** Have students look at the model photograph. Set the scene: "A customer is talking to a pharmacist in a drug store."

3. **LISTENING:** With books closed, have students listen to the model conversation—presented

by you, by a pair of students, or on the audio program. Check students' understanding of the situation and the vocabulary.

4. **CLASS PRACTICE:** With books still closed, model each line, and have the whole class practice in unison.

5. **READING:** With books open, have students follow along as two students present the model.

6. **PAIR PRACTICE:** In pairs, have students practice the model conversation.

THE CONVERSATION EXERCISES
10 MINUTES

1. **THE SKELETAL DIALOG:** Write the "skeletal dialog" on the board. Fill in a replacement to show students how the guided conversation method works. Call on a few pairs of students to practice the dialog, using the skeletal framework on the board.

> A. Excuse me. Where can I find <u>aspirin</u>?
> B. Look in Aisle <u>2</u>.
> A. Thank you.

2. **EXERCISE PRACTICE:** (optional) Have pairs of students simultaneously practice the conversation, starting with *Aisle 1.*

3. **EXERCISE PRESENTATIONS:** Call on pairs of students to present their conversations to the class.

EXPANSION

1. **True or False?** ✶
PHOTO CARDS 212–217

Show students various Photo Cards. Make a false statement about the item, and have students correct it. For example:

> Teacher: [*showing the class Photo Card 213*] This is cough syrup.
> Students: No. It's aspirin.
>
> Teacher: [*showing the class Photo Card 214*] These are throat lozenges.
> Students: No. They're ear drops.

2. **Finish the Sentence!** ✶
Divide the class into two teams. Begin sentences, and have members of each team take turns finishing them with an appropriate kind of medicine. For example:

> When I have a headache, I use . . . *aspirin.*
> When I have a sore throat, I use . . . *throat lozenges.*

The team with the most correctly completed sentences wins.

3. **Alphabetize!** ✶
ACTIVITY MASTER 90

a. Make copies of Activity Master 90 and cut them into cards.

b. Have students work in pairs. Give each pair a set of cards, and have them work together to place the medicines in alphabetical order.

c. Have the first pair to complete the alphabetization write their list on the board. Go over the list with the class.

4. **Match Game** ✶✶
ACTIVITY MASTER 91

a. Make a copy of Activity Master 91, cut it into cards, and distribute the cards randomly, one to each student.

b. Have students memorize the sentence on their card and leave their cards on their desks. Then have students circulate around the room, saying their lines until they find their match.

c. When students have found their match, have them compare their cards and come show you.

5. **Medical Advice** ✶✶

a. Tell students to think of an ailment. Then call on individual students to tell what they *have.* For example:

> I have a cold.
> I have a cough.

b. Other students then give advice. For example:

> You should use cold medicine.
> You should use cough syrup.

6. **Name That Brand!** ✶✶✶

a. With the help of the class, make a list of popular name brands, such as:

> aspirin: Bayer®
> throat lozenges: Hall's®
> antacid tablets: Tum's®
> cough syrup: Robitussin®

b. As a class, in pairs, or in small groups, have students tell which popular brands they use.

7. **How Much Are They?** ✶✶✶
Bring in drug store flyers and distribute to pairs of students. Have students locate ads for the

(continued)

medicines on student book page 148 and write down the prices for these medicines.

8. Comparison Shopping ✭✭✭

ACTIVITY MASTER 92

a. Make multiple copies of Activity Master 92 and give one to each student.

b. Explain to students that *brand-name* products are usually more expensive than *generic* products. They are made by different companies, but the medicine is the same. If possible, bring in an example of a brand-name product and its generic counterpart.

c. Have students visit a local drug store and write down the prices of generic and brand-name medicines to complete their charts.

d. In the next class, have students compare their results.

9. The Local Drug Store ✭✭✭

a. Have students visit a neighborhood drug store and write down the aisle numbers of the following items:

   aspirin
   ear drops
   throat lozenges
   cold medicine
   antacid tablets

b. Write on the board the names of the drug stores they visited and ask students where the medicines are located at this store. Students answer according to the information they found. For example:

   Teacher: Where can I find aspirin at
            Well-Mart?
   Student: Look in Aisle 4.

LESSON OBJECTIVE

FOCUS

Making a doctor's appointment
Injuries
Medicine

VOCABULARY

appointment
doctor's office

face
wrist

broke (irregular past of *break*)
burned (regular past of *burn*)
cut (irregular past of *cut*)
sprained (regular past of *sprain*)

GETTING READY   10 MINUTES

1. Review ailments and injuries.

   a. Write the following on the board:

   > What's the problem?

   b. Mime an ailment for students—for example, a stomachache. Encourage students to ask: "What's the problem?" You answer: "I have a stomachache."

   c. Ask for several student volunteers to mime ailments, and have the class ask: "What's the problem?"

2. Review time expressions by drawing clock faces on the board and asking students: "What time is it?"

THE MODEL CONVERSATION   10 MINUTES

1. **SETTING THE SCENE:** Have students look at the model photographs. Set the scene: "Someone is calling the doctor's office."

2. **LISTENING:** With books closed, have students listen to the model conversation—presented by you, by a pair of students, or on the audio program. Check students' understanding of the situation and the vocabulary.

3. **CLASS PRACTICE:** With books still closed, model each line, and have the whole class practice in unison.

4. **READING:** With books open, have students follow along as two students present the model.

5. **PAIR PRACTICE:** In pairs, have students practice the model conversation.

THE CONVERSATION EXERCISES   10 MINUTES

1. **THE SKELETAL DIALOG:** Write the "skeletal dialog" on the board. Fill in replacements to show students how the guided conversation method works. Call on a few pairs of students to practice the dialog, using the skeletal framework on the board.

   > A. Doctor's Office.
   > B. Hello. This is _(name of student in the class)_. I want to make an appointment.
   > A. What's the problem?
   > B. *I have a fever.*
   > A. Can you come in tomorrow at 10:30?
   > B. Yes. That's fine.

2. **EXERCISE PRACTICE:** (optional) Have pairs of students simultaneously practice the conversation, using ailments they have learned in Unit 11.

3. **EXERCISE PRESENTATIONS:** Call on pairs of students to present their conversations to the class.

LISTENING   5–10 MINUTES

Listen and write the number under the correct picture.

1. A. What's the problem?
   B. I have an earache.
2. A. What's the problem?
   B. My back hurts.
3. A. What's the matter?
   B. My neck hurts.
4. A. What's the problem?
   B. I have a stomachache.
5. A. What's the matter?
   B. My arm hurts.

Answers

3 5 2 4 1

WHAT HAPPENED?

GETTING READY
5 MINUTES

1. Introduce the following body vocabulary: *wrist* and *face*. Point to that part of the body, say its name, and have students repeat.

2. Use the photos on student book page 151 and appropriate body language to introduce the medical injuries. Model the pronunciation of each sentence, and have students repeat chorally and individually.

THE CONVERSATION EXERCISES
10 MINUTES

1. **THE SKELETAL DIALOG:** Write the "skeletal dialog" on the board. Fill in the replacement from Exercise 1 to show students how the guided conversation method works. Call on a few pairs of students to practice Exercise 1, using the skeletal framework on the board.

> A. What happened?
> B. I broke my arm.
> A. I'm sorry to hear that.

2. **EXERCISE PRACTICE:** (optional) Have pairs of students simultaneously practice all the exercises.

3. **EXERCISE PRESENTATIONS:** Call on pairs of students to present their conversations to the class.

COMMUNITY CONNECTIONS
10–15 MINUTES

Make a chart on the board similar to the chart on student book page 151. Model each line of the conversation (using *a headache* in the first speaker's line), and have the whole class practice in unison. Call on two students to present the conversation. Have a student come to the board and write *Boyer Aspirin* next to *headache* in the chart.

Have students visit a drug store in their community, use the model in the book to ask for the pharmacist's recommendations, and then complete the chart in the book. Have students then report back to the class. Make a master list on the board of all the pharmacists' recommendations.

EXPANSION

1. **Disappearing Dialog** ★
   Write the model conversation on the board and ask for two student volunteers to read the conversation. Erase a few of the words from the dialog, and have two different students read the conversation. Erase more words and call on two more students to read the conversation. Continue erasing words and calling on pairs of students until everyone has had a turn and the dialog has disappeared.

2. **Concentration** ★
   PHOTO CARDS 218–223 (TWO SETS)

   a. Shuffle the cards and place them face-down in two rows of 6 each.

   b. Divide the class into two teams. The object of the game is for students to find the matching cards and identify the vocabulary item. Both teams should be able to see the cards, since *concentrating* on their location is an important part of playing the game.

   c. A student from Team 1 turns over two cards, and if they match, the student must identify the item. If the student correctly identifies the item, that team keeps the cards, and the student takes another turn. If they don't match or if the student isn't able to correctly identify the item, the student turns them face-down, and a member of Team 2 takes a turn.

   d. The game continues until all the cards have been matched. The team with the most correct *matches* wins the game.

   Variation:
   PHOTO CARDS 218–223
   ACTIVITY MASTER 93

   Have the class play with one set of Photo Cards and one set of Word Cards.

3. **Miming Game** ★★
   ACTIVITY MASTER 93

   Make multiple copies of Activity Master 93 and cut them into cards. Place the cards on a desk or table in the front of the classroom. Have students take turns coming to the front of the room, picking a card, and pantomiming the injury on the card. Ask the class: "What happened?" Have the class try to guess the injury.

   Variation: Do the activity as a game with teams. Set a 30-second time limit for each turn. If the team can't guess the injury within the time limit, the card is returned to the pile and the other team takes its turn with a new card.

4. **Telephone** ★★
   a. Have students sit in a circle or semicircle. Make up two sentences, using the new

vocabulary in this lesson, and whisper them to Student 1. For example:

> I want to make an appointment. I sprained my wrist and cut my hand.

b. The first student whispers what he or she heard to the second student, who whispers it to the third student, and so forth. When the message gets to the last student, that person says it aloud. Is it the same message you started with?

Give each student in the class a chance to start his or her own message.

5. Scrambled Sentences ✷✷

ACTIVITY MASTER 94

Divide the class into pairs. Make enough copies of Activity Master 94 for half the class, cut them into cards, and distribute one set to each pair of students. Have students take turns picking up a prompt and then saying the complete sentence.

Variation: Students can write their complete sentences and compare their answers with other pairs.

6. What's the Problem? ✷✷

In pairs, have students practice the model conversation on student book page 150, but this time talk about injuries, using the vocabulary on student book page 151. Have several pairs present their conversations to the class.

7. What Do You Do? ✷✷✷

a. Write the following on the board:

> call 911
> call the doctor
> go to the drug store
> go to the emergency room

b. Call out situations such as the following, and have students tell you what to do. For example:

> I have a cold. What should I do?
> I broke my leg. What should I do?
> I cut my eye. What should I do?
> I have a stomachache and a fever. What should I do?
> My grandmother broke her arm. What should I do?
> I hurt my back. What should I do?
> I have an earache and a sore throat. What should I do?
> My daughter sprained her wrist. What should I do?
> My son has a headache. What should I do?

Variation: Write the situations on the board. Divide the class into groups and have them decide on the best action to take in each situation and then share their ideas with the class.

8. First-Aid ✷✷✷

Have someone certified in basic first-aid visit your classroom. Have students prepare questions before the visit. For example: "What should I do when I burn my hand?"

LESSON OBJECTIVE

FOCUS

Medical advice
Staying healthy
Calling for an ambulance

VOCABULARY

ambulance
checkup
exercise
glass of water
healthy
meal
vitamin

a day
every day/night

fell (past of *fall*)
move
try

GETTING READY   5 MINUTES

Use the illustrations on student book page 152 to introduce the following new vocabulary: *exercise, eat 3 healthy meals a day, drink 6 glasses of water a day, take 1 vitamin a day,* and *sleep 8 hours every night.*

THE MODEL CONVERSATION   10 MINUTES

1. **SETTING THE SCENE:** Have students look at the model photograph. Set the scene: "A doctor and a patient are talking."

2. **LISTENING:** With books closed, have students listen to the model conversation—presented by you, by a pair of students, or on the audio program. Check students' understanding of the situation and the vocabulary.

3. **CLASS PRACTICE:** With books still closed, model each line, and have the whole class practice in unison.

4. **READING:** With books open, have students follow along as two students present the model.

5. **PAIR PRACTICE:** In pairs, have students practice the model conversation.

THE CONVERSATION EXERCISES   10 MINUTES

1. **THE SKELETAL DIALOG:** Write the "skeletal dialog" on the board. Fill in the replacement from Exercise 1 to show students how the guided conversation method works. Call on a few pairs of students to practice Exercise 1, using the skeletal framework on the board. Point out that Student B only repeats the words in purple (the predicate) and not the verb.

> A. I think you should 3 healthy meals a day.
> B. Three healthy meals a day?
> A. Yes.

2. **VOCABULARY PRESENTATION:** Present the vocabulary words in the exercises. Point to the illustrations, and have the class repeat the sentences chorally and individually. Check students' understanding and pronunciation of the vocabulary.

3. **EXERCISE PRACTICE:** (optional) Have pairs of students simultaneously practice all the exercises.

4. **EXERCISE PRESENTATIONS:** Call on pairs of students to present their conversations to the class.

CLOZE READING   10 MINUTES

Remind students that a "cloze reading" is a story with words missing. Tell students that their task is to write the correct words in the blanks. Have students complete the paragraph and then compare answers with a partner.

Option: This is a good opportunity to have students practice checking off items as they move through an exercise. Call on a student to read the example sentence. Have all students check off the word *eat* in the box. Call on a student to read and complete the next sentence. Then have all students check off the word *drink* in the box.

Answers

1. eat
2. drink
3. take
4. exercise
5. sleep
6. go

LANGUAGE IN *MOTION*

1. Model the pronunciation of the questions, and have students repeat after you chorally and individually. Interview one student and write his or her name and responses on the board.

2. Have students circulate around the classroom, interviewing four other students. Set a ten-minute time limit for the survey portion of this activity.

3. Have students share their answers with the class. As a class, in pairs, or in small groups, have students discuss the health survey. Have the class decide if students have good health habits.

Variation: Have each student ask only one question of all his or her classmates and then report the findings to the class. For example: "Three students eat four meals a day. Nine students eat three meals a day. And four students eat two meals a day."

CALLING FOR AN AMBULANCE

15 MINUTES

1. **GETTING READY:** Introduce the new vocabulary: *fell, hurt,* and *ambulance.*

2. **SETTING THE SCENE:** Have students look at the model photograph. Set the scene: "An Emergency Operator is talking to someone who has an emergency."

3. **THE SKELETAL DIALOG:** Write the "skeletal dialog" on the board. Fill in replacements to show students how the guided conversation method works. Call on a few pairs of students to practice the dialog, using the skeletal framework on the board.

> A. Emergency Operator.
> B. My <u>daughter</u> just fell and hurt her head very badly. She can't move. Please send an ambulance.
> A. What's your address?
> B. <u>23 Main Street, Apartment 4A</u>.
> A. And your telephone number?
> B. <u>212-656-3538</u>.
> A. Okay. An ambulance is on the way.

4. **CONVERSATION PRACTICE:** (optional) Have pairs of students simultaneously practice the dialog, using any injury and personal information they wish.

5. **CONVERSATION PRESENTATIONS:** Call on pairs of students to present their conversations to the class.

EXPANSION

1. **Missing Letters** ★

   a. Divide the class into two teams. Draw a series of blanks on the board to represent the letters in a phrase from student book page 152.

   b. Have students from each team take turns calling out letters. If the letter is correct, put it in the appropriate blank and give the team one point. If the letter is incorrect, put it on a list to the side. The team that gets the most points wins the game.

2. **Telephone** ★

   a. Have students sit in a circle or semicircle. Make up four sentences, using the new vocabulary in this lesson, and whisper them to Student 1. For example:

      > I try to stay healthy. I exercise 30 minutes a day. I take a vitamin every day. I go to the doctor every year for a checkup.

   b. The first student whispers what he or she heard to the second student, who whispers it to the third student, and so forth. When the message gets to the last student, that person says it aloud. Is it the same message you started with?

   Give each student a chance to start his or her own message.

3. **Dictation Game** ★★

   a. In large print on a piece of paper, write a list of three or four healthy habits from the lesson. For example:

      > Drink 6 glasses of water a day.
      > Sleep 8 hours a night.
      > Exercise 30 minutes a day.
      > Eat 3 healthy meals a day.

   b. Divide the class into pairs—Student A and Student B. Have all the Student A's come outside the classroom with you. Show them the list of healthy habits, and have them spend a few minutes looking at it and trying to remember the phrases.

   c. Have the Student A's return to the classroom and give them four minutes to dictate what they remembered from the list to their Student B partners. The pair that has the most phrases wins the game.

   d. For correction, have different pairs call out a phrase on their list. Write that phrase

(continued)

on the board so students can check their spelling.

e. Repeat the game with a new list for Student B's to dictate to their Student A partners.

4. Sequencing ★★
ACTIVITY MASTER 95

Divide the class into pairs. Make multiple copies of Activity Master 95, cut them into cards, and distribute one set to every pair. Have the pairs put the telephone conversation in order. Have one pair of students read their correct telephone sequence aloud, as the other students listen and check their sequence.

5. Find the Right Person! ★★★
ACTIVITY MASTER 96

a. Make copies of Activity Master 96 and give one copy to each student.

b. Review the pronunciation of the questions, and have the class repeat chorally and individually. (*Note*: Students are already familiar with the questions. They are from the Health Survey on student book page 153.)

c. Have students walk around the classroom, interviewing their classmates.

d. The first student to complete all the sentences wins the game. Have that student then report back to the class about all the people he or she interviewed.

LESSON OBJECTIVE

Focus

Dosages

Vocabulary

caplet
capsule
pill
tablespoon
tablet
teaspoon

after each meal
before each meal
once
twice

GETTING READY 15 MINUTES

1. Use your own visuals, the illustrations on student book page 154, or the actual objects themselves to introduce the following medicine vocabulary: *pill, tablet, capsule, caplet, teaspoon,* and *tablespoon.*

2. Teach time expressions *once a day, twice a day,* and so on.

   a. Draw a calendar for one week on the board, writing in the times as indicated:

Monday	Tuesday	Wednesday	Thursday	Friday
9:00	9:00	9:00	9:00	9:00

   b. Point to the calendar and say: "I take a pill every day at 9:00. I take a pill *once a day.*" Have students repeat after you chorally and individually.

   c. Add another time to each day on the calendar. For example:

Monday	Tuesday	Wednesday	Thursday	Friday
9:00	9:00	9:00	9:00	9:00
12:00	12:00	12:00	12:00	12:00

   d. Point to the times on the calendar and say to students: "I take a pill every day at 9:00 and at 12:00. I take a pill *twice a day.*" Have students repeat after you chorally and individually.

   e. Continue in the same fashion, adding a third time and fourth time to each day on the calendar.

3. Point out the abbreviations on the medicine bottles:

   1X = once a day
   2X = twice a day
   3X = three times a day
   4X = four times a day

4. Explain:

   1 tablespoon = 3 teaspoons

THE MODEL CONVERSATION 10 MINUTES

1. **SETTING THE SCENE:** Have students look at the model photograph. Set the scene: "A pharmacist and a patient are talking in a drug store."

2. **LISTENING:** With books closed, have students listen to the model conversation—presented by you, by a pair of students, or on the audio program. Check students' understanding of the situation and the vocabulary.

3. **CLASS PRACTICE:** With books still closed, model each line, and have the whole class practice in unison.

4. **READING:** With books open, have students follow along as two students present the model.

5. **PAIR PRACTICE:** In pairs, have students practice the model conversation.

THE CONVERSATION EXERCISES 10 MINUTES

1. **THE SKELETAL DIALOG:** Write the "skeletal dialog" on the board. Fill in the replacement from Exercise 1 to show students how the guided conversation method works. Call on a few pairs of students to practice Exercise 1, using the skeletal framework on the board.

   > A. Here's your medicine. Take <u>one tablet four times a day</u>.
   > B. I understand. <u>One tablet four times a day</u>.
   > A. That's right.

2. **VOCABULARY PRESENTATION:** Present the vocabulary words in the exercises. Point to the illustration of each item, say the word, and have the class repeat it chorally and

individually. Check students' understanding and pronunciation of the vocabulary.

3. **EXERCISE PRACTICE:** (optional) Have pairs of students simultaneously practice all the exercises.

4. **EXERCISE PRESENTATIONS:** Call on pairs of students to present their conversations to the class.

EXPANSION

1. Scrambled Words ★

a. Choose words from the lesson and write them on the board or on a card with the letters scrambled out of order. For example:

b. Have students take turns guessing what the word is. [capsule]

Variation 1: Do the activity in pairs or small groups, with students taking turns scrambling words for others to guess.

Variation 2: Do the activity as a class game with competing teams.

2. Drawing Game ★
ACTIVITY MASTER 97

You will need either an hourglass or a watch with a second hand for the following activity.

a. Make three copies of Activity Master 97. Cut them into cards and place the three sets of cards in three piles on a table or desk in the front of the classroom. Also, have a pad of paper and pencil next to each pile.

b. Divide the class into three teams. Have each team sit together in a different part of the room.

c. When you say: "Go!," a person from each team picks a card from the pile and draws the object. The rest of the team then guesses what the object is.

d. When a team correctly guesses the object, another team member picks a card and draws the object on that card.

e. Continue until each team has guessed all of the objects in their pile.

The team that guesses the objects in the shortest time wins the game.

3. Telephone ★★

a. Have students sit in a circle or semicircle. Make up two sentences, using the new vocabulary in this lesson, and whisper them to Student 1. For example:

> Here's your medicine. Take one teaspoon twice a day.

b. The first student whispers what he or she heard to the second student, who checks to make sure he or she understood it before passing it on: For example:

> Student A: Here's your medicine. Take one teaspoon twice a day.
> Student B: One teaspoon twice a day?
> Student A: That's right.
> Student B: [*to Student C*] Here's your medicine. Take one teaspoon twice a day.

When the message gets to the last student, that person says it aloud. Is it the same message you started with?

Give each student in the class a chance to start his or her own message.

4. Listen and Write ★★

Divide the class into pairs. Say the following dosages, and have students write them in abbreviated forms. Then have the pairs check each other's abbreviations.

> once a day (1X/day)
> twice a day (2X/day)
> three times a day (3X/day)
> four times a day (4X/day)

5. Medicine Label Concentration ★★
ACTIVITY MASTER 98

a. Divide the class into pairs. Make multiple copies of Activity Master 98, cut them into cards, and give each pair of students one set of cards. Have students shuffle the cards and place them face-down in two rows of 10 each.

b. The object of the game is for students to find the matching cards. Both students should be able to see the cards, since *concentrating* on their location is an important part of playing the game.

c. Student A turns over two cards, and if they match, the student keeps the cards. If the cards don't match, the student turns them face-down and Student B takes a turn.

d. The play continues until all the cards have been matched. The student with the most correct *matches* wins the game.

Variation: For lower-level students, make Activity Master 98 into two sets, with ten cards in each set. This simplifies the game. Pairs can then play two games of concentration, once with each set of cards.

6. **Medicine Label Match Game** ✯✯✯

ACTIVITY MASTER 98

a. Make a copy of Activity Master 98, cut it into cards, and distribute the cards randomly, one to each student.

b. Have students look at their card and identify the dosages. Then have students circulate around the room, saying their dosage until they find their match. Make sure students don't show their cards to their classmates since this is a listening and speaking exercise.

c. When students have found their match, have them compare their cards and come show you.

7. **Questions to Ask Your Pharmacist** ✯✯✯

Talk to students about the kinds of questions they should ask a pharmacist about their medication. For example:

How often should I take this medicine?
How long should I take it?
Should I take it with food?
Are there any side effects?

LANGUAGE EXPERIENCE JOURNAL

Have students write about what they do when they are sick. Depending on your students' writing abilities, either have them write in their journal or dictate their story for you to write. Then students should read what they have written to a classmate. If time permits, you may also want to write a response in each student's journal, sharing your own opinions and experiences as well as reacting to what the student has written.

Different Cultures/ *Different Ways* 10 MINUTES

Have students first work in pairs or small groups, reacting to the photographs and responding to the questions. Then have students share with the class what they have talked about.

PUT IT TOGETHER 15–20 MINUTES

In this activity, students talk with each other to find out information about a drug store.

1. Divide the class into pairs: Student A and Student B.

2. Tell all the Student A's to look at Part A of the activity on student book page 155. Tell all the Student B's to look at Part B on page 156.

3. Have everybody look at the first item on the directory: *aspirin.*

   a. In Student B's directory, next to *aspirin,* it says, *Aisle 3.* Therefore, when Student A asks: "Where can I find aspirin?", Student B answers: "Look in Aisle 3."

   b. Ask all the Student B's: "Where can I find aspirin?" Have all the Student B's respond in unison: "Look in Aisle 3."

4. Have everybody look at the second item on the directory: *cold medicine.*

   a. Have all the Student A's look at their directory. In their directory next to *cold medicine,* it says, *Aisle 4.* Therefore, when Student B asks: "Where can I find cold medicine?", Student A answers: "Look in Aisle 4."

   b. Ask all the Student A's: "Where can I find cold medicine?" Have all the Student A's respond in unison: "Look in Aisle 4."

5. The Student A and Student B pairs are now ready to continue the activity with the rest of the words on their directory.

6. When the pairs have completed the activity, have them check each other's answers.

VOCABULARY FOUNDATIONS 5–10 MINUTES

Have students review the list of words they have learned in this unit. Encourage students to get a small notebook where they can write down vocabulary that is new for them. If students have personal copies of dictionaries or picture dictionaries, have them look up these words in the dictionary and highlight them with a marker. Encourage them to look at their notebooks or dictionaries frequently to review what they have learned.

For additional practice, have students do one or more of the following activities.

1. **Taking Notes** ★

   In their vocabulary notebooks or on a piece of paper, have students write all the words in one column. In a second column, have them write notes, draw pictures, or write the word in a sentence that will help them remember the meaning of the words.

2. **Body Part Review** ★

   a. Write the following alphabet letters on the board:

   b. Have students take turns calling out the names of body parts that begin with each letter of the alphabet written on the board. Either you or a student volunteer can write the words on the board next to the appropriate letter. For example:

3. **Scrambled Words** ★

   a. Choose words from the unit and write them on the board or on a card with the letters scrambled out of order. For example:

   b. Have students take turns guessing what the word is. [cold medicine]

   Variation 1: Do the activity in pairs or small groups, with students taking turns scrambling words for others to guess.

   Variation 2: Do the activity as a class game with competing teams.

4. Category Dictation ★★

a. Have students make four columns on a piece of paper:

> body parts
> injuries
> ailments
> medicine

b. Dictate words from Vocabulary Foundations, and have students write them in the appropriate column. Make sure all students have covered the vocabulary items on student book page 156 with a piece of paper so they don't refer to that list.

c. As a class, in pairs, or in small groups, have students check their work.

5. Theme Matching Game ★★

ACTIVITY MASTER 99

a. Make a copy of Activity Master 99, cut it into cards, and give one to each student. Half of the cards are theme headings and half of the cards are lists of items that belong under those theme headings.

b. Have students walk around the room, telling each other the items on their cards until they find their match.

6. Match Game ★★★

ACTIVITY MASTER 100

a. Make a copy of Activity Master 100, cut it into cards, and distribute the cards randomly, one to each student.

b. Have students memorize the question or response on their card and leave their cards on their desks. Then have students circulate around the room, saying their lines until they find their match.

c. When students have found their match, have them compare their cards and come show you.

7. Remedies I Know ★★★

a. Write the following list on the board:

> headache
> stomachache
> sore throat
> backache
> cold
> cough
> earache

b. In pairs or small groups, have students from different cultures discuss what remedies they would use in their countries for these problems.

LANGUAGE SKILL FOUNDATIONS
10–15 MINUTES

Explain to students that this is a list of skills they have learned in the unit. Students should become familiar with the vocabulary of describing their skills, but they don't need to master all the terms. For each speaking skill on the list, read the skill aloud to students, and have them demonstrate it. For example:

Teacher: I can identify ways to stay healthy.
Students: You should exercise 30 minutes a day.

(If students don't understand the vocabulary of a particular speaking skill, give them a concrete example rather than a description or explanation, and then have students practice your example and others.)

Have students put a check next to each skill if they feel they have learned it. Use this information to determine which lessons you may want to review or reinforce for the entire class or for particular students. The Getting Ready and Expansion activities for this unit and the CD-ROM's Activity Bank of supplemental worksheets are excellent resources for additional practice. It may also be helpful to have stronger students or, if available, a classroom aide or volunteer, work with students who need more practice.

Talk About It! ▶▶▶ (Page 157)
20–30 MINUTES

(Page 157 is also available as a transparency.)

Use the scenes in this illustration to review the vocabulary, conversations, and grammar in the unit. Have students first work in pairs or small groups to talk about the illustration and answer the questions posed at the bottom of the page. Then discuss as a class.

For additional motivating practice, students will enjoy doing one or more of the following activities.

These activities review Unit 11 vocabulary:

1. Listen and Point ★

Say any of the following sentences, and have students listen and point to the person in the illustration you're describing.

> She broke her leg.
> She sprained her arm.
> He cut his hand.
> She burned her hand.
> He hurt his back.
> He sprained his wrist.
> He has a fever.
> She has a sore throat.

(continued)

She has a toothache.
He has a stomachache
She has an earache.
He has a cough.
He has a headache.

2. The Longest List ✳✳

a. Call out a category. For example:

> Injuries
> Ailments
> Medicines

b. In pairs, have students write all the examples in that category they see in the scenes on student book page 157. Tell students to cover the list of words on student book page 156 with a piece of paper so they don't refer to that list. (Set a one-minute time limit for this activity.)

c. Tell students to stop when the one minute is up. Ask students to count the number of items on their lists. Who has the longest list? Continue the activity, calling out other categories.

d. Check students' answers by calling on students to name items on their lists. Write the words on the board, and have students check their spelling.

3. Remember the Words! ✳✳

a. Tell students to spend two minutes looking carefully at the scenes on student book page 157.

b. Have students close their books and write down everything they remember from the illustration.

c. Have students compare notes with a partner and then look at the scenes again to see how well they remembered them.

This activity reviews Unit 11 conversations and grammar:

4. Look Again! ✳✳

a. Have students look at the scenes on student book page 157 for one minute.

b. Tell students to close their books. Make statements about the scenes, using words from the lesson and have students decide if the statements are true or false. If the statement is false, have students correct it. For example:

> There are five patients in the doctor's office. [False. There are six.]
> The dosage for the patient in the drug store is to take one tablet twice a day. [False. Take one tablet three times a day.]
> There are six customers in the drug store. [True.]

c. Then have students *look again* at the illustration to see if they are right.

5. The "Write" Person! ✳✳

a. Divide the class into pairs. Have each pair choose one character in the illustration on student book page 157 and write several sentences describing that person. For example:

> [*the woman with the blue shirt in the doctor's office*]
> She broke her leg.
> She's sitting.
> She's reading a magazine.

b. Have the pairs read their sentences to the class and see if students can guess who is being described.

6. What Are They Saying? ✳✳✳

a. Have pairs or small groups of students look at the transparency or the illustration on student book page 157.

b. Divide the class into pairs or small groups. Point to two characters in one of the scenes, and have the students in each pair or group work together to create a conversation between those characters.

c. Call on students to present their conversations to the class.

d. One at a time, point to another two people talking on page 157 until students have created and presented conversations between the three pairs of characters talking to one another in the illustration.

Variation 1: Have pairs or small groups of students create a conversation based on one of the scenes, present it to the class, and the other students point to the appropriate scene in the book or on the transparency.

Variation 2: Have students write out the conversations they created for each scene.

This activity expands upon Unit 11 vocabulary:

7. Vocabulary Expansion ✳✳✳

Write the following words on the board, and have students identify these objects in the illustration on student book page 157 or on the overhead transparency.

bandage	sling
cast	thermometer
crutches	tissues

LESSONS & UNIT ACTIVITIES	OBJECTIVES	TEXT	TEACHER'S GUIDE
Vocabulary Preview	School personnel • School locations • School subjects • Extracurricular activities	158–159	202–203
LESSON 1 That's the English teacher.	School personnel • School locations	160–161	204–206
LESSON 2 What's your favorite subject?	School subjects	162–163	207–208
LESSON 3 I have band practice.	Extracurricular activities	164–165	209–210
LESSON 4 NUMBERS: A Class Schedule	Review: Cardinal and ordinal Numbers	166	211–212
Language Experience Journal	Writing about your school	166	212
Different Cultures / Different Ways	School in different countries	167	213
Put It Together	Information Gap / Teamwork activity	167–168	213
Vocabulary Foundations / Language Skill Foundations	Review & skills checklist	168	213–214
Talk About It!	Review, conversations, activities, & games	169	214–215

UNIT RESOURCES

Audio Program:
Audio CD 4: Tracks 29–40
Audio Cassette 4A

Workbooks:
Activity Workbook
Literacy Workbook

Lesson Planner CD-ROM:
Activity Masters 101–105
Activity Bank Unit 12 Worksheets

Vocabulary Photo Cards: 224–252

Transparency: Color Overhead for Unit 12, page 169

SCHOOL PERSONNEL AND LOCATIONS (PAGE 158)

PREVIEW
5 MINUTES

Activate students' prior knowledge of school personnel vocabulary. Have students tell you school personnel they know. (Prompt them by asking: "Who works in our school? What does he/she do?") Then have students tell you the words they know. As they tell you the words, write them on the board.

Also have students tell you school locations they know. (Prompt them by asking: "What places do we have in our school building? Do we have a cafeteria?") Then have students tell you the words they know. As they tell you the words, write them on the board.

PRESENT
5 MINUTES

Using the photographs on student book page 158, point to each photo or say its number, say the word, and have the class repeat it chorally and individually. (You can also play the audio program.) Check students' understanding and pronunciation of the vocabulary. (*Note: P.E.* stands for *Physical Education.*)

PRACTICE
5 MINUTES

As a class, in pairs, or in small groups, have students practice the vocabulary in either or both of the following ways:

- Say or write a word, and have students point to the item in their books or tell the number. Or say the name of an occupation of a person in your school, and have students tell the name of the person. For example:

    Teacher: P.E. teacher
    Students: Mr. Rivera

- Point to a photograph in the book or give the number, and have students say the word. Or say the name of a school employee, and have students tell that person's occupation. For example:

    Teacher: Ms. Cardinelli
    Students: Guidance counselor

SPELLING PRACTICE
5 MINUTES

Say a word, and have students spell it aloud or write it. Or point to a photo in the student book, and have students write the word. You can also spell a portion of a word on the board, and have students come to the board to complete it.

SCHOOL SUBJECTS AND EXTRACURRICULAR ACTIVITIES (PAGE 159)

PREVIEW
5 MINUTES

Activate students' prior knowledge of the vocabulary. Have students tell you school subjects they know. (Prompt them by asking: "What do students study in school?") As they tell you the words, write them on the board.

Also have students tell you extracurricular activities they know. (Prompt them by asking: "What do students do after school? Are there any after-school activities at our school?") As they tell you the words, write them on the board.

PRESENT
5 MINUTES

Using the photographs on student book page 159, point to each photo or say its number, say the word, and have the class repeat it chorally and individually. (You can also play the audio program.) Check students' understanding and pronunciation of the vocabulary.

PRACTICE
5 MINUTES

As a class, in pairs, or in small groups, have students practice the vocabulary in either or both of the following ways:

- Say or write a word, and have students point to the item in their books or tell the number.
- Point to a photograph in the book or give the number, and have students say the word.

SPELLING PRACTICE
5 MINUTES

Say a word, and have students spell it aloud or write it. Or point to a photo in the student book, and have students write the word. You can also spell a portion of a word on the board, and have students come to the board to complete it.

EXPANSION

1. Tell and Show ⭑

Photo Cards 224–252 (TWO SETS)

a. Divide the class into pairs. Distribute all the Photo Cards randomly so every pair receives at least five or six cards.

b. Have Student A in each pair select a Photo Card and tell Student B the school word. Have Student B point to the photograph on student book page 158 or 159.

c. As the pairs finish using their Photo Cards, have them trade their sets with another pair and then continue the activity. Have students reverse roles each time they get a new set of cards.

2. Match Game ⭑

Photo Cards 231–252 (TWO SETS)

a. Choose duplicate copies of any Photo Cards 231–252 and distribute them randomly, one to each student.

b. Have students look at their card and identify the school location, subject, or extracurricular activity. Then have students circulate around the room, saying the name of the school location, subject, or extracurricular activity on their card until they find their match. Make sure students don't show their cards to their classmates since this is a listening and speaking exercise.

c. When students have found their match, have them compare their cards and come show you. Then give each student another card to keep the game going. Continue until students have found all the matches.

3. True or False? ⭑⭑

Photo Cards 224–252

Show students various Photo Cards. Make a false statement about the item, and have students correct it. For example:

Teacher: [*showing the class Photo Card 241*] These students are studying math.
Students: No. They're studying social studies.

Teacher: [*showing the class Photo Card 236*] This is the nurse's office.
Students: No. It's the principal's office.

Variation: Make false statements about your school's personnel, and have students correct them. For example:

Teacher: Mr. Wong is the school librarian.
Students: No. He's the principal.

LESSON OBJECTIVE

Focus

School personnel
School locations

Vocabulary

custodian
English teacher
guidance counselor
P.E. teacher
principal
school librarian
school nurse

auditorium
cafeteria
guidance office
gym
library
nurse's office
office
principal's office

GETTING READY   5 MINUTES

Use your own visuals or the photos on student book page 160 to introduce the following school personnel: *English teacher, principal, school nurse, P.E. teacher, guidance counselor, custodian,* and *school librarian.* Say each word, and have the class repeat it chorally and individually. Check students' understanding and pronunciation of the vocabulary.

THE MODEL CONVERSATION   10 MINUTES

1. **SETTING THE SCENE:** Have students look at the model photographs. Set the scene: "Two students are talking."

2. **LISTENING:** With books closed, have students listen to the model conversation—presented by you, by a pair of students, or on the audio program. Check students' understanding of the situation and the vocabulary.

3. **CLASS PRACTICE:** With books still closed, model each line, and have the whole class practice in unison.

4. **READING:** With books open, have students follow along as two students present the model.

5. **PAIR PRACTICE:** In pairs, have students practice the model conversation.

THE CONVERSATION EXERCISES   10 MINUTES

1. **THE SKELETAL DIALOG:** Write the "skeletal dialog" on the board. Fill in the replacement from Exercise 1 to show students how the guided conversation method works. Call on a few pairs of students to practice Exercise 1, using the skeletal framework on the board.

    > A. Who's that?
    > B. That's the <u>principal</u>.

2. **VOCABULARY PRESENTATION:** Present the vocabulary words in the exercises. Point to the photograph of each item, say the word, and have the class repeat it chorally and individually. Check students' understanding and pronunciation of the vocabulary.

3. **EXERCISE PRACTICE:** (optional) Have pairs of students simultaneously practice all the exercises.

4. **EXERCISE PRESENTATIONS:** Call on pairs of students to present their conversations to the class.

PLACES AT SCHOOL

GETTING READY   5 MINUTES

Use the photos on student book page 161 to introduce the following school locations: *library, cafeteria, gym, auditorium, office, principal's office, nurse's office,* and *guidance office.* Say each phrase, and have the class repeat it chorally and individually. Check students' understanding and pronunciation of the vocabulary.

THE MODEL CONVERSATION   10 MINUTES

1. **SETTING THE SCENE:** Have students look at the model photograph. Set the scene: "Two people are talking in the hallway."

2. **LISTENING:** With books closed, have students listen to the model conversation—presented by you, by a pair of students, or on the audio program. Check students' understanding of the situation and the vocabulary.

3. **CLASS PRACTICE:** With books still closed, model each line, and have the whole class practice in unison.

4. **READING:** With books open, have students follow along as two students present the model.

5. **PAIR PRACTICE:** In pairs, have students practice the model conversation.

THE CONVERSATION EXERCISES
10 MINUTES

1. **THE SKELETAL DIALOG:** Write the "skeletal dialog" on the board. Fill in the replacement from Exercise 1 to show students how the guided conversation method works. Call on a few pairs of students to practice Exercise 1, using the skeletal framework on the board.

> A. Where are you going?
> B. I'm going to the library.

2. **VOCABULARY PRESENTATION:** Present the vocabulary words in the exercises. Point to the photograph of each item, say the word, and have the class repeat it chorally and individually. Check students' understanding and pronunciation of the vocabulary.

3. **EXERCISE PRACTICE:** (optional) Have pairs of students simultaneously practice all the exercises.

4. **EXERCISE PRESENTATIONS:** Call on pairs of students to present their conversations to the class.

MATCHING
5 MINUTES

Have students complete the activity and then compare answers with a partner.

Answers
1. principal's office.
2. library.
3. nurse's office.
4. guidance office
5. gym.

EXPANSION

1. **Concentration** ★

   PHOTO CARDS 224–230 (TWO SETS)

   a. Shuffle the cards and place them face-down in two rows of 7 each.

   b. Divide the class into two teams. The object of the game is for students to find the matching cards and identify the vocabulary item. Both teams should be able to see the cards, since *concentrating* on their location is an important part of playing the game.

   c. A student from Team 1 turns over two cards, and if they match, the student must identify the item. If the student correctly identifies the item, that team keeps the cards, and the student takes another turn. If they don't match or if the student isn't able to correctly identify the item, the student turns them face-down, and a member of Team 2 takes a turn.

   d. The game continues until all the cards have been matched. The team with the most correct *matches* wins the game.

   Variation:
   PHOTO CARDS 224–230
   ACTIVITY MASTER 101

   Have the class play with one set of Photo Cards and one set of Word Cards.

2. **Missing Letters** ★

   a. Divide the class into two teams. Draw a series of blanks on the board to represent the letters in a word from student book page 160 or 161.

   b. Have students from each team take turns calling out letters. If the letter is correct, put it in the appropriate blank and give the team one point. If the letter is incorrect, put it on a list to the side. The team that gets the most points wins the game.

3. **Name That Place!** ★

   Ask students about various school locations, and have them guess the location you're asking about. For example:

   Teacher: Where do students eat?
   Students: The cafeteria.

4. **What Can You Do There?** ★★

   a. Divide the class into pairs or small groups. Have students make a list of the places in a school on student book page 161, and for each place, write several activities they can do there. For example:

   library: [study/read books/use the Internet]
   gym: [take P.E./watch a basketball game]

   b. Call on pairs to present their list to the class and compare everybody's ideas. Write a master list of ideas on the board, and have students copy the words in their notebooks.

(continued)

5. Association Game ✴✴

Divide the class into several teams. Call out a place from student book page 161. Have the students in each team work together to see how many words they can associate with that place. For example:

cafeteria: [food/friends/noise]

The team with the most correct items wins.

6. True or False? ✴✴

Make statements about school locations, and have students decide if the statements are true or false. If the statement is false, have students correct it. For example:

You go to the guidance counselor's office when you have a problem. [True.]

You go to the cafeteria when you're sick. [False. You go to the nurse's office when you're sick.]

7. People or Places? ✴✴

a. Have students take out a piece of paper and draw a line down the center of the page. At the top of the left column, have them write People, and at the top of the right column, have them write Places.

b. Dictate various school words. Have students write the words in the appropriate column, depending on whether they are *people* or *places*. For example:

People	Places
custodian	cafeteria
guidance counselor	principal's office
P.E. teacher	gym

c. At the end of the dictation, have students compare their lists.

8. Who Am I? ✴✴

Choose one of the school personnel from student book page 160. Tell what that person does, and have students guess who the person is. For example:

Teacher: I help students choose their courses.
Students: The guidance counselor.

Teacher: I teach students how to exercise and play sports.
Students: The P.E. teacher.

Variation: You can also do the activity in pairs or small groups, or as a game with competing teams.

9. Who Is It? ✴✴✴

a. Divide the class into pairs. Have each pair choose one person from student book page 160 and write three sentences describing what that person does. For example:

[*principal*]
This person is in charge of the school.
This person helps when there are problems in the school.
This person talks to parents and students.

b. Have one student from each pair read the sentences to the class and see if students can guess who is being described.

10. School Directory ✴✴✴

Send pairs of students out of the classroom to find out the names and office numbers of your school's personnel. Have students report their findings to the class and then compile a master list.

LESSON OBJECTIVE

Focus

School subjects

VOCABULARY

art	science
English	social studies
math	technology
music	

GETTING READY
5 MINUTES

Use your own visuals or the photos on student book page 162 to introduce the following vocabulary items: *math, English, social studies, science, art, music,* and *technology.* Say each word, and have the class repeat it chorally and individually. Check students' understanding and pronunciation of the vocabulary.

THE MODEL CONVERSATION
10 MINUTES

1. **SETTING THE SCENE:** Have students look at the model photographs. Set the scene: "Two students are talking."

2. **LISTENING:** With books closed, have students listen to the model conversation—presented by you, by a pair of students, or on the audio program. Check students' understanding of the situation and the vocabulary.

3. **CLASS PRACTICE:** With books still closed, model each line, and have the whole class practice in unison.

4. **READING:** With books open, have students follow along as two students present the model.

5. **PAIR PRACTICE:** In pairs, have students practice the model conversation.

THE CONVERSATION EXERCISES
10 MINUTES

1. **THE SKELETAL DIALOG:** Write the "skeletal dialog" on the board. Fill in the replacement from Exercise 1 to show students how the guided conversation method works. Call on a few pairs of students to practice Exercise 1, using the skeletal framework on the board.

A. What's your favorite subject?
B. English.

2. **VOCABULARY PRESENTATION:** Present the vocabulary words in the exercises. Point to the photograph of each item, say the word, and have the class repeat it chorally and individually. Check students' understanding and pronunciation of the vocabulary.

3. **EXERCISE PRACTICE:** (optional) Have pairs of students simultaneously practice all the exercises.

4. **EXERCISE PRESENTATIONS:** Call on pairs of students to present their conversations to the class.

LISTENING
5 MINUTES

Listen and write the number under the correct picture.

1. My favorite subject is music.
2. My favorite subject is social studies.
3. My favorite subject is math.
4. My favorite subject is science.
5. My favorite subject is English.
6. My favorite subject is technology.

Answers

2	6	1
4	3	5

UNSCRAMBLE THE SUBJECTS
5 MINUTES

Tell students that their task is to rearrange the letters to spell a school subject. Have students complete the activity and then compare answers with a partner.

Answers

1. art	4. science
2. math	5. English
3. music	6. technology

LANGUAGE IN *MOTION*
10 MINUTES

Have students circulate around the classroom, asking and answering the question: "What's your favorite subject?" Have each student interview eight students and complete the chart on student book page 163 by writing the name and favorite subject of each of those students. Set a ten-minute limit to this activity. When time is up, have all the students sit down, and then tell the class what they learned about their classmates.

EXPANSION

1. **Beanbag Toss** ✶

   Have students sit or stand in a circle. Say the name of a school subject and throw a beanbag
   (continued)

to Student 1. Student 1 says the name of another school subject and throws the beanbag to another student. Continue around the circle until everyone has had a turn.

2. Alphabetize! ✷

ACTIVITY MASTER 102

a. Make copies of Activity Master 102 and cut them into cards.

b. Have students work in pairs. Give each pair a set of cards, and have them work together to place the words in alphabetical order.

c. Have the first pair to complete the alphabetization write their list on the board. Go over the list with the class.

3. The Letter Game ✷

Divide the class into teams. Say: "I'm thinking of a school subject that starts with *t*." The first person to raise his or her hand and guess correctly (*technology*), wins a point for that team. Continue with other letters of the alphabet.

4. Dictation Game ✷✷

a. In large print on a piece of paper, write a list of seven school subjects from the lesson. For example:

math	music
English	art
social studies	science
technology	

b. Divide the class into pairs—Student A and Student B. Have all the Student A's come outside the classroom with you. Show them the list of words, and have them spend a few minutes looking at it and trying to remember the words.

c. Have the Student A's return to the classroom and give them three minutes to dictate what they remembered from the list to their Student B partners. The pair that has written the most words wins the game.

d. For correction, have each pair call out one word on their list. Write that word on the board so students can check their spelling.

e. Repeat the game with a new list for Student B's to dictate to their Student A partners.

5. Likes and Dislikes ✷✷

a. Have students take out a piece of paper and draw a line down the center of the page. At the top of the left column, have them write I like to study, and at the top of the right column, have them write I don't like to study.

b. Dictate school subjects, and have students write the words in either the left or right column, depending on whether they *like to study* or *don't like to study* them.

c. At the end of the dictation, have students compare their lists to see which school subjects people *like* and *don't like*.

6. Game: Name That Subject! ✷✷✷

a. Bring to class books in different subject areas. Divide the class into two teams.

b. For each book, name a topic from the table of contents or show the class a page from the book, and have a student from Team 1 try to guess the subject. If he or she guesses correctly, that team gets one point. If the student doesn't take a guess or guesses incorrectly, a student from Team 2 has a chance to guess.

The team that gets the most correct answers wins the game.

7. The Hardest Subject ✷✷✷

a. Have students look at the school subjects on student book page 162. Tell everyone to think about which of these subjects are the hardest for them and which are the easiest.

b. Have students then rank these items from one to seven, with one being the hardest. For example:

1. science
2. math
3. social studies
4. English
5. music
6. technology
7. art

c. As a class, in pairs, or in small groups, have students compare their lists.

8. What's Most Important For Kids Today? ✷✷✷

Divide the class into small groups. Have each group look at the subjects listed on student book page 162 and decide which are the most important for young people to study. Have each group rank the subjects in order of importance, with one being the most important. Have the class compare their lists and discuss the different rankings.

LESSON OBJECTIVE

FOCUS

Extracurricular activities

VOCABULARY

band	football
basketball	orchestra
choir	soccer
drama	

GETTING READY
5 MINUTES

1. Explain that extracurricular activities are activities that students do after their classes. Then use your own visuals or the photos on page 164 of the student book to introduce the following new vocabulary: *band, orchestra, choir, drama, football, soccer,* and *basketball.*

2. Introduce the concept of *practice.* Write the following on the board:

Activity	Practice
band	band practice
orchestra	orchestra practice
drama	drama practice
football	football practice

Explain that to play football well, for example, you have to practice. *Practice* happens after school. It is not an actual football game. The same is true for band, orchestra, drama, soccer, and basketball.

THE MODEL CONVERSATION
10 MINUTES

1. **SETTING THE SCENE:** Have students look at the model photographs. Set the scene: "Two students are talking."

2. **LISTENING:** With books closed, have students listen to the model conversation—presented by you, by a pair of students, or on the audio program. Check students' understanding of the situation and the vocabulary.

3. **CLASS PRACTICE:** With books still closed, model each line, and have the whole class practice in unison.

4. **READING:** With books open, have students follow along as two students present the model.

5. **PAIR PRACTICE:** In pairs, have students practice the model conversation.

THE CONVERSATION EXERCISES
10 MINUTES

1. **THE SKELETAL DIALOG:** Write the "skeletal dialog" on the board. Fill in the replacement from Exercise 1 to show students how the guided conversation method works. Call on a few pairs of students to practice Exercise 1, using the skeletal framework on the board.

> A. What are you going to do after school today?
> B. I have <u>orchestra</u> practice.

2. **VOCABULARY PRESENTATION:** Present the vocabulary words in the exercises. Point to the photograph of each item, say the word, and have the class repeat chorally and individually. Check students' understanding and pronunciation of the vocabulary.

3. **EXERCISE PRACTICE:** (optional) Have pairs of students simultaneously practice all the exercises.

4. **EXERCISE PRESENTATIONS:** Call on pairs of students to present their conversations to the class.

LISTENING
5 MINUTES

Listen and write the number under the correct picture.

1. I have orchestra practice after school today.
2. I play basketball with my friends after school.
3. My daughter is in the band at her school.
4. We have soccer practice every afternoon.
5. The choir is practicing in the music room.
6. My son practices football every day after school.

Answers

6	3	2
1	5	4

SCHOOL VOCABULARY
10 MINUTES

Tell students that their task is to circle the correct word to complete each sentence. Have students complete the activity and then compare answers with a partner.

Answers

1. music	4. nurse's
2. auditorium	5. basketball
3. custodian	6. P.E.

**10–15
MINUTES**

Divide the class into small groups. Have students
share what they know about schools in the
community and complete the chart. Have them
write the name of the school, its location, and the
type of students who go there. If students don't
know much about schools in the community, have
them interview other students in the school and
then report what they learned in small groups.

EXPANSION

1. Concentration ★

PHOTO CARDS 246–252 (TWO SETS)

a. Shuffle the cards and place them face-down
   in two rows of 7 each.

b. Divide the class into two teams. The object
   of the game is for students to find the
   matching cards and identify the vocabulary
   item. Both teams should be able to see the
   cards, since *concentrating* on their location
   is an important part of playing the game.

c. A student from Team 1 turns over two cards,
   and if they match, the student must identify
   the item. If the student correctly identifies
   the item, that team keeps the cards, and
   the student takes another turn. If they
   don't match or if the student isn't able to
   correctly identify the item, the student turns
   them face-down, and a member of Team 2
   takes a turn.

d. The game continues until all the cards have
   been matched. The team with the most
   correct *matches* wins the game.

Variation:
PHOTO CARDS 246–252
ACTIVITY MASTER 103

Have the class play with one set of Photo Cards
and one set of Word Cards.

2. Guess the Word! ★

a. Divide the class into two teams. Choose a
   vocabulary word from the lesson, and on
   the board, write a blank for each letter in
   the word. For example: *orchestra*.

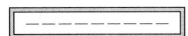

b. Give students a clue about the word. For
   example: "This is a group of people who
   play classical music together." The team
   that guesses the word gets one point. The
   team with the most points wins the game.

3. Telephone ★★

a. Have students sit in a circle or semicircle.
   Make up two sentences, using the words in
   this lesson, and whisper them to Student 1.
   For example:

   Today after school, I have drama practice and
   football practice. My sister has basketball
   practice.

b. The first student whispers what he or she
   heard to the second student, who whispers
   it to the third student, and so forth. When
   the message gets to the last student, that
   person says it aloud. Is it the same message
   you started with?

Give each student in the class a chance to start
his or her own message.

4. Game: Name That Activity! ★★

Divide the class into two teams. Describe an
extracurricular activity, and have a student
from Team 1 try to guess the activity. If the
student guesses correctly, that team gets one
point. If the student guesses incorrectly, a
student from Team 2 has a chance to guess. For
example:

Teacher: You perform a play with other people
          on a stage.
Student: Drama.

The team that gets the most correct answers
wins the game.

5. Likes and Dislikes ★★

a. Have students take out a piece of paper and
   draw a line down the center of the page. At
   the top of the left column, have them write
   I like, and at the top of the right column,
   have them write I don't like.

b. Dictate various extracurricular activities
   from the lesson, and have students write
   the activities in either the left or the right
   column, depending on whether they *like* or
   don't like them.

c. At the end of the dictation, have
   students compare their lists to see which
   extracurricular activities people *like* and
   don't like.

6. What Activities are Best for Kids? ★★★

Divide the class into small groups. Have
each group look at the activities listed on
student book page 164 and decide which
are the best for young people to take part
in. Have each group rank the activities in
order of importance, with one being the most
important. Have the class compare their lists
and discuss the different rankings.

LESSON OBJECTIVE

Focus

Review: Cardinal & ordinal numbers

Vocabulary

period

GETTING READY

10 MINUTES

1. Review ordinal numbers. Have students look at student book page 166. Read the numbers *first* through *sixth* aloud as students repeat chorally or individually.

2. Review saying large numbers. Write three-digit numbers on the board. Read the first few examples to the class. Then invite students to read the remaining examples. For example:

123	331
241	215
101	319

Teacher: one twenty-three
Teacher: two forty-one
Teacher: one oh one

Student 1: three thirty-one
Student 2: two fifteen
Student 3: three nineteen

3. Introduce the new vocabulary. Explain that *period* means "the time a class meets." Most high school students have six to seven periods in a day. Each period lasts as long as 60 minutes. At the end of each period, the school bell rings and students change classes. The new period begins when the school bell rings again.

THE MODEL CONVERSATION

10 MINUTES

1. **SETTING THE SCENE:** Have students look at the model photograph. Set the scene: "Two students are talking."

2. **LISTENING:** With books closed, have students listen to the model conversation—presented by you, by a pair of students, or on the audio program. Check students' understanding of the situation and the vocabulary.

3. **CLASS PRACTICE:** With books still closed, model each line, and have the whole class practice in unison.

4. **READING:** With books open, have students follow along as two students present the model.

5. **PAIR PRACTICE:** In pairs, have students practice the model conversation.

THE CONVERSATION EXERCISES

10 MINUTES

1. **THE SKELETAL DIALOG:** Write the "skeletal dialog" on the board. Fill in the replacement from the class schedule to show students how the guided conversation method works. Call on a few pairs of students to practice the dialog, using the skeletal framework on the board.

> A. What class do you have <u>second</u> period?
> B. <u>Science</u>.
> A. In which classroom?
> B. Room <u>124</u>.

2. **VOCABULARY PRESENTATION:** Go over the class schedule. Have students practice saying the ordinal numbers 1st through 6th, the subjects, the teachers' names, and the room numbers. Check students' understanding and pronunciation of the vocabulary.

3. **EXERCISE PRACTICE:** (optional) Have pairs of students simultaneously practice all the conversations.

4. **EXERCISE PRESENTATIONS:** Call on pairs of students to present their conversations to the class.

EXPANSION

1. **Listen for the Class Period** ★
   a. Read the following sentences, and have students write down the ordinal or cardinal number number they hear:

   I have science first period.
   I have art third period.
   I have technology fifth period.
   I have social studies in Room 311.
   I have music second period.
   I have English sixth period.
   She has math fourth period.
   The principal's office is Room 101.
   The guidance office is Room 214
   The nurse's office is Room 192.

   b. Have pairs of students check each others' answers. *(continued)*

2. Chain Game ★★

Have students sit in a circle. Begin the activity by saying: "First period I have math." Student 1 repeats what you said and adds another period—for example: "First period I have math. Second period I have English." Student 2 repeats what you and Student 1 said and adds another period—for example: "First period I have math. Second period I have English. Third period I have social studies." Continue around the circle in this fashion, with each student repeating what the previous student said and adding another period. After six periods, do the activity again, beginning and ending with different students.

3. Telephone ★★

a. Have students sit in a circle or semicircle. Make up a sentence, using the vocabulary in this lesson, and whisper it to Student 1. For example:

> First period I have English, second period I have technology, third period I have music, and fourth period I have science.

b. The first student whispers what he or she heard to the second student, who whispers it to the third student, and so forth. When the message gets to the last student, that person says it aloud. Is it the same message you started with?

Give each student in the class a chance to start his or her own message.

4. Information Gap ★★★

ACTIVITY MASTER 104

a. Make multiple copies of Activity Master 104 and cut them in half (Schedule A and Schedule B).

b. Divide the class into pairs. Give each partner a different schedule—A or B. Have students share their information and fill in their class schedules. For example:

> A. What class do we have first period?
> B. English. In which classroom do we have English?
> A. Room three forty-five.

c. When students have finished completing their schedules, have them look at their partner's schedule to make sure they have written the information correctly.

LANGUAGE EXPERIENCE JOURNAL

Have students write about their schools. Depending on your students' writing abilities, either have them write in their journal or dictate their story for you to write. Then students should read what they have written to a classmate. If time permits, you may also want to write a response in each student's journal, sharing your own opinions and experiences as well as reacting to what the student has written.

Different Cultures/ *Different Ways* 10 MINUTES

Have students first work in pairs or small groups, reacting to the photographs and responding to the questions. Then have students share with the class what they have talked about.

For additional practice, have students do the following activity.

Class Discussion

As a class, in pairs, or in small groups, have students discuss any or all of the following questions about schools in their country:

> How old are children when they start school?
> How many years is elementary school? How old are students when they start elementary school? How old are they when they finish?
> How about middle school and high school?
> Do students in your country need to take a special exam to graduate from high school? What is that exam called?
> How many years is university? Are there different kinds of universities? What is the largest university in your country?
> Are private schools popular in your country?
> How much do students pay to go to school in your country?

PUT IT TOGETHER 15–20 MINUTES

In this activity, students talk with each other to find out information about a school schedule.

1. Divide the class into pairs: Student A and Student B.
2. Tell all the Student A's to look at Part A of the activity on student book page 167. Tell all the Student B's to look at Part B on page 168.
3. Have everybody look at the first item on the schedule: *science.*
   a. In Student B's schedule, next to *science,* it says, *8:15–9:00.* Therefore, when Student A asks: "What time is science class?", Student B answers: "From 8:15 to 9:00."
   b. Ask all the Student B's: "What time is science class?" Have all the Student B's respond in unison: "From 8:15 to 9:00."
4. Have everybody look at the second item on the schedule: *math.*
   a. Have all the Student A's look at their schedule. In their schedule next to *math,* it says, *9:05–9:50.* Therefore, when Student B

asks: "What time is math class?", Student A answers: "From 9:05 to 9:50."
   b. Ask all the Student A's: "What time is math class?" Have all the Student A's respond in unison: "From 9:05 to 9:50."
5. The Student A and Student B pairs are now ready to continue the activity with the rest of the subjects on their schedules.
6. When the pairs have completed the activity, have them check each other's answers.

VOCABULARY FOUNDATIONS 5–10 MINUTES

Have students review the list of words they have learned in this unit. Encourage students to get a small notebook where they can write down vocabulary that is new for them. If students have personal copies of dictionaries or picture dictionaries, have them look up these words in the dictionary and highlight them with a marker. Encourage them to look at their notebooks or dictionaries frequently to review what they have learned.

For additional practice, have students do one or more of the following activities.

1. **Taking Notes** ✮
   In their vocabulary notebooks or on a piece of paper, have students write all the words in one column. In a second column, have them write notes, draw pictures, or write the word in a sentence that will help them remember the meaning of the words.

2. **Guess the Word!** ✮✮
   a. Divide the class into two teams. Choose a vocabulary word from the unit, and on the board, write a blank for each letter in the word. For example: *gym*

   b. Give students a clue about the word. For example: "You take P.E. class here." The team that guesses the word gets one point. The team with the most points wins the game.

3. **Finish the Sentence!** ✮✮
   Divide the class into two teams. Begin sentences, and have students from each team take turns finishing them with appropriate words from the unit. For example:

The guidance counselor is in the . . . *guidance office.*

The librarian is in the . . . *library.*

The P.E. teacher is in the . . . *gym.*

The principal is in the . . . *principal's office.*

The school nurse is in the . . . *nurse's office.*

An activity after school is called an . . . *extracurricular activity.*

Three after-school sports are . . . *soccer, basketball, and football.*

Students study computers in . . . *technology class.*

The person who directs the school is the . . . *principal.*

The person who helps students choose classes is the . . . *guidance counselor.*

The team with the most correctly completed sentences wins.

4. Category Dictation ★★★

a. Have students make four columns on a piece of paper:

> people
> places
> subjects
> extracurricular activities

b. Dictate words from Vocabulary Foundations, and have students write them in the appropriate column. Make sure students have covered the vocabulary items on student book page 168 with a piece of paper so they don't refer to that list.

c. As a class, in pairs, or in small groups, have students check their work.

5. Match Game ★★★

ACTIVITY MASTER 105

a. Make a copy of Activity Master 105, cut it into cards, and distribute the cards randomly, one to each student.

b. Have students memorize the phrases on their card and leave their cards on their desks. Then have students circulate around the room, saying their lines until they find their match.

c. When students have found their match, have them compare their cards and come show you.

LANGUAGE SKILL FOUNDATIONS   10–15 MINUTES

Explain to students that this is a list of skills they have learned in the unit. Students should become familiar with the vocabulary of describing their skills, but they don't need to master all the terms.

For each speaking skill on the list, read the skill aloud to students, and have them demonstrate it. For example:

> Teacher: I can name school personnel.
> Students: That's the custodian.

(If students don't understand the vocabulary of a particular speaking skill, give them a concrete example rather than a description or explanation, and then have students practice your example and others.)

Have students put a check next to each skill if they feel they have learned it. Use this information to determine which lessons you may want to review or reinforce for the entire class or for particular students. The Getting Ready and Expansion activities for this unit and the CD-ROM's Activity Bank of supplemental worksheets are excellent resources for additional practice. It may also be helpful to have stronger students or, if available, a classroom aide or volunteer, work with students who need more practice.

Talk About It! ▶▶▶   (Page 169)   20–30 MINUTES

(Page 169 is also available as a transparency.)

Use the scenes in this illustration to review the vocabulary, conversations, and grammar in the unit. Have students first work in pairs or small groups to talk about the illustration and answer the questions posed at the bottom of the page. Then discuss as a class.

For additional motivating practice, students will enjoy doing one or more of the following activities.

These activities review Unit 12 vocabulary:

1. School Locations ★

a. Divide the class into pairs or small groups. Have students make a list of all the locations they see in the scenes on student book page 169. (Set a one-minute time limit for this activity.)

b. Tell students to stop when one minute is up. Have students tell you what they saw. For example:

> cafeteria
> library
> guidance office
> nurse's office
> auditorium
> gym
> classrooms (English and science)

2. **School Personnel** ✮

   a. Divide the class into pairs or small groups. Have students make a list of all the school personnel they see in the scenes on student book page 169. (Set a one-minute time limit for this activity.)

   b. Tell students to stop when one minute is up. Have students tell you who they saw. For example:

   > science teacher
   > custodian
   > librarian
   > guidance counselor
   > school nurse
   > English teacher
   > P.E. teacher

These activities review Unit 12 grammar and conversations.

3. **What Are They Doing?** ✮✮

   a. Write the following on the board:

   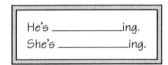

   b. In pairs, have students talk about what the characters in the scenes are doing. One student points to a character and the other describes what he or she is doing. Then reverse roles.

Variation: One student describes what a character in one of the scenes is doing and the other student points to that person.

4. **Where Are They?** ✮✮

   In pairs, have students talk about where the characters in the illustration are. One student points to a character and the other describes where he or she is. Then reverse roles.

   Variation: One student describes where a character is and the other student points to that person.

5. **The "Write" Person!** ✮✮✮

   a. Divide the class into pairs. Have each pair choose one character in the illustration on student book page 169 and write two sentences describing that person. For example:

   > [*the boy with the green shirt*]
   >
   > He's a student.
   > He's talking to the librarian.

   b. Have the pairs read their sentences to the class and see if students can guess who is being described.

LESSONS & UNIT ACTIVITIES	OBJECTIVES	TEXT	TEACHER'S GUIDE
Vocabulary Preview	Occupations	170–171	217
LESSON 1 What do you do?	Occupations • Help Wanted signs	172–173	218–220
LESSON 2 Can you drive a bus?	Occupations • Job skills	174–175	221–223
LESSON 3 Where do you work?	Places of employment • Want ads • Job application form	176–177	224–226
LESSON 4 Can you assemble components?	Job skills • Calling in sick	178–179	227–229
LESSON 5 Where's the supply room?	Workplace locations • Reading a diagram • Help Wanted signs	180–181	230–231
LESSON 6 Careful!	Workplace safety • Warning & safety signs	182–183	232–233
LESSON 7 NUMBERS: Work schedules & Paychecks	Time • Money	184	234–235
Language Experience Journal	Writing about a workplace	184	235
Different Cultures / Different Ways	Jobs in different cultures	185	236
Put It Together	Information Gap / Teamwork activity	185–186	236
Vocabulary Foundations / Language Skill Foundations	Review & skills checklist	186	236–237
Talk About It!	Review, conversations, activities, & games	187	237–238

UNIT RESOURCES

Audio Program:
  Audio CD 5: Tracks 2–21
  Audio Cassette 4A

Workbooks:
  Activity Workbook
  Literacy Workbook

Lesson Planner CD-ROM:
  Activity Masters 106–116
  Activity Bank Unit 13 Worksheets

Vocabulary Photo Cards: 253–294

Transparency: Color Overhead for Unit 13, page 187

PREVIEW
5 MINUTES

Activate students' prior knowledge of occupations by doing either or both of the following:

1. Have students brainstorm occupations and write them on the board.
2. Have students look at the photographs on student book pages 170 and 171 while they cover the words at the bottom of the page. Have students identify the words they already know.

PRESENT
10 MINUTES

Using the photographs on student book pages 170 and 171, point to each item, say the word, and have the class repeat it chorally and individually. (You can also play the audio program.) Check students' understanding and pronunciation of the vocabulary.

PRACTICE
10 MINUTES

As a class, in pairs, or in small groups, have students practice the vocabulary in either or both of the following ways:

- Say or write a word, and have students point to the occupation in their books or tell the number.
- Point to a photograph in the book or give the number, and have students say the occupation.

SPELLING PRACTICE
5 MINUTES

Say an occupation, and have students spell it aloud or write it. Or point to an occupation in the student book, and have students write the word. You can also spell a portion of a word on the board, and have students come to the board to complete it.

EXPANSION

1. Tell and Show ★
PHOTO CARDS 253–280

Place the Photo Cards in a pile at the front of the classroom. Have students take turns coming up to the front of the class, selecting a Photo Card, and telling the class the item without showing the card. Have the rest of the students point to the item on student book page 170 or 171.

2. Match Game ★
PHOTO CARDS 253–280 (TWO SETS)

a. Choose duplicate copies of any Photo Cards 253–280 and distribute them randomly, one to each student.

b. Have students look at their card and identify the occupation. Then have students circulate around the room, saying the occupation on their card until they find their match. Make sure students don't show their cards to their classmates since this is a listening and speaking exercise.

c. When students have found their match, have them compare their cards and come show you. Then give each student another Photo Card to keep the game going. Continue until students have found all the matches.

3. Listen and Point ★★

Divide the class into pairs. Have Student A cover the words on student book pages 170 and 171 and look just at the photos. Have Student B read the words in random order. Student A must point to the appropriate photo. Then reverse roles.

4. True or False? ★★
PHOTO CARDS 253–280

Show students various Photo Cards. Make statements about the item, and have students decide if the statements are true or false. If a statement is false, have students correct it.

Teacher: [*showing the class Photo Card 263*] He's a baker.
Students: False. He's a bus driver.

Teacher: [*showing the class Photo Card 275*] She's a housekeeper.
Students: True.

LESSON OBJECTIVE

FOCUS

Occupations
Help Wanted signs

VOCABULARY

cashier
construction worker
cook
custodian
delivery person
electrician
gardener
police officer
repairperson
security guard

GETTING READY
5 MINUTES

Use your own visuals or the photos on student book page 172 to introduce the following vocabulary: *cook, custodian, gardener, cashier, electrician, repairperson, delivery person, security guard, police officer,* and *construction worker.* Say each occupation, and have the class repeat it chorally and individually. Check students' understanding and pronunciation of the vocabulary.

THE MODEL CONVERSATION
10 MINUTES

1. **SETTING THE SCENE:** Have students look at the model photograph. Set the scene: "Two people are talking. One is telling his occupation."

2. **LISTENING:** With books closed, have students listen to the model conversation—presented by you, by a pair of students, or on the audio program. Check students' understanding of the situation and the vocabulary.

3. **CLASS PRACTICE:** With books still closed, model each line, and have the whole class practice in unison.

4. **READING:** With books open, have students follow along as two students present the model.

5. **PAIR PRACTICE:** In pairs, have students practice the model conversation.

THE CONVERSATION EXERCISES
10 MINUTES

1. **THE SKELETAL DIALOG:** Write the "skeletal dialog" on the board. Fill in the replacement from Exercise 1 to show students how the guided conversation method works. Call on a few pairs of students to practice Exercise 1, using the skeletal framework on the board.

> A. What *do you do?*
> B. I'm *a custodian.*

2. **VOCABULARY PRESENTATION:** Present the vocabulary words in the exercises. Point to the photograph of each occupation, say the word, and have the class repeat it chorally and individually. Check students' understanding and pronunciation of the vocabulary.

3. **EXERCISE PRACTICE:** (optional) Have pairs of students simultaneously practice all the exercises.

4. **EXERCISE PRESENTATIONS:** Call on pairs of students to present their conversations to the class.

WHAT KIND OF JOB ARE YOU LOOKING FOR?

THE MODEL CONVERSATION
10 MINUTES

1. **SETTING THE SCENE:** Have students look at the model photograph. Set the scene: "Someone is looking for a job."

2. **THE SKELETAL DIALOG:** Write the "skeletal dialog" on the board. Fill in an occupation word to show students how the guided conversation method works. Call on a few pairs of students to practice the dialog, using the skeletal framework on the board.

> A. What kind of job are you looking for?
> B. I'm looking for a job as *a cashier.*

3. **EXERCISE PRACTICE:** (optional) Have pairs of students simultaneously practice the conversation, using the jobs on student book page 172.

4. **EXERCISE PRESENTATIONS:** Call on pairs of students to present their conversations to the class.

LISTENING

5–10 MINUTES

Listen and write the number under the correct Help Wanted sign.

1. A. What kind of job are you looking for?
   B. I'm looking for a job as a cashier.
2. A. What kind of job are you looking for?
   B. I'm looking for a job as a delivery person.
3. A. What kind of job do you want?
   B. I'm looking for a job as a cook.
4. A. What kind of job are you looking for?
   B. I'm looking for a job as a gardener.
5. A. What kind of work are you looking for?
   B. I'm looking for a job as a construction worker.
6. A. What kind of work do you want to do?
   B. I want to work as a custodian.

Answers

3	1	5
2	6	4

MISSING LETTERS

5–10 MINUTES

Point out that there are letters missing from the occupation words and students have to figure out what those missing letters are and write them in the blanks. Have students complete the activity and then compare answers with a partner.

Answers

1. cashier
2. custodian
3. electrician
4. carpenter
5. repairperson
6. police officer
7. security guard
8. delivery person

EXPANSION

1. Concentration ✶

PHOTO CARDS 253–262 (TWO SETS)

a. Shuffle the cards and place them face-down in two rows of 10 each.

b. Divide the class into two teams. The object of the game is for students to find the matching cards and identify the vocabulary item. Both teams should be able to see the cards, since *concentrating* on their location is an important part of playing the game.

c. A student from Team 1 turns over two cards, and if they match, the student must identify the item. If the student correctly identifies the item, that team keeps the cards, and the student takes another turn. If they don't match or if the student isn't able to correctly identify the item, the student turns them face-down, and a member of Team 2 takes a turn.

d. The game continues until all the cards have been matched. The team with the most correct *matches* wins the game.

Variation:
PHOTO CARDS 253–262
ACTIVITY MASTER 106

Have the class play with one set of Photo Cards and one set of Word Cards.

2. Scrambled Occupations ✶

a. Choose words from the lesson and write them on the board or on a card with the letters scrambled out of order. For example:

> d r a g n e e r

b. Have students take turns guessing what the word is. [gardener]

Variation 1: Do the activity in pairs or small groups, with students taking turns scrambling words for others to guess.

Variation 2: Do the activity as a class game with competing teams.

3. Beanbag Toss ✶

Stand in a circle. Say the name of an occupation and throw the beanbag to Student 1. Student 1 says another occupation and throws the beanbag to another student. Continue around the circle until everyone has had a turn.

4. Dictation Game ✶✶

a. In large print on a piece of paper, write a list of seven to nine vocabulary words from the lesson. For example:

> cook
> gardener
> repairperson
> construction worker
> security guard
> cashier
> electrician

(continued)

b. Divide the class into pairs—Student A and Student B. Have all the Student A's come outside the classroom with you. Show them the list of words, and have them spend a few minutes looking at it and trying to remember the words.

c. Have the Student A's return to the classroom and give them three minutes to dictate what they remembered from the list to their Student B partners. The pair that has written the most words wins the game.

d. For correction, have each pair call out one word on their list. Write that word on the board so students can check their spelling.

e. Repeat the game with a new list for Student B's to dictate to their Student A partners.

5. Indoor or Outdoor Work? ★★★

a. Have students take out a piece of paper and draw a line down the center of the page. At the top of the left column, have them write Indoors, and at the top of the right column, have them write Outdoors.

b. Dictate various occupations from student book page 172, and have students write the occupations in the appropriate column, depending on whether they are *indoor* or *outdoor* jobs. Some occupations can include both—for example: *police officer.*

c. At the end of the dictation, have students compare their lists.

6. Who Is It? ★★★

a. Divide the class into pairs. Have each pair choose one occupation from student book page 172 and write three sentences describing what that person does. For example:

> [*cashier*]
> She works in a store.
> She takes money.
> She makes change.

b. Have one student from each pair read the sentences to the class and see if students can guess who is being described.

7. Which Pays Best? ★★★

Write the following occupations on the board: *construction workers, police officers, cashiers,* and *electricians.* Have students rank them from the most pay to least pay, with one being the most. As a class, in pairs, or in small groups, have students compare their lists. *Note:* Here is the list according to the U.S. Department of Labor in 2000:

1. police officers
2. electricians
3. construction workers
4. cashiers

8. Who Do You Know? ★★★

a. Make two columns on the board. At the top of the left column, write Occupations, and the top of the right column, write Names. Write the occupations from student book page 172 in the left column.

b. Call out an occupation. Have students tell you the name of a person they know who works in that occupation along with their relationship to that person. For example:

> Teacher: cook
> Student A: my brother Mario
> Student B: my friend Christina

c. Write that information on the board. For example:

Occupations	Names
cook	Juan's brother Mario
	Maria's friend Christina

d. In pairs, have students ask each other about the information on the board. For example:

> A. What does Juan's brother do?
> B. He's a cook.

LESSON OBJECTIVE

FOCUS

Occupations
Job Skills

VOCABULARY

baker	bake
bus driver	drive
carpenter	fix
mechanic	paint
painter	repair
plumber	teach
secretary	type
taxi driver	
truck driver	
teacher	

GETTING READY
5 MINUTES

1. Introduce *can*.

   a. Write on the board:

   > A. Can you _____?
   > B. Yes, I can.

   b. Ask about activities you know they can do. For example:

   > Can you speak *Spanish*?
   > Can you spell your first name?
   > Can you drive a car?

2. Use your own visuals or the photos on student book page 174 to introduce the following occupations: *bus driver, painter, teacher, baker, secretary, taxi driver, truck driver, plumber, mechanic,* and *carpenter.*

THE MODEL CONVERSATION
5 MINUTES

1. **SETTING THE SCENE:** Have students look at the model photographs. Set the scene: "Someone is at a job interview."

2. **LISTENING:** With books closed, have students listen to the model conversation—presented by you, by a pair of students, or on the audio program. Check students' understanding of the situation and the vocabulary.

3. **CLASS PRACTICE:** With books still closed, model each line, and have the whole class practice in unison.

4. **READING:** With books open, have students follow along as two students present the model.

5. **PAIR PRACTICE:** In pairs, have students practice the model conversation.

THE CONVERSATION EXERCISES
10–15 MINUTES

1. **THE SKELETAL DIALOG:** Write the "skeletal dialog" on the board. Fill in the replacement from Exercise 1 to show students how the guided conversation method works. Call on a few pairs of students to practice Exercise 1, using the skeletal framework on the board.

   > A. Can you <u>paint</u>?
   > B. Yes, I can. I'm an experienced <u>painter</u>.

2. **VOCABULARY PRESENTATION:** Present the vocabulary words in the exercises. Point to the photo of each occupation and skill, say the words, and have the class repeat them chorally and individually. Check students' understanding and pronunciation of the vocabulary.

3. **EXERCISE PRACTICE:** (optional) Have pairs of students simultaneously practice all the exercises.

4. **EXERCISE PRESENTATIONS:** Call on pairs of students to present their conversations to the class.

WHAT CAN YOU DO?

THE MODEL CONVERSATION
10 MINUTES

1. **SETTING THE SCENE:** Have students look at the model photograph. Set the scene: "Someone is at a job interview."

2. **THE SKELETAL DIALOG:** Write the "skeletal dialog" on the board. Fill in a job skill from student book page 174 to show students how the guided conversation method works. Call on a few pairs of students to practice the conversation, using the skeletal framework on the board.

   > A. Tell me about your job skills. What can you do?
   > B. I can <u>fix sinks</u>.

3. **EXERCISE PRACTICE:** (optional) Have pairs of students simultaneously practice the conversation, using the job skills on student book page 174.

4. **EXERCISE PRESENTATIONS:** Call on pairs of students to present their conversations to the class.

LISTENING
5–10 MINUTES

Listen and write the number under the correct want ad.

1. I can drive a taxi.
2. I can bake.
3. I can type.
4. I can fix cars.
5. I can paint.

Answers

3   2   5   4   1

MATCHING
5–10 MINUTES

Have students complete the activity individually, and then share their answers in pairs, small groups, or as a class.

Answers

1. I can drive a bus.
2. I can paint.
3. I can fix sinks.
4. I can type.
5. I can fix cars.
6. I can repair buildings.

LANGUAGE IN *MOTION*
10 MINUTES

1. Write on the board:

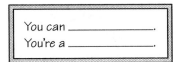

You can _____.
You're a _____.

2. Have students take turns standing in the front of the classroom, pantomiming a job skill, and asking: "What can I do? What's my job?" Other students respond, using the phrases on the board.

EXPANSION

1. Concentration ★
PHOTO CARDS 263–272 (TWO SETS)

a. Shuffle the cards and place them face-down in two rows of 10 each.

b. Divide the class into two teams. The object of the game is for students to find the matching cards and identify the vocabulary

item. Both teams should be able to see the cards, since *concentrating* on their location is an important part of playing the game.

c. A student from Team 1 turns over two cards, and if they match, the student must identify the item. If the student correctly identifies the item, that team keeps the cards, and the student takes another turn. If they don't match or if the student isn't able to correctly identify the item, the student turns them face-down, and a member of Team 2 takes a turn.

d. The game continues until all the cards have been matched. The team with the most correct *matches* wins the game.

Variation:
PHOTO CARDS 263–272
ACTIVITY MASTER 107

Have the class play with one set of Photo Cards and one set of Word Cards.

2. Missing Letters

a. Divide the class into two teams. Draw a series of blanks on the board to represent the letters in a word from student book page 174.

b. Have students from each team take turns calling out letters. If the letter is correct, put it in the appropriate blank and give the team one point. If the letter is incorrect, put it on a list to the side. The team that gets the most points wins the game.

3. Alphabetize! ★
ACTIVITY MASTER 108

a. Make copies of Activity Master 108 and cut them into cards.

b. Have students work in pairs. Give each pair a set of cards, and have them work together to place the words in alphabetical order.

c. Have the first pair to complete the alphabetization write their list on the board. Go over the list with the class.

4. Dictation Game ★★

a. In large print on a piece of paper, write a list of seven to nine job skills from the lesson. For example:

> paint
> drive a bus
> bake
> drive a taxi
> fix sinks
> repair buildings
> fix cars

b. Divide the class into pairs—Student A and Student B. Have all the Student A's come outside the classroom with you. Show them the list of words, and have them spend a few minutes looking at it and trying to remember the words.

c. Have the Student A's return to the classroom and give them three minutes to dictate what they remembered from the list to their Student B partners. The pair that has written the most words wins the game.

d. For correction, have each pair call out one word on their list. Write that word on the board so students can check their spelling.

e. Repeat the game with a new list for Student B's to dictate to their Student A partners.

5. **Category Dictation** ★★

a. Have students make two columns on a piece of paper. Have them write <u>Occupations</u> at the top of the left column and <u>Job Skills</u> at the top of the right column.

b. Dictate items from the lesson, and have students write the word or phrase in the appropriate column. For example:

<u>Occupations</u>	<u>Job Skills</u>
truck driver	type
mechanic	bake

c. After students have written down the word or phrase, write it on the board so students can correct their work.

6. **Associations** ★★★

a. Divide the class into small groups. Call out a word or expression from the lesson, and have the groups write down as many associations as they can think of. For example:

plumber: [fix/sinks/toilets/water]
carpenter: [repair/buildings/wood]

b. Have the groups call out their words and make a common list on the board.

7. **Class Story** ★★★

a. Have students look at a photograph on student book page 174. Ask questions about the person to help them imagine a storyline. For example:

Who is he/she?
What is his/her occupation?
Where does he/she work?
What does he/she do at work every day?
Is the job interesting? Why or why not?
Does he/she like the job?
How many hours a week does he/she work?
What time of day does he/she work?

b. Have students dictate the story to you as you write it on the board. Ask them how to spell various words as they're dictating the story to you. Also ask the class to point out any grammar errors they find in the story.

8. **Who Is It?** ★★★

a. Divide the class into pairs. Have each pair choose one occupation from student book page 174 and write three sentences describing what that person does. For example:

[*secretary*]
She works in an office.
She types letters.
She uses a computer.

b. Have one student from each pair read the sentences to the class and see if the students can guess who is being described.

9. **Interesting Occupations** ★★★

In pairs, have students look at student book page 174 and answer the following questions:

On this page, which occupation would you most like? Why?
What skills do you need for this occupation?
Do you know someone who has this occupation?

10. **One Minute Talks** ★★★

ACTIVITY MASTER 107

Make a copy of Activity Master 107, cut it into cards, and distribute one to each student. Have each student speak to the class for one minute about that occupation.

LESSON OBJECTIVE

Focus

Places of employment
Want ads
Job application form

Vocabulary

assembler
doctor
housekeeper
pharmacist
salesperson
waiter
waitress

A. What's your occupation?
B. I'm a waiter.
A. Where do you work?
B. At Danny's Restaurant.

GETTING READY
5 MINUTES

Use your own visuals or the photos on student book page 176 to introduce the following occupations: *waitress, waiter, housekeeper, assembler, doctor, salesperson,* and *pharmacist.*

THE MODEL CONVERSATION
10 MINUTES

1. **SETTING THE SCENE:** Have students look at the model photograph. Set the scene: "Two people are talking. One is telling about her occupation and where she works."

2. **LISTENING:** With books closed, have students listen to the model conversation—presented by you, by a pair of students, or on the audio program. Check students' understanding of the situation and the vocabulary.

3. **CLASS PRACTICE:** With books still closed, model each line, and have the whole class practice in unison.

4. **READING:** With books open, have students follow along as two students present the model.

5. **PAIR PRACTICE:** In pairs, have students practice the model conversation.

THE CONVERSATION EXERCISES
10 MINUTES

1. **THE SKELETAL DIALOG:** Write the "skeletal dialog" on the board. Fill in the replacement from Exercise 1 to show students how the guided conversation method works. Call on a few pairs of students to practice Exercise 1, using the skeletal framework on the board.

2. **VOCABULARY PRESENTATION:** Present the vocabulary words in the exercises. Point to the illustrations, say the occupation and the places, and have the class repeat them chorally and individually. Check students' understanding and pronunciation of the vocabulary.

3. **EXERCISE PRACTICE:** (optional) Have pairs of students simultaneously practice all the exercises.

4. **EXERCISE PRESENTATIONS:** Call on pairs of students to present their conversations to the class.

READING: WANT ADS
10 MINUTES

Set the context: "These people are looking for a job. They're reading want ads in the newspaper." Have students look at the ads and find the numbers they should call. Have students write the numbers and then compare their answers in pairs.

Answers

1. 668–4950
2. 974–3500
3. 684–2222
4. 684–9733
5. 663–2777

JOB APPLICATION FORM
15 MINUTES

1. Go over the application form. Use yourself (or a hypothetical person) as an example. Point to each item and explain what you would write on each line. For the lines about jobs, ask several individual students what they will write. Give the class many examples, including *self-employed.*

2. Have students complete the form. Circulate around the classroom, answering questions as necessary.

3. Have students share their job applications in pairs.

Option: You may want to make some additional copies of the form for students who make multiple mistakes and want to start over again on a clean form.

EXPANSION

1. Concentration ★

PHOTO CARDS 273–279 (TWO SETS)

a. Shuffle the cards and place them face-down in two rows of 7 each.

b. Divide the class into two teams. The object of the game is for students to find the matching cards and identify the vocabulary item. Both teams should be able to see the cards, since *concentrating* on their location is an important part of playing the game.

c. A student from Team 1 turns over two cards, and if they match, the student must identify the item. If the student correctly identifies the item, that team keeps the cards, and the student takes another turn. If they don't match or if the student isn't able to correctly identify the item, the student turns them face-down, and a member of Team 2 takes a turn.

d. The game continues until all the cards have been matched. The team with the most correct *matches* wins the game.

Variation:
PHOTO CARDS 273–279
ACTIVITY MASTER 109

Have the class play with one set of Photo Cards and one set of Word Cards.

2. Telephone ★★

a. Have students sit in a circle or semicircle. Make up three sentences, using language from the lesson, and whisper them to Student 1. For example:

> I'm a secretary. I can type. I work at the Ajax Company.

b. The first student whispers what he or she heard to the second student, who whispers it to the third student, and so forth. When the message gets to the last student, that person says it aloud. Is it the same message you started with?

Give each student in the class a chance to start his or her own message.

3. Category Dictation ★★

a. Have students make two columns on a piece of paper. Have them write Occupations at the top of the left column and Places at the top of the right column.

b. Dictate the words from the lesson, and have students write the words in the appropriate column. For example:

Occupations	Places
waiter	pharmacy
housekeeper	department store
assembler	restaurant

c. After students have written down the word or phrase, write it on the board so students can correct their work.

4. Association Game ★★★

a. Divide the class into several teams. Call out an occupation from student book page 176. Have the students in each team work together to see how many words they can associate with that occupation. For example:

> housekeeper: [hotel/clean/bed/bathroom/ vacuum cleaner]
>
> doctor: [hospital/patient/sick/ medicine]

b. Set a time limit for the game. When the time limit is up, call on the teams to read their list of associations to the class. The team with the most correct items wins.

5. Who Is It? ★★★

a. Divide the class into pairs. Have each pair choose one occupation from student book page 176 and write three sentences describing what that person does. For example:

> [*housekeeper*]
> She works in a hotel.
> She vacuums rugs.
> She makes beds.

b. Have one student from each pair read the sentences, and have the class guess who is being described.

6. Class Story ★★★

a. Have students look a photograph on student book page 176. Ask questions about the person to help them imagine a storyline. For example:

> Who is he/she?
> What is his/her occupation?
> Where does he/she work?
> What does he/she do at work every day?
> Is the job interesting? Why or why not?
> Does he/she like the job?
> How many hours a week does he/she work?
> What time of day does he/she work?

(continued)

b. Have students dictate the story to you as you write it on the board. Ask them how to spell various words as they're dictating the story to you. Also, ask the class to point out any grammar errors they find in the story.

7. Find the Right Person! ★★★

ACTIVITY MASTER 110

a. Make copies of Activity Master 110 and give one copy to each student.

b. Review the pronunciation of the questions, and have the class repeat chorally and individually.

c. Have students walk around the classroom, interviewing their classmates.

d. The first student to complete all the sentences wins the game. Have that student then report back to the class about all the people he or she interviewed.

8. Interesting Occupations ★★★

In pairs, have students look at student book page 176 and answer the following questions:

On this page, which occupation would you most like? Why?
What skills do you need for this occupation?
Do you know someone who has this occupation?

9. One Minute Talks ★★★

ACTIVITY MASTER 109

Make a copy of Activity Master 109, cut it into cards, and distribute one to each student. Have each student speak to the class for one minute about that occupation.

LESSON OBJECTIVE

Focus

Job skills
Calling in sick

Vocabulary

assemble components
cook
cut hair
operate equipment
repair watches
sell clothing
use a cash register

GETTING READY
10 MINUTES

1. Preview *can't*.
   a. Write on the board:

   > A. Can you _____?
   > B. No, I can't.

   b. Have students repeat: "No, I can't" chorally and individually. Ask about things you are sure they *can't* do. For example: "Can you lift this desk?" Have students respond: "No, I can't."

2. Use your own visuals or the photos on student book page 178 to introduce the following vocabulary items: *assemble components, cook, sell clothing, cut hair, repair watches, operate equipment,* and *use a cash register.*

THE MODEL CONVERSATION
10 MINUTES

1. **SETTING THE SCENE:** Have students look at the model photographs. Set the scene: "Someone is at a job interview."

2. **LISTENING:** With books closed, have students listen to the model conversation—presented by you, by a pair of students, or on the audio program. Check students' understanding of the situation and the vocabulary.

3. **CLASS PRACTICE:** With books still closed, model each line, and have the whole class practice in unison.

4. **READING:** With books open, have students follow along as two students present the model.

5. **PAIR PRACTICE:** In pairs, have students practice the model conversation.

THE CONVERSATION EXERCISES
10 MINUTES

1. **THE SKELETAL DIALOG:** Write the "skeletal dialog" on the board. Fill in the replacement from Exercise 1 to show students how the guided conversation method works. Call on a few pairs of students to practice Exercise 1, using the skeletal framework on the board.

   > A. Can you <u>cook</u>?
   > B. No, I can't. But I'm sure I can learn quickly.

2. **VOCABULARY PRESENTATION:** Present the vocabulary words in the exercises. Point to the photograph of each job skill, say the word, and have the class repeat it chorally and individually. Check students' understanding and pronunciation of the vocabulary.

3. **EXERCISE PRACTICE:** (optional) Have pairs of students simultaneously practice all the exercises.

4. **EXERCISE PRESENTATIONS:** Call on pairs of students to present their conversations to the class.

I CAN'T COME TO WORK TODAY.

THE MODEL CONVERSATION
10 MINUTES

1. **SETTING THE SCENE:** Have students look at the model photographs. Set the scene: "Someone is sick and can't come to work."

2. **LISTENING:** With books closed, have students listen to the model conversation—presented by you, by a pair of students, or on the audio program. Check students' understanding of the situation and the vocabulary.

3. **CLASS PRACTICE:** With books still closed, model each line, and have the whole class practice in unison.

4. **READING:** With books open, have students follow along as two students present the model.

5. **PAIR PRACTICE:** In pairs, have students practice the model conversation.

GRAMMAR

1. Contrast the pronunciation of *can* and *can't*. *Can* is shorter in duration compared to *can't*. Have students repeat after you chorally and individually.

2. Explain that the task is to complete the sentence with the words *can* or *can't*. Have students complete the exercise. Call on individual students for their answers. Pay special attention to their pronunciation of the words *can* and *can't*.

Answers

1. can	4. Can
2. can't	5. can
3. can	6. can't

LANGUAGE IN *MOTION*

1. Model the activity. With students' books closed, write the first line of the chart on the board (assemble things), and then interview students, asking: "Can you assemble things?" When a student finally answers: "Yes, I can," write his or her name next to the phrase *assemble things*.

2. Have students circulate around the classroom, asking others if they can do each of the work skills, and completing the chart with those people's names. Listen in on student conversations and provide help if necessary.

EXPANSION

1. Disappearing Dialog ★

Write the model conversation on the board and ask for two student volunteers to read the conversation. Erase a few of the words from the dialog, and have two different students read the conversation. Erase more words and call on two more students to read the conversation. Continue erasing words and calling on pairs of students until everyone has had a turn and the dialog has disappeared.

2. Concentration ★

PHOTO CARDS 281–287 (TWO SETS)

a. Shuffle the cards and place them face-down in two rows of 7 each.

b. Divide the class into two teams. The object of the game is for students to find the matching cards and identify the vocabulary item. Both teams should be able to see the cards, since *concentrating* on their location is an important part of playing the game.

c. A student from Team 1 turns over two cards and if they match, the student must identify the item. If the student correctly identifies the item, that team keeps the cards, and the student takes another turn. If they don't match or if the student isn't able to correctly identify the item, the student turns them face-down, and a member of Team 2 takes a turn.

d. The game continues until all the cards have been matched. The team with the most correct *matches* wins the game.

Variation:
PHOTO CARDS 281–287
ACTIVITY MASTER 111

Have the class play with one set of Photo Cards and one set of Word Cards.

3. Beanbag Toss ★

Have students stand in a circle. Say a job skill and throw a beanbag to Student 1. Student 1 says another job skill and throws the beanbag to another student. Continue around the circle until all students have mentioned a different job skill.

4. Listening Contrast ★

a. Write the following on the board:

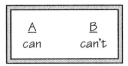

b. Read a sentence, and have students tell you whether it is A (*can*) or B (*can't*). For example:

Teacher: I can type.
Students: A

Teacher: I can't cook.
Students: B

5. What Can You Do? ★★

a. Write on the board:

I can	I can't

b. Tell some things about yourself. For example: "I can speak English. I can't speak Portuguese."

c. Have students take a piece of paper and draw a line down the middle to create two columns. At the top of the left column, have them write I can and at the top of the right column, have them write I can't.

d. Tell students to write five things they *can* do and five things they *can't* do, using the verbs on student book pages 174 and 176 along with other verbs they know. For example:

I can	I can't
type	repair buildings
cook	fix cars
drive a car	drive a truck

e. Have students share their lists in pairs, small groups, or as a class.

6. Match Game ★★★

ACTIVITY MASTER 112

a. Make a copy of Activity Master 112, cut it into cards, and distribute the cards randomly, one to each student.

b. Have students memorize the line on their card and leave their cards on their desks. Then have students circulate around the room, saying their lines until they find their match.

c. When students have found their match, have them compare their cards and come show you.

LESSON OBJECTIVE

FOCUS

Workplace locations
Reading a diagram
Help Wanted signs

VOCABULARY

bathroom
cafeteria
employee lounge
mailroom
personnel office
supply room
vending machine

GETTING READY

5–10 MINUTES

1. Introduce *down the hall*, using school locations. Open the door to your classroom, and have students look down the hallway. Ask students about locations that are down the hall—for example: "Where's the principal's office? Where's the cafeteria?" Model for students: "Down the hall."

2. Use your own visuals or the photos on student book page 180 to introduce the following vocabulary items: *supply room, cafeteria, mailroom, bathroom, employee lounge, personnel office*, and *vending machine*.

THE MODEL CONVERSATION

10 MINUTES

1. **SETTING THE SCENE:** Have students look at the model photographs. Set the scene: "A new employee is asking a question."

2. **LISTENING:** With books closed, have students listen to the model conversation—presented by you, by a pair of students, or on the audio program. Check students' understanding of the situation and the vocabulary.

3. **CLASS PRACTICE:** With books still closed, model each line, and have the whole class practice in unison.

4. **READING:** With books open, have students follow along as two students present the model.

5. **PAIR PRACTICE:** In pairs, have students practice the model conversation.

THE CONVERSATION EXERCISES

10–20 MINUTES

1. **THE SKELETAL DIALOG:** Write the "skeletal dialog" on the board. Fill in the replacement from Exercise 1 to show students how the guided conversation method works. Call on a few pairs of students to practice Exercise 1, using the skeletal framework on the board.

> A. Excuse me. Where's the <u>cafeteria</u>?
> B. Down the hall.
> A. Thanks.

2. **VOCABULARY PRESENTATION:** Present the vocabulary words in the exercises. Point to the photograph of the workplace location, say the word, and have the class repeat it chorally and individually. Check students' understanding and pronunciation of the vocabulary.

3. **EXERCISE PRACTICE:** (optional) Have pairs of students simultaneously practice all the exercises.

4. **EXERCISE PRESENTATIONS:** Call on pairs of students to present the exercises.

A WORKPLACE DIAGRAM

10 MINUTES

1. Explain that this is a diagram of a workplace. If students have a difficult time interpreting it, provide an example on the board of your classroom and how it relates to other neighboring rooms in your school.

2. Tell students that the task is to name the room that is described in each statement. Have students complete the exercise and then compare their answer in pairs.

Answers
1. cafeteria
2. mailroom
3. cafeteria
4. supply room
5. personnel office

COMMUNITY CONNECTIONS

15–20 MINUTES

Brainstorm with the class the types of businesses that would have Help Wanted signs—for example: barber shops, restaurants, drug stores, bakeries, gas stations, and supermarkets. For homework, have students find two Help Wanted signs in their community, write what they see, and the name of the workplace. In the next class, have students discuss the jobs and workplaces in pairs or small groups.

EXPANSION

1. Concentration ⭐

PHOTO CARDS 288–294 (TWO SETS)

a. Shuffle the cards and place them face-down in two rows of 7 each.

b. Divide the class into two teams. The object of the game is for students to find the matching cards and identify the vocabulary item. Both teams should be able to see the cards, since *concentrating* on their location is an important part of playing the game.

c. A student from Team 1 turns over two cards, and if they match, the student must identify the item. If the student correctly identifies the item, that team keeps the cards, and the student takes another turn. If they don't match or if the student isn't able to correctly identify the item, the student turns them face-down, and a member of Team 2 takes a turn.

d. The game continues until all the cards have been matched. The team with the most correct *matches* wins the game.

Variation:
PHOTO CARDS 288–294
ACTIVITY MASTER 113

Have the class play with one set of Photo Cards and one set of Word Cards.

2. Alphabetizing ⭐

ACTIVITY MASTER 113

a. Make a copy of Activity Master 113 and cut it into cards.

b. Have students work in pairs. Give each pair a set of cards, and have them work together to alphabetize the cards. Then call on students to read their alphabetized lists for the class to verify.

Variation: Do the activity as a game. The first pair of students to successfully alphabetize their words wins.

3. Associations ⭐⭐

a. Divide the class into small groups. Call out a workplace location from student book page 180, and have the groups write down as many associations as they can think of. For example:

cafeteria: [lunch/coffee/food]

personnel office: [application forms/calling in sick/benefits]

b. Have the groups call out their words and make a common list on the board.

4. School Diagram ⭐⭐

Have students draw a diagram of where different rooms in the school are located. If necessary, have students walk around the school or ask school personnel where the various rooms are. In pairs, have students compare their diagrams.

5. Where I Work ⭐⭐⭐

Have students draw diagrams of where they work, showing where the different rooms are. In pairs, have students tell about their diagrams.

LESSON OBJECTIVE

FOCUS

Workplace safety

Warning & safety signs

VOCABULARY

safety glasses

GETTING READY
5 MINUTES

Use the photos on student book page 182 to introduce the safety warnings: *The floor is wet! Put on your safety glasses! Don't stand there! Don't go in that room!* and *Don't smoke in here!* Point to the photograph of each situation, say the phrase, and have the class repeat it chorally and individually. Check students' understanding and pronunciation of the vocabulary.

THE MODEL CONVERSATION
10 MINUTES

1. **SETTING THE SCENE:** Have students look at the model photograph. Set the scene: "Somebody is warning someone else about a wet floor."

2. **LISTENING:** With books closed, have students listen to the model conversation—presented by you, by a pair of students, or on the audio program. Check students' understanding of the situation and the vocabulary.

3. **CLASS PRACTICE:** With books still closed, model each line, and have the whole class practice in unison.

4. **READING:** With books open, have students follow along as two students present the model.

5. **PAIR PRACTICE:** In pairs, have students practice the model conversation.

THE CONVERSATION EXERCISES
10 MINUTES

1. **THE SKELETAL DIALOG:** Write the "skeletal dialog" on the board. Fill in the replacement from Exercise 1 to show students how the guided conversation method works. Call on a few pairs of students to practice Exercise 1, using the skeletal framework on the board.

A. Careful!
B. Excuse me?
A. <u>Put on your safety glasses!</u>
B. Okay. Thanks for telling me.

---

2. **VOCABULARY PRESENTATION:** Present the sentences in the exercises. Point to the photograph, say the sentence, and have the class repeat it chorally and individually. Check students' understanding and pronunciation of the vocabulary.

3. **EXERCISE PRACTICE:** (optional) Have pairs of students simultaneously practice all the exercises.

4. **EXERCISE PRESENTATIONS:** Call on pairs of students to present their conversations to the class.

SAFETY SIGNS AT WORK
5 MINUTES

1. Tell students that their task is to match the signs to the warnings. Have them work individually to complete the exercise, and then call on individual students for their answers.

Answers

1. Wear a helmet.
2. Don't smoke.
3. Wear safety glasses
4. Don't stand there.
5. The floor is wet.
6. Don't go that way.

2. Have students look for safety signs for homework or during a five-minute break from class. Have them draw the signs in their student books. In class, have students meet in small groups to share their signs.

EXPANSION

1. Scrambled Sentences ★

ACTIVITY MASTER 114

Divide the class into pairs. Make enough copies of Activity Master 114 for half the class, cut them into cards, and distribute one set to each pair of students. Have students take turns picking up a sentence card, and then saying the complete sentence.

Variation: Students can write their complete sentences and compare their answers with other pairs.

2. **Telephone** ★★

   a. Have students sit in a circle. Make up a message, using the safety warnings in this lesson and whisper it to Student 1.

   b. The first student whispers the message to the second student, who asks: "Excuse me?" Upon hearing the message again, the second student whispers the message to the third student, and so forth. For example:

   > Student 1: Put on your safety glasses! Wear your helmet! And don't go in that room!
   > Student 2: Excuse me?
   > Student 1: Put on your safety glasses! Wear your helmet! And don't go in that room!
   > Student 2: Okay. [*to Student 3*] Put on your safety glasses! Wear your helmet! And don't go in that room!
   > Student 3: Excuse me?
   >   Etc.

   c. When the message gets to the last student, that person says it aloud. Is it the same message you started with?

   Give each student a chance to start his or her own message.

3. **Chain Game** ★★

   Begin the activity by saying: "Careful! The floor is wet!" Student 1 repeats what you said and adds another safety warning—for example: "Careful! The floor is wet! And put on your safety glasses!" Student 2 repeats what you and Student 1 said and adds another warning—for example: "Careful! The floor is wet! Put on your safety glasses. And wear your helmet!" Continue around the room in this fashion, with students repeating what the previous student said and adding another safety warning. Do the activity again, beginning and ending with different students.

   Variation: To aid in the memorization of the phrases—and to increase the fun—have students mime a gesture with each warning. For example:

   > Careful! The floor is wet! [*Student points to floor.*]
   > Put on your safety glasses. [*Student mimes putting on glasses.*]
   > And wear your helmet! [*Student mimes putting on a helmet.*]

4. **School Rules** ★★★

   a. In small groups, have students write a list of rules for their classroom and school.

   b. Have the groups share their lists with the class. Write their sentences on the board. For example:

   > Don't sit on the tables!
   > Don't eat in the classroom!
   > Don't smoke in here!

   c. Then have pairs of students create dialogs based on the model conversation on student book page 182, using these expressions.

5. **Important Safety Tips** ★★★

   In pairs or small groups, have students make a list of important home safety rules. Write students' ideas on the board. For example:

   > Don't smoke in bed!
   > Turn off the stove when you leave the house!
   > Don't put too many plugs in one outlet!

6. **Class Interview** ★★★

   Invite someone from OSHA (Occupational Safety and Health Administration) to visit your classroom. Before the visit, have students prepare questions for the guest about common workplace safety concerns.

LESSON OBJECTIVE

Focus
Time
Money

Vocabulary
deductions
federal taxes
gross pay
health plan
Medicare taxes
pay period
social security (FICA)
state taxes

WORK SCHEDULE

15–20
MINUTES

1. Have students look at the work schedule on student book page 184. Set the scene: "This is Yolanda's work schedule."

2. Ask students the following comprehension questions about the work schedule:

    How many days does Yolanda work?
    When does she start work on Sunday?
    When does she end work on Sunday?
    When does she start work on Monday?
    When does she end work on Monday?

3. Tell students that their task is to write the correct numbers in the blanks based on the work schedule. Have students complete the paragraph on their own, and then compare their answers in pairs.

Answers

1. 6
2. Wednesday
3. 7
4. 5
5. 8
6. Thursday
7. 40

PAYCHECK

20–25
MINUTES

1. Have students look at the paycheck on student book page 184. Set the scene: "This is Yolanda's paycheck."

2. Introduce the following vocabulary:

    deductions: the money taken out of Yolanda's paycheck before she gets the check.

federal taxes: the money that goes to the U.S. government for education, police, security, highways, and other federal government responsibilities.

state taxes: money that goes to Yolanda's state government to pay for education, police, security, highways, and other state government responsibilities.

health plan: a health insurance plan that the employer buys for Yolanda. Yolanda pays $24.80 a week for the plan and the company pays for the rest (usually another $50–$75).

Medicare taxes: the money that goes to the U.S. government Medicare health program.

social security (FICA): money that the U.S. government saves for Yolanda's retirement. When Yolanda stops working, she can get a monthly check from social security. (FICA stands for the Federal Insurance Contributions Act.)

gross pay: the total amount of money Yolanda made before deductions were taken out.

net pay: the final amount of money Yolanda gets after taxes and other deductions.

3. Tell students that their task is to write the correct money amounts in the blanks based on the paycheck information. Have students complete the paragraph on their own and then compare their answers in pairs.

Answers

8. $13.00
9. $520.00
10. $52.00
11. $41.60
12. $26.00
13. $24.50
14. $375.90

EXPANSION

1. Listen for the Money ★

a. Read the paragraph about Yolanda's paycheck again, but with different money figures. For example:

    8. $10.00
    9. $400.00
    10. $45.00
    11. $36.00
    12. $21.00
    13. $24.50
    14. $ 273.50

b. Have students listen and write down the amounts they hear. When you are done with the paragraph, have students compare their figures in pairs.

2. Retell the Story ★★

Divide the class into pairs. Have students look at the work schedule and paycheck illustrations on student book page 184, but have them cover the text. Have the students take turns retelling the story in their own words, referring to the information in the illustrations.

3. Telephone ★★

a. Have students sit in a circle or semicircle. Make up sentences using the new vocabulary in this lesson and whisper them to Student 1. For example:

> Jim makes 600 dollars in gross pay a week. He has 200 dollars in deductions. His net pay is 400 dollars a week.

b. The first student whispers what he or she heard to the second student, who whispers it to the third student, and so forth. When the message gets to the last student, that person says it aloud. Is it the same message you started with?

Give each student in the class a chance to start his or her own message.

4. True or False? ★★

Make statements about the paycheck on student book page 184, and have students decide if the statements are true or false. If a statement is false, have students correct it. For example:

> Yolanda paid $41.60 to Social Security. [True.]
> Yolanda's gross pay is $144.10. [False. Her gross pay is $520.00.]

Variation: Do the activity as a game with competing teams.

5. True or False Definitions ★★★

Give the following definitions of terms on a paycheck, and have students decide whether the definitions are true or false. If a definition is false, have students correct it. For example:

> *deduction*: the money taken out of a paycheck before the person receives the check. [True.]
> *gross pay*: the total amount of money before deductions were taken out. [True.]
> *federal taxes*: the money that goes to the state government. [False. It's the money that goes to the federal government.]

> *health plan*: a health insurance program the employer helps pay for. [True.]
> *Medicare taxes*: the money that goes to the U.S. government Medicare health program. [True.]
> *net pay*: the final amount of money before deductions were taken out. [False. It's the final amount of money *after* deductions were taken out.]
> *social security (FICA)*: money that goes to the social security program. [True.]
> *state taxes*: money that goes to the state government. [True.]

Variation: Do the activity as a game with competing teams.

LANGUAGE EXPERIENCE JOURNAL

Have students write about a workplace. Depending on your students' writing abilities, either have them write in their journal or dictate their story for you to write. Then students should read what they have written to a classmate. If time permits, you may also want to write a response in each student's journal, sharing your own opinions and experiences as well as reacting to what the student has written.

Different Cultures / Different Ways
10 MINUTES

Have students first work in pairs or small groups, reacting to the photographs and responding to the questions. Then have students share with the class what they have talked about.

PUT IT TOGETHER
15–20 MINUTES

In this activity, students talk with each other to find out what job skills their partner has.

1. Divide the class into pairs: Student A and Student B.

2. Tell all the Student A's to look at Part A of the activity on page 185. Have the Student A's check off the job skills they have on this list under the column *You*.

3. Tell all the Student B's to look at Part B on page 186. Have the Student B's check off the job skills they have on this list under the column *You*.

4. When students have finished, have everybody look at the first item on the list: *cook*. Student A asks Student B: "Can you cook?" Student B answers: "Yes, I can," or "No, I can't." Student A writes *yes* or *no* next to *cook*, depending on Student B's answer.

5. The Student A and Student B pairs are now ready to continue the activity with the rest of the skills on their lists.

6. When the pairs have completed the activity, have them check each other's answers.

VOCABULARY FOUNDATIONS
5–10 MINUTES

Have students review the list of words they have learned in this unit. Encourage students to get a small notebook where they can write down vocabulary that is new for them. If students have personal copies of dictionaries or picture dictionaries, have them look up these words in the dictionary and highlight them with a marker. Encourage them to look at their notebooks or dictionaries frequently to review what they have learned.

For additional practice, have students do one or more of the following activities.

1. Taking Notes ✴
In their vocabulary notebooks or on a piece of paper, have students write all the words in one column. In a second column, have them write notes, draw pictures, or write the word in a sentence that will help them remember the meaning of the words.

2. Beanbag Toss ✴
Have students stand in a circle. Say an occupation and throw a beanbag to Student 1. Student 1 says another occupation and throws the beanbag to another student. Continue around the circle until everyone has had a turn.

3. Guess the Word! ✴✴
a. Divide the class into two teams. Choose a vocabulary word from the unit, and on the board, write a blank for each letter in the word. For example: *teach*

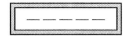

b. Give students a clue about the word. For example: "I do this every class." The team that guesses the word gets one point. The team with the most points wins the game.

4. Finish the Sentence! ✴✴
Divide the class into two teams. Begin sentences, and have students from each team take turns finishing them with appropriate words from the unit. For example:

I drive a taxi. I'm a . . . *taxi driver.*
I fix sinks. I'm a . . . *plumber.*
I teach English. I'm a . . . *teacher.*
I cook in a restaurant. I'm a . . . *cook.*
I cut hair. I'm a . . . *barber.*
I type letters. I'm a . . . *secretary.*
I assemble components. I'm an . . . *assembler.*
I sell clothing. I'm a . . . *salesperson.*
I use a cash register. I'm a . . . *cashier.*
I clean rooms in a hotel. I'm a . . . *housekeeper.*
I clean buildings. I'm a . . . *custodian.*

The team with the most correctly completed sentences wins the game.

5. Category Dictation ✴✴✴
a. Have students make three columns on a piece of paper:

   occupations
   job skills
   workplace locations

b. Dictate words from Vocabulary Foundations, and have students write them in the appropriate column. Make sure all students have covered the vocabulary items on student book page 186 with a piece of paper so they don't refer to that list.

c. As a class, in pairs, or in small groups, have students check their work.

6. Match Game: Occupations ★★★

ACTIVITY MASTER 115

a. Make a copy of Activity Master 115, cut it into cards, and distribute the cards randomly, one to each student.

b. Have students memorize the question or response on their card and leave their cards on their desks. Then have students circulate around the room, saying their lines until they find their match.

c. When students have found their match, have them compare their cards and come show you.

7. Scrambled Phrase Game ★★★

ACTIVITY MASTER 116

a. Divide the class into groups of four. Make a copy of Activity Master 116 for each group. Cut the Activity Masters into cards and place them in two piles—one for verbs and the other for object phrases. Distribute the two sets of cards to each group.

b. Have students take turns picking up one card from each pile and reading the phrase to the group. For example:

```
drive        hair
```

The group decides if the phrase makes sense or doesn't make sense.

c. After all the cards have been picked, have the group lay out all the cards and put together all the phrase combinations that make sense.

LANGUAGE SKILL FOUNDATIONS   10–15 MINUTES

Explain to students that this is a list of skills they have learned in the unit. Students should become familiar with the vocabulary of describing their skills, but they don't need to master all the terms. For each speaking skill on the list, read the skill aloud to students, and have them demonstrate it. For example:

Teacher: I can describe job skills.
Students: I can drive a taxi.

(If students don't understand the vocabulary of a particular speaking skill, give them a concrete example rather than a description or explanation, and then have students practice your example and others.)

Have students put a check next to each skill if they feel they have learned it. Use this information to determine which lessons you may want to review or reinforce for the entire class or for particular students. The Getting Ready and Expansion activities for this unit and the CD-ROM's Activity Bank of supplemental worksheets are excellent resources for additional practice. It may also be helpful to have stronger students or, if available, a classroom aide or volunteer, work with students who need more practice.

Talk About It! ▶▶▶   (Page 187)   20–30 MINUTES

(Page 187 is also available as a transparency.)

Use the scenes in this illustration to review the vocabulary, conversations, and grammar in the unit. Have students first work in pairs or small groups to talk about the illustration and answer the question posed at the bottom of the page. Then discuss as a class.

For additional motivating practice, students will enjoy doing one or more of the following activities.

These activities review Unit 13 vocabulary:

1. The Longest List ★★

a. In pairs, have students write all the occupations they see in the scenes on student book page 187. Tell students to cover the list of words on student book page 186 with a piece of paper so they don't refer to that list. (Set a three-minute time limit for this activity.)

b. Tell students to stop when the three minutes are up. Ask students to count the number of items on their list. Who has the longest list?

c. Check students' answers by calling on students to name items on their lists. Write the words on the board, and have students check their spelling.

2. Remember the Words! ★★

a. Tell students to spend two minutes looking carefully at the scenes on student book page 187.

(continued)

b. Have students close their books and write down all the occupations they remember from the illustration.

c. Have students compare notes with a partner and then look at the scenes again to see how well they remembered them.

3. Do You Remember? ★★

Tell students to spend two minutes looking carefully at the illustration on student book page 187. Then have students close their books. Ask students questions about the scenes. For example:

> How many people are driving?
> Who is crossing the street?
> Where is the police officer?
> Where is the teacher?
> What's the teacher doing?
> How many people work in the restaurant?
> How many customers are in the restaurant?

These activities review Unit 13 conversations and grammar:

4. Class Story ★

a. Have students look at a character in one of the two scenes on student book page 187. Ask questions about the character to help the class imagine a storyline. For example:

> What's his/her occupation?
> What's his/her name?
> Where does he/she work?
> What hours does he/she work?
> Does this person like his/her job?

b. Have students dictate the story to you as you write it on the board. Ask them how to spell various words as they're dictating the story to you. Also, ask the class to point out any grammar errors they find in the story.

Variation: As a review of the vocabulary, erase all the unit vocabulary from the story, and have students come to the board and fill in the words.

5. True or False? ★★

Point to characters in the scenes on student book page 187, make statements about them, and have students decide if the statements are true or false. If a statement is false, have students correct it. For example:

> This woman is a painter. [True.]
> This man is a bus driver. [False. He's a taxi driver.]
> This women is a gardener. [True.]
> These people are mechanics. [False. They're construction workers.]

6. The "Write" Person! ★★

a. Write the following skeletal sentences on the board:

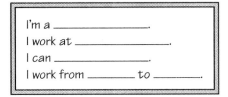

b. Have students each choose one character in one of the scenes on student book page 187 and complete the four sentences.

c. Have students read their sentences to the class and see if students can guess who is being described.

Variation: ★★★ To challenge students, don't provide the skeletal sentences on the board. Have students compose their own sentences to read to the class.

LESSONS & UNIT ACTIVITIES	OBJECTIVES	TEXT	TEACHER'S GUIDE
Vocabulary Preview	Types of Public Transportation • Prepositions of Location • Traffic signs	188–189	240–241
LESSON 1 How do I get there?	Locating places • Asking for & giving directions	190–191	242–243
LESSON 2 Take Bus Number 7.	Public transportation • Asking for & giving information	192–193	244–245
LESSON 3 Where do I get off?	Public transportation • Asking about a destination	194–195	246–247
LESSON 4 The sign says, "Speed Limit 30."	Traffic signs • Driving safely	196–197	248–249
LESSON 5 NUMBERS: A Bus Schedule	Time • Reading a schedule	198	250–251
Language Experience Journal	Writing about transportation.	198	251
Different Cultures / Different Ways	Identifying types of transportation in different countries	199	252
Put It Together	Information Gap / Teamwork activity	199–200	252
Vocabulary Foundations / Language Skill Foundations	Review & skills checklist	200	252–253
Talk About It!	Review, conversations, activities, & games	201	253–254

UNIT RESOURCES

Audio Program:
Audio CD 5: Tracks 22–35
Audio Cassette 4B

Workbooks:
Activity Workbook
Literacy Workbook

Lesson Planner CD-ROM:
Activity Masters 117–122
Activity Bank Unit 14 Worksheets

Transparency: Color Overhead for Unit 14, page 201

TYPES OF TRANSPORTATION (PAGE 188)

PREVIEW
5 MINUTES

Activate students' prior knowledge of types of transportation vocabulary by doing either or both of the following:

1. Have students brainstorm types of transportation and write them on the board.
2. Have students look at the photographs on student book page 188 while they cover the words at the bottom of the page. Have students identify the words they already know.

PRESENT
10 MINUTES

Using the photographs on student book page 188, point to each item or say its number, say the word or phrase, and have the class repeat it chorally and individually. (You can also play the audio program.) Check students' understanding and pronunciation of the vocabulary.

PRACTICE
10 MINUTES

As a class, in pairs, or in small groups, have students practice the vocabulary in either or both of the following ways:

- Say or write a word or phrase, and have students point to the item in their books or tell the number.
- Point to a photograph in the book or give the number, and have students say the word or phrase.

PREPOSITIONS OF LOCATION (PAGE 189)

PREVIEW
5 MINUTES

Activate students' prior knowledge of prepositions by brainstorming prepositions and writing them on the board.

PRESENT
10 MINUTES

Using the map on student book page 189, point to each location, say the word, and have the class repeat it chorally and individually. (You can also play the audio program.) Check students' understanding and pronunciation of the vocabulary.

PRACTICE
5 MINUTES

Move about the classroom, make statements about your "location," and have students complete the sentences. For example:

> [*standing face to face with a student*] I am . . . *across from Carlos.*
> [*standing next to a student*] I am . . . *next to Carlos.*
> [*standing between two students*] I am . . . *between Carlos* and *Monica.*

TRAFFIC SIGNS (PAGE 189)

PREVIEW
5 MINUTES

Activate students' prior knowledge of traffic signs by doing either or both of the following:

1. Have students brainstorm traffic signs and draw them on the board.
2. Have students look at the photographs on student book page 189 while they cover the words at the bottom of the page. Have students identify the traffic signs they already know.

PRESENT
5 MINUTES

Using the photographs on student book page 189, point to each item, say the phrase, and have the class repeat it chorally and individually. (You can also play the audio program.) Check students' understanding and pronunciation of the vocabulary.

PRACTICE
5 MINUTES

As a class, in pairs, or in small groups, have students practice the vocabulary in either or both of the following ways:

- Say or write the meaning of a traffic sign, and have students point to the traffic sign in their books or tell the number.
- Point to a traffic sign in the book or give the number, and have students say the word.

SPELLING PRACTICE
5 MINUTES

Say a word or phrase, and have students spell it aloud or write it. Or point to photographs on student book pages 188 and 189, and have students write the word or phrase. You can also spell a portion of a word or phrase on the board, and have students come to the board to complete it.

1. Listen and Point ★

Divide the class into pairs. Have Student A cover the phrases and look just at the photographs. Have Student B read the phrases in random order. Student A must point to the appropriate photograph or location on the map. Then reverse roles.

2. True or False? ★★

Point to the photographs and the map on student book pages 188 and 189. Make false statements, and have students correct them. For example:

Teacher: [*pointing to #4*] This is a train.
Students: No. It's a bus.

Teacher: [*pointing to #15*] This sign says, "No right turn."
Students: No. It says, "No left turn."

LESSON OBJECTIVE

FOCUS

Locating places
Asking for & giving directions

VOCABULARY

across from
next to
on the left
on the right

walk

GETTING READY

1. Use the photos from Unit 6 on student book pages 76 and 77 to review the following community locations: *post office, clinic, library, bus station, park, movie theater, train station, hospital, bank,* and *laundromat.*

2. Introduce *left* and *right.*

   a. Demonstrate *left* and *right.* With your back to the class, raise your left hand, and have the class repeat: "left." Then raise your right hand, and have the class repeat: "right."

   b. Have students look at one of the illustrations on student book page 190 or draw a similar diagram on the board. Say: "The post office is on the left. The clinic is on the right."

THE MODEL CONVERSATION   10 MINUTES

There are two model conversations. Introduce and practice the first model before going on to the second. For each model:

1. **SETTING THE SCENE:** Have students look at the model photograph. Set the scene: "Someone is asking for directions."

2. **LISTENING:** With books closed, have students listen to the model conversation—presented by you, by a pair of students, or on the audio program. Check students' understanding of the situation and the vocabulary.

3. **CLASS PRACTICE:** With books still closed, model each line, and have the whole class practice in unison.

4. **READING:** With books open, have students follow along as two students present the model.

5. **PAIR PRACTICE:** In pairs, have students practice the model conversation.

THE CONVERSATION EXERCISES   10–20 MINUTES

1. **THE SKELETAL DIALOG:** Write the "skeletal dialog" on the board. Fill in the replacement from Exercise 1 to show students how the guided conversation method works. Call on a few pairs of students to practice Exercise 1, using the skeletal framework on the board.

   > A. Excuse me. How do I get to the library?
   > B. Walk that way. The library is on the left.

2. **VOCABULARY PRESENTATION:** Present the vocabulary words in the exercises. Point to each diagram, say the word, and have the class repeat it chorally and individually. Check students' understanding and pronunciation of the vocabulary.

3. **EXERCISE PRACTICE:** (optional) Have pairs of students simultaneously practice all the exercises.

4. **EXERCISE PRESENTATIONS:** Call on pairs of students to present their conversations to the class.

WHERE IS IT?   10 MINUTES

1. Review *next to, across from,* and *between.*

   a. Draw a diagram of the buildings around your school or *invent* a neighborhood on the board. For example:

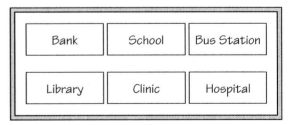

   b. Ask students questions. For example:

   What's across from the school? [The clinic.]
   What's next to the bus station? [The school.]
   What's between the library and the hospital? [The clinic.]

2. Have students complete the exercise on student book page 191 and compare their answers in pairs.

Answers

1. left
2. right
3. across from
4. next to
5. between

Look at the map above. Listen and circle the correct place.

1. It's on the left.
2. It's on the right.
3. It's across from the laundromat.
4. It's next to the bus station.
5. It's on the right, across from the hospital.
6. It's on the left, across from the train station.
7. It's on the right, next to the park.
8. It's on the left, between the library and the hospital.

Answers

1. library
2. laundromat
3. bank
4. library
5. park
6. bus station
7. laundromat
8. bank

EXPANSION

1. Alphabetize! ★

a. Divide the class into pairs. Have each pair take out a piece of paper and write down the names of the places on the map on student book page 191. Then have them work together to rewrite the list in alphabetical order.

b. Have the first pair to complete the task write their list on the board. Go over the list with the class.

2. True or False: Left or Right? ★

Make statements about the places in the diagrams on student book page 190, and have students decide if the statements are true or false. If a statement is false, have students correct it. For example:

The post office is on the right. [False. It's on the left.]
The clinic is on the right. [True.]

3. Guessing Game ★★

a. Write the following on the board:

```
It's next to _____.
It's across from _____.
It's between _____ and _____.
```

b. Have students choose a building in the school neighborhood and write two sentences, describing the building's location.

c. Have students read their sentences to the class without saying what the building is.

The class then tries to identify the building. For example:

Student 1: It's between the park and the supermarket.
It's across from the gas station.
Student 2: The library.
Student 1: That's right.

4. Listen and Draw ★★

ACTIVITY MASTERS 117, 118

a. Make a copy of Activity Masters 117 and 118 for all the students in your class.

b. Divide the class into pairs. Have all the students fold the sheet in half so they only see the A or B section. Have the B Students read the sentences aloud as the A Students listen and complete the map.

c. After the pairs complete Activity Master 117, have them compare their maps with another pair of students. Then have students reverse roles for Activity Master 118.

Variation: To simplify this activity, pairs can work individually or together to read the sentences and complete the maps.

5. Giving Directions ★★

a. Show the class the map on student book page 191 and mark "You are here" in front of the park in the lower right corner of the map. Have all the students mark the same spot on their maps.

b. In pairs, have students ask for and give directions from that spot to the following places on the map: *the train station, the post office, the library, the bus station, the laundromat,* and *the bank.*

c. Have several pairs of students present their conversations to the class.

6. Neighborhood Map ★★★

a. Draw on the board a simple map of the neighborhood around your school, writing in the names of streets and buildings. Mark a spot on the map and say: "You are here."

b. Have students ask for directions to different places in the neighborhood, using the prepositions *on the left, on the right, next to, between,* and *across from.* For example:

A. How do I get to the parking lot?
B. Walk that way. It's on the left, next to the bank.

LESSON OBJECTIVE

Focus

Public transportation
Asking for & giving information

GETTING READY 5 MINUTES

Have students look at the bus illustrations on student book page 192. Say each bus destination and bus number, and have students repeat chorally and individually.

THE MODEL CONVERSATION 10 MINUTES

1. **SETTING THE SCENE:** Have students look at the model photograph. Set the scene: "Two people are talking at the bus stop."

2. **LISTENING:** With books closed, have students listen to the model conversation—presented by you, by a pair of students, or on the audio program. Check students' understanding of the situation and the vocabulary.

3. **CLASS PRACTICE:** With books still closed, model each line, and have the whole class practice in unison.

4. **READING:** With books open, have students follow along as two students present the model.

5. **PAIR PRACTICE:** In pairs, have students practice the model conversation.

THE CONVERSATION EXERCISES 10–15 MINUTES

1. **THE SKELETAL DIALOG:** Write the "skeletal dialog" on the board. Fill in the replacement from Exercise 1 to show students how the guided conversation method works. Call on a few pairs of students to practice Exercise 1, using the skeletal framework on the board.

   A. Excuse me. How do I get to the <u>hospital</u>?
   B. Take Bus Number <u>12</u>.
   A. Bus Number <u>12</u>? Thank you.

2. **EXERCISE PRACTICE:** (optional) Have pairs of students simultaneously practice all the exercises.

3. **EXERCISE PRESENTATIONS:** Call on pairs of students to present their conversations to the class.

TAKE THE BLUE LINE.

GETTING READY 5 MINUTES

Have students look at the subway map in the photograph on student book page 193. Point to different subway lines and say their names—for example: the Blue Line, the Red Line, the Orange Line. If applicable, show a subway transit map for your area and point to the different subway lines. Have students tell you their names—for example: the Green Line.

THE MODEL CONVERSATION 10 MINUTES

1. **SETTING THE SCENE:** Have students look at the model photograph. Set the scene: "Two people are talking in a subway station."

2. **LISTENING:** With books closed, have students listen to the model conversation—presented by you, by a pair of students, or on the audio program. Check students' understanding of the situation and the vocabulary.

3. **CLASS PRACTICE:** With books still closed, model each line, and have the whole class practice in unison.

4. **READING:** With books open, have students follow along as two students present the model.

5. **PAIR PRACTICE:** In pairs, have students practice the model conversation.

THE CONVERSATION EXERCISES 10 MINUTES

1. **THE SKELETAL DIALOG:** Write the "skeletal dialog" on the board. Fill in the replacement from Exercise 1 to show students how the guided conversation method works. Call on a few pairs of students to practice Exercise 1, using the skeletal framework on the board.

   A. Excuse me. How do I get to <u>Central Square</u>?
   B. Take the <u>Red Line</u>.
   A. The <u>Red Line</u>? Thank you.

2. **VOCABULARY PRESENTATION:** Present the vocabulary words in the exercises. Point to

the illustrations, say the names of the train lines and their destinations, and have the class repeat them chorally and individually. Check students' understanding and pronunciation of the vocabulary.

3. **EXERCISE PRACTICE:** (optional) Have pairs of students simultaneously practice all the exercises.

4. **EXERCISE PRESENTATIONS:** Call on pairs of students to present their conversations to the class.

LISTENING

10 MINUTES

Listen and write the number under the correct picture.

1. A. Excuse me. How do I get to the mall?
   B. Take Bus Number 11.
   A. Bus Number 11? Thank you.

2. A. Excuse me. How do I get to City Hall?
   B. Take the E Train.
   A. The E Train? Thanks.

3. A. Excuse me. How do I get to the Midtown Hospital?
   B. Take the C Train.
   A. The C Train?
   B. Yes.
   A. Thank you.

4. A. Excuse me. How do I get to the airport?
   B. Take the Blue Line.
   A. The Blue Line? Thanks.

5. A. Excuse me. How do I get to the library?
   B. Take Bus Number 23.
   A. Number 23? Thanks.

Answers

5 1 3 2 4

EXPANSION

1. Disappearing Dialog ✶

Write one of the two model conversations from this lesson on the board and ask for two student volunteers to read the conversation. Erase a few of the words from the dialog, and have two different students read the conversation. Erase more words and call on two more students to read the conversation. Continue erasing words and calling on pairs of students until everyone has had a turn and the dialog has *disappeared.*

2. Read the Map! ✶✶

If applicable, bring in maps of local public transportation. Ask students questions about how to get to different destinations, using the maps. Make sure students are always starting from the same common point (downtown or the school location). For example:

Teacher: How do I get to Benson Hospital (from our school)?
Student: Take Bus Number 77 to Georgia Avenue. Then take Bus Number 54 to the hospital.

3. True or False? ✶✶

Make statements about public transportation service in your community, and have students decide if the statements are true or false. If a statement is false, have students correct it. For example:

The Green Line goes to the airport. [False. The Blue Line goes to the airport.]
The Red Line goes to Broadway. [True.]

4. How Do I Get There? ✶✶✶

a. In pairs, have students write a list of places they usually go to. Then distribute maps of local public transportation.

b. Have students figure out how to get to those places with public transportation.

c. Have students tell the class any new routes or transportation ideas they learned.

Variation: If there is no local public transportation in your community, choose a larger community in your area that has public transportation and that students sometimes visit. With class input, list all the places students might visit there—for example: the hospital, the airport, the bus station, a theater, a museum, a shopping mall. Download public transportation maps of that community, copy them, and distribute to the class. Have students figure out which buses and subways go to their most common destinations.

LESSON OBJECTIVE

Focus

Public transportation
Asking about a destination

Vocabulary

get off

THE MODEL CONVERSATION

10 MINUTES

1. **SETTING THE SCENE:** Have students look at the model photograph. Set the scene: "Two passengers are talking on a subway."

2. **LISTENING:** With books closed, have students listen to the model conversation—presented by you, by a pair of students, or on the audio program. Check students' understanding of the situation and the vocabulary.

3. **CLASS PRACTICE:** With books still closed, model each line, and have the whole class practice in unison.

4. **READING:** With books open, have students follow along as two students present the model.

5. **PAIR PRACTICE:** In pairs, have students practice the model conversation.

THE CONVERSATION EXERCISES

10 MINUTES

1. **THE SKELETAL DIALOG:** Write the "skeletal dialog" on the board. Fill in the replacement from Exercise 1 to show students how the guided conversation method works. Call on a few pairs of students to practice Exercise 1, using the skeletal framework on the board.

> A. Excuse me. Where do I get off for
>   the Midtown Clinic?
> B. Get off at 30th Street.
> A. Thanks very much.

2. **VOCABULARY PRESENTATION:** Present the destination words in the exercises. Point to the illustrations, say the words, and have the class repeat them chorally and individually. Check students' understanding and pronunciation of the vocabulary.

3. **EXERCISE PRACTICE:** (optional) Have pairs of students simultaneously practice all the exercises.

4. **EXERCISE PRESENTATIONS:** Call on pairs of students to present their conversations to the class.

CONVERSATIONS ABOUT PLACES IN THE COMMUNITY

10 MINUTES

1. Brainstorm with students places they go in community. Write their ideas on the board.

2. Have pairs of students practice the skeletal conversation, using the destinations on the board.

3. Call on pairs of students to present their conversations to the class.

LISTENING

10 MINUTES

Listen and write the number under the correct sign.

1. A. Excuse me. Where do I get off for City Hall?
   B. Get off at K Street.
   A. K Street? Thank you.

2. A. Excuse me. Where do I get off for the West Town Mall?
   B. Get off at 11th Avenue.
   A. 11th Avenue? Thanks.

3. A. Excuse me. Where do I get off for Jefferson Memorial Hospital?
   B. Get off at 7th Avenue.
   A. 7th Avenue? Thank you.

4. A. Excuse me. Where do I get off for the central library?
   B. Get off at J Street.
   A. J Street? Thanks.

5. A. Excuse me. Where do I get off for Miller's Department Store?
   B. Get off at 2nd Avenue.
   A. 2nd Avenue? Thanks.

Answers

2 5 1 4 3

LANGUAGE IN *MOTION* SURVEY

10 MINUTES

1. Use your own visuals or the photographs on student book page 188 to review the following vocabulary: *walk, take a bus, take a subway, take a taxi, drive a car,* and *ride a bicycle.*

2. Have students walk around the classroom, asking each other: "How do you get to school?" Have students mark one line in the right column of the chart on student book page 195 for every person who answers positively for each type of transportation.

3. Have students report back to the class what they found out. For example: "Four students take the bus."

COMMUNITY CONNECTIONS **15 MINUTES**

Have students complete the chart for homework. In the next class, have students compare their information in small groups. Write the following questions on the board to guide their group conversations:

> Where do you go on public transportation?
> How do you get there?
> What's the route number?
> Where do you get off?

EXPANSION

1. Associations ★

a. Divide the class into small groups. Call out a verb from Lessons 1–3, and have the groups write down as many associations as they can think of. For example:

> take: [a taxi/a bus/a subway]
> drive: [a car]
> ride: [a bus/a bicycle/a motorcycle]
> get: [on/off/to]

b. Have the groups call out their words and make a common list on the board.

2. Student Survey: Getting to Work ★★
ACTIVITY MASTER 119

Make multiple copies of Activity Master 119 and distribute them to students. Have students survey other students in the school, or friends, neighbors, and co-workers, and record their results on Activity Master 119. Have students report their findings to the class.

3. True or False? ★★

Make statements about how to get to a destination on public transportation in your community, and have students decide if the statements are true or false. If a statement is false, have students correct it. For example:

> Get off the bus at 10th Street to get to City Hall. [True.]
> Get off the subway at Harrison Street to get to Memorial Hospital. [False. Get off at Center Street.]

4. Connecting with the Community ★★★

Have students interview other students in the school, or friends, neighbors, and co-workers, using the same table and questions in Community Connections.

5. Pair Interviews ★★★
ACTIVITY MASTER 120

Make multiple copies of Activity Master 120 and distribute one to each student. In pairs, have students write a report about his or her interview. For example:

> Alicia likes to walk.
> It's a good way to exercise.
> She walks every day.
> She walks to the subway.

LESSON OBJECTIVE

Focus
Traffic signs
Driving safety

Vocabulary
Slow down
train tracks

Do Not Enter
No Turn on Red
No U-turn
One Way
Speed Limit
Stop

GETTING READY
5 MINUTES

1. Brainstorm with students all the traffic signs they know. Write their ideas on the board.
2. Use your own visuals or the photos on student book page 189 to introduce or review the following traffic signs: *Do Not Enter, No Left Turn, No Right Turn, No Turn on Red, No U-Turn, One Way, Speed Limit,* and *Stop.*

THE MODEL CONVERSATION
10 MINUTES

1. **SETTING THE SCENE:** Have students look at the model photographs. Set the scene: "A passenger is talking to a driver."
2. **LISTENING:** With books closed, have students listen to the model conversation—presented by you, by a pair of students, or on the audio program. Check students' understanding of the situation and the vocabulary.
3. **CLASS PRACTICE:** With books still closed, model each line, and have the whole class practice in unison.
4. **READING:** With books open, have students follow along as two students present the model.
5. **PAIR PRACTICE:** In pairs, have students practice the model conversation.

THE CONVERSATION EXERCISES
10 MINUTES

1. **THE SKELETAL DIALOG:** Write the "skeletal dialog" on the board. Fill in the replacement from Exercise 1 to show students how the guided conversation method works. Call on

a few pairs of students to practice Exercise 1, using the skeletal framework on the board.

> A. Slow down!
> B. What?
> A. Slow down!
>   The sign says, "Speed Limit 25."
> B. Thanks.

2. **VOCABULARY PRESENTATION:** Present the vocabulary words in the exercises. Point to the photograph of each sign, say the phrase below and what the sign says, and have the class repeat it chorally and individually. Check students' understanding and pronunciation of the vocabulary.
3. **EXERCISE PRACTICE:** (optional) Have pairs of students simultaneously practice all the exercises.
4. **EXERCISE PRESENTATIONS:** Call on pairs of students to present their conversations to the class.

TRAFFIC SIGNS
10 MINUTES

Point out that the task is to match the signs to the phrases. Have students work individually to complete the exercise, and then compare answers in pairs.

Answers
1. There's a school nearby.
2. No left turn.
3. No right turn.
4. There are train tracks ahead.
5. Look for people in the street.
6. No U-turn.

WHAT OTHER TRAFFIC SIGNS DO YOU SEE IN YOUR COMMUNITY?
15 MINUTES

Have students look for and draw three signs for homework. In the next class, have students compare their drawings in small groups. Then ask each student to draw one sign on the board to explain to the class.

EXPANSION

1. **Listen and Point** ★
Divide the class into pairs. Have Student A cover the words and look just at the signs on

student book pages 196 and 197. Have Student B say what the signs mean in random order. Student A must point to the appropriate sign. Then reverse roles.

2. **Beanbag Toss** ✮

Have students stand in a circle. Describe a traffic sign—for example: "There are train tracks ahead"—and throw a beanbag to Student 1. Student 1 describes another traffic sign and throws the beanbag to another student. Continue around the circle until all students have described a traffic sign.

3. **Telephone** ✮

a. Have students sit in a circle or semicircle. Make up two sentences, using the vocabulary in this lesson and whisper them to Student 1. For example:

   Don't turn yet! The sign says, "No turn on red!"

b. The first student whispers what he or she heard to the second student, who whispers it to the third student, and so forth. When the message gets to the last student, that person says it aloud. Is it the same message you started with?

Give each student in the class a chance to start his or her own message.

4. **Do You Remember?** ✮✮

Tell students to spend two minutes looking carefully at student book pages 196 and 197. Then have students close their books. Have students write down all the kinds of signs they can remember. (There are thirteen different signs on these student book pages.) They can draw the signs or write phrases to explain the signs.

5. **Ranking** ✮✮✮

a. Have students look at the signs on student book pages 196 and 197 and choose the five signs they see the most. Have students rank these signs from one to five, with one being the one they see the most. For example:

   1. one way
   2. stop
   3. speed limit 25
   4. no turn on red
   5. look for people in the street

b. As a class, in pairs, or in small groups, have students compare their lists.

6. **Drawing Dictation** ✮✮✮

Call out the meaning of a sign, and have students draw the sign with the correct shape. For example:

   Teacher: Stop!
   Students: [*draw a hexagonal stop sign with* stop *in capital letters*]

   Teacher: You can't go that way! It's one way!
   Students: [*draw a sign with an arrow inside a rectangle and* one way *in capital letters*]

LESSON OBJECTIVE

Focus

Time

Reading a schedule

Vocabulary

first

next

last

GETTING READY   10 MINUTES

1. Review telling time. Write the following times on the board. Point to each time, say it, and have the class repeat it chorally and individually. For example:

   2:00 (two o'clock)   2:30 (two–thirty)
   2:10 (two–ten)   2:40 (two–forty)
   2:15 (two–fifteen)   2:50 (two–fifty)
   2:20 (two–twenty)

2. Point to the illustrations of the bus stop and bus schedule on student book page 198. Ask students: "Where do you see bus schedules? Where can you get your own copy of a bus schedule? Where do you see train schedules? Where can you get your own copy of a train schedule?"

READING   10–15 MINUTES

1. Go over the schedule with the class. Ask students: "Where does the bus stop? When does the first bus leave Center Street? When does the last bus leave Center Street?"

2. Read the text aloud, and have students cover it up, listen, and point to the parts of the schedule you mention from the text.

3. Read the text again as students read along silently.

4. In pairs or in small groups, have students read the text to each other.

5. Then have students complete the exercise below the bus schedule.

Answers

1. 6:50   5. 2:00
2. 7:20   6. 6:15
3. 8:30   7. 8:00
4. 8:40   8. 8:50

EXPANSION

1. **Listen for the Time** ★

   a. Read the following sentences, and have students write down the times they hear:

      The last bus leaves Center Street at 8:40.
      The next bus arrives at Main Street at 11:14.
      The next bus arrives at 3:15.
      The last bus arrives at 9:50.
      The next bus arrives at Washington Avenue at 6:30.
      The first bus leaves Downtown Crossing at 5:13.
      The next bus arrives at 10:10.

   b. Have pairs of students check each others' answers.

2. **More Comprehension Exercises** ★★

   Activity Master 121

   Make multiple copies of Activity Master 121 and distribute them to students. Have students work individually to answer the questions, and then compare their answers in pairs.

3. **True or False?** ★★

   Make statements about the schedule on student book page 198, and have students decide if the statements are true or false. If a statement is false, have students correct it. For example:

      The last bus arrives at River Road at 7:15.
        [False. It arrives at River Road at 8:15.]
      It's 4:00. The next bus leaves School Street at 4:40.
        [True.]

   Variation: Do the activity as a game with competing teams.

4. **Bus Schedules** ★★★

   Write the following questions on the board, filling in the blanks with the names of real places in your community. Bring to class bus schedules from your community. In pairs, have students look at the schedule and ask and answer the questions.

When does the first bus leave _____?

When does the last bus leave _____?

When does the first bus arrive at _____?

When does the last bus arrive at _____?

It's 10 A.M. When does the next bus arrive at _____?

It's 12:30 P.M. When does the next bus arrive at _____?

It's 5:15 P.M. When does the next bus arrive at _____?

LANGUAGE EXPERIENCE JOURNAL

Have students write about how they get around town. Depending on your students' writing abilities, either have them write in their journal or dictate their story for you to write. Then students should read what they have written to a classmate. If time permits, you may also want to write a response in each student's journal, sharing your own opinions and experiences as well as reacting to what the student has written.

Different Cultures *Different Ways*   10 MINUTES

Have students first work in pairs or small groups, reacting to the photographs and responding to the questions. Then have students share with the class what they have talked about.

PUT IT TOGETHER   15–20 MINUTES

In this activity, students talk with each other to find out information about a bus schedule.

1. Divide the class into pairs: Student A and Student B.

2. Tell all the Student A's to look at Part A of the activity on page 199. Tell all the Student B's to look at Part B on page 200.

3. Have everybody look at the first item on the schedule: *San Diego.*

   a. In Student B's schedule, under *San Diego,* it says, *9:30.* Therefore, when Student A asks: "When does the bus to San Diego leave?," Student B answers: "It leaves at 9:30."

   b. Ask all the Student B's: "When does the bus to San Diego leave?" Have all the Student B's respond in unison: "It leaves at 9:30."

4. Have everybody look at the second item on the schedule: *San Francisco.*

   a. Have all the Student A's look at their list. In their list under *San Francisco,* it says, *10:15.* Therefore, when Student B asks: "When does the bus to San Francisco leave?," Student A answers: "It leaves at 10:15."

   b. Ask all the Student A's: "When does the bus to San Francisco leave?" Have all the Student A's respond in unison: "It leaves at 10:15."

5. The Student A and Student B pairs are now ready to continue the activity with the rest of the words on their lists.

6. When the pairs have completed the activity, have them check each other's answers.

VOCABULARY FOUNDATIONS   5–10 MINUTES

Have students review the list of words they have learned in this unit. Encourage students to get a small notebook where they can write down vocabulary that is new for them. If students have personal copies of dictionaries or picture dictionaries, have them look up these words in the dictionary and highlight them with a marker.

Encourage them to look at their notebooks or dictionaries frequently to review what they have learned.

For additional practice, have students do one or more of the following activities.

1. **Taking Notes** ✶

   In their vocabulary notebooks or on a piece of paper, have students write all the words in one column. In a second column, have them write notes, draw pictures, or write the word in a sentence that will help them remember the meaning of the words.

2. **Scrambled Words** ✶

   a. Choose words from the unit and write them on the board or on a card with the letters scrambled out of order. For example:

   b. Have students take turns guessing what the word is. [between]

   Variation 1: Do the activity in pairs or small groups, with students taking turns scrambling words for others to guess.

   Variation 2: Do the activity as a class game with competing teams.

3. **Listen and Point** ✶

   To review the vocabulary on the list, have students return to the Vocabulary Preview on student book pages 188 and 189. Divide the class into pairs. Have Student A cover the words at the bottom of student book pages 188 and 189 and look just at the photographs or the diagram. Have Student B read the phrases in random order. Student A must point to the appropriate photo or illustration. Then reverse roles.

4. **Category Dictation** ✶✶

   a. Have students make two columns on a piece of paper:

      verbs
      preposition

   b. Dictate words from Vocabulary Foundations, and have students write them in the appropriate column. Make sure all students have covered the vocabulary items on student book page 200 with a piece of paper so they don't refer to that list.

c. As a class, in pairs, or in small groups, have students check their work.

Variation: Other possible categories are: *types of transportation, traffic signs.*

5. Scrambled Sentences ✶✶✶

ACTIVITY MASTER 122

Divide the class into pairs. Make enough copies of Activity Master 122 for half the class, cut them into cards, and distribute one set to each pair of students. Have students take turns picking up a prompt, and then saying the complete sentence.

Variation: Students can write their complete sentences and compare their answers with other pairs.

LANGUAGE SKILL FOUNDATIONS   10–15 MINUTES

Explain to students that this is a list of skills they have learned in the unit. Students should become familiar with the vocabulary of describing their skills, but they don't need to master all the terms. For each speaking skill on the list, read the skill aloud to students, and have them demonstrate it. For example:

Teacher: I can ask for and give directions.
Students: How do I get to the mall? Walk that way. The mall is on the left.

(If students don't understand the vocabulary of a particular speaking skill, give them a concrete example rather than a description or explanation, and then have students practice your example and others.)

Have students put a check next to each skill if they feel they have learned it. Use this information to determine which lessons you may want to review or reinforce for the entire class or for particular students. The Getting Ready and Expansion activities for this unit and the CD-ROM's Activity Bank of supplemental worksheets are excellent resources for additional practice. It may also be helpful to have stronger students or, if available, a classroom aide or volunteer, work with students who need more practice.

Talk About It! ▶▶▶   (Page 201)   20–30 MINUTES

(Page 201 is also available as a transparency.)

Use the scenes in this illustration to review the vocabulary, conversations, and grammar in the unit. Have students first work in pairs or small groups to talk about the illustration and answer the questions posed at the bottom of the page. Then discuss as a class.

For additional motivating practice, students will enjoy doing one or more of the following activities.

These activities review Unit 14 vocabulary:

1. The Longest List ✶✶

a. In pairs, have students write all the things they see in the scenes on student book page 201. Tell students to cover the list of words on student book page 200 with a piece of paper so they don't refer to that list. (Set a three-minute time limit for this activity.)

b. Tell students to stop when the three minutes are up. Ask students to count the number of items on their lists. Who has the longest list?

c. Check students' answers by calling on students to name items on their lists. Write the words on the board, and have students check their spelling.

2. What Are They Doing? ✶✶

a. Tell students to spend two minutes looking carefully at the scenes on student book page 201.

b. Have students close their books and write down all the actions they remember from the illustration. For example:

taking a subway
walking home
asking for directions
driving
giving directions
riding a bus
reading a schedule
riding a bicycle

c. Have students compare notes with a partner and then look at the illustration again to see how well they remembered the actions.

This activity reviews Unit 14 conversations and grammar:

3. Who Is It? ✶

a. Have students look at the transparency or the illustration on student book page 201.

b. Say the following sentences, and have students point to a character in the illustration to identify who is speaking.

Teacher: Excuse me. How do I get to the laundromat?
Students: [*Point to the man with the laundry basket.*]

(continued)

Teacher: The sign says, "Speed Limit 30."
Students: [*Point to the police officer.*]

Teacher: Excuse me. Where do I get off for the Main Street Clinic?
Students: [*Point to the mother with the son who hurt himself.*]

Teacher: Excuse me. How do I get to the post office?
Students: [*Point to the woman with the package.*]

Teacher: Excuse me. How do I get to General Hospital?
Students: [*Point to the woman with the flowers.*]

Teacher: Excuse me. How do I get to the Washington Monument?
Students: [*Point to the man with the camera and map.*]

Teacher: Excuse me. When does the bus leave for Miami?
Students: [*Point to the woman at the bus station.*]

Teacher: Taxi! Taxi!
Students: [*Point to the man holding his hand out.*]

Teacher: Excuse me. When is the next bus to the park?
Students: [*Point to the boys holding the baseball glove and bat.*]

4. **True or False?** ★★

Point to characters in the illustration on student book page 201, make statements about them, and have students decide if the statements are true or false. If a statement is false, have students correct it. For example:

This woman is riding a bus. [True.]
This man is asking for directions. [False. He's giving directions.]
This man was driving too fast. [True.]
These women are at a train station. [False. They're at a bus station.]

5. **What Are They Saying?** ★★★

a. Have pairs or small groups of students look at the transparency or the illustration on student book page 201.

b. Point to two characters in one of the scenes, and have the students in each pair or group work together to create a conversation between those characters.

c. Call on students to present their conversations to the class.

d. One at a time, point to another two people talking on student book page 201 until students have created and presented conversations between all the characters who are having conversations.

Variation 1: Have pairs or small groups of students create a conversation based on one of the scenes, present it to the class, and the other students point to the appropriate scene in the book or on the transparency.

Variation 2: Have students write out the conversations they created for each scene.

6. **The "Write" Person!** ★★★

a. Divide the class into pairs. Have each pair choose one character in one of the scenes on student book page 201 and write a few sentences describing that person. For example:

He's on the street.
He's holding a map.
He's asking for directions.

b. Have the pairs read their sentences to the class and see if students can guess who is being described.

LESSONS & UNIT ACTIVITIES	OBJECTIVES	TEXT	TEACHER'S GUIDE
Vocabulary Preview	Recreation & entertainment activities	202–203	256
LESSON 1 I like to play soccer.	Recreation activities • Expressing likes	204–205	257–259
LESSON 2 I'm going to see a movie.	Recreation activities • Expressing future plans	206–207	260–262
LESSON 3 I went to a concert.	Recreation activities • Describing past actions	208–209	263–264
LESSON 4 NUMBERS: Using a Calendar	Time expressions • Calendar	210	265–266
Language Experience Journal	Writing about weekend plans	210	266
Different Cultures / Different Ways	Recreation activities around the world	211	267
Put It Together	Information Gap / Teamwork activity	211–212	267
Vocabulary Foundations / Language Skill Foundations	Review & skills checklist	212	267–268
Talk About It!	Review, conversations, activities, & games	213	268–269

UNIT RESOURCES

Audio Program:
Audio CD 5: Tracks 36–45
Audio Cassette 4B

Workbooks:
Activity Workbook
Literacy Workbook

Lesson Planner CD-ROM:
Activity Masters 123–133
Activity Bank Unit 14 Worksheets

Vocabulary Photo Cards: 295–313

Transparency: Color Overhead for Unit 14, page 213

PREVIEW
5 MINUTES

Activate students' prior knowledge of recreation vocabulary by doing either or both of the following:

1. Have students brainstorm activities they do in their free time and write them on the board.

2. Have students look at the photographs on student book pages 202 and 203 while they cover the words at the bottom of the page. Have students identify the recreation activities they already know.

PRESENT
10 MINUTES

Using the photographs on student book pages 202 and 203, point to each photograph, say the phrase, and have the class repeat it chorally and individually. (You can also play the audio program.) Check students' understanding and pronunciation of the vocabulary.

PRACTICE
10 MINUTES

As a class, in pairs, or in small groups, have students practice the vocabulary in either or both of the following ways:

• Say or write a word, and have students point to the item in their books or tell the number.

• Point to a photograph in the book or give the number, and have students say the word.

SPELLING PRACTICE
5 MINUTES

Say a phrase, and have students spell it aloud or write it. Or point to an item in the student book, and have students write the phrase. You can also spell a portion of a phrase on the board, and have students come to the board to complete it.

EXPANSION

1. Tell and Show ✶
PHOTO CARDS 295–313

Place the Photo Cards in a pile at the front of the classroom. Have students take turns coming up to the front of the class, selecting a Photo Card, and telling the class the recreation activity without showing the card. Have the rest of the students point to the item on student book page 202 or 203.

2. Listen and Point ✶

Divide the class into pairs. Have Student A cover the words and look just at the photos. Have Student B read the words in random order. Student A must point to the appropriate photo. Then reverse roles.

3. Match Game ✶
PHOTO CARDS 295–313 (TWO SETS)

a. Choose duplicate copies of any Photo Cards 295–313 and distribute them randomly, one to each student.

b. Have students look at their card and identify the item. Then have students circulate around the room, saying the name of the recreation activity on their card until they find their match. Make sure students don't show their cards to their classmates since this is a listening and speaking exercise.

c. When students have found their match, have them compare their cards and come show you. Then give each student another Photo Card to keep the game going. Continue until students have found all the matches.

LESSON OBJECTIVE

FOCUS

Recreation activities
Expressing likes

VOCABULARY

exercise
go dancing
go jogging
go rollerblading
go swimming
listen to music
play basketball
play soccer
play tennis
watch TV

GETTING READY
5 MINUTES

Use your own visuals or the photographs on student book page 204 to introduce the following vocabulary items: *play soccer, play basketball, play tennis, watch TV, listen to music, exercise, go jogging, go swimming, go rollerblading,* and *go dancing.* Say each word, and have the class repeat it chorally and individually. Check students' understanding and pronunciation of the vocabulary.

THE MODEL CONVERSATION
10 MINUTES

1. **SETTING THE SCENE:** Have students look at the model photographs. Set the scene: "Two co-workers are talking in the cafeteria."

2. **LISTENING:** With books closed, have students listen to the model conversation—presented by you, by a pair of students, or on the audio program. Check students' understanding of the situation and the vocabulary.

3. **CLASS PRACTICE:** With books still closed, model each line, and have the whole class practice in unison.

4. **READING:** With books open, have students follow along as two students present the model.

5. **PAIR PRACTICE:** In pairs, have students practice the model conversation.

THE CONVERSATION EXERCISES
10–20 MINUTES

1. **THE SKELETAL DIALOG:** Write the "skeletal dialog" on the board. Fill in the replacement from Exercise 1 to show students how the guided conversation method works. Call on a few pairs of students to practice Exercise 1, using the skeletal framework on the board.

> A. What do you like to do in your free time?
> B. I like to <u>play basketball</u>.

2. **VOCABULARY PRESENTATION:** Present the vocabulary words in the exercises. Point to the photograph of each recreation activity, say the word, and have the class repeat it chorally and individually. Check students' understanding and pronunciation of the vocabulary.

3. **EXERCISE PRACTICE:** (optional) Have pairs of students simultaneously practice all the exercises.

4. **EXERCISE PRESENTATIONS:** Call on pairs of students to present their conversations to the class.

LISTENING
5–10 MINUTES

Listen and write the number under the correct picture.

1. I like to go swimming.
2. I like to play tennis.
3. I like to go dancing.
4. I like to play soccer.
5. I like to go jogging.

Answers

1   4   3   2   5

MATCHING
5 MINUTES

Have students complete the activity individually and then share their answers in pairs, small groups, or as a class.

Answers

1. music
2. TV
3. swimming
4. soccer

MISSING LETTERS

5 MINUTES

Point out that there are letters missing in these words and students have to figure out what those missing letters are and write them in the blanks. Have students fill in the missing letters and then compare answers with a partner.

Answers

1. soccer
2. tennis
3. basketball
4. exercise
5. swimming

LANGUAGE IN *MOTION* SURVEY

15 MINUTES

1. Have students walk around the classroom, asking each other: "What do you like to do in your free time?" Have the interviewer write the activity the classmate mentions in the left column of the chart and then mark one line in the corresponding right column for every classmate who mentions that same activity.

2. Have students count their responses and then report back to the class what they found out. For example: "Nine students like to watch TV in their free time."

EXPANSION

1. Concentration ★

PHOTO CARDS 295–304 (TWO SETS)

a. Shuffle the Photo Cards and place them face-down in four rows of 5 each.

b. Divide the class into two teams. The object of the game is for students to find the matching cards and identify the vocabulary item. Both teams should be able to see the cards, since *concentrating* on their location is an important part of playing the game.

c. A student from Team 1 turns over two cards, and if they match, the student must identify the item. If the student correctly identifies the item, that team keeps the cards, and the student takes another turn. If they don't match or if the student isn't able to correctly identify the item, the student turns them face-down, and a member of Team 2 takes a turn.

d. The game continues until all the cards have been matched. The team with the most correct *matches* wins the game.

Variation:
PHOTO CARDS 295–304
ACTIVITY MASTER 123

Have the class play with one set of Photo Cards and one set of Word Cards.

2. Scrambled Words ★

a. Choose words from the lesson and write them on the board or on a card with the letters scrambled out of order. For example:

```
yalp blestakalb
```

b. Have students take turns guessing what the words are. [play basketball]

Variation 1: Do the activity in pairs or small groups, with students taking turns scrambling words for others to guess.

Variation 2: Do the activity as a class game with competing teams.

3. Alphabetize! ★

ACTIVITY MASTER 123

a. Make copies of Activity Master 123 and cut them into cards.

b. Have students work in pairs. Give each pair a set of cards, and have them work together to place the phrases in alphabetical order.

c. Have the first pair to complete the alphabetization write their list on the board. Go over the list with the class.

4. Miming Game ★★

ACTIVITY MASTER 123

Make a copy of Activity Master 123 and cut it into cards. Place the cards on a desk or table in the front of the classroom. Have students take turns coming to the front of the room, picking a card, and pantomiming the recreation activity on the card. The class tries to guess the action.

Variation: Do the activity as a game with teams. Set a 30-second time limit for each turn. If the team can't guess the recreation activity within the time limit, the card is returned to the pile and the other team takes its turn with a new card.

5. Chain Game ★★

Begin the activity by saying: "In my free time, I like to play basketball." Student 1 repeats what you said and adds another activity—for example: "In my free time, I like to play basketball and listen to music." Student 2 repeats what you and Student 1 said and adds another activity—for example: "In my free time, I like to play basketball, listen to music, and go jogging." Continue around the room in this fashion, with each student repeating what the previous student said and adding another activity. Do the game again, beginning and ending with different students.

6. Likes and Dislikes ★★

a. Have students take out a piece of paper and draw a line down the center of the page. At the top of the left column, have them write <u>I like to</u>, and on the top of the right column, have them write <u>I don't like to</u>.

b. Dictate recreation activities, and have students write the words in either of the columns, depending on whether they *like to* or *don't like to* do them.

c. At the end of the dictation, have students compare their lists to see which activities people *like to* and *don't like to* do.

7. Find the Right Person! ★★★

ACTIVITY MASTER 124

a. Duplicate Activity Master 124 and give one copy to each student.

b. Practice questions of the type on the questionnaire. For example:

> Do you like to play basketball?
> Do you like to watch TV?

c. Have students walk around the classroom, interviewing other students. When a student gets a *yes* answer to the first question, that student writes the other person's name and then continues interviewing others until getting a *yes* answer to the second question, and so on.

d. The first student to fill in names for all the questions wins the game. Have that student then report back to the class about all the people he or she interviewed.

8. Ranking ★★★

a. Have students look at the vocabulary on student book page 204 and choose their five favorite recreation activities. Have students rank these activities from one to five, with one being the one they like the most. For example:

1. watch TV
2. listen to music
3. go dancing
4. exercise
5. go swimming

b. As a class, in pairs, or in small groups, have students compare their lists.

9. Pair Interviews ★★★

ACTIVITY MASTER 125

Make multiple copies of Activity Master 125 and distribute one to each student. In pairs, have students interview one another about what they do in their free time. Have the pairs write a report about their interview. For example:

> Melanie likes to watch TV.
> She watches TV every day.
> She watches TV in her living room with her family.

LESSON OBJECTIVE

Focus

Recreation activities

Expressing future plans

GETTING READY

10 MINUTES

1. Introduce the future with *going to*.

   a. Write the following on the board:

   > I'm going to _____.

   b. Model the following sentences, and have students repeat chorally and individually:

   > After class, I'm going to eat lunch.
   > After class, I'm going to go to the library.
   > After class, I'm going to go home.

   c. Then ask individual students: "What are you going to do after class?"

2. Use your own visuals or the photos on student book page 206 to introduce the following vocabulary items: *see a movie, go to the park, see a play, go to a concert, play baseball, play golf, go to a ballgame, go to a museum,* and *go to the zoo.*

THE MODEL CONVERSATION

10 MINUTES

1. **SETTING THE SCENE:** Have students look at the model photographs. Set the scene: "Two friends are talking."

2. **LISTENING:** With books closed, have students listen to the model conversation—presented by you, by a pair of students, or on the audio program. Check students' understanding of the situation and the vocabulary.

3. **CLASS PRACTICE:** With books still closed, model each line, and have the whole class practice in unison.

4. **READING:** With books open, have students follow along as two students present the model.

5. **PAIR PRACTICE:** In pairs, have students practice the model conversation.

THE CONVERSATION EXERCISES

10–15 MINUTES

1. **THE SKELETAL DIALOG:** Write the "skeletal dialog" on the board. Fill in the replacement from Exercise 1 to show students how the guided conversation method works. Call on a few pairs of students to practice Exercise 1, using the skeletal framework on the board.

   > A. What are you going to do tomorrow?
   > B. I'm going to <u>see a play</u>. How about you?
   > A. I'm going to <u>go to a concert</u>.

2. **VOCABULARY PRESENTATION:** Present the vocabulary words in the exercises. Point to the photographs, say the words, and have the class repeat them chorally and individually. Check students' understanding and pronunciation of the vocabulary.

3. **EXERCISE PRACTICE:** (optional) Have pairs of students simultaneously practice all the exercises.

4. **EXERCISE PRESENTATIONS:** Call on pairs of students to present their conversations to the class.

LISTENING

5 MINUTES

Listen and write the number under the correct picture.

1. A. What are you going to do tomorrow?
   B. I'm going to go to the park.

2. A. What are you going to do tomorrow?
   B. I'm going to see a movie.

3. A. What are you going to do tomorrow?
   B. I'm going to play baseball.

4. A. What are you going to do tomorrow?
   B. I'm going to see a play.

5. A. What are you going to do tomorrow?
   B. I'm going to go to the zoo.

Answers

5 4 2 3 1

GRAMMAR

10 MINUTES

Read the words in the word box aloud to the class. Tell students that their task is to write the correct words in the blanks. Have students complete the exercise and compare answers with a partner, a small group, or the whole class.

Answers

1. you, I'm
2. do, to
3. are, going, go

COMMUNITY CONNECTIONS

15 MINUTES

1. Model the activity. Ask the class: "Where can you go to play soccer?" Write students' ideas on the board. Then tell students to write those places in the chart after "play soccer."

2. Divide the class into small groups. Have students work together to think about places they can go in their community to do the other activities in the chart.

3. After students have completed their charts, ask about each activity, and have the groups report to the class the places in the community they identified for that activity.

EXPANSION

1. Concentration ✷

PHOTO CARDS 301, 305–313 (TWO SETS)

a. Shuffle the cards and place them face-down in four rows of 5 each.

b. Divide the class into two teams. The object of the game is for students to find the matching cards and identify the vocabulary item. Both teams should be able to see the cards, since *concentrating* on their location is an important part of playing the game.

c. A student from Team 1 turns over two cards, and if they match, the student must identify the item. If the student correctly identifies the item, that team keeps the cards, and the student takes another turn. If they don't match or if the student isn't able to correctly identify the item, the student turns them face-down, and a member of Team 2 takes a turn.

d. The game continues until all the cards have been matched. The team with the most correct *matches* wins the game.

Variation:
PHOTO CARDS 301, 305–313
ACTIVITY MASTER 126

Have the class play with one set of Photo Cards and one set of Word Cards.

2. Scrambled Words ✷

a. Choose words from the lesson and write them on the board or on a card with the letters scrambled out of order. For example:

b. Have students take turns guessing what the words are. [play baseball]

Variation 1: Do the activity in pairs or small groups, with students taking turns scrambling words for others to guess.

Variation 2: Do the activity as a class game with competing teams.

3. Clap in Rhythm ✷

Object: Once a clapping rhythm is established, the students must continue naming different recreation activities.

a. Have students sit in a circle.

b. Establish a steady, even beat: one-two-three-four, one-two-three-four, etc., by having students clap their hands to their laps twice and then clap their hands together twice. Repeat throughout the game, maintaining the same rhythm.

c. The object is for each student in turn to name a different recreation activity *each time their hands are clapped together*. Nothing is said when students clap their hands on their laps.

Note: The beat never stops! If a student misses a beat, he or she can either wait for the next beat or pass to the next student.

4. Miming Game ✷✷

ACTIVITY MASTER 126

Make a copy of Activity Master 126 and cut it into cards. Place the cards on a desk or table in the front of the classroom. Have students take turns coming to the front of the room, picking a card, and pantomiming the recreation activity on the card. The class tries to guess the action.

Variation: Do the activity as a game with teams. Set a 30-second time limit for each turn. If the team can't guess the recreation activity within the time limit, the card is returned to the pile and the other team takes its turn with a new card.

(continued)

5. Verb Completions ★★

Write the verbs *go, see,* and *play* on the board. Have students write down activities that begin with each of these verbs. For example: *go to a concert, see a movie, play baseball.* Have students compare lists in pairs, small groups, or as a class.

6. Chain Game ★★

Begin the activity by saying: "Next weekend I'm going to play basketball." Student 1 repeats what you said and adds another activity—for example: "Next weekend I'm going to play basketball and see a play." Student 2 repeats what you and Student 1 said and adds another activity—for example: "Next weekend I'm going to play basketball, see a play, and go to a museum." Continue around the room in this fashion, with each student repeating what the previous student said and adding another activity. Do the activity again, beginning and ending with different students.

7. Circle Game: What Are You Going to Do? ★★

Have students sit in a circle. Ask students: "What are you going to do next weekend?" Go around the circle, with each student saying what he or she is going to do.

8. Likes and Dislikes ★★

a. Have students take out a piece of paper and draw a line down the center of the page. At the top of the left column, have them write <u>I like to</u>, and on the top of the right column, have them write <u>I don't like to</u>.

b. Dictate recreation activities. (Be sure to change the singular activities into general plurals.) Have students write the words in either column, depending on whether they *like to* or *don't like to* do them. For example:

<u>I like to</u>	<u>I don't like to</u>
see movies	see plays
go to concerts	go to museums
go to ballgames	go to zoos

c. At the end of the dictation, have students compare their lists to see which activities people *like to* and *don't like to* do.

9. Find the Right Person! ★★★

ACTIVITY MASTER 127

a. Duplicate Activity Master 127 and give one copy to each student.

b. Practice questions of the type on the questionnaire. For example:

> Are you going to play baseball next weekend?
> Are you going to go to the zoo next weekend?

c. Have students walk around the classroom interviewing other students. When a student gets a *yes* answer to the first question, that student writes in the other person's name and then continues interviewing others until getting a *yes* answer to the second question, and so on.

d. The first student to fill in names for all the questions wins the game. Have that student then report back to the class about all the people he or she interviewed.

10. Ranking ★★★

a. Have students look at the vocabulary on student book page 206 and choose their four favorite recreation activities. Have students rank these activities from one to four, with one being the one they like the most. For example:

1. go to a movie
2. go to a museum
3. go to a concert
4. see a play

b. As a class, in pairs, or in small groups, have students compare their lists.

LESSON OBJECTIVE

FOCUS
Recreation activities
Describing past actions

VOCABULARY
yesterday

GETTING READY
10 MINUTES

1. Introduce the regular past tense and *yesterday*.

   a. Write on the board:

   > Every day I _____.
   > Yesterday I _____.

   b. Model the following, and have students repeat chorally and individually:

   > Every day I play basketball.
   > Yesterday I played basketball.

   c. Fill in the verbs forms on the board:

   > Every day I play basketball.
   > Yesterday I played basketball.

   d. Do the same for the verbs *listen to music* and *watch TV*.

2. Introduce the irregular verbs *see* and *go* following steps a–d above.

THE MODEL CONVERSATION
10 MINUTES

1. **SETTING THE SCENE:** Have students look at the model photographs. Set the scene: "Two co-workers are talking in the cafeteria."

2. **LISTENING:** With books closed, have students listen to the model conversation—presented by you, by a pair of students, or on the audio program. Check students' understanding of the situation and the vocabulary.

3. **CLASS PRACTICE:** With books still closed, model each line, and have the whole class practice in unison.

4. **READING:** With books open, have students follow along as two students present the model.

5. **PAIR PRACTICE:** In pairs, have students practice the model conversation.

THE CONVERSATION EXERCISES
10 MINUTES

1. **THE SKELETAL DIALOG:** Write the "skeletal dialog" on the board. Fill in the replacement from Exercise 1 to show students how the guided conversation method works. Call on a few pairs of students to practice Exercise 1, using the skeletal framework on the board.

   > A. What did you do yesterday?
   > B. I played soccer.

2. **VOCABULARY PRESENTATION:** Present the vocabulary words in the exercises. Point to the photographs, say the words, and have the class repeat them chorally and individually. Check students' understanding and pronunciation of the vocabulary.

3. **EXERCISE PRACTICE:** (optional) Have pairs of students simultaneously practice all the exercises.

4. **EXERCISE PRESENTATIONS:** Call on pairs of students to present their conversations to the class.

GRAMMAR
10 MINUTES

1. Read the sentences in the left column of the word box aloud to the class. Point out to students that these verbs are *regular*—the past tense is formed with *–ed*. Then read the sentences in the right column aloud to the class. Point out that these verbs are *irregular*—the past tense has a different form. In pairs, have students practice reading the sentences in the left column and then in the right column.

2. Tell students that their task is to circle the correct verbs in the sentences below. Have students complete the exercise and compare answers with a partner.

Answers

1. play	5. went	9. exercised
2. played	6. go	10. go
3. listened	7. played	11. went
4. listen	8. exercise	12. saw

LISTENING
5 MINUTES

Listen and circle the correct word.

1. I went to the zoo yesterday.
2. I like to listen to music.
3. I exercised yesterday morning.
4. I exercise every day.
5. I like to go dancing.

6. I played soccer this morning.
7. I went to the park.
8. I saw a movie.

Answers

1. went	5. go
2. listen	6. played
3. exercised	7. went
4. exercise	8. saw

EXPANSION

1. Past Tense Concentration ★

PHOTO CARDS 295–304 (TWO SETS) OR
PHOTO CARDS 305–313 (TWO SETS)

a. Shuffle the cards and place them face-down in four rows of 5 each.

b. Divide the class into two teams. The object of the game is for students to find the matching cards and identify the vocabulary item. Both teams should be able to see the cards, since *concentrating* on their location is an important part of playing the game.

c. A student from Team 1 turns over two cards, and if they match, the student must identify the item. If the student correctly identifies the item, that team keeps the cards, and the student takes another turn. If they don't match or if the student isn't able to correctly identify the item, the student turns them face-down, and a member of Team 2 takes a turn.

d. The game continues until all the cards have been matched. The team with the most correct *matches* wins the game.

Variation:

PHOTO CARDS 295–304	PHOTO CARDS 305–313
ACTIVITY MASTER 128	ACTIVITY MASTER 129

Have the class play first with one set of Photo Cards 295–304 and Activity Master 128 and then with Photo Cards 305–313 and Activity Master 129.

2. Listen for the Verb ★

a. Write the following on the board:

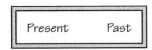

b. Say sentences using present tense and past tense verbs, and have the class tell you whether the statements are past tense or present tense. For example:

Teacher: I play soccer.
Students: Present.

Teacher: I played soccer yesterday.
Students: Past.

Teacher: I went to the park.
Students: Past.

Teacher: I go to the park.
Students: Present.

3. My Own Sentences ★★

a. Write the following on the board, and have students complete them any way they wish:

I like to _____.	I saw _____.
I like to _____.	I played _____.
I like to _____.	I went _____.

b. In pairs or small groups, have students read their sentences to each other.

4. Chain Game ★★

Begin the activity by saying: "Yesterday I saw a movie." Student 1 repeats what you said and adds another activity—for example: "Yesterday I saw a movie and went to a ballgame." Student 2 repeats what you and Student 1 said and adds another activity—for example: "Yesterday I saw a movie, went to a ballgame, and played tennis." Continue around the room in this fashion, with each student repeating what the previous student said and adding another activity. Do the activity again, beginning and ending with different students.

5. Category Dictation ★★★

a. Have students make three columns on a piece of paper. Have them write <u>Yesterday</u> at the top of the left column, <u>Every Day</u> at the top of the middle column, and <u>Tomorrow</u> at the top of the right column.

b. Dictate sentences from the lesson, and have students write the sentences in the appropriate column. For example:

<u>Yesterday</u>	<u>Every Day</u>	<u>Tomorrow</u>
I exercised.	I exercise.	I'm going to exercise.

c. After students have written down the sentences, write them on the board so students can correct their work.

6. Class Survey ★★★

ACTIVITY MASTER 130

Make a copy of Activity Master 130 and give a copy to each student. Have students walk around the classroom, asking each another: "What did you do yesterday?" Have the interviewer write the activity the classmate mentions, and then mark one line for every classmate who mentions that same activity. Have students count their responses and report back to the class.

LESSON OBJECTIVE

FOCUS

Time expressions
Calendar

VOCABULARY

once
twice

GETTING READY
10 MINUTES

1. Review the meaning of *once* and *twice* by writing the following on the board:

once = one time
twice = two times

2. Go over the schedule on student book page 210 with the class. To help students get oriented to the calendar, ask the following questions: "What month is it? What day of the week is the first of January? What day of the week is the 18th of January? What day of the week is the 21st of January? What is the third Wednesday in January? What is the second Thursday in January? How many Sundays are in this January? How many Tuesdays are in this January?"

READING
10–15 MINUTES

Have students read the paragraph and circle the correct words to complete the story. In pairs or in small groups, have students read the completed text to each other.

Answers

1. five
2. once
3. twice
4. 11th
5. fourth
6. month
7. dancing
8. four

MAKE A CALENDAR FOR THIS MONTH.
25 MINUTES

ACTIVITY MASTER 131

Make multiple copies of Activity Master 131 and distribute them to students. Have students complete the calendar according to their plans for the next month. Have students talk in pairs about their plans for the next month.

EXPANSION

1. Listen and Point ★

Read the following phrases, and have students listen and point to the appropriate part of the calendar on student book page 210.

   the first Tuesday of the month
   the first Monday of the month
   the second Wednesday of the month
   the third Saturday of the month
   the fourth Sunday of the month
   the fifth Thursday of the month
   the 18th of January
   the 24th of January
   January 5th
   January 15th

2. Writing Practice ★

Have students write four more sentences about Martin's calendar.

3. Verb Practice ★★

Have students rewrite the paragraph about Martin's calendar in the past tense. Introduce the regular verb *worked* before they start rewriting.

4. True or False? ★★

Make statements about the calendar on student book page 210, and have students decide if the statements are true or false. If a statement is false, have students correct it. For example:

   Martin is going to work 23 days in the month of January. [True.]
   Martin is going to swim twelve times in the month of January. [False. He's going to swim ten times.]

Variation: Do the activity as a game with competing teams.

5. Information Gap ★★★

ACTIVITY MASTERS 132, 133

a. Make multiple copies of Activity Masters 132 and 133 and cut each one in half (Calendar A and Calendar B).

(continued)

b. Divide the class into pairs. Give each partner a different calendar—A or B. Have students share their information and fill in their calendars. For example:

> Student A: What are you going to do on Tuesday, June 3rd?
> Student B: I'm going to work and swim.

c. When the pairs have finished completing their calendars, have them look at their partner's calendar to make sure they have written the information correctly.

d. Then distribute Activity Master 133. Have students reverse roles and repeat steps a–c.

Variation: Students can also practice the past tense in this activity. They can ask one another: "What did you do Tuesday, June 3rd?

LANGUAGE EXPERIENCE JOURNAL

Have students write about their plans for next weekend. Depending on your students' writing abilities, either have them write in their journal or dictate their story for you to write. Then students should read what they have written to a classmate. If time permits, you may also want to write a response in each student's journal, sharing your own opinions and experiences as well as reacting to what the student has written.

Different Cultures / Different Ways   10 MINUTES

Have students first work in pairs or small groups, reacting to the photographs and responding to the question. Then have students share with the class what they have talked about.

PUT IT TOGETHER   15–20 MINUTES

In this activity, students talk with each other to find out information about a person's plans for tomorrow.

1. Divide the class into pairs: Student A and Student B.

2. Tell all the Student A's to look at Part A of the activity on page 211. Tell all the Student B's to look at Part B on page 212.

3. Have everybody look at the first item on the calendar: *8:00 AM*.

   a. In Student B's calendar, next to *8:00 AM*, it says, *exercise*. Therefore, when Student A asks: "What's Linda going to do tomorrow at 8:00?", Student B answers: "She's going to exercise."

   b. Ask all the Student B's: "What's Linda going to do tomorrow at 8:00?" Have all the Student B's respond in unison: "She's going to exercise."

4. Have everybody look at the second item on the calendar: *9:00 AM*.

   a. Have all the Student A's look at their calendar. In their calendar next to *9:00 AM*, it says, *clean the apartment*. Therefore, when Student B asks: "What's Linda going to do tomorrow at 9:00?", Student A answers: "She's going to clean the apartment."

   b. Ask all the Student A's: "What's Linda going to do tomorrow at 9:00?" Have all the Student A's respond in unison: "She's going to clean the apartment."

5. The Student A and Student B pairs are now ready to continue the activity with the rest of the activities on their calendars.

6. When the pairs have completed the activity, have them check each other's answers.

VOCABULARY FOUNDATIONS   5–10 MINUTES

Have students review the list of words they have learned in this unit. Encourage students to get a small notebook where they can write down vocabulary that is new for them. If students have personal copies of dictionaries or picture dictionaries, have them look up these words in the dictionary and highlight them with a marker. Encourage them to look at their notebooks or dictionaries frequently to review what they have learned.

For additional practice, have students do one or more of the following activities.

1. **Taking Notes** ⭑

   In their vocabulary notebooks or on a piece of paper, have students write all the words in one column. In a second column, have them write notes, draw pictures, or write the word in a sentence that will help them remember the meaning of the words.

2. **Scrambled Words** ⭑

   a. Choose words from the unit and write them on the board or on a card with the letters scrambled out of order. For example:

   scxeeeri

   b. Have students take turns guessing what the word is. [exercise]

   Variation 1: Do the activity in pairs or small groups, with students taking turns scrambling words for others to guess.

   Variation 2: Do the activity as a class game with competing teams.

3. **Listen and Point** ⭑

   To review the vocabulary on the list, have students return to the Vocabulary Preview on student book pages 202 and 203. Divide the class into pairs. Have Student A cover the words at the bottom of student book pages 202 and 203 and look just at the photos. Have Student B read the words in random order. Student A must point to the appropriate photo. Then reverse roles.

4. **Categorizing Words** ⭑⭑

   a. Have students make two columns on a piece of paper. Have them write <u>Activities I did last weekend</u> at the top of the left column, and <u>Activities I'm going to do tomorrow or next weekend</u> at the top of the right column.

   b. Have students look at the list of recreation activities on student book page 212 and write the activities in the appropriate

(continued)

column. Then have students compare their lists in pairs.

Variation: Other possible categories are: *Activities I like to do alone, Activities I like to do with family or friends.*

5. Category Dictation ✵✵

a. Have students make two columns on a piece of paper. Have them write <u>go</u> at the top of the left column and <u>play</u> at the top of the right column.

b. Dictate phrases from Vocabulary Foundations, and have students write the phrases in the appropriate column. For example:

<u>go</u>	<u>play</u>
rollerblading	soccer
to the park	tennis

c. After students have written down a phrase, write it on the board so students can correct their work.

LANGUAGE SKILL FOUNDATIONS
10–15 MINUTES

Explain to students that this is a list of skills they have learned in the unit. Students should become familiar with the vocabulary of describing their skills, but they don't need to master all the terms. For each speaking skill on the list, read the skill aloud to students and have them demonstrate it. For example:

Teacher: I can express what I like to do.
Students: I like to play soccer.

(If students don't understand the vocabulary of a particular speaking skill, give them a concrete example rather than a description or explanation, and then have students practice your example and others.)

Have students put a check next to each skill if they feel they have learned it. Use this information to determine which lessons you may want to review or reinforce for the entire class or for particular students. The Getting Ready and Expansion activities for this unit and the CD-ROM's Activity Bank of supplemental worksheets are excellent resources for additional practice. It may also be helpful to have stronger students or, if available, a classroom aide or volunteer, work with students who need more practice.

Talk About It! ▶▶▶ (Page 213)
20–30 MINUTES

(Page 213 is also available as a transparency.)

Use the scenes in this illustration to review the vocabulary, conversations, and grammar in the unit. Have students first work in pairs or small groups to talk about the illustration and answer the question posed at the bottom of the page. Then discuss as a class.

For additional motivating practice, students will enjoy doing one or more of the following activities.

These activities review Unit 15 vocabulary:

1. The Longest List ✵✵

a. In pairs, have students write all the activities they see they see in the scenes on student book page 213. Tell students to cover the list of words on student book page 212 with a piece of paper so they don't refer to that list. (Set a three-minute time limit for this activity.)

b. Tell students to stop when the three minutes are up. Ask students to count the number of items on their lists. Who has the longest list?

c. Check students' answers by calling on students to name items on their lists. Write the words on the board, and have students check their spelling.

2. Remember the Words! ✵✵

a. Tell students to spend two minutes looking carefully at the scenes on student book page 213.

b. Have students close their books and write down all the things they remember from the scenes.

c. Have students compare notes with a partner and then look at the scenes again to see how well they remembered them.

These activities review Unit 15 conversations and grammar:

3. Who Is It? ✵

a. Have students look at student book page 213.

b. Say the following sentences, and have students point to a person in one of the scenes to identify who is speaking.

"I went dancing with my boyfriend last night."
"I went to a ballgame with my father yesterday."
"I like to watch TV."
"I'm going to go to the park with my friend Amy to play baseball."
"I saw a movie with my girlfriend last weekend."
"I went to a museum yesterday."
"I went rollerblading for the first time in my life!"
"I went to the zoo with my son last weekend."
"I like to go swimming."
"I exercise every morning."

4. True or False? ★★

Point to characters in the illustration on student book page 213 or on the transparency. Make statements about them, and have students decide if the statements are true or false. If a statement is false, have students correct it. For example:

These women are playing soccer. [True.]
This man is seeing a movie. [False. He's at a museum.]
This woman is playing tennis. [True.]
This man is playing basketball. [False. He's playing baseball.]

5. The "Write" Person! ★★★

a. Divide the class into pairs. Have each pair choose a character in one of the scenes on student book page 213 and write a few sentences describing that person. For example:

He's on the floor.
He's exercising.
He exercises every day.

b. Have the pairs read their sentences to the class and see if students can guess who is being described.

The *Foundations* Vocabulary Photo Cards offer students a motivating way to learn, review, and expand their vocabulary. This set of 313 cards can be used for classroom instruction, games and activities, and individual students' practice in school and at home.

The Vocabulary Photo Cards depict key life skills vocabulary related to home, school, community, and work introduced in the *Foundations* program. They can be used as flash cards to introduce and practice vocabulary items. They can also be used to play card games such as Gin Rummy, Go Fish, and other games popular with students.

It may be useful to create with index cards a set of word cards that correspond to the items on the Vocabulary Photo Cards. Together, these word and photo cards can be used to play Lotto and other matching games and activities. (You can also use the Flash Cards on the *Foundations* Multilevel Activity CD-ROM for this purpose. Each unit has a set of word cards that you can reproduce and cut up to create flash cards for vocabulary practice and games.)

In addition, try some of these activities for vocabulary practice that is effective, enjoyable, and playful. Have fun!

ASK ME A QUESTION!

Give each student a different card from the same category (e.g., food, clothing, work). Have students, keeping their cards hidden from other students, walk around and try to guess each other's words by asking yes/no questions.

For example:

Is it a vegetable?	No.
Is it a fruit?	Yes.
Is it yellow?	No.
Is it red?	Yes.
Is it an apple?	Yes.

You can also do this activity as a game by dividing the class into two teams. One person comes to the front of the room and picks a card, and the two teams compete against each other, trying to guess the item by asking yes/no questions.

ASSOCIATION GAME

Divide the class into two teams. Place a pile of cards face down on a table or desk in front of the room. Each team picks a card and team members work together to write down as many associations as they can think of for that word without naming the word. They read their associations aloud and the other team tries to guess what the word is.

BLEEP!

Place some cards in a pile face down on a table or desk in front of the room. (The cards can come from the same category or from different categories.) Divide the class into pairs. Have each pair come to the front of the room, pick two cards from the pile, and create a conversation in which they use those two words. Call on the pairs to present their conversations to the class, saying *bleep* instead of their two words when they come up in the conversation. Other students then try to guess the *bleeped* words.

CONCENTRATION

(You will need two decks of cards for this activity.) Select nine or more of the same cards from each deck. Shuffle the matching cards you have selected and place them face down. Divide the class into two teams. The object of the game is for students to find the matching pairs. Both teams should be able to see the cards, since *concentrating* on their location is an important part of playing the game.

A student from Team 1 turns over two cards. If they match, the student must identify the item. If the student correctly identifies the item, that team gets a point and the student takes another turn. If they don't match, or if the student isn't able to identify the item correctly, the student turns them face down and a member of Team 2 takes a turn. The play continues until all the cards have been matched. The team with the most correct matches wins the game.

Alternative: Play the game with one set of Vocabulary Photo Cards and a set of corresponding word flash cards. You can either create word cards with index cards or use the Flash Cards provided on the CD-ROM.

DRAWING GAME

Divide the class into two teams, and have each team sit in a different part of the room. Place an equal number of cards face down in a pile near each team. Give each team a pad of paper and a marker or pencil.

When you say "Go!" a person from each team comes to the front of his or her team, picks a card from the pile, and draws the object or action shown on the card. The rest of the team then guesses what the word is. When a team correctly guesses a word, another team member picks a card and draws the object or action shown on that card.

Continue until each team has guessed all of the words in their pile. The team that guesses the words in the shortest time wins the game.

GUESS THE WORD

Have students take turns picking a card from a pile and giving a clue about the vocabulary word. Other students guess what the word is. This can also be played as a game between competing teams.

HOT SPOT!

Divide the class into two teams. Place a pile of cards face down on a table or desk in the front of the room. Have one member from each team come to the front and sit facing his or her teammates in the *hot spot*. That person picks a card from the pile, *doesn't* look at the card, and shows it to his or her teammates. The team members then give clues to their teammate, who tries to guess the word. Repeat with the other team. Continue until each team member has had a chance to sit in the *hot spot* and guess a word.

Scoring: Each team earns a point for each clue given before the word is guessed. Low score wins the game.

MIME GAME

Students take turns picking a card from a pile and pantomiming the activity or what somebody would do with the object. Other students then guess what the word is. This can also be played as a game between competing teams.

TRUE OR FALSE?

Have students take turns picking a card from a pile and making a statement about the vocabulary word. The statement may be true or false. If a statement is false, have students correct it. This may also be played as a game between competing teams.

WORD CLUES

Choose 10 cards to use in this game. Divide the class into two teams. Have a member from each team come to the front of the room and sit facing his or her team. Show one of the cards to the two players without showing it to the rest of the class. The two players take turns giving one-word clues to their teams so that they can guess the word. For example:

The word is *cashier.*

Team 1 Player: *"occupation"*
[Team 1 guesses.]

Team 2 Player: *"store"*
[Team 2 guesses.]

Team 1 Player: *"cash register"*
[Team 1 guesses.]

Tell each team to listen carefully to the opposing team's clues. Do the same for the remaining nine cards. The team that guesses the most words wins the game.

VOCABULARY PHOTO CARDS LIST

Classroom Objects
1. pen
2. pencil
3. book
4. notebook
5. ruler
6. eraser
7. calculator
8. bookshelf
9. desk
10. board
11. chalk
12. map
13. globe
14. TV
15. computer
16. bulletin board
17. overhead projector
18. table
19. chair
20. clock
21. screen

Classroom Actions
22. Stand up.
23. Go to the board.
24. Write your name.
25. Erase your name.
26. Sit down.
27. Take out your book.
28. Open your book.
29. Raise your hand.
30. Close your book.
31. Put away your book.

Everyday Activities
32. get up
33. take a shower
34. brush my teeth
35. comb my hair
36. get dressed
37. eat breakfast
38. go to work
39. eat lunch
40. go to school
41. come home
42. cook dinner
43. read
44. watch TV
45. get undressed
46. go to bed
47. make breakfast
48. make lunch
49. make dinner
50. clean
51. wash the dishes
52. do the laundry
53. iron
54. feed the baby
55. walk the dog
56. study
57. exercise
58. listen to music
59. play the guitar
60. play basketball

Weather
61. sunny
62. cloudy
63. hot
64. cold
65. raining
66. snowing
67. foggy

Money
68. penny
69. nickel
70. dime
71. quarter
72. half dollar
73. dollar bill
74. five-dollar bill
75. ten-dollar bill
76. twenty-dollar bill

Home
77. living room
78. kitchen
79. bedroom
80. bathroom
81. dining room
82. balcony
83. patio
84. refrigerator
85. shower
86. closet
87. fireplace
88. stove
89. window
90. bathtub
91. table
92. sofa
93. bed
94. chair
95. rug
96. lamp
97. cabinet

Places in the Community
98. laundromat
99. bank
100. clinic
101. bakery
102. library
103. gas station
104. bus station
105. drug store
106. grocery store
107. post office
108. supermarket
109. hospital
110. park
111. restaurant
112. shopping mall
113. movie theater
114. train station
115. department store

Describing People
116. young
117. middle-aged
118. old
119. tall
120. average height
121. short
122. thin
123. average weight
124. heavy
125. single
126. married
127. divorced
128. widowed

Describing Feelings
129. afraid
130. angry
131. happy
132. hungry
133. sad
134. sick
135. thirsty
136. tired

Food
137. cookie
138. banana
139. carrot
140. tomato
141. potato
142. peach
143. apple
144. orange
145. egg
146. onion
147. bread
148. cheese
149. milk
150. cereal
151. butter
152. sugar
153. lettuce
154. soup
155. soda
156. ice cream
157. a box of cookies
158. a bunch of bananas
159. a jar of mayonnaise
160. a dozen eggs
161. hamburger

162. hot dog
163. sandwich
164. cheeseburger
165. taco
166. pizza
167. donut
168. lemonade
169. coffee
170. tea

Clothing

171. shirt
172. coat
173. suit
174. belt
175. jacket
176. tie
177. sweater
178. umbrella
179. blouse
180. dress
181. watch
182. necklace
183. skirt
184. shoes
185. pants
186. socks
187. jeans
188. gloves
189. mittens
190. pajamas

Bank

191. bank book
192. ATM card
193. deposit slip
194. withdrawal slip
195. check
196. checkbook
197. credit card

Post Office

198. stamps
199. package
200. registered letter
201. money order
202. air letter

Health Ailments

203. backache
204. cold
205. cough
206. earache
207. fever
208. headache
209. sore throat
210. stomachache
211. toothache

Medicine

212. cough syrup

213. aspirin
214. ear drops
215. cold medicine
216. antacid tablets
217. throat lozenges

Injuries

218. broke my arm
219. broke my leg
220. burned my hand
221. cut my face
222. cut my finger
223. sprained my wrist

School Personnel

224. English teacher
225. principal
226. school nurse
227. P.E. teacher
228. guidance counselor
229. custodian
230. school librarian

Places at School

231. auditorium
232. cafeteria
233. gym
234. library
235. office
236. principal's office
237. nurse's office
238. guidance office

School Subjects & Activities

239. math
240. English
241. social studies
242. science
243. art
244. music
245. technology
246. band
247. orchestra
248. choir
249. drama
250. football
251. soccer
252. basketball

Occupations

253. cook
254. custodian
255. gardener
256. cashier
257. electrician
258. repairperson
259. delivery person
260. security guard
261. police officer
262. construction worker
263. bus driver

264. painter
265. teacher
266. baker
267. secretary
268. taxi driver
269. truck driver
270. plumber
271. mechanic
272. carpenter
273. waitress
274. waiter
275. housekeeper
276. assembler
277. doctor
278. salesperson
279. pharmacist
280. barber

Job Skills

281. assemble components
282. cook
283. sell clothing
284. cut hair
285. repair watches
286. operate equipment
287. use a cash register

Workplace Locations

288. supply room
289. cafeteria
290. mailroom
291. bathroom
292. employee lounge
293. personnel office
294. vending machine

Recreation & Entertainment

295. play soccer
296. play basketball
297. play tennis
298. watch TV
299. listen to music
300. exercise
301. go jogging
302. go swimming
303. go rollerblading
304. go dancing
305. see a movie
306. go to the park
307. see a play
308. go to a concert
309. play baseball
310. play golf
311. go to a ballgame
312. go to a museum
313. go to the zoo

Activity Masters

The *Foundations* Activity Masters are provided on the Multilevel Activity CD-ROM included with this Teacher's Guide. In order to download and print these resources, you need to have Adobe Acrobat Reader installed on your computer. If you do not have a copy of the Reader installed, please visit www.adobe.com and download and install the free Adobe Acrobat Reader program.

The instructional resources on the CD-ROM are organized in a set of convenient folders designed for easy access and flexible use. You can find the Activity Masters in their own Activity Master folder, or you can go to the folder for a particular unit and find the Activity Masters and other resources for that unit assembled in one place.

See the CD-ROM User's Guide at the back of this volume for a complete description of the *Foundations* instructional resources and how to access them.

Unit 1

1 Capital Alphabet Letters I
2 Capital Alphabet Letters II
3 Lower Case Alphabet Letters I
4 Lower Case Alphabet Letters II
5 Numbers 0–10
6 Numbers 0–10 in Words

Unit 2

7 Classroom Object Word Cards I
8 Classroom Object Word Cards II
9 Classroom Action Word Cards
10 Numbers 11–19
11 Numbers 11–19 in Words

Unit 3

12 Everyday Activities
13 Everyday Activities Phrase Cards
14 Everyday Actions
15 Everyday Actions Phrase Cards
16 Everyday Activities Sentence Prompts
17 Weather Word Cards
18 Numbers 20–100
19 Numbers 20–100 in Words
20 Temperature Information Gap
21 Unit 3 Match Game

Unit 4

5 Numbers 0–10
6 Numbers 0–10 in Words

10 Numbers 11–19
11 Numbers 11–19 in Words
18 Numbers 20–100
19 Numbers 20–100 in Words
22 Days of the Week Word Cards
23 Months of the Year Word Cards
24 Large Number Cards
25 Addition Match Cards
26 Tic Tac Grid
27 Clock Faces
28 Pair Interview: *What Time?*
29 Weekly Schedules
30 Ordinal Number Cards I
31 Ordinal Number Cards II
32 Ordinal Number Cards III
33 Information Gap: *The Smith Family Apartment Building*
34 Month and Number Cards I
35 Month and Number Cards II
36 Dates Match Game
37 Money Word Cards
38 Money Match Game
39 Unit 4 Match Game

Unit 5

40 Rooms in the Home Word Cards
41 Home Appliances & Features Word Cards
42 Pair Interview: *In Your Home*
43 Furniture Word Cards
44 Home Theme Matching Game

Unit 6

45 Places in the Community Word Cards I
46 Places in the Community Word Cards II
47 Listen and Draw I
48 Listen and Draw II
49 Street Numbers Information Gap
50 Unit 6 Match Game

Unit 7

51 Describing Age and Height Word Cards
52 Describing Hair Color and Eye Color Word Cards
53 Describing Marital Status Word Cards
54 Information Gap: *Describing People*
55 Describing Feelings Word Cards
56 Match Game: *Countries and Languages*
57 Describing Weight Word Cards
58 Match Game: *Age, Height, and Weight*
59 Match Game: *Questions and Answers*
60 Questions for *Talk About It!*

Unit 8

26 Tic Tac Grid
61 Food Word Cards I
62 Food Word Cards II
63 Information Gap: *At the Supermarket*

275

FOUNDATIONS UNIT TESTS

The following pages contain 15 reproducible unit achievement tests—one for each unit of *Foundations*. Additional test resources are also provided: listening scripts (pages 309–312), an answer sheet (page 313), and an answer key (pages 315–317).

These test materials are also available as downloadable and reproducible files on the Multilevel Activity CD-ROM included with this Teacher's Guide. The CD-ROM also offers additional assessment tools:

- A Needs Assessment questionnaire in an easy pictorial format enables students to indicate their needs and interests to guide the teacher's lesson planning.
- A Performance-Based Lesson Assessment form is a tool for evaluating and documenting student participation and performance.
- A Learner Progress Chart enables students to record their test scores and chart their progress.

GOAL OF THE UNIT TESTS

The *Foundations* unit achievement tests are designed to assess student progress and prepare students for the types of standardized tests and performance assessments used by many instructional programs. Such tests have become common tools for assessing students' educational advancement and for evaluating programs' effectiveness in meeting outcome-based performance standards.

TEST CONTENT

All 15 tests have a consistent two-page format. The first page contains three listening activities. In the first activity, students listen to a statement and choose the correct picture. In the second activity, students listen to a question and choose the correct written answer. The third activity exclusively involves listening, as students listen to a question and three possible answers and then select the correct spoken answer. (Scripts for the listening activities are provided on pages 309–312 of this Teacher's Guide and also on the CD-ROM.) The second page of each test includes two activities: a

reading activity in which students choose a word or answer a question based on a picture; and a writing activity in which students complete sentences with words provided in a choice box.

Students can record their answers in two ways. An Answers Box on each test page enables students to practice "bubbling in" their answers, and students can answer the sentence-completion activity by writing words directly on the blank lines. Or you can have students use the separate Unit Tests Answer Sheet, which offers them practice placing their answers on a separate sheet rather than in a test booklet. (The Unit Tests Answer Sheet can be used with any of the tests.)

USING THE TESTS

You can use the tests in a variety of ways to carefully develop students' test-taking skills. For the first few tests, it will be helpful to do each section of the test separately. Go over each section as a class and then have students answer the questions in that section. Make sure students understand the question format. Then for the next few tests, preview all the sections at once, make sure students understand all the formats, and then have them take the test in its entirety. For the remaining tests, have students answer all the questions without any preview of the material, in order to more closely simulate a real test-taking situation.

Over time, you can modify other aspects of the test-taking experience in order to develop students' skills. For example, for the first few tests, you may want to allow students to ask for help when they have difficulty understanding a question format. Later, it will be better to not allow students to ask for help during a test. Also, you may want to have students do some or most of the tests on an untimed basis, allowing them as much time as they need to answer all the questions. Eventually, though, it will be good practice for students to take some of the tests on a timed basis, especially if they will experience timed tests in your program. (If you use timed tests, let students complete the unfinished items later in class or at home so they benefit from the practice.)

(continued)

TEST-TAKING STRATEGIES FOR STUDENTS

As students work with the tests, focus on strategies they need to develop in order to perform well on authentic tests. Work on these strategies at a pace and intensity that is appropriate for the needs and abilities of your students.

BUBBLING IN THE BUBBLE: Make sure students know how to use a pencil to fill in a bubble completely on an answer grid so that the answer is recorded. Explain how the answer sheet on a standardized test is scored by a machine. (You may want to have a supply of Number 2 pencils available for test-taking practice.)

ERASURES AND STRAY MARKS: Students should be sure to erase completely any bubbled-in answer that they wish to change. They should also be sure to erase any stray marks they may have accidentally made on a page.

BUBBLING IN ON THE CORRECT LINE OF THE ANSWER SHEET: Make sure students avoid a common mistake when recording their answers on the answer sheet. If they skip a question, they need to be sure to also skip the corresponding line on the answer sheet. (Encourage students to make a mark on the test page next to any question they have skipped, so they can quickly locate these questions when they come back to them.)

MULTIPLE-CHOICE STRATEGIES: When students don't know the answer to a multiple-choice question, they should learn to eliminate the choice or choices that they know are wrong. By doing this, they might arrive at the correct answer, or they may narrow down the number of possible answers and then guess. (If you wish, have students actually cross out on the test page the letters of answer choices they can eliminate, so that they can focus on the narrowed-down set of choices.)

CHECKING ANSWERS: Make sure students allow enough time to go over their work before handing in a test. They should first try to answer any questions they have skipped, and they should then go over their work to check it. Caution students to not change an answer unless they know it is incorrect. If they have guessed an answer and they are still not sure of the correct choice, their first guess is more likely to be right

OTHER FORMS OF ASSESSMENT

In addition to using these achievement tests, you should plan to use a variety of other forms of assessment with your students. Alternative assessment activities that involve students performing classroom or real-life tasks, playing games, or participating in role plays, simulations, and other performance-based activities should be part of a well-rounded assessment program, especially for students at the beginning-literacy and low-beginning level. Using portfolio assessment strategies to keep files of student work (for example, homework, in-class writing, creative projects, teacher evaluations, and student self-evaluations) creates a much more comprehensive picture of student achievement and progress than is represented in a set of test scores.

INTEGRATING SCANS SKILLS

For programs that integrate the objectives of the Secretary's Commission on Achieving Necessary Skills, it is very appropriate to give students responsibility for the day-to-day management of classroom logistics, such as recording attendance, obtaining supplies and equipment, or making copies of lesson handouts. Students can also take responsibility for aspects of their assessment, including scoring the Unit Achievement Tests, copying blank answer sheets, graphing their performance on their Learner Progress Chart, and maintaining their student portfolios.

A. Listen and choose the correct picture.

A

B

C

1.

A

B

C

2.

A

B

C

3.

A

B

C

4.

	ANSWERS		
1	(A)	(B)	(C)
2	(A)	(B)	(C)
3	(A)	(B)	(C)
4	(A)	(B)	(C)
5	(A)	(B)	(C)
6	(A)	(B)	(C)
7	(A)	(B)	(C)
8	(A)	(B)	(C)
9	(A)	(B)	(C)
10	(A)	(B)	(C)

B. Listen and choose the correct answer.

5. A. Mary.
   B. M-A-R-Y.
   C. Nice to meet you.

6. A. 8D.
   B. 10 Center Street.
   C. 249–1115.

7. A. Yes, that's right.
   B. Did you say 9C?
   C. Nice to meet you, too.

C. Listen and answer numbers 8–10 on the answer sheet.

© 2007 Pearson Education, Inc.
Duplication for classroom use is permitted.

Name: _____ Date: _____

D. Read and answer.

  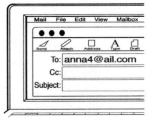

11. **A.** sister
     B. daughter
     C. husband
     D. wife

12. **A.** three Elm Street
     B. two Elm Street
     C. ten Elm Street
     D. eight Elm Street

13. **A.** e-mail address
     B. address
     C. cell phone number
     D. social security number

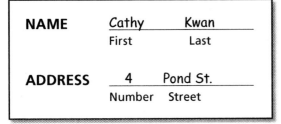

NAME	Cathy	Kwan
	First	Last
ADDRESS	4	Pond St.
	Number	Street

Joe Green
7 Elm Rd.
Los Angeles, CA 90036

14. What's her last name?
     A. Cathy.
     B. Kwan.
     C. Four.
     D. Pond.

15. What's his zip code?
     A. 7 Elm Road.
     B. Los Angeles.
     C. California.
     D. 90036.

E. Write.

address	apartment	name	son	telephone

16. My _____ is Anna.

17. My _____ number is 7B.

18. My _____ is 9 Main Street.

19. My _____ number is 862–9104.

20. My _____ is 4 years old.

ANSWERS

11	Ⓐ	Ⓑ	Ⓒ	Ⓓ
12	Ⓐ	Ⓑ	Ⓒ	Ⓓ
13	Ⓐ	Ⓑ	Ⓒ	Ⓓ
14	Ⓐ	Ⓑ	Ⓒ	Ⓓ
15	Ⓐ	Ⓑ	Ⓒ	Ⓓ

© 2007 Pearson Education, Inc.
Duplication for classroom use is permitted.

A. Listen and choose the correct picture.

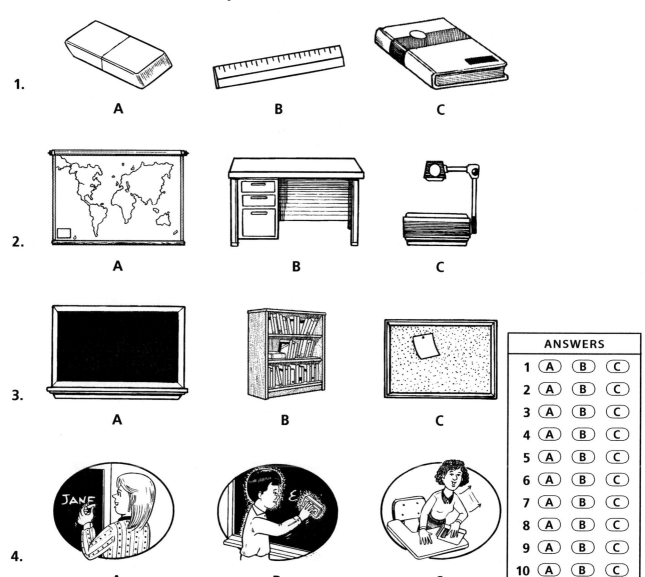

1.
   A   B   C

2.
   A   B   C

3.
   A   B   C

4.
   A   B   C

ANSWERS

1 Ⓐ Ⓑ Ⓒ
2 Ⓐ Ⓑ Ⓒ
3 Ⓐ Ⓑ Ⓒ
4 Ⓐ Ⓑ Ⓒ
5 Ⓐ Ⓑ Ⓒ
6 Ⓐ Ⓑ Ⓒ
7 Ⓐ Ⓑ Ⓒ
8 Ⓐ Ⓑ Ⓒ
9 Ⓐ Ⓑ Ⓒ
10 Ⓐ Ⓑ Ⓒ

B. Listen and choose the correct answer.

5. **A.** Next to the teacher.
   B. Sixteen.
   C. There are two erasers.

6. **A.** A pencil.
   B. Twelve students.
   C. The classroom.

7. **A.** A wall.
   B. A desk.
   C. A TV.

C. Listen and answer numbers 8–10 on the answer sheet.

© 2007 Pearson Education, Inc.
Duplication for classroom use is permitted.

Name: _____   Date: _____

D. Read and answer.

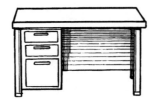

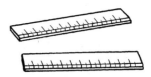

11. **A.** calculator
    B. bulletin board
    C. eraser
    D. notebook

12. **A.** table
    B. bookshelf
    C. desk
    D. screen

13. **A.** pens
    B. rulers
    C. pencils
    D. chalk

14. Where's the pen?
    A. On the eraser.
    B. Next to the eraser.
    C. On the chalk.
    D. Next to the pencil.

15. Where's the globe?
    A. Next to the calculator.
    B. Next to the computer.
    C. Next to the map.
    D. On the calculator.

E. Write.

Close	Erase	Go	Raise	Sit

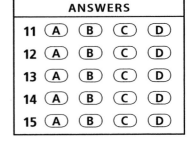

ANSWERS
11 Ⓐ Ⓑ Ⓒ Ⓓ
12 Ⓐ Ⓑ Ⓒ Ⓓ
13 Ⓐ Ⓑ Ⓒ Ⓓ
14 Ⓐ Ⓑ Ⓒ Ⓓ
15 Ⓐ Ⓑ Ⓒ Ⓓ

16. _____ your hand.

17. _____ to the board.

18. _____ down.

19. _____ your name.

20. _____ your book.

© 2007 Pearson Education, Inc.
Duplication for classroom use is permitted.

A. Listen and choose the correct picture.

1.

A   B   C

2.

A   B   C

3.

A   B   C

4.

A   B   C

ANSWERS		
1 (A)	(B)	(C)
2 (A)	(B)	(C)
3 (A)	(B)	(C)
4 (A)	(B)	(C)
5 (A)	(B)	(C)
6 (A)	(B)	(C)
7 (A)	(B)	(C)
8 (A)	(B)	(C)
9 (A)	(B)	(C)
10 (A)	(B)	(C)

B. Listen and choose the correct answer.

5. **A.** My son watches TV.
   B. It's hot.
   C. I go to work.

6. **A.** It's raining.
   B. I'm studying.
   C. I clean every day.

7. **A.** I'm taking a shower.
   B. I play the guitar.
   C. It's cloudy.

C. Listen and answer numbers 8–10 on the answer sheet.

© 2007 Pearson Education, Inc.
Duplication for classroom use is permitted.

Name: _____ Date: _____

D. Read and answer.

11. **A.** I wash the dishes.
    B. I do the laundry.
    C. I take a shower.
    D. I clean the house.

12. **A.** I comb my hair.
    B. I go to bed.
    C. I get dressed.
    D. I come home.

13. **A.** I'm playing the guitar.
    B. I'm exercising.
    C. I'm listening to music.
    D. I'm making lunch.

14. What's the weather?
    A. It's snowing.
    B. It's raining.
    C. I'm cleaning.
    D. It's foggy.

15. What do you do every day?
    A. It's sunny.
    B. I do the laundry.
    C. I play the guitar.
    D. I play basketball.

E. Write.

cloudy	cold	hot	raining	sunny

16. It's _____ in Denver.

17. It's _____ in Chicago.

18. It's _____ in New York.

19. It's _____ in Miami.

20. It's _____ in Los Angeles.

ANSWERS				
11	Ⓐ	Ⓑ	Ⓒ	Ⓓ
12	Ⓐ	Ⓑ	Ⓒ	Ⓓ
13	Ⓐ	Ⓑ	Ⓒ	Ⓓ
14	Ⓐ	Ⓑ	Ⓒ	Ⓓ
15	Ⓐ	Ⓑ	Ⓒ	Ⓓ

© 2007 Pearson Education, Inc.
Duplication for classroom use is permitted.

A. Listen and choose the correct picture.

1.
    A   B   C

2.
    A   B   C

3.
    A   B   C

ANSWERS		
1 (A)	(B)	(C)
2 (A)	(B)	(C)
3 (A)	(B)	(C)
4 (A)	(B)	(C)
5 (A)	(B)	(C)
6 (A)	(B)	(C)
7 (A)	(B)	(C)
8 (A)	(B)	(C)
9 (A)	(B)	(C)
10 (A)	(B)	(C)

4.
    A   B   C

B. Listen and choose the correct answer.

5. A. Sunday.
   B. March.
   C. 11:15.

6. A. October 21.
   B. Ten cents.
   C. 9:00.

7. A. 8.
   B. $26.00.
   C. 2:30.

C. Listen and answer numbers 8–10 on the answer sheet.

© 2007 Pearson Education, Inc.
Duplication for classroom use is permitted.

Name: _____ Date: _____

D. Read and answer.

11. A. a dollar bill
   B. $1.05
   C. $1.01
   D. $1.10

12. A. $31.00
   B. 31¢
   C. 21¢
   D. 36¢

13. A. It's seven fifteen.
   B. It's six forty-five.
   C. It's seven thirty.
   D. It's eight thirty.

Chicago	3:45
Miami	6:30
Dallas	7:15
New York	9:30

14. What month is it?
   A. January.
   B. June.
   C. January 14.
   D. 9:45.

15. What time does the train to Miami leave?
   A. Three forty-five.
   B. Seven fifteen.
   C. Nine thirty.
   D. Six thirty.

E. Write.

Tuesday	Wednesday	Thursday	Friday	Saturday

16. May fourth is on _____.

17. May ninth is on _____.

18. May fifteenth is on _____.

19. May twenty-sixth is on _____.

20. May thirty-first is on _____.

ANSWERS

11 (A) (B) (C) (D)
12 (A) (B) (C) (D)
13 (A) (B) (C) (D)
14 (A) (B) (C) (D)
15 (A) (B) (C) (D)

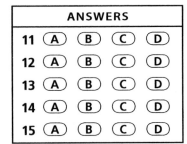

MAY

SUN	MON	TUE	WED	THU	FRI	SAT
		1	2	3	4	5
6	7	8	9	10	11	12
13	14	15	16	17	18	19
20	21	22	23	24	25	26
27	28	29	30	31		

© 2007 Pearson Education, Inc.
Duplication for classroom use is permitted.

A. Listen and choose the correct picture.

1.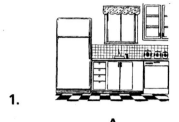

   A   B   C

2.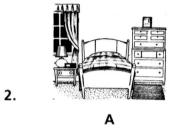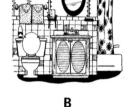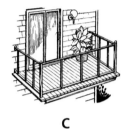

   A   B   C

3.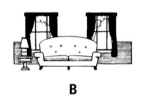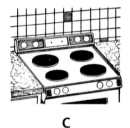

   A   B   C

ANSWERS
1 (A) (B) (C)
2 (A) (B) (C)
3 (A) (B) (C)
4 (A) (B) (C)
5 (A) (B) (C)
6 (A) (B) (C)
7 (A) (B) (C)
8 (A) (B) (C)
9 (A) (B) (C)
10 (A) (B) (C)

4.

   A   B   C

B. Listen and choose the correct answer.

5. **A.** There's a nice bathtub.
   B. There are two bedrooms.
   C. There's one bathroom.

6. **A.** In the living room.
   B. In the kitchen.
   C. In the bathroom.

7. **A.** There are five apartments.
   B. There are four rooms.
   C. There are three windows.

C. Listen and answer numbers 8–10 on the answer sheet.

© 2007 Pearson Education, Inc.
Duplication for classroom use is permitted.

Name: _____ Date: _____

D. Read and answer.

11. A. table
    B. lamp
    C. picture
    D. rug

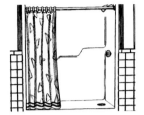

12. A. shower
    B. stove
    C. shelter
    D. chair

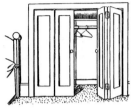

13. A. cabinet
    B. closet
    C. refrigerator
    D. patio

14. Where do you live?
    A. In a mobile home.
    B. In a duplex.
    C. In an apartment building.
    D. In a house.

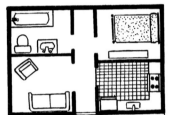

15. How many rooms are there?
    A. One.
    B. Two.
    C. Three.
    D. Four.

ANSWERS				
11	Ⓐ	Ⓑ	Ⓒ	Ⓓ
12	Ⓐ	Ⓑ	Ⓒ	Ⓓ
13	Ⓐ	Ⓑ	Ⓒ	Ⓓ
14	Ⓐ	Ⓑ	Ⓒ	Ⓓ
15	Ⓐ	Ⓑ	Ⓒ	Ⓓ

E. Write.

apartment	closet	living room	refrigerator	shower

16. I live in a very nice _____ .

17. There's a large _____ in the kitchen.

18. There's a bathtub and there's a _____ in the bathroom.

19. There's a nice sofa in the _____ .

20. There's a large _____ in the bedroom.

© 2007 Pearson Education, Inc.
Duplication for classroom use is permitted.

A. Listen and choose the correct picture.

1.
   A   B   C

2.
   A   B   C

3.
   A   B   C

4.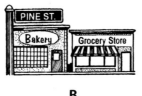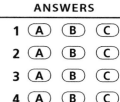
   A   B   C

ANSWERS

1 (A) (B) (C)
2 (A) (B) (C)
3 (A) (B) (C)
4 (A) (B) (C)
5 (A) (B) (C)
6 (A) (B) (C)
7 (A) (B) (C)
8 (A) (B) (C)
9 (A) (B) (C)
10 (A) (B) (C)

B. Listen and choose the correct answer.

5. **A.** Next to the post office.
   B. On Center Street.
   C. On Tuesday.

6. **A.** Put it in the living room.
   B. I'm cleaning.
   C. I'm going to the bank.

7. **A.** The restaurant.
   B. I'm reading a book.
   C. It's next to the bakery.

C. Listen and answer numbers 8–10 on the answer sheet.

© 2007 Pearson Education, Inc.
Duplication for classroom use is permitted.

Name: _____ Date: _____

D. Read and answer.

11. **A.** restaurant
    B. park
    C. movie theater
    D. bakery

12. **A.** grocery store
    B. supermarket
    C. drug store
    D. department store

13. **A.** bank
    B. bakery
    C. library
    D. hospital

14. Where's the library?
    A. Across from the post office.
    B. On Central Avenue.
    C. Between the post office and the park.
    D. In the park.

15. Where's the bus station?
    A. Next to the clinic.
    B. Next to the restaurant.
    C. Across from the restaurant.
    D. On Fifth Street.

E. Write.

ANSWERS
11 (A) (B) (C) (D)
12 (A) (B) (C) (D)
13 (A) (B) (C) (D)
14 (A) (B) (C) (D)
15 (A) (B) (C) (D)

clinic   grocery store   hospital   laundromat   park

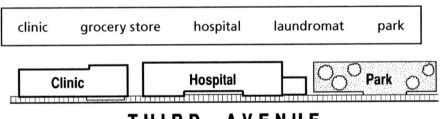
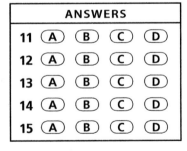

THIRD   AVENUE

16. The grocery store is across from the _____.

17. The laundromat is next to the _____.

18. The drug store is across from the _____.

19. The hospital is between the clinic and the _____.

20. The park is across from the _____.

© 2007 Pearson Education, Inc.
Duplication for classroom use is permitted.

A. Listen and choose the correct picture.

1.

A

B

C

2.

A

B

C

3.

A

B

C

4.

A

B

C

ANSWERS

1	Ⓐ	Ⓑ	Ⓒ
2	Ⓐ	Ⓑ	Ⓒ
3	Ⓐ	Ⓑ	Ⓒ
4	Ⓐ	Ⓑ	Ⓒ
5	Ⓐ	Ⓑ	Ⓒ
6	Ⓐ	Ⓑ	Ⓒ
7	Ⓐ	Ⓑ	Ⓒ
8	Ⓐ	Ⓑ	Ⓒ
9	Ⓐ	Ⓑ	Ⓒ
10	Ⓐ	Ⓑ	Ⓒ

B. Listen and choose the correct answer.

5. A. Brown.
B. Blond.
C. Red.

6. A. She's married.
B. She's thirsty.
C. She's tall, with gray hair.

7. A. He's average height.
B. He's old.
C. He's average weight.

C. Listen and answer numbers 8–10 on the answer sheet.

© 2007 Pearson Education, Inc.
Duplication for classroom use is permitted.

Name: _____ Date: _____

D. Read and answer.

11. **A.** She has blond hair.
   B. She has gray hair.
   C. She has white hair
   D. She has curly hair.

12. **A.** He's thin.
   B. He has black hair.
   C. He's heavy.
   D. He's angry.

13. **A.** She's upset.
   B. She's happy.
   C. She's afraid.
   D. She's sad.

NAME:	Pierre Nadal
HEIGHT:	6 feet 3 inches
WEIGHT:	250 pounds
AGE:	35 years old

NAME:	Marta Amado
COUNTRY OF ORIGIN:	Brazil
HEIGHT:	5 feet 2 inches
HAIR COLOR:	brown
MARITAL STATUS:	divorced

14. How tall is Pierre?
   A. Two hundred fifty pounds.
   B. Middle-aged.
   C. Six feet three inches.
   D. Average height.

15. What does Marta look like?
   A. She's tall.
   B. She has black hair.
   C. She's divorced.
   D. She's short, with brown hair.

E. Write.

| Arabic | hair | height | Morocco | single |

| ANSWERS |
| 11 Ⓐ Ⓑ Ⓒ Ⓓ |
| 12 Ⓐ Ⓑ Ⓒ Ⓓ |
| 13 Ⓐ Ⓑ Ⓒ Ⓓ |
| 14 Ⓐ Ⓑ Ⓒ Ⓓ |
| 15 Ⓐ Ⓑ Ⓒ Ⓓ |

16. Fatima is from _____.

17. She speaks _____.

18. She has brown _____ and green eyes.

19. She's five feet six inches tall. She's average _____.

20. She isn't married. She's _____.

© 2007 Pearson Education, Inc.
Duplication for classroom use is permitted.

A. Listen and choose the correct picture.

1.   A   B   C

2.   A   B   C

3.   A   B   C

 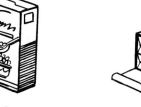 

4.   A   B   C

ANSWERS
1 (A) (B) (C)
2 (A) (B) (C)
3 (A) (B) (C)
4 (A) (B) (C)
5 (A) (B) (C)
6 (A) (B) (C)
7 (A) (B) (C)
8 (A) (B) (C)
9 (A) (B) (C)
10 (A) (B) (C)

B. Listen and choose the correct answer.

5. A. Aisle 7.
   B. A dozen eggs.
   C. A cheeseburger.

6. A. Yes. I'd like a taco, please.
   B. Yes. Sugar is in Aisle 6.
   C. Sorry. There aren't any
      more bananas.

7. A. Cheese is over there.
   B. Pizza is in Aisle 2.
   C. Peaches are in Aisle 5.

C. Listen and answer numbers 8–10 on the answer sheet.

© 2007 Pearson Education, Inc.
Duplication for classroom use is permitted.

Name: _____ Date: _____

D. Read and answer.

11. **A.** a jar
    B. a can
    C. a box
    D. a bottle

12. **A.** a potato
    B. a tomato
    C. an apple
    D. an egg

13. **A.** a hamburger
    B. a sandwich
    C. a donut
    D. a hot dog

3 tomatoes
3 lbs. onions
1/2 lb. cheese
1 doz. eggs

14. What do we need at the supermarket?
    A. Three pounds of tomatoes.
    B. Half a dozen eggs.
    C. Half a pound of cheese.
    D. Three onions.

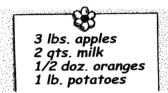

3 lbs. apples
2 qts. milk
1/2 doz. oranges
1 lb. potatoes

15. What do we need at the supermarket?
    A. Three quarts of milk.
    B. Three apples.
    C. A pound of tomatoes.
    D. Six oranges.

E. Write.

bag	bottle	bunch	jar	loaf

ANSWERS
11 (A) (B) (C) (D)
12 (A) (B) (C) (D)
13 (A) (B) (C) (D)
14 (A) (B) (C) (D)
15 (A) (B) (C) (D)

Shopping List

16. a _____ of mayonnaise

17. a _____ of sugar

18. a _____ of bananas

19. a _____ of bread

20. a _____ of soda

© 2007 Pearson Education, Inc.
Duplication for classroom use is permitted.

A. Listen and choose the correct picture.

1.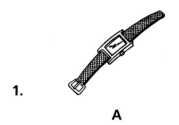

    A   B   C

2.

    A   B   C

3.

    A   B   C

4.

    A   B   C

ANSWERS
1 (A) (B) (C)
2 (A) (B) (C)
3 (A) (B) (C)
4 (A) (B) (C)
5 (A) (B) (C)
6 (A) (B) (C)
7 (A) (B) (C)
8 (A) (B) (C)
9 (A) (B) (C)
10 (A) (B) (C)

B. Listen and choose the correct answer.

5. **A.** Size 10.
   B. Brown.
   C. Thirty-six fifty.

6. **A.** Skirts are on the second floor.
   B. Shirts are on the third floor.
   C. I'm wearing a shirt.

7. **A.** Yes. I'm looking for a watch.
   B. Yes. Pajamas are over there.
   C. Yes. I'm wearing a yellow blouse.

C. Listen and answer numbers 8–10 on the answer sheet.

© 2007 Pearson Education, Inc.
Duplication for classroom use is permitted.

Name: _____ Date: _____

D. Read and answer.

11. **A.** The shirt is small.
    B. The shirt is medium.
    C. The shirt is large.
    D. The shirt is extra-large.

12. **A.** He's wearing a jacket.
    B. He's wearing jeans.
    C. He's wearing a tie.
    D. He's wearing a black shirt.

13. **A.** They're too large.
    B. They're too long.
    C. They're too big.
    D. They're too short.

STORE DIRECTORY			
Department	**Floor**	**Department**	**Floor**
Belts	2	Shoes	1
Coats	3	Ties	2
Jackets	3	Umbrellas	3
Men's Shirts	2	Watches	1
Necklaces	1	Women's Blouses	4

14. Where are the umbrellas?
    A. On the first floor.
    B. On the second floor.
    C. On the third floor.
    D. On the fourth floor.

15. Where are the necklaces?
    A. On the first floor.
    B. On the second floor.
    C. On the third floor.
    D. On the fourth floor.

E. Write.

Dresses	Pants	Shoes	Ties	Watches

16. _____ are thirty-six fifty.

17. _____ are fourteen ninety-five.

18. _____ are sixty-five dollars.

19. _____ are fifty-three twenty-five.

20. _____ are twenty-seven fifty.

ANSWERS				
11	Ⓐ	Ⓑ	Ⓒ	Ⓓ
12	Ⓐ	Ⓑ	Ⓒ	Ⓓ
13	Ⓐ	Ⓑ	Ⓒ	Ⓓ
14	Ⓐ	Ⓑ	Ⓒ	Ⓓ
15	Ⓐ	Ⓑ	Ⓒ	Ⓓ

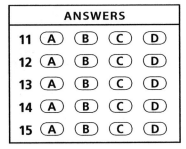

$27⁵⁰ $14⁹⁵ $36⁵⁰ $53²⁵ $65⁰⁰

© 2007 Pearson Education, Inc.
Duplication for classroom use is permitted.

A. Listen and choose the correct picture.

1.
   A   B   C

2.
   A   B   C

 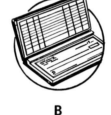 

3.
   A   B   C

ANSWERS
1 (A) (B) (C)
2 (A) (B) (C)
3 (A) (B) (C)
4 (A) (B) (C)
5 (A) (B) (C)
6 (A) (B) (C)
7 (A) (B) (C)
8 (A) (B) (C)
9 (A) (B) (C)
10 (A) (B) (C)

4.
   A   B   C

B. Listen to the conversation and choose the next line.

5. A. You can buy a money order at the next window.
   B. You can send a registered letter at window number 1.
   C. You can buy an air letter at window number 2.

6. A. For shirts and pants.
   B. For fifty-six dollars.
   C. To Flint's Department Store.

7. A. Your change is one dollar.
   B. Your change is two dollars.
   C. Your change is five cents.

C. Listen and answer numbers 8–10 on the answer sheet.

© 2007 Pearson Education, Inc.
Duplication for classroom use is permitted.

Name: _____ Date: _____

D. Read and answer.

11. **A.** a stamp
    B. a deposit slip
    C. a bank account
    D. a money order

12. **A.** an air letter
    B. a package
    C. a letter to Dan Wong
    D. a letter from Dan Wong

13. **A.** seventy-five sixty
    B. sixty-seven fifty
    C. sixty-five seventeen
    D. sixty-five seventy

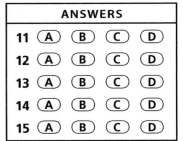

14. What's the return address?
    A. Olga Garcia.
    B. 1220 Lincoln Avenue.
    C. Carol Benedict.
    D. 925 Park Street.

15. How much is your change?
    A. Ten dollars.
    B. Nine fifty.
    C. Nine dollars.
    D. Fifty cents.

E. Write.

ANSWERS			
11 Ⓐ	Ⓑ	Ⓒ	Ⓓ
12 Ⓐ	Ⓑ	Ⓒ	Ⓓ
13 Ⓐ	Ⓑ	Ⓒ	Ⓓ
14 Ⓐ	Ⓑ	Ⓒ	Ⓓ
15 Ⓐ	Ⓑ	Ⓒ	Ⓓ

Fifty-four and 00/100   lamp   Mitchell's Department Store
                    June 21   54.00

```
                                                        16
                                         _____ 2009

PAY TO THE                               17 ┌──────────┐ 18
ORDER OF _____$│          │

                                              19
_____ ⌐ dollars

                      20
FOR _____    Donald Raniere
    ⑆ 210000021  990  507931  0233
```

© 2007 Pearson Education, Inc.
Duplication for classroom use is permitted.

A. Listen and choose the correct picture.

1. 　　

　　A　　　　　　　B　　　　　　　C

2. 　　

　　A　　　　　　　B　　　　　　　C

3. 　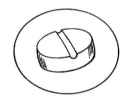　

　　A　　　　　　　B　　　　　　　C

4.

　　A　　　　　　　B　　　　C

ANSWERS
1 Ⓐ Ⓑ Ⓒ
2 Ⓐ Ⓑ Ⓒ
3 Ⓐ Ⓑ Ⓒ
4 Ⓐ Ⓑ Ⓒ
5 Ⓐ Ⓑ Ⓒ
6 Ⓐ Ⓑ Ⓒ
7 Ⓐ Ⓑ Ⓒ
8 Ⓐ Ⓑ Ⓒ
9 Ⓐ Ⓑ Ⓒ
10 Ⓐ Ⓑ Ⓒ

B. Listen and choose the correct answer.

5. **A.** I have a stomach.
   B. I have a backache.
   C. I have throat lozenges.

6. **A.** Look in Aisle 2.
   B. Come in tomorrow at 3:15.
   C. Take two capsules three times a day.

7. **A.** You should exercise.
   B. You should use eye drops.
   C. You should use antacid tablets.

C. Listen and answer numbers 8–10 on the answer sheet.

© 2007 Pearson Education, Inc.
Duplication for classroom use is permitted.

Name: _____ Date: _____

D. Read and answer.

11. A. My eye hurts.
    B. I cut my face.
    C. I have a sore throat.
    D. I have an earache.

12. A. I broke my leg.
    B. I broke my arm.
    C. I broke my neck.
    D. I sprained my wrist.

13. A. Take two tablets twice a day.
    B. Take two tablets once a day.
    C. Take two tablespoons once a day.
    D. Take one tablespoon twice a day.

Medicine	Aisle	Medicine	Aisle
Antacid Tablets	6	Cold Medicine	2
Aspirin	3	Ear Drops	5
Cough Syrup	4	Throat Lozenges	1

14. Where can you find it?
    A. In Aisle 4.
    B. In Aisle 6.
    C. In Aisle 2.
    D. In Aisle 1.

15. Where can you find it?
    A. In Aisle 3.
    B. In Aisle 6.
    C. In Aisle 5.
    D. In Aisle 4.

E. Write.

arm	back	hand	head	stomach

16. _____

17. _____

18. _____

19. _____

20. _____

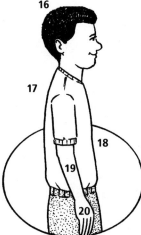

ANSWERS				
11	Ⓐ	Ⓑ	Ⓒ	Ⓓ
12	Ⓐ	Ⓑ	Ⓒ	Ⓓ
13	Ⓐ	Ⓑ	Ⓒ	Ⓓ
14	Ⓐ	Ⓑ	Ⓒ	Ⓓ
15	Ⓐ	Ⓑ	Ⓒ	Ⓓ

© 2007 Pearson Education, Inc.
Duplication for classroom use is permitted.

A. Listen and choose the correct picture.

1.

   A   B   C

2.

   A   B   C

3.

   A   B   C

4.

   A   B   C

ANSWERS

1	A	B	C
2	A	B	C
3	A	B	C
4	A	B	C
5	A	B	C
6	A	B	C
7	A	B	C
8	A	B	C
9	A	B	C
10	A	B	C

B. Listen and choose the correct answer.

5. A. Football.
   B. My English teacher.
   C. Social studies.

6. A. In the guidance office.
   B. In the gym.
   C. In the library.

7. A. In the cafeteria.
   B. In the office.
   C. In the auditorium.

C. Listen and answer numbers 8–10 on the answer sheet.

© 2007 Pearson Education, Inc.
Duplication for classroom use is permitted.

Name: _____ Date: _____

D. Read and answer.

11. **A.** orchestra
    B. choir
    C. band
    D. drama

12. **A.** technology
    B. science
    C. social studies
    D. math

13. **A.** library
    B. auditorium
    C. cafeteria
    D. gym

Period	Class	Room
1st	math	225
2nd	art	307
3rd	English	104
4th	music	222
5th	science	126

14. Which class is third period?
    A. Art.
    B. Math.
    C. Science.
    D. English.

15. In which classroom is music class?
    A. Room 307.
    B. Room 225.
    C. Room 222.
    D. Room 104.

E. Write.

English	math	science	social studies	technology

Time	Class	Teacher	Room
8:15–9:00	science	Mrs. Park	115
9:05–9:50	social studies	Mr. Kanda	108
9:55–10:40	math	Miss Lewis	325
10:45–11:30	English	Mr. Burger	216
12:00–12:45	technology	Ms. Garcia	301

16. The _____ class is in Room 325.

17. The _____ class is from twelve to twelve forty-five.

18. Mr. Burger is the _____ teacher.

19. The _____ class is in Room 108.

20. The _____ class is from eight fifteen to nine o'clock.

ANSWERS			
11 Ⓐ	Ⓑ	Ⓒ	Ⓓ
12 Ⓐ	Ⓑ	Ⓒ	Ⓓ
13 Ⓐ	Ⓑ	Ⓒ	Ⓓ
14 Ⓐ	Ⓑ	Ⓒ	Ⓓ
15 Ⓐ	Ⓑ	Ⓒ	Ⓓ

© 2007 Pearson Education, Inc.
Duplication for classroom use is permitted.

| UNIT **13** TEST | Name: _____ | Date: _____ | Score: _____ |

A. Listen and choose the correct picture.

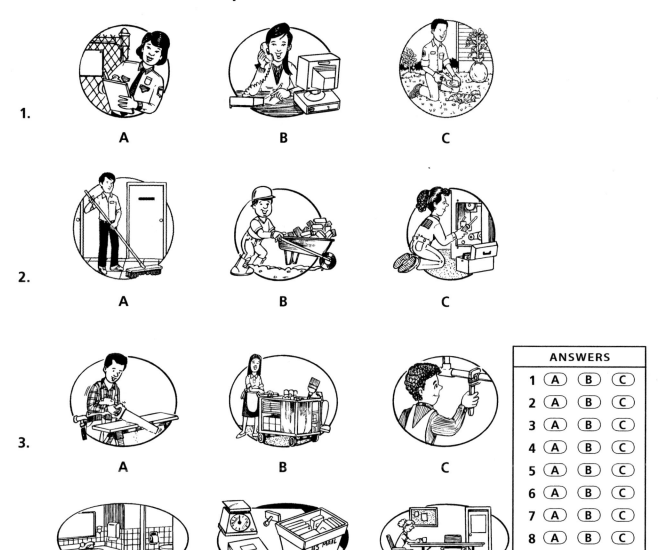

1.　A　B　C

2.　A　B　C

3.　A　B　C

4.　A　B　C

ANSWERS

1　Ⓐ　Ⓑ　Ⓒ
2　Ⓐ　Ⓑ　Ⓒ
3　Ⓐ　Ⓑ　Ⓒ
4　Ⓐ　Ⓑ　Ⓒ
5　Ⓐ　Ⓑ　Ⓒ
6　Ⓐ　Ⓑ　Ⓒ
7　Ⓐ　Ⓑ　Ⓒ
8　Ⓐ　Ⓑ　Ⓒ
9　Ⓐ　Ⓑ　Ⓒ
10　Ⓐ　Ⓑ　Ⓒ

B. Listen and choose the correct answer.

5. **A.** I'm sick.
   B. I'm a cashier.
   C. Wear a helmet.

6. **A.** At the Park Hotel.
   B. As a painter.
   C. I can fix cars.

7. **A.** I can learn quickly.
   B. I'm a pharmacist.
   C. Rosedale Hospital.

C. Listen and answer numbers 8–10 on the answer sheet.

© 2007 Pearson Education, Inc.
Duplication for classroom use is permitted.

Name: _____ Date: _____

D. Read and answer.

11. A. mechanic
 B. electrician
 C. assembler
 D. repairperson

12. A. delivery person
 B. waitress
 C. salesperson
 D. barber

13. A. He sells watches.
 B. He operates equipment.
 C. He types.
 D. He uses a cash register.

Day	SUN	MON	TUE	WED	THU	FRI	SAT
Start		9:00 AM	4:00 PM		9:00 AM	12:00 PM	5:00 PM
End		5:00 PM	9:00 PM		5:00 PM	6:00 PM	11:00 PM

14. How many days does she work?
 A. She works three days a week.
 B. She works four days a week.
 C. She works five days a week.
 D. She works six days a week.

15. How many hours does she work on Tuesday?
 A. She works eight hours.
 B. She works four hours.
 C. She works six hours.
 D. She works five hours.

E. Write.

cafeteria   employee lounge   mailroom   personnel office
supply room

personnel office | employee lounge | cafeteria
supply room | mailroom | bathroom

ANSWERS
11 Ⓐ Ⓑ Ⓒ Ⓓ
12 Ⓐ Ⓑ Ⓒ Ⓓ
13 Ⓐ Ⓑ Ⓒ Ⓓ
14 Ⓐ Ⓑ Ⓒ Ⓓ
15 Ⓐ Ⓑ Ⓒ Ⓓ

16. The cafeteria is next to the _____.

17. The _____ is across from the personnel office.

18. The _____ is across from the bathroom.

19. The supply room is next to the _____.

20. The employee lounge is between the _____ and the cafeteria.

© 2007 Pearson Education, Inc.
Duplication for classroom use is permitted.

A. Listen and choose the correct picture.

1.
   A

   B

   C

2.
   A

   B

   C

3.
   A

   B

   C

4.
   A

   B

   C

ANSWERS
1 Ⓐ Ⓑ Ⓒ
2 Ⓐ Ⓑ Ⓒ
3 Ⓐ Ⓑ Ⓒ
4 Ⓐ Ⓑ Ⓒ
5 Ⓐ Ⓑ Ⓒ
6 Ⓐ Ⓑ Ⓒ
7 Ⓐ Ⓑ Ⓒ
8 Ⓐ Ⓑ Ⓒ
9 Ⓐ Ⓑ Ⓒ
10 Ⓐ Ⓑ Ⓒ

B. Listen and choose the correct answer.

5. **A.** Every day.
   B. I take a bus.
   C. On Elm Avenue.

6. **A.** Across from the post office.
   B. Drive a car.
   C. Take bus number 8.

7. **A.** Take the A train.
   B. Get off at Tenth Avenue.
   C. On the left.

C. Listen and answer numbers 8–10 on the answer sheet.

© 2007 Pearson Education, Inc.
Duplication for classroom use is permitted.

Name: _____ Date: _____

D. Read and answer.

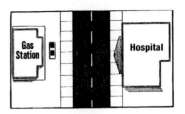

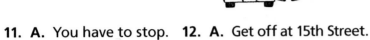

11. A. You have to stop.
   B. Don't turn yet.
   C. You can't go that way.
   D. Slow down.

12. A. Get off at 15th Street.
   B. Take Bus Number 5.
   C. Get off at 5th Street.
   D. Take Train Number 15.

13. A. The gas station is next to the hospital.
   B. The hospital is on the right.
   C. The hospital is on the left.
   D. The gas station is on the right.

Route 42			
Bay Street	**Center Street**	**Western Avenue**	**Clinton Avenue**
6:30 AM	6:45 AM	7:00 AM	7:15 AM
8:00 AM	8:15 AM	8:30 AM	8:45 AM
9:30 AM	9:45 AM	10:00 AM	10:15 AM
11:00 AM	11:15 AM	11:30 AM	11:45 AM

14. When does the first bus in the morning leave Center Street?
   A. At seven fifteen.
   B. At eight fifteen.
   C. At six thirty.
   D. At six forty-five.

15. When does the last bus in the morning leave Bay Street?
   A. At eleven forty-five.
   B. At eleven o'clock.
   C. At eight o'clock.
   D. At nine thirty.

E. Write.

Adams Street	Fourth Avenue	Line Street
Spring Street	Third Avenue	

Spring Street	Adams Street	Third Avenue	Fourth Avenue	Line Street
1:15 PM	1:30 PM	1:45 PM	2:00 PM	2:15 PM
3:30 PM	3:45 PM	4:00 PM	4:15 PM	4:30 PM
5:45 PM	6:00 PM	6:15 PM	6:30 PM	6:45 PM
8:00 PM	8:15 PM	8:30 PM	8:45 PM	9:00 PM

ANSWERS

11	(A)	(B)	(C)	(D)
12	(A)	(B)	(C)	(D)
13	(A)	(B)	(C)	(D)
14	(A)	(B)	(C)	(D)
15	(A)	(B)	(C)	(D)

16. The first bus in the afternoon leaves _____ at one fifteen.

17. The next bus arrives at _____ at four thirty.

18. It's six o'clock. The next bus arrives at _____ at six thirty.

19. The last bus leaves _____ at eight fifteen.

20. The last bus arrives at _____ at eight thirty.

Foundations
Unit 14 Test

© 2007 Pearson Education, Inc.
Duplication for classroom use is permitted.

| UNIT **15** TEST | Name: _____ Date: _____ Score: _____ |

A. Listen and choose the correct picture.

1.

A

B

C

2.

A

B

C

3.

A

B

C

4.

A
B
C

```
ANSWERS

 1  (A)  (B)  (C)
 2  (A)  (B)  (C)
 3  (A)  (B)  (C)
 4  (A)  (B)  (C)
 5  (A)  (B)  (C)
 6  (A)  (B)  (C)
 7  (A)  (B)  (C)
 8  (A)  (B)  (C)
 9  (A)  (B)  (C)
10  (A)  (B)  (C)
```

B. Listen and choose the correct answer.

5. **A.** I like to go swimming.
   B. I went to a concert.
   C. I saw a movie.

6. **A.** I went to a ballgame.
   B. I'm going to exercise.
   C. I played basketball.

7. **A.** Swimming.
   B. Baseball.
   C. Rollerblading.

C. Listen and answer numbers 8–10 on the answer sheet.

© 2007 Pearson Education, Inc.
Duplication for classroom use is permitted.

Name: _____ Date: _____

D. Read and answer.

11. **A.** I saw a movie.
    B. I went to a concert.
    C. I saw a play.
    D. I went to a ballgame.

12. **A.** I play soccer.
    B. I play golf.
    C. I play basketball.
    D. I play baseball.

13. **A.** I'm going to go to a museum.
    B. I'm going to see a play.
    C. I'm going to go to the zoo.
    D. I'm going to go to the park.

July						
Sunday	**Monday**	**Tuesday**	**Wednesday**	**Thursday**	**Friday**	**Saturday**
	1 basketball	2 swimming	3 soccer	4 concert: Grant Hall	5 dancing: Music Cafe	6 movie: Rex Theater

14. It's July third. What's she going to do tomorrow?
    A. She's going to go swimming.
    B. She's going to go dancing.
    C. She's going to go to a concert.
    D. She's going to play soccer.

15. It's July third. What did she do yesterday?
    A. She went swimming.
    B. She played soccer.
    C. She went to a movie.
    D. She played basketball.

ANSWERS				
11	Ⓐ	Ⓑ	Ⓒ	Ⓓ
12	Ⓐ	Ⓑ	Ⓒ	Ⓓ
13	Ⓐ	Ⓑ	Ⓒ	Ⓓ
14	Ⓐ	Ⓑ	Ⓒ	Ⓓ
15	Ⓐ	Ⓑ	Ⓒ	Ⓓ

E. Write.

goes jogging	goes swimming	plays baseball
sees a play	works	

Sunday	Monday	Tuesday	Wednesday	Thursday	Friday	Saturday
1	2 work swimming	3 work jogging	4 work swimming	5 work jogging	6 work swimming	7 baseball
8 play: Royal Theater	9 work swimming	10 work jogging	11 work swimming	12 work jogging	13 work swimming	14 baseball

16. He _____ five days a week.

17. He _____ twice a week.

18. He _____ once a week.

19. He _____ three times a week.

20. He _____ once a month.

© 2007 Pearson Education, Inc.
Duplication for classroom use is permitted.

FOUNDATIONS UNIT TESTS LISTENING SCRIPTS

Unit 1 Test

A. Listen and choose the correct picture.
1. My phone number is (323) 456–8917.
2. My address is 5 Main Street.
3. This is my brother.
4. My daughter is 8 years old.

B. Listen and choose the correct answer.
5. How do you spell your name?
6. What's your apartment number?
7. Nice to meet you.

C. Listen to the question and the three answers. Which answer is correct: A, B, or C?
8. What's your address?
   A. California.
   B. D-R-A-K-E.
   C. 2 Main Street.
9. What's your first name?
   A. That's correct.
   B. Maria.
   C. My last name is Sanchez.
10. How old is your son?
   A. He's four years old.
   B. His name is Carlos.
   C. 8G.

Unit 2 Test

A. Listen and choose the correct picture.
1. Open your book.
2. There's a map in my classroom.
3. The bookshelf is over there.
4. Write your name.

B. Listen and choose the correct answer.
5. How many students are there in your class?
6. What's on your desk?
7. What's on the table?

C. Listen to the question and the three answers. Which answer is correct: A, B, or C?
8. How many books are there?
   A. There are 15 desks.
   B. There are 18 books.
   C. Put away your books.
9. Where's the teacher?
   A. On the globe.
   B. On the clock.
   C. Over there.
10. Where's the computer?
   A. On the calculator.
   B. On the table.
   C. On the chalk.

Unit 3 Test

A. Listen and choose the correct picture.
1. I'm eating dinner.
2. I brush my teeth every day.
3. I'm watching TV.
4. I'm making lunch.

B. Listen and choose the correct answer.
5. What do you do every day?
6. What are you doing right now?
7. What's the weather?

C. Listen to the question and the three answers. Which answer is correct: A, B, or C?
8. What are you doing right now?
   A. I'm twenty years old.
   B. I'm listening to music.
   C. It's snowing.
9. What's the weather today in New York?
   A. It's sunny.
   B. I'm cleaning.
   C. I'm reading.
10. It's hot in Los Angeles. What's the temperature?
   A. Thirty years old.
   B. Ninety degrees.
   C. Five degrees.

Unit 4 Test

A. Listen and choose the correct picture.
1. It's five o'clock.
2. My birthday is September 10th.
3. I just found a quarter.
4. My English class is in Room 215.

B. Listen and choose the correct answer.
5. What month is it?
6. What time is it?
7. How much is two plus six?

C. Listen to the question and the three answers. Which answer is correct: A, B, or C?
8. What floor do you live on?
   A. At 6 o'clock.
   B. 1722 Central Avenue.
   C. The third floor.
9. What's today's date?
   A. It's February.
   B. It's September 12th.
   C. On Friday at 4 o'clock.
10. What time does the train leave?
   A. At 8:45.
   B. On Wednesday.
   C. Twenty dollars.

Unit 5 Test

A. Listen and choose the correct picture.
1. The apartment has a nice kitchen.
2. This is a very nice bathroom.
3. There's a fireplace in the living room.
4. There are two windows.

B. Listen and choose the correct answer.
5. How many bathrooms are there?
6. Where do you want this sofa?
7. How many rooms are there in the apartment?

C. Listen to the question and the three answers. Which answer is correct: A, B, or C?
8. Where do you cook?
   A. In the kitchen.
   B. In the bedroom.
   C. In the dining room.
9. How many floors are there in the building?
   A. I live on the fourth floor.
   B. There are six floors.
   C. It has a nice rug.
10. Where do you want this table?
   A. Put it in the cabinet.
   B. Put it in the fireplace.
   C. Put it in the dining room.

Unit 6 Test

A. Listen and choose the correct picture.
1. I'm going to the laundromat.
2. The shopping mall is on Main Street.
3. The bus station is over there.
4. The grocery store is across from the bakery.

B. Listen and choose the correct answer.
5. Where's the post office?
6. Where are you going?
7. What's across from the library?

C. Listen to the question and the three answers. Which answer is correct: A, B, or C?
8. Where's the supermarket?
   A. In the movie theater.
   B. Next to the drug store.
   C. Between the gas station.
9. Is there a park nearby?
   A. Yes. There's a bank on Pine Street.
   B. Yes. There's a clinic on Central Avenue.
   C. Yes. There's a park on Tenth Street.
10. Excuse me. Where's the school?
   A. The school is across from the park.
   B. The zoo is on Third Avenue.
   C. There are 30 students in the school.

Unit 7 Test

A. Listen and choose the correct picture.
1. He's young.
2. She's average height.
3. I'm angry.
4. She's short, with black hair.

B. Listen and choose the correct answer.
5. What color eyes does he have?
6. What does she look like?
7. What's his age?

C. Listen to the question and the three answers. Which answer is correct: A, B, or C?
8. Where are you from?
   A. I speak Portuguese.
   B. I speak Arabic.
   C. I'm from Korea.
9. What's your marital status?
   A. I'm average height.
   B. I'm single.
   C. I weigh 150 pounds.
10. How tall are you?
   A. I'm 5 feet 4 inches.
   B. I'm middle-aged.
   C. I'm average weight.

Unit 8 Test

A. Listen and choose the correct picture.
1. I'm looking for onions.
2. Carrots are in Aisle 7.
3. Please get a quart of milk.
4. We need a box of cereal.

B. Listen and choose the correct answer.
5. What do we need at the supermarket?
6. Can I help you?
7. Excuse me. Where are the peaches?

C. Listen to the question and the three answers. Which answer is correct: A, B, or C?
8. What do we need at the supermarket?
   A. A quart of bananas.
   B. A can of mayonnaise.
   C. A bottle of soda.
9. What are you looking for?
   A. A pound of milk.
   B. A bag of sugar.
   C. A loaf of cheese.
10. What vegetables do we need?
   A. We need potatoes and lettuce.
   B. We need cookies and bread.
   C. We need apples and oranges.

Unit 9 Test

A. Listen and choose the correct picture.
1. I'm looking for a belt.
2. I'm looking for a pair of gloves.
3. She's wearing a suit.
4. Sweaters are over there.

B. Listen and choose the correct answer.
5. What's the price of the shoes?
6. Where are men's shirts?
7. May I help you?

C. Listen to the question and the three answers. Which answer is correct: A, B, or C?
8. What are you wearing today?
   A. A red umbrella.
   B. A blouse and a skirt.
   C. A pair of dresses.
9. What's the matter with the jacket?
   A. It's too big.
   B. It's on the third floor.
   C. Five dollars.
10. What size do you wear?
   A. Too short.
   B. White.
   C. Medium.

Unit 10 Test

A. Listen and choose the correct picture.
1. I'm writing a check.
2. I want to send a registered letter.
3. I'm looking for my bank book.
4. Your change is $2.25.

B. Listen to the conversation and choose the next line.
5. —May I help you?
   —Yes. I want to buy an air letter.
6. —I'm writing a check.
   —For how much?
7. —That's four dollars.
   —Here's five dollars.

C. Listen to the question and the three answers. Which answer is correct: A, B, or C?
8. What do we need at the post office?
   A. A withdrawal slip.
   B. A money order.
   C. A bank book.
9. How much is a hamburger?
   A. Here's $4.00.
   B. Your change is $1.25.
   C. A hamburger is $3.50.
10. Where can I mail a package?
   A. At the post office.
   B. At the bank.
   C. At the train station.

Unit 11 Test

A. Listen and choose the correct picture.
1. I have a headache.
2. I have a cough.
3. Take one capsule twice a day.
4. I burned my hand.

B. Listen and choose the correct answer.
5. What's the matter?
6. Where can I find cold medicine?
7. I have a stomachache. What should I do?

C. Listen to the question and the three answers. Which answer is correct: A, B, or C?
8. What's the matter?
   A. I have a finger.
   B. I have a fever.
   C. I have ear drops.
9. What do you recommend for a toothache?
   A. Cough syrup.
   B. Cold medicine.
   C. Aspirin.
10. What happened?
   A. I broke my eye.
   B. I broke my arm.
   C. I sprained my throat.

Unit 12 Test

A. Listen and choose the correct picture.
1. That's the principal.
2. I'm going to the nurse's office.
3. My favorite subject is science.
4. I have choir practice after school today.

B. Listen and choose the correct answer.
5. What's your favorite subject?
6. Where is basketball practice?
7. Where do the students eat lunch?

C. Listen to the question and the three answers. Which answer is correct: A, B, or C?
8. Who cleans the school?
   A. The librarian.
   B. The custodian.
   C. The P.E. teacher.
9. Where do you go when you have a bad headache?
   A. To the guidance office.
   B. To the auditorium.
   C. To the nurse's office.
10. Where is band practice?
   A. In the principal's office.
   B. In the auditorium.
   C. In the library.

Unit 13 Test

A. Listen and choose the correct picture.

1. I'm a security guard.
2. I'm looking for a job as a construction worker.
3. I can fix sinks.
4. The mailroom is down the hall.

B. Listen and choose the correct answer.

5. What do you do?
6. Where do you work?
7. What's your occupation?

C. Listen to the question and the three answers. Which answer is correct: A, B, or C?

8. What kind of job are you looking for?
   - A. The employee lounge.
   - B. Down the hall.
   - C. A job as a cook.
9. Can you repair buildings?
   - A. Yes, I can. I'm an experienced mechanic.
   - B. Yes, I can. I'm an experienced carpenter.
   - C. Yes, I can. I'm an experienced assembler.
10. Can you type?
    - A. Yes, I can. I'm an experienced secretary.
    - B. Yes, I can. I'm an experienced electrician.
    - C. Yes, I can. I'm an experienced truck driver.

Unit 14 Test

A. Listen and choose the correct picture.

1. There are train tracks ahead.
2. No left turn.
3. Get off at Second Street.
4. Take the C train to Pine Street.

B. Listen and choose the correct answer.

5. How do you get to school?
6. Excuse me. How do I get to the train station?
7. Where do I get off for the Midtown Mall?

C. Listen to the question and the three answers. Which answer is correct: A, B, or C?

8. How do I get to the West Street Clinic?
   - A. Look for people in the street.
   - B. There's a school nearby.
   - C. Take Bus Number 6.
9. How do I get to Washington Street?
   - A. At 6:00 PM.
   - B. Take the Red Line.
   - C. Turn on red.
10. When does the bus to San Francisco leave?
    - A. At 10:00 AM.
    - B. At the bus station.
    - C. Walk that way.

Unit 15 Test

A. Listen and choose the correct picture.

1. I like to go jogging.
2. I'm going to play tennis tomorrow.
3. I went dancing yesterday.
4. I'm going to see a play.

B. Listen and choose the correct answer.

5. What do you like to do in your free time?
6. What are you going to do tomorrow?
7. What do you like to play?

C. Listen to the question and the three answers. Which answer is correct: A, B, or C?

8. What do you like to do in your free time?
   - A. I like to brush my teeth.
   - B. I like to use a cash register.
   - C. I like to play soccer.
9. What do you like to do when it's raining?
   - A. I like to listen to music.
   - B. I like to go to the park.
   - C. I like to play golf.
10. What are you going to do at home?
    - A. I'm going to go to a concert.
    - B. I'm going to go to a museum.
    - C. I'm going to watch TV.

FOUNDATIONS UNIT TESTS ANSWER SHEET

Name: _____ Date: _____ Score: _____

1 Ⓐ Ⓑ Ⓒ

2 Ⓐ Ⓑ Ⓒ

3 Ⓐ Ⓑ Ⓒ

4 Ⓐ Ⓑ Ⓒ

5 Ⓐ Ⓑ Ⓒ

6 Ⓐ Ⓑ Ⓒ

7 Ⓐ Ⓑ Ⓒ

8 Ⓐ Ⓑ Ⓒ

9 Ⓐ Ⓑ Ⓒ

10 Ⓐ Ⓑ Ⓒ

11 Ⓐ Ⓑ Ⓒ Ⓓ

12 Ⓐ Ⓑ Ⓒ Ⓓ

13 Ⓐ Ⓑ Ⓒ Ⓓ

14 Ⓐ Ⓑ Ⓒ Ⓓ

15 Ⓐ Ⓑ Ⓒ Ⓓ

16 _____

17 _____

18 _____

19 _____

20 _____

© 2007 Pearson Education, Inc.
Duplication for classroom use is permitted.

FOUNDATIONS UNIT TESTS ANSWER KEY

Unit 1 Test
1. B
2. A
3. B
4. C
5. B
6. A
7. C
8. C
9. B
10. A
11. C
12. B
13. A
14. B
15. D
16. name
17. apartment
18. address
19. telephone
20. son

Unit 2 Test
1. C
2. A
3. B
4. A
5. B
6. A
7. C
8. B
9. C
10. B
11. D
12. C
13. B
14. B
15. A
16. Raise
17. Go
18. Sit
19. Erase
20. Close

Unit 3 Test
1. B
2. A
3. C
4. A
5. C
6. B
7. C
8. B
9. A
10. B
11. C
12. D
13. C
14. A
15. D
16. raining
17. cold
18. cloudy
19. sunny
20. hot

Unit 4 Test
1. C
2. B
3. C
4. A
5. B
6. C
7. A
8. C
9. B
10. A
11. D
12. B
13. C
14. A
15. D
16. Friday
17. Wednesday
18. Tuesday
19. Saturday
20. Thursday

Unit 5 Test
1. A
2. B
3. A
4. C
5. C
6. A
7. B
8. A
9. B
10. C
11. B
12. A
13. B
14. C
15. D
16. apartment
17. refrigerator
18. shower
19. living room
20. closet

Unit 6 Test
1. C
2. A
3. B
4. A
5. B
6. C
7. A
8. B
9. C
10. A
11. C
12. D
13. B
14. C
15. A
16. hospital
17. grocery store
18. clinic
19. park
20. laundromat

Unit 7 Test

1. A
2. B
3. C
4. B
5. A
6. C
7. B
8. C
9. B
10. A
11. D
12. C
13. B
14. C
15. D
16. Morocco
17. Arabic
18. hair
19. height
20. single

Unit 8 Test

1. B
2. A
3. C
4. A
5. B
6. A
7. C
8. C
9. B
10. A
11. B
12. A
13. D
14. C
15. D
16. jar
17. bag
18. bunch
19. loaf
20. bottle

Unit 9 Test

1. C
2. A
3. B
4. A
5. C
6. B
7. A
8. B
9. A
10. C
11. C
12. B
13. D
14. C
15. A
16. Watches
17. Ties
18. Dresses
19. Shoes
20. Pants

Unit 10 Test

1. C
2. B
3. A
4. B
5. C
6. B
7. A
8. B
9. C
10. A
11. D
12. C
13. D
14. B
15. D
16. June 21
17. Mitchell's Department Store
18. 54.00
19. FIfty-four and 00/100
20. lamp

Unit 11 Test

1. A
2. C
3. C
4. A
5. B
6. A
7. C
8. B
9. C
10. B
11. D
12. A
13. B
14. D
15. C
16. head
17. back
18. stomach
19. arm
20. hand

Unit 12 Test

1. B
2. C
3. A
4. B
5. C
6. B
7. A
8. B
9. C
10. B
11. C
12. D
13. B
14. D
15. C
16. math
17. technology
18. English
19. social studies
20. science

Unit 13 Test
1. A
2. B
3. C
4. B
5. B
6. A
7. B
8. C
9. B
10. A
11. C
12. A
13. D
14. C
15. D
16. employee lounge
17. supply room
18. cafeteria
19. mailroom
20. personnel office

Unit 14 Test
1. C
2. A
3. B
4. A
5. B
6. C
7. B
8. C
9. B
10. A
11. D
12. C
13. B
14. D
15. B
16. Spring Street
17. Line Street
18. Fourth Avenue
19. Adams Street
20. Third Avenue

Unit 15 Test
1. B
2. A
3. B
4. C
5. A
6. B
7. B
8. C
9. A
10. C
11. D
12. B
13. A
14. C
15. A
16. works
17. goes jogging
18. plays baseball
19. goes swimming
20. sees a play

Multilevel Activity CD-ROM User's Guide

The CD-ROM included with this Teacher's Guide provides a wealth of downloadable, printable instructional resources for use with the *Foundations* program, including activity masters, tests, and an Activity Bank with hundreds of supplemental worksheets offering practice in preliteracy, literacy, evidence-based reading instruction, handwriting, vocabulary, and numeracy.

ASSESSMENT AND TEST FOLDERS

Unit Achievement Tests assess student progress and prepare students for standardized tests. Reproducible resources include a two-page test for each unit, listening scripts, an answer sheet, and an answer key. Teacher Notes offer suggestions for using the tests and strategies for developing students' test-taking skills.

A **Needs Assessment** questionnaire in an easy pictorial format enables students to indicate their needs and interests to guide the teacher's lesson planning.

A **Performance-Based Lesson Assessment** form is a tool for evaluating and documenting student participation and performance with a simple scoring rubric. The form contains text fields* that enable instructors to enter up to 23 student names prior to printing the form.

A **Learner Progress Chart** enables students to record their test scores and chart their progress.

ACTIVITY MASTERS, FLASH CARDS, & LABELS

Activity Masters include ready-to-use word cards and activity sheets for the multilevel activities and games suggested in the Teacher's Guide.

Flash Cards on reproducible masters provide an economical vocabulary study tool for students.

Classroom Labels with large print can be posted next to key classroom objects and furnishings.

WORKSHEETS ACTIVITY BANK

Phonemic Awareness activities offer students systematic, explicit instruction in how to detect the individual speech sounds that make up words.

Basic Reading Practice activities provide evidence-based reading instruction in decoding, concepts of print (letters/words/sentences), and fluency.

Preliteracy and **Literacy Practice** worksheets focus on shape, letter, and word recognition.

Vocabulary Practice worksheets review key unit vocabulary.

Handwriting Practice worksheets help learners master manuscript and cursive letter-formation.

Number Practice worksheets develop students' numeracy skills.

RESOURCES BY UNIT

For convenience and ease-of-use, all resources that are organized by type in their respective folders may also be accessed by unit. Instructors can therefore find the various resources related to a specific unit in one convenient folder.

The resources contained on this disk may be reproduced for classroom use only in conjunction with the *Foundations* instructional program.

You need to have Adobe Acrobat Reader® installed on your computer in order to use the CD-ROM files. If you do not have a copy of the Reader installed, please visit www.adobe.com and download and install the free Adobe Acrobat Reader® program. You will then be able to view and print the files on the CD-ROM.

*The full version of Adobe Acrobat® is required in order to retain the names entered in form fields by saving the file. Saving forms without the full version of Adobe Acrobat® will NOT retain the data within the form fields.